THE MODEL RAILROAD TRACK PLAN BOOK

No. 1106
$12.95

THE MODEL RAILROAD TRACK PLAN BOOK

BY JOHN H. ARMSTRONG

TAB BOOKS
BLUE RIDGE SUMMIT, PA. 17214

FIRST EDITION

FIRST PRINTING—JANUARY 1980

Printed in the United States of America

Library of Congress Cataloging in Publication Data

Armstrong, John H.
The model railroad track plan book.
Includes index.
1. Railroads—Models, I. Title.
TF197.A68 625.1'9 78-26493
ISBN 0-8306-9829-9
ISBN 0-8306-1106-1 (pbk.)

Contents

Introduction 7

1 **Trackwork Fundamentals and Standards** 11
Personal Standards—Track Curvature vs. Rolling Stock—Radius vs. Scale—Beautiful Curves—Superelevation and Easements—Centrifugal Force—Tilt or No Tilt?—Track Centers and Clearances—Why Keep Em Close?—What About Narrow Gauge?—Vertical Clearances—Side Clearances—Grades and Tonnage—Vertical Curves—Trackwork—Turnouts—Ladder Tracks—Turnouts on Curves—N and HO Turnout Recommendations—Minimum Isn't the Maximum!—Hand-Laid, Pre-Fab or Sectional Track?—Crossings

2 **Types of Model Railroad Layouts** 51
What Type of Railroad Are You Modeling?—The Period Railroad—Choosing a Schematic—Combination Schematics—Accentuating the Positive—Convertible Schematic Plans—Progressive Pike Planning—Double-Track vs. Single—How Is It Built?—Tabletop Construction— Layout Configurations— How High Is Enough?— Electrical Controls and the Track Plan

3 **Track Plans For Small Layouts** 80
Character Profiles—Let's Get Started—The Improved Oval—The Little Big Time—The Prairie Division Point—Shelf-Style Switching Layouts—Constricted Connecting Railroad—Hammerlock Industrial District—Big Scale in a Small Package—Twice Around, Two Ways—Coffee Table Railroads—The Iron Ranger—The Accessible Waterwings—The Underbed Special—Traditional Coffee Table Railroad—Long Trains for the Coffee Table—The Coffee Table Upper Limit—Grand Central Junior—Centennial Peak Branch

4 **Medium Size Track Plans** 129
The Medium Big Time—The Pretzel—A Progressive Pike Trilogy—The Limits of Sharp Curves—The Happy Acorn—Long Trains with a Push—The Long, Long Trail—The Super Switching Railroad—Around-the-Wall Plans—The Collector's Friend—A Two-Layer Roomful—Spaghetti on the Rolling Pin—Notching the L—The Exhibitionist—Another Medium Big Time Railroad—Both Sides of the Mountain—All the Essentials

5 **Larger Track Plans** 173
Garage Railroads—A Garage Full of Way Freight Fun—Two Stalls, One Automobile, Two Railroads—The Big Z—Big Trains You Can Live With

6 **Modifying and Combining Track Plans** 189
Changing Scale or Gauge—Inappropriate Changes—Changing Curvature Standards—Effect on Grade—It's All Approximate—Changing Character—Dieseling or Steamizing—More Freight Car Capacity—Let Yourself Go!

Glossary of Railroad Terms....213
Appendix A—Freight Car Insignias of Major Railroads.... 219
Appendix B—Rules and Regulations....220
Appendix C—Connecting Power to the Rails.... 224
Appendix D—Preventive Maintenance for Locomotives....231
Index....239

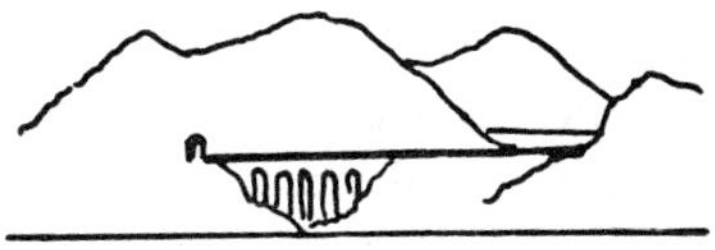

Introduction

You can buy or build a model of a Union Pacific "Big Boy" 4-8-8-4 that's strictly scale size in every dimension—133 ft. 3¼ in. over the coupler pulling faces, 16 ft. 2½ in. high over the stack, and 10 ft. 10 in. wide.

You can build or buy accurately scaled models of freight cars large and small, manhole covers, signal bridges, fire plugs, stations, and all the other thousands of items that make up the railroad scene. You can lay track itself with rail and ties of scale cross-section, correctly spaced.

Nevertheless, there's one thing you *can't* build to scale—the railroad itself! Even if your choice as a prototype is the Narragansett Pier Railroad, its five-mile main line would scale out to 166 ft. in N gauge or to the length of a football field in HO. At the least, that track is going to have to be coiled or folded up if it's going to fit into any likely space. Anything beyond the shortest of short line railroads will have to be drastically condensed in the lengthwise dimension. This isn't necessarily all bad, of course. There are long stretches on any line which aren't particularly scenic or interesting, and our "modeler's license" naturally includes the right to leave out such sections and pick the best parts for miniaturization.

Because a railroad is so long and narrow, the *track plan* is the element in model railroading where you have the greatest need and the greatest opportunity to be original. Various models of Santa Fe caboose 999047 or of a Canadian National Class Two combination station built by a dozen different modelers will all look much the same, but *model railroads* patterned after the AT&SF or CN, even for spaces of the same general size, can be entirely different. All must depart from strict scaling in such matters as the proportion of curved to straight track and the radius of those arcs, but each railroad can be successful in capturing something of the essence of its prototype line's appearance and operating practices. To the extent that its track plan and scenery overcome these necessary deviations from simply miniaturizing the whole railroad, each layout, large or small, becomes a truly one-of-a-kind expression of its builder's creativity and imagination—and that's pretty much what model railroading is all about!

Over the years, certain particularly effective ways of condensing a railroad and its operations into commonly-available areas have evolved and become recognized. This book presents a large number of track plans based on these principles. These plans put as much railroading as possible within reach, considering the three limitations that affect us all: space, time and money.

Space is the most common excuse for being an "armchair" modeler! Many of the track plans in this book are for apartment-size spaces, or for railroads that must be put away between operating sessions. The difference between a well-thought-out plan and a haphazard jumble of track can be the difference between having railroading fun and retreating to model-building only because "I just don't have enough space." In larger areas, the best track plans are still those that make good use of every square foot, squeezing in a lot of action without *looking* overcrowded.

Time-saving techniques for translating a track plan into reality are covered thoroughly in other model railroading books and magazines, and much of the efforts of manufacturers in developing and improving their products is in this direction. Model railroading is so unlimited in its opportunities for continuing enjoyment that you need never fear getting through too soon with some one of its aspects. Plans in this book are designed to be compatible with the use of prefabricated track components. But improvements possible through individual efforts are discussed for your consideration where final results are more important than speed in getting into operation.

On both full-size and model railroads, two track switches *cost* a lot more than one, so if there is a way to move the traffic without requiring that second switch it will and should be used. The same principle applies to space for the right-of-way, too. While a model railroad powered with a variety of brass locomotives may have only a small fraction of its capital tied up in track and plywood, careful planning pays off so that you can have the most railroading enjoyment for the money you have available.

Model railroading is such an absorbing hobby that to some it becomes almost a way of life, with its many social aspects and supporting interests such as history, photography, art and even music adding themselves to the model building and train operating. In many ways the design of a track plan is like the architecture of a home. A home should be designed to meet the needs of the family who lives in it, not just now but over a period of time. A track plan should fit the model railroading desires of its builder, now and later as his abilities and interests grow and change. No one house design is best. The particular combination of rooms, location, style, appliances, price and so on that comes closest to anyone's ideal is bound to vary, and any house that's lived in until it becomes a home will undergo many changes, if only in paint scheme and furniture, as part of the process. Let's look at some of the ways the processes of finding an ideal house and an ideal track plan resemble each other.

First, a house must provide the rooms your family needs. It's basically a place you can live in; and that means sleeping, cooking, eating, bathing and living areas, all connected so you can get from one to another as occasion demands. Similarly, the first thing a track plan must let you do is *run trains*! As we've already noted, it can't let you run them over the hundreds of scale miles equivalent to a railroad route, but the track it does have must be so arranged that several of the operations involved in railroad transportation—picking up loaded cars, taking them in trains from one point to another, and the like—can be duplicated. The equivalent of the floor plan of a house is the track plan *schematic*, the possible routes over which trains can move. In a small house the most practical design may have to combine kitchen and dining room to provide space for a second small bedroom; and track plans often must use a single yard to represent both ends of a railroad route—maybe not what you'd prefer in either case, but at least it works.

The direction in which these compromises are made determines the *character* of the plan. The Galloping Gourmet is going to have a big kitchen if he has to sleep on a fold-down bed in the living room, and the model railroader who likes long trains will have to favor main-line trackage over branch lines or yards. The architect to be preferred, whether designing a home or a layout, of course, is the one who can best arrange things so that much of the space (or track) can *comfortably* serve more than one purpose. Maybe it's just a matter of locating the dining space so its use as a hall doesn't interfere with the table, or connecting switches so both passenger and freight locomotives can use the same track to get to the engine terminal without blocking the main line.

Once past the toy-train oval, or its equivalent log-cabin stage, we begin to realize that there are some artistic considerations. A house shouldn't be just a box, and layout should if at all possible provide places where the trains can run through a scenic setting that matches their own realistic appearance. Model railroaders have a peculiarly broad definition of *scenery*, including all sorts of "railroady" things like steel mills and junk yards that wouldn't qualify so far as the nature lovers are concerned but which are definitely an essential and interesting part of the railroad's environment.

Right here there's some conflict. A quaint English cottage with dormer windows simply can't have as much living space as a two-story cube, and completely filling the layout with track won't leave room for the fields, hills and buildings that are needed to let the train look as though it's climbing through picturesque rural New England. Again, the better track plans are those that use all manner of tricks to combine track routing variety with apparently uncrowded scenes, just as the good architect hides a lot of closet space under those attractive eaves.

Sometimes the difference between an ugly house and an equally spacious but attractive one is mostly a matter of some artfully chosen decorative touches, and often a whole new scene can be created on a small layout by simply adding a backdrop or view-block to separate some of its trackage from adjacent lines. This book doesn't attempt to cover layout scenicking (word you won't find in the dictionary, though it's perfectly clear what it means), but the *top level trackage* only plans included with many of the layouts provide one example of the many approaches possible. Imaginative scenic treatments can improve any track plan, but the good track plan is designed to help rather than challenge the scenic planner.

At best, some choice must be made between scenic emphasis and the maximum in trackage and operational possibilities. The best balance is a highly personal matter, to be made on the basis of your preference for running trains in a complex pattern vs. watching individual units doing their thing in more realistic surroundings. Some plans lean in one direction, some in the other. To help you find ones that are more likely to suit your desires, a *character profile* is included with each. The length of the five bars shows the *relative* emphasis on the different aspects of track plan design. If you want your railroad, whether it's on the large or the small side, to provide some spacious, almost museum-like settings for showing off your trains in action, look for those plans whose profiles have a relatively long center bar.

It's got to fit, of course. If you want a mansion with spacious grounds and located right downtown, you're simply out of your mind. Most of us realize from the beginning that only certain combinations are practical and that it's either a town house in close or a boondocks location if there's to be an acre or more to call your own. Similarly, most track plan thoughts start out with the space available rather rigidly defined. If there's a good possibility that the layout will have to be moved sometime, there may be some further constraints on its dimensions and construction.

Real estate agents faced with the job of selling very cramped houses often make things sound a little better by referring to them as "fine starter houses," which provide a way for a young couple to move into something now rather than later, even though a move will become pretty essential later on. Well, let's face it! Many of the track plans in this book are *starters*, small enough for any apartment. They provide similar options later on: trackwork and materials can be worked into a second pike, the third dimension can be exploited in developing them into a much more elaborate railroad in the same space, or they can be expanded by major additions into *full size* layouts for whatever areas may later become available. Since there's nothing like experience when it comes to learning which aspects of model railroading are most enjoyable to you, the starter approach has a lot going for it.

Many of the plans are for the traditional smaller sizes, such as 4 × 8 ft. as dictated by the proportions of the standard sheet of plywood. Such common sizes don't necessarily represent the best match between portability or construction ease and desirable track radii, though, so other small plans are of more unconventional shapes. Perhaps some of these oddballs will stimulate a second look at your space possibilities and lead to something better right now than you thought could be in the cards.

The larger track plans are matched to such likely areas as one-car garages. The larger a layout, the smaller the chance that it will be an exact fit, but the more flexible it may be as far as modification is concerned. Some of these plans include markings to indicate points where you can take a *tuck* in the main line if things are a little too tight or add length should such a blissful opportunity present itself.

The efficient house plan recognizes the fact that it's a lot cheaper to let its dimensions match available standard-size building-blocks than to come in an inch or a foot off almost everywhere. Likewise, doors are the size they are because people need to walk through them; and since most people fall within certain height and width limits, most doors can be built to stock sizes.

Similarly, it's possible to assemble an infinite variety of track plans from just a few standard-geometric pieces of trackwork, so most of these layouts are designed so that they can be built using available standard turnouts and crossings. Many can also be built using sectional-track curved and straight sections, but the economy and reduced number of joints resulting from using flexible prefabricated track, cut to fit from longer lengths, encourages its use in most cases.

By reducing every dimension on an HO track plan by the ratio of 87 to 160, the same layout can be duplicated in N scale. In all but the smallest railroads, though, this leads to certain problems. The space between adjacent layers of track may get so small that retrieving cars is impossible, or access hatches may shrink to the point you can't fit through them. Conversely, if an N gauge plan is built in HO scale, some parts of it may become inaccessible unless different arrangements, such as access hatches or moving it away from the wall, are made. Various items of trackwork may be common in one scale but unavailable in another.

For these reasons, track plans in Chapters 3, 4 and 5 of this book are planned on the basis of a specific gauge and scale. Some of the most useful plans have been presented in more than one gauge and are completely re-engineered in each case to make them most compatible with the constant-size model railroaders who may be building and operating them.

With suitable adjustments, using the basic principles discussed in Chapters 1 and 2, it is possible to convert many plans from one scale to another or even from standard to narrow gauge or vice versa. Chapter 6 includes a tabulation of all the possible conversions, with the resulting dimensions so you can see what will and won't fit, and explains how such translations can be made should a plan you like be in the "wrong" scale. The effects of changing the minimum track radius to accommodate your rolling stock is also presented for each plan.

Just as a rectangular cracker-box home is easier and cheaper to build than the equivalent-size version of the House of the Seven Gables, a flat railroad fitting a standard-size plywood sheet lets you get quickly to the point of running trains and working on scenic effects far more quickly than if you have multiple levels of benchwork to plan and build before you can start laying track. A flat railroad can be a perfectly good one, particularly if it's patterned after a prototype route in a level section of the country, but the more complex pike naturally has greater possibilities for the future. The fifth bar on the character profile indicates the *relative* ease of construction of each track plan to help you pick one best suited to your situation.

All plans have been designed somewhat conservatively; that is, the track will easily fit into the area called for, and there are a minimum of tight spots where unusually careful and accurate work would be necessary to fit things together satisfactorily. This means that you can often squeeze some additional railroading into the space if you're willing to make some personal modifications as you go along. The model railroading magazines are fruitful sources of ideas, but you'll undoubtedly find that your own inventiveness will come to the fore during the later stages of construction. Every operating layout is a personal expression of its builder—good luck!

John H. Armstrong

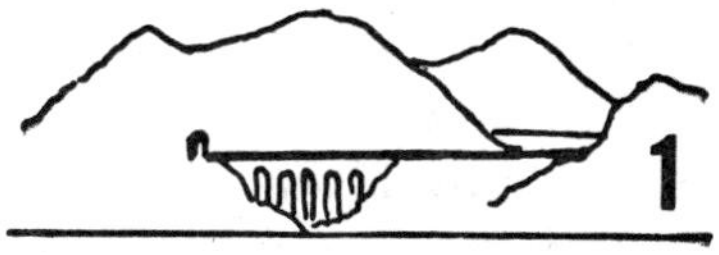

1

Trackwork Fundamentals and Standards

Going far beyond other craft hobbies, model railroading miniaturizes an *operating system*—the railroad, an aggregation of thousands of separate elements which must all work together smoothly to produce transportation. A lot of the railroader's continuing fun and satisfaction comes from the fact that track and rolling stock from many different sources is interchangeable. In any of the more common scales and track gauges you are not limited to the products of a single manufacturer but can combine items, including those you make yourself, in an infinite number of ways.

The basis for much of this standardization is the degree of uniformity required by full-size railroad rolling-stock interchange. Cars from a thousand different private railroad owners move freely throughout North America on rails 4 ft. 8½ in. apart, except on a handful of narrow gauge lines. These Association of American Railroads (AAR) standards, with modifications as necessary to provide good tracking over our vastly sharper curves, have been reduced to corresponding model standards in various scaled reductions from full size. In most cases these wheel and track dimensions, along with voltage, polarity and insulation requirements to permit electric propulsion, have been standardized by the National Model Railroad Association (NMRA), P.O. Box 2186, Indianapolis, IN 46206.

You don't have to be a member of NMRA to get the benefits of this standardization, which insures that an HO train with cars from all over the world will run together as a unit and that all locomotives will in fact move in the same direction with the same reverse switch position, but the details contained in its standards, recommended practices, and data sheets are extremely helpful as you progress in the hobby.

PERSONAL STANDARDS

Things that *must* work together, principally individual car and locomotive wheels and mating parts of the track, are covered by standards with appropriate tolerances so that the widest-spaced wheels, for example, will still not bind when running through a section of track whose rails are at the minimum allowable spacing (gauge). These matters are mandatory for satisfactory operation and no originality is encouraged! Railroads and the steel companies that manufacture components for building track and trackwork (turnouts and crossings which we'll discuss in more detail later on) can't afford to have an infinite variety of parts in stock, so the civil engineers have long ago standardized on a few angles of the frogs used to let wheels cross another rail. Model railroad practice follows a similar course, using standard angles except where the advantages of a special component are worth the extra trouble and expense.

When it comes to such matters as the route that a railroad uses to get across a mountain range or the alignment of a spur track to enter a factory, though, ingenuity and originality come back into the picture. Trains can accommodate themselves to different sharpnesses of track curvature by running at different speeds, and the railroad location engineer must balance the cost of straightening out the line or digging a long tunnel to reduce the grade against the saving in time, fuel, and wear and tear over the years. Track which must withstand loaded coal trains at 50 mph will be much more solidly constructed than that which serves a two-carloads-a-week feed mill.

Similarly, NMRA standards don't set a single limit on such matters as rail size or track curvature, which would vary in the prototype, but merely provide information on dimensions typical in various railroad situations. In planning a layout, you must select particular values that match *your* needs and desires. This chapter discusses some of the most important matters and their significance in determining how much railroading you can fit into your own situation. Each layout in subsequent chapters includes specific data on the standards to which it has been designed, so you can compare it with what your rolling stock requires. It's a good idea to have personal standards in mind, particularly if your interests are strongly in the direction of some definite type of railroading, when you shop for a suitable trackplan, but some of the discussion on specific points may help you consider the possible advantages of some flexibility.

TRACK CURVATURE VS ROLLING STOCK

"What minimum radius are you using?" That's likely to be one of the very first questions one model railroader will ask another in comparing notes on their layouts, and with good reason. As much as anything else, the answer tells the story so far as the character of the railroad is concerned. Since track can be laid to an infinite number of different radii, it has become traditional to pick a few dividing limits of curve sharpness, give them arbitrary names, and thus get a quick handle on the situation. Table 1-1 is one such set of values, with comments on the effect of curvature on two aspects of modeling: the lower limit and appearance of trains.

Lower Limits

There is a lower limit below which a "scale model" cannot round the curve. Typical main-line steam and long (six-axle), E or SD) diesel locomotives, at very restricted speed, must be able to squeal around curves in the 20 to 23-degree range so that they can pass through turnouts and other typical sharp curves in reaching the engine terminal for fuel and service. This corresponds to our *super broad* curves! With some minor modifications, which don't change the engine's appearance noticeably such as using an engine-tender drawbar pivoted farther back on each unit but keeping the spacing between cab and tank at the correct scale distance, it is usually possinle to get even fairly large engines (4-8-4's, for example) to go around *conventional* curves. A four-axle prototype diesel (GP-40-2, B-30-7 or earlier equivalent) is built to do somewhat better and tolerate 150 ft. radius if not coupled to another unit, so running a model of one of these around *sharp* curves needn't mean mutilating its appearance.

Passenger cars and the new generation of special-purpose freight cars such as tri-level auto-racks, piggyback flats and high-cube box cars are from 85 to 94 ft. long over the couplers. They're entitled by AAR standards to require as much as 350 ft. radius (more than super broad) curvature when coupled to a standard 40 ft. car. With practical coupler-mounting modifications, though, model railroaders have found it practical to match curves and rolling stock in accordance with Table 1-2. Some compromises are necessary, chiefly in the direction of spacing units a little farther apart than strict scaling would permit.

Electric street and interurban railways had no choice but to modify their equipment to negotiate whatever curves their urban surroundings dictated, so even some heavy 50-ft. or longer cars might find themselves rounding super-extra-sharp curves in the 60 to 90-ft. radius class. Steam railroad freight cars up to 50 feet in length have enough truck swing to tolerate 150 ft. curves when not coupled, so some industrial lines in particularly cramped areas have almost streetcar-like bends and there is a place for sharp or even extra sharp standards in some of our auxiliary trackage.

Railroad main-line curves are almost impossibly broad. Table 1-3 shows why by indicating the speed restrictions necessary with radii far above our super-broad standards. Operationally, these restrictions don't apply in the model. Once you get

Table 1-1. Curvature Classes For Various Scales.

CURVATURE CLASS (MODEL)	RADIUS OF CURVE (PROTOTYPE)	DEGREE OF CURVE (PROTOTYPE)	RADIUS OF CURVE IN MODEL SCALES: Z(1/220) SCALE	N(1/160) SCALE	HO(1/87) SCALE	S(1/64) SCALE	O(1/48) SCALE
TYPICAL MINIMUM FOR SECTIONAL TRACK	105 FT. (APPROXIMATE)	54°	5¾ in.	7⅝ in.	15 in.	21 in.	24 in.
EXTRA SHARP							
	130 FT.	44°	7 in.	9¾ in.	18 in.	24 in.	33 in.
SHARP							
	175 FT.	32°	9½ in.	13 in.	24 in.	33 in.	44 in.
CONVENTIONAL							
	220 FT.	26°	12 in.	16 in.	30 in.	41 in.	54 in.
BROAD							
	260 FT.	22°	14 in.	19 in.	36 in.	49 in.	64 in.
SUPER-BROAD							
"SWEEPING"	1145 FT	5°	62 in.	86 in.	158 in.	215 in.	288 in.

all the obstacles to free tracking removed so that a combination of cars can crawl around a curve without binding or hanging up at any point, the laws of physics are such that the same consist can zip around the bend at any reasonable speed. So, making the schedule isn't a problem so far as our unreasonably sharp curves are concerned.

Appearance of Trains

Appearance of trains on minimum-radius curves is an important consideration. The vast majority of published pictures of trains show them on gentle curves because that's where you can see them best and where they look most graceful. On the sharpest real curves, 85 ft. passenger cars already begin to look a bit awkward; and on the model they may get around conventional radius bends safely, but they look horrible doing it. One attraction for really short cars, such as the 24 ft. jimmies used to roll iron ore to Lake Superior in solid trains, is their flowing appearance on curves. As radius increases, the point at which a miniature of the local freight with its mixture of 40 and 50 ft. boxcars or the Amtrak limited with its 85 footers begin to look reasonably realistic is a matter of individual choice, but Table 1-2 shows some average opinions. In some cases appearance calls for considerably more liberal curvature that does operation. This suggests that it may well be wise to have two different standards for main-line curves, one for hidden trackage and a larger radius for places where trains are in full view.

RADIUS VS SCALE

Table 1-1 translates our classes of curvature into specific radius values for several common model scales. In some cases the figures have been rounded off a bit to match commercially-available sectional track, since the distinction between classes isn't all that sharp. Now you can know when an HO-gauger tells you that he's using 18 inch curves that he's not interested in running 2-10-2's.

Since many industrial, yard and branch-line tracks on railroads operating in congested or rugged country are restricted from use by all but small locomotives and short cars, it makes sense to use different minimums for main line and secondary trackage on the model. Track plans in this book usually maintain a single standard for tracks used by through trains but indicate any points where sharper curves are necessary.

Why so much fuss about curve standards? Wouldn't it be better to pick a liberal figure and not have to worry about what runs where? Well, adding even a few percent to the minimum radius often completely changes the amount of railroading that can be fitted into the room available—particularly in the larger walk-in track plans, where using bigger curves may mean having to duck under the layout or squeeze through an inadequate aisle.

BEAUTIFUL CURVES

On the other hand, it's often possible to use a wide, swinging curve on which any full-scale train would feel comfortable instead of a stretch of straight track. The realism of such a scene has to be seen to be believed, and is well worth the trouble it takes to lay out such a gentle bend. As the second line of Table 1-3 shows, a curve around which a train might run 50 mph is still pretty big, even in the tinest (Z-gauge, 1/220, not currently available commercially except in European prototypes) scales. You're not likely to be able to fit in a horseshoe of such radius, but a few degrees of a *sweeping* curve along one side of the layout can add a lot.

Is there anything that can be done to help save space without impairing the ability of a layout to accommodate those long cars and big locomotives? Yes, there is.

SUPERELEVATION AND EASEMENTS

As Table 1-3 indicates, centrifugal force requires that main-line railroad curves be *banked* or *superelevated* by raising the outer rail if high speeds are to be allowed. Since the two rails should be level on straight track, referred to as tangent in civil engineering terminology, there would be a sudden requirement to go from zero to maximum superelevation upon entering a curve unless the tangent and curved sections were joined by a section of gradually changing sharpness (Fig. 1-1). As the train passes through this *easement* section, also referred to as a *spiral* since it's mathematically a curve of that shape, the radius and supereleva-

Table 1-2. Track Curvature VS. Rolling Stock Performance and Appearance.

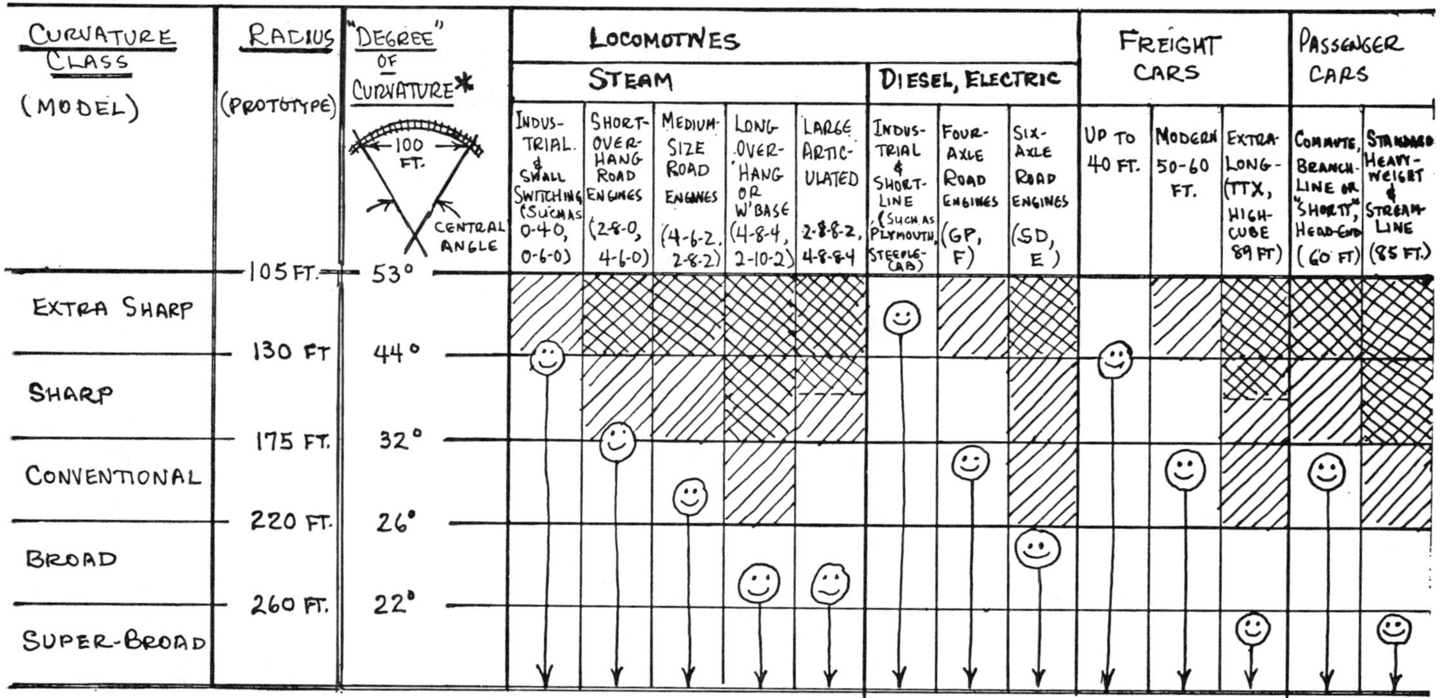

* RAILROAD CIVIL ENGINEERS DEFINE THE "DEGREE" OF A CURVE AS THE CENTRAL ANGLE THRU WHICH THE TRACK CURVES IN 100 FT.

KEY:

OPERATION VIRTUALLY IMPOSSIBLE WITHOUT MAKING "TOY TRAIN" MODIFICATIONS (SUB-STANDARD SIZE & LENGTH, GROSSLY OVERSIZE WHEEL FLANGES, ETC.)

OPERATION REQUIRES MAJOR MODIFICATIONS (ENGINE-TENDER SPACING, COUPLER SWING, ETC.) BUT OPERATION OF FULLY SCALE EQUIPMENT OF LENGTHS INDICATED IS PRACTICAL IF CLEARANCES CAN BE SUITABLY INCREASED.

OPERATION VIRTUALLY UNRESTRICTED WITH ONLY THOSE DEVIATIONS FROM STRICT SCALE (E.G MODIFIED TRAILER-TRUCK SUSPENSION) CONSIDERED "NORMAL" IN SCALE MODEL RAILROADING PRACTICE.

☺ APPEARANCE OF EQUIPMENT ON CURVES REASONABLY REALISTIC

Table 1-3. Prototype VS. Model Curves VS. Speed.

PROTOTYPE: SPEED LIMIT (TYPICAL, WITH 6″ MAX. SUPERELEVATION OF OUTER RAIL)	PROTOTYPE: "DEGREE" OF CURVE (CURVATURE/100 FT.)	PROTOTYPE: RADIUS, FT.	MODEL: RADIUS, INCHES Z	N	HO	S	O	CURVATURE CLASS
100 + M.P.H.	1°	5729	312	430	830	1070	1430	
45-50 M.P.H.	5°	1146	63	86	157	215	286	SUPER-BROAD
30-35 M.P.H.	10°	573	31	43	79	107	143	SUPER-BROAD
20 M.P.H.	22°	260	14	19	36	49	64	BROAD
10-15 M.P.H.	26°	220	12	16	30	41	54	CONVENTIONAL
6 M.P.H.	32°	175	9½	13	24	33	44	SHARP
4 M.P.H.	44°	130	7	9¾	18		33	EXTRA SHARP

26°–44°: OFF LIMITS TO ALL BUT SHORT FREIGHT CARS IN MOST CASES

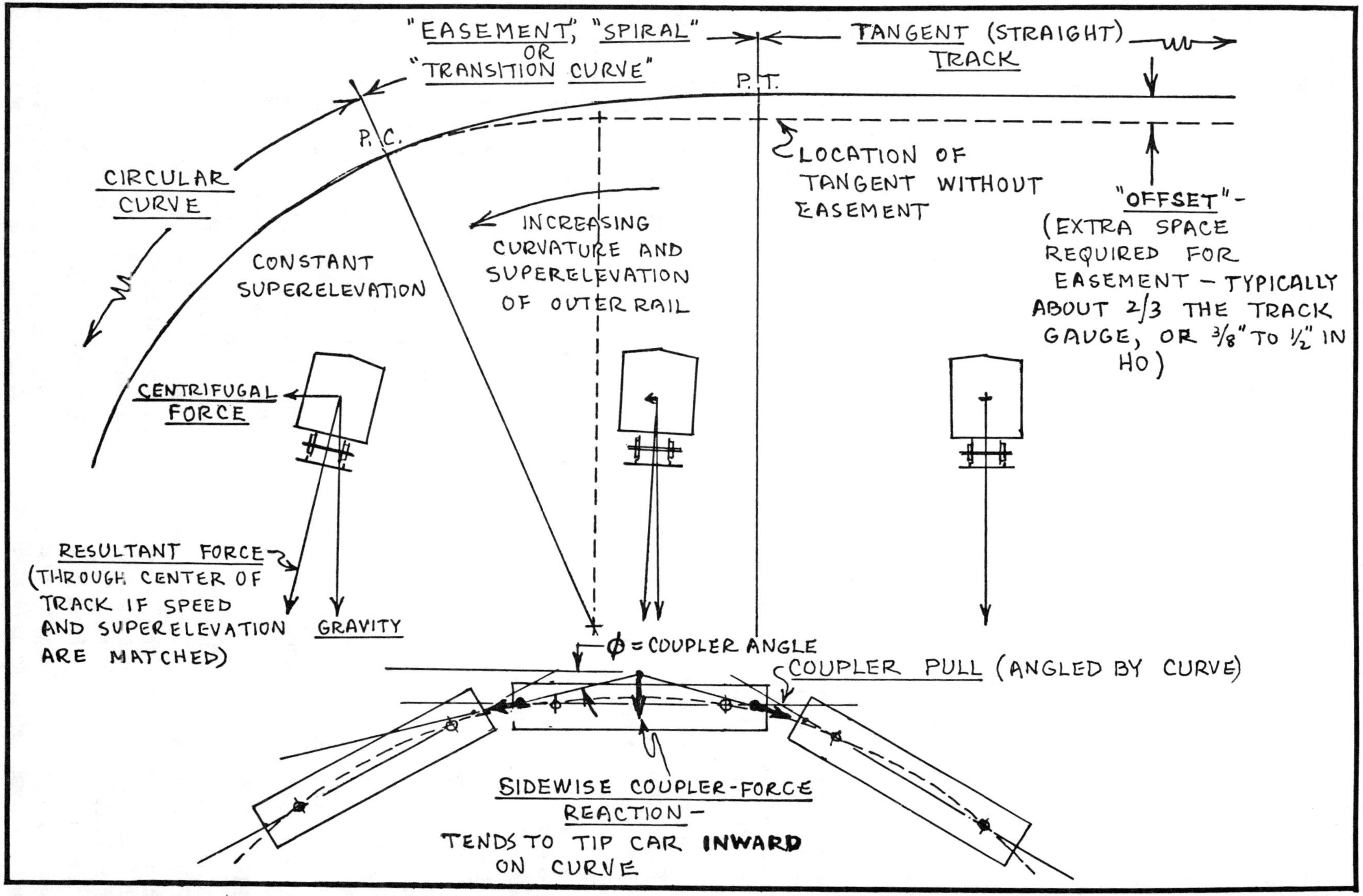

Fig. 1-1. Easements and superelevation.

tion can change so that it remains in equilibrium and runs smoothly throughout the transition.

As Fig. 1-2 shows, on our excessively sharp model railroad curves there's another reason for using curves with easements; they greatly reduce misalignment and coupler swing as *long* cars enter minimum-radius sections. This not only greatly improves appearance but tracking as well, reducing the likelihood of derailment, especially when backing up, and even allowing the use of a smaller minimum radius with a given amount of coupler swing.

Prototype railroad spirals are figured very precisely, and for high-speed operation are often hundreds of feet in length. They'd run off the end of our 4 × 8 layout before even reaching the circular part of one curve! Without getting that fancy, the major benefits of an easement can be achieved on a small track plan with conventional or sharp curve standards by introducing one section of larger-radius track at the beginning of any minimum-radius bend. Most of the track plans in this book provide space for doing this on all trackage where rolling stock other than short (40 ft. or less) freight cars would be expected to operate.

On less cramped layouts, easements should also be used in the interest of better appearance and smoother running. More sophisticated but still very practical methods for laying out easements are covered in books, magazine articles and NMRA publications on trackwork. Since the benefits of eased curves are not just a matter of appearance, they should be used on hidden trackage, too. Since many curves begin at the point where a track leaves the tangent via a turnout, the selection of a turnout with an appropriate sharpness of curvature is also important for smooth train action and good appearance. This is discussed later with trackwork components.

CENTRIFUGAL FORCE

As Fig. 1-1 illustrates, an individual car in a train is subjected to several forces working against each other. On prototype railroads it has been found that about six inches of superelevation on standard-gauge track is the most that it's practical to use in balancing centrifugal force. If the train could always be sure of continuing at the designed speed until passing beyond the curve, much more severely banked curves could be used. But since it may be necessary to stop anywhere in an emergency, the tilt must be limited. Restarting the train must not pull its cars *inward*, and with the extremely long piggyback and high-cube cars now in use this is a real possibility, even on the relatively gentle curves typical of main lines.

In the model, our curves are much sharper, making the angular coupler-pull forces bigger in proportion to the car weight. At the same time, centrifugal force does an almost complete fade out; at the same scale speed, it's less than 1/9th as much in HO as it would be in full size. Superelevation simply isn't necessary on the model unless you are determined to run at toy-train speeds except as a matter of appearance. There are few things that add as much to the impressiveness and realism of a well-detailed model in operation on an artistically scenic layout as its smooth inward cant as it rolls around a neatly-ballasted curve.

TILT OR NO TILT

On the other hand, it is considerably easier to lay track precisely if it's flat, and superelevated curves require some freedom and flexibility in locomotive and car suspensions if derailment tendencies are to be avoided. The possibilities of momentary shorts between wheels and car body parts are increased, too. For most model railroaders, the best percentage play is *to avoid any superelevation on trackage where the trains are out of sight* but to bank other curved sections as they would be in the prototype. This will require some extra care and effort in track laying and rolling-stock check-out for reliable operation, but the overall effect on realism will be well worth it.

From the track-plan standpoint, the only effect of superelevation, apart from the need for using easements at the ends of curves, shows up in terms of clearances between trains if they are tilted differently on adjacent trackage. Track plans in this book have been adjusted to allow for superelevation, as indicated on Fig. 1-3. That brings up another major matter affecting the traffic a model railroad can handle—clearances!

TRACK CENTERS AND CLEARANCES

Standard-gauge railroads usually space parallel tracks on 13 or 14 ft. centers, and main-line

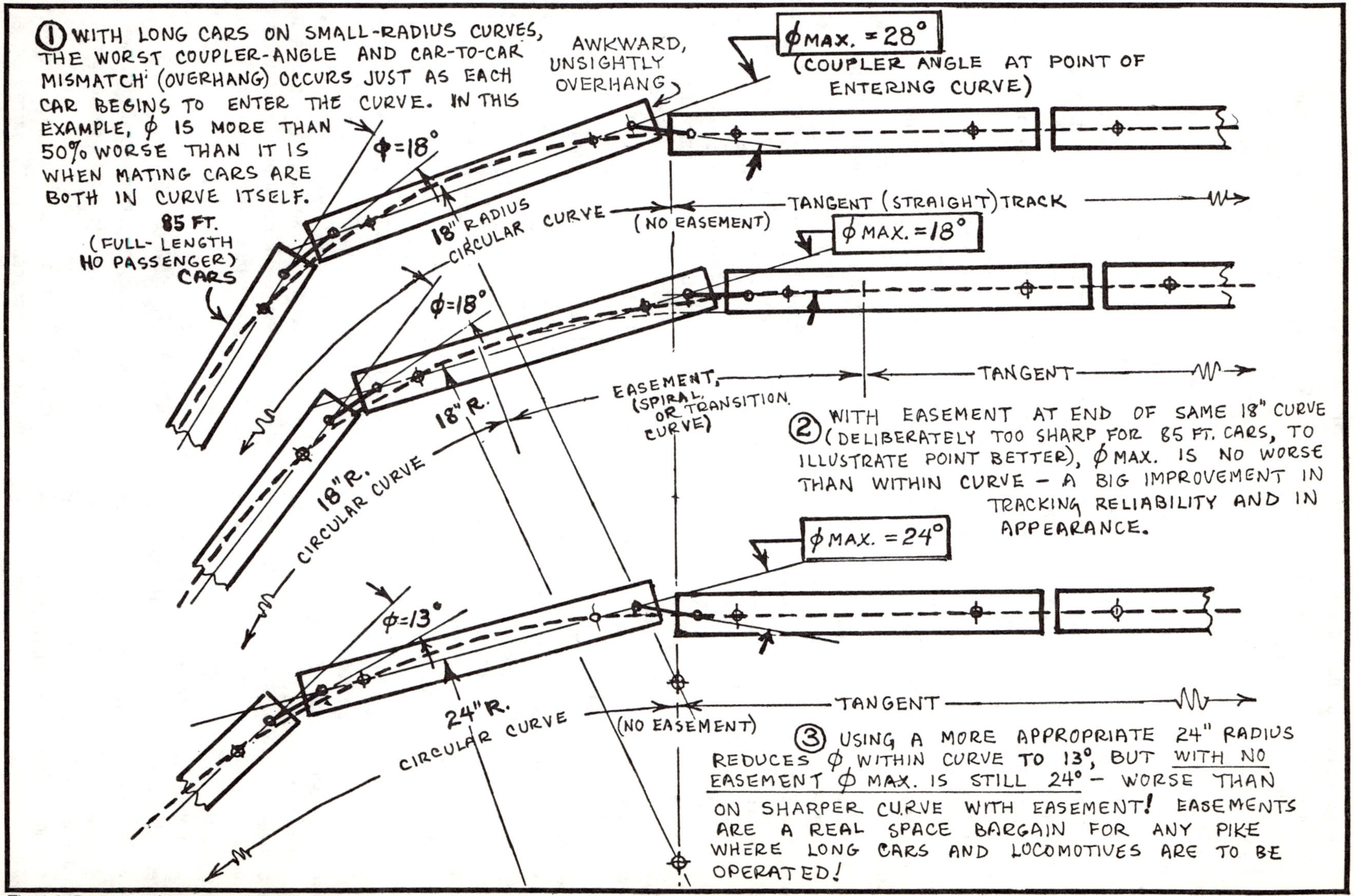

Fig. 1-2. Better running on smaller radius?

curves are gentle enough that car and locomotive overhang isn't usually much of a problem. In model railroading, our curves are so sharp in comparison that it's necessary to increase track spacing considerably to avoid side-swiping. Table 1-4 pretty well tells the story in terms of the different classes of curve sharpness and common model railroad scales.

The sharper the curve, the more any particular piece of rolling stock overhangs and the wider the track centers must be if that horrid scraping sound is to be avoided. On the other hand, the very tightest curves will only accommodate the shorter classes of cars and locomotives, so it would be a waste of space to allow "Big Boy" clearances between tracks on a pike built to sharp-curve standards.

Track plans in this book use track-center spacing corresponding to the "normal" selection of rolling stock for their curvature class, as shown in Table 1-4. These standards are based on the critical *swingout* on curves. On long passenger or freight cars, the inward movement at the center of the car on the outer track in combination with the outward swing of the car corner on the inside track is what usually governs the space required. On layouts with broad or superbroad standards where large steam locomotives are likely to be operated, it's the outward swing of the cab (on engines with a long rear overhang, such as 4-8-4's) or of the boiler (on articulateds) which represents the worst case, in combination with a long passenger car on the outer track. Since it is possible, and to "big steam" fans almost irresistible, to operate modified engines on what should logically be considered way too sharp curves, these extreme requirements for extra wide track spacing are also known.

There must be some allowance for clearance beyond the theoretical sum of *swing-in* and *swing-out* measurements, of course, and Table 1-4 adds 3/16 in. for this *in all scales*. The larger proportional allowance in N and HO, relative to the larger scales, is to take account of the fact that there is a considerably larger clearance between wheel flanges and track in these sizes. This permits a considerably greater angle between track and carbody to develop, for which space must be allowed.

WHY KEEP 'EM CLOSE?

Why not just allow plenty of clearance and be done with it? Compared with the effect of using an extra six inches of curve radius, adding a half inch between tracks won't have much effect on how much railroad will fit in the space, and then there will be no clearance problems to worry about! Well, it's primarily a matter of appearance. As mentioned before, with the wide-swinging curves typical of a steam railroad it's not necessary to widen spacing on curves, so the increased spacing in the model tends to make it look too much like a street-car arrangement.

In yards, widening out the track centers *does* greatly inflate the space requirement as the number of parallel tracks increases. Here the limiting factor is usually not car clearance, unless the yard is on a sharp curve, but rather it's likely to be finger clearance. If you do much switching, and after all that's what yards are for, it's important to be able to couple and uncouple cars on the parallel tracks. Doing this by hand would require widening out the track centers by a huge proportion in N or HO scales, since there's no evidence that model railroaders working in the smaller gauges have fingers that are proportionately skinnier.

Fortunately, automatic couplers and uncoupling ramps of reasonable reliability can take care of the yard uncoupling situation with closely-spaced tracks. There are some requirements regarding track curvature at the points where coupling and uncoupling is desired. These have been taken into consideration in the track plans in this book or are mentioned in the commentary section where there are particular problems. The narrow *alley* represented by an empty yard track between two strings of boxcars is one of the "railroady" scenes we seek to reproduce, so yard-track spacing in most plans assumes the use of automatic couplers and follows prototype standards of 14 or 14½ ft. centers.

WHAT ABOUT NARROW GAUGE?

Narrow-gauge equipment is both narrower and shorter than its standard-gauge counterparts, though not proportionally so; 3 ft. gauge track is 36 percent skinnier than standard but typical cars are only about 20 percent slimmer. Narrow-gauge

Table 1-4. Minimum Track Centers on Curves.

CURVATURE CLASS (MODEL)	GOVERNING CLASS OF ROLLING STOCK	THEORETICAL MINIMUM TK. CENTERS (SCALE FT.)	TRACK CENTERS (INCHES)			
			N	HO	S	O
EXTRA SHARP (7⅝″ N, 15″ HO)	NORMAL EQUIPMENT* (40′ FGT. CARS)	13′2″	1¼	2	2⅝	3½
	EXTREME (65′ PSGR. CARS)	14′10″	1 5/16	2¼	3	3⅞
SHARP (9¾″ N, 18″ HO)	NORMAL (65′ PSGR. CARS)	13′8″	1¼	2	2¾	3⅝
	EXTREME (85′ PSGR. CARS)	17′4″	1½	2 9/16	3 7/16	4½
CONVENTIONAL (13″ N, 24″ HO)	NORMAL (85″PSGR. CARS)	16′0″	1⅜	2 5/16	3 3/16	4 3/16
	EXTREME (LARGE 4-8-4 & 85′ PSGR. CARS)	18′2″	1 9/16	2 11/16	3⅝	4 7/16
BROAD (16″ N, 30″ HO)	NORMAL (LARGE 4-8-4 & 85′ PSGR. CARS)	15′11″	1⅜	2 5/16	3 3/16	4 3/16
	EXTREME (UP "BIG BOY" & 85′ PSGR. CARS)	16′11″	1 7/16	2½	3⅜	4 7/16
SUPER-BROAD (19″ N, 36″ HO)	NORMAL (U.P. "BIG BOY" & 85″ PSGR. CARS)	15′8″	1⅜	2 5/16	3⅛	4⅛
	EXTREME (SAME AS ABOVE)	15′8″	″	″	″	″
TANGENT TRACK	ANY	13′-14′	1¼	2	2⅝	3½†

* LARGEST EQUIPMENT LOGICALLY USED ON TRACKAGE OF CURVATURE-CLASS INDICATED.
† 4″ IN YARDS IF NON-AUTOMATIC COUPLERS USED.

trainmen, like HOn-3 or On-3 model railroaders, weren't any smaller than those on the wide gauge lines and protruded just as far from the boxcar when hanging on a grabiron en route down the yard, so track centers were kept at about a 12 ft. minimum. To preserve the distinctive wide-spaced appearance of Fig. 1-4, narrow-gauge track plans in this book use this standard.

VERTICAL CLEARANCES

The height between railheads required for one track to pass over another can have a profound effect on the track arrangement and operating characteristics of an entire layout. Furthermore, the advent of piggyback trailer-on-flat-car, multi-level auto rack and high-cube boxcar traffic in the 1960's resulted in a rather sudden increase in the maximum height of freight cars from 15 ft. above the rail to 17, 18 and even 19 feet. A corresponding increase in minimum vertical had to take place on most main lines, even if it meant lowering the floor of tunnels or getting rid of them entirely. The problem was most acute in the East, since most of the Western railroads already had larger clearances and fewer old, low overpasses. What this means to the modeler, of course, is that he must make an early decision if he wants to be able to run modern freight and passenger bi-level or dome equipment on his pike. Figure 1-5 shows how prototype practice affects our modeling standards. We don't have to worry about decapitating brakemen, but every extra foot of clearance we decide to provide does affect the whole track plan unless, of course, the purposes of the railroad can be satisfied with a flat or single-level layout.

Figure 1-6 shows how much the clearance between railheads as one track crosses over another may affect the grade it takes to do the trick. If the crossing takes place where the tracks are hidden, we can forget the fact that bridges must have a floor structure strong and rigid enough to transfer the weight of the train from the rails to the bridge structure and that this is usually several feet thick. In the smaller gauges, the track itself will bridge a 20-(scale) foot gap and support any likely train weight. Out where it shows, thin-floor bridges can be used, usually without too much loss of realism.

Track plans in this book are generally based on providing vertical separation of at least 24 scale feet where tracks cross each other, railhead to railhead. Where this raises the grade to an awkward steepness, the remedies of thin-floor construction and restrictions on equipment selection are available. Having some trackage which will not accommodate the high loads is far from unrealistic. As long as you have one route over which such cars can move on your modern-era railroad, the special rules and switching involved in keeping the new Chevvys from being flattened by the low clearance on Track 2 can add an authentic flavor and variety to your operations!

SIDE CLEARANCES

As Fig. 1-5 indicates, *width* of railroad equipment has not increased in recent years. Aside from track spacing, which we have previously considered and which the extra-long cars have greatly affected, side clearances are more a matter of scenery than track plan design. There are a few situations to watch out for, as indicated on Fig. 1-7, which have generally been taken care of in our track plans either by providing extra track spacing or a cautionary note in the commentary.

GRADES AND TONNAGE

There are two distinctly different situations calling for *grades* on model railroads; in one of them, the grade is a villain, while in the other it's the hero.

To let one track *cross* over another is the first and most common reason for introducing a grade. If one line doesn't cross another *at grade*, there's no alternative but to have it somehow attain a level somewhere from 12 to 28 feet higher so it can pass above with proper clearance, as we saw in the discussion on vertical clearances (Fig. 1-6). Usually such grades are incidental to achieving a desired track plan within space limits, and the extra hauling power they demand from our locomotives is a necessary evil. If one of the tracks involved must remain level for some reason, such as being located on a nice flat sheet of plywood forming the basic layout, the other has to do the whole job itself and is about twice as steep (Fig. 1-8) as it needs to be if a split the difference approach with both

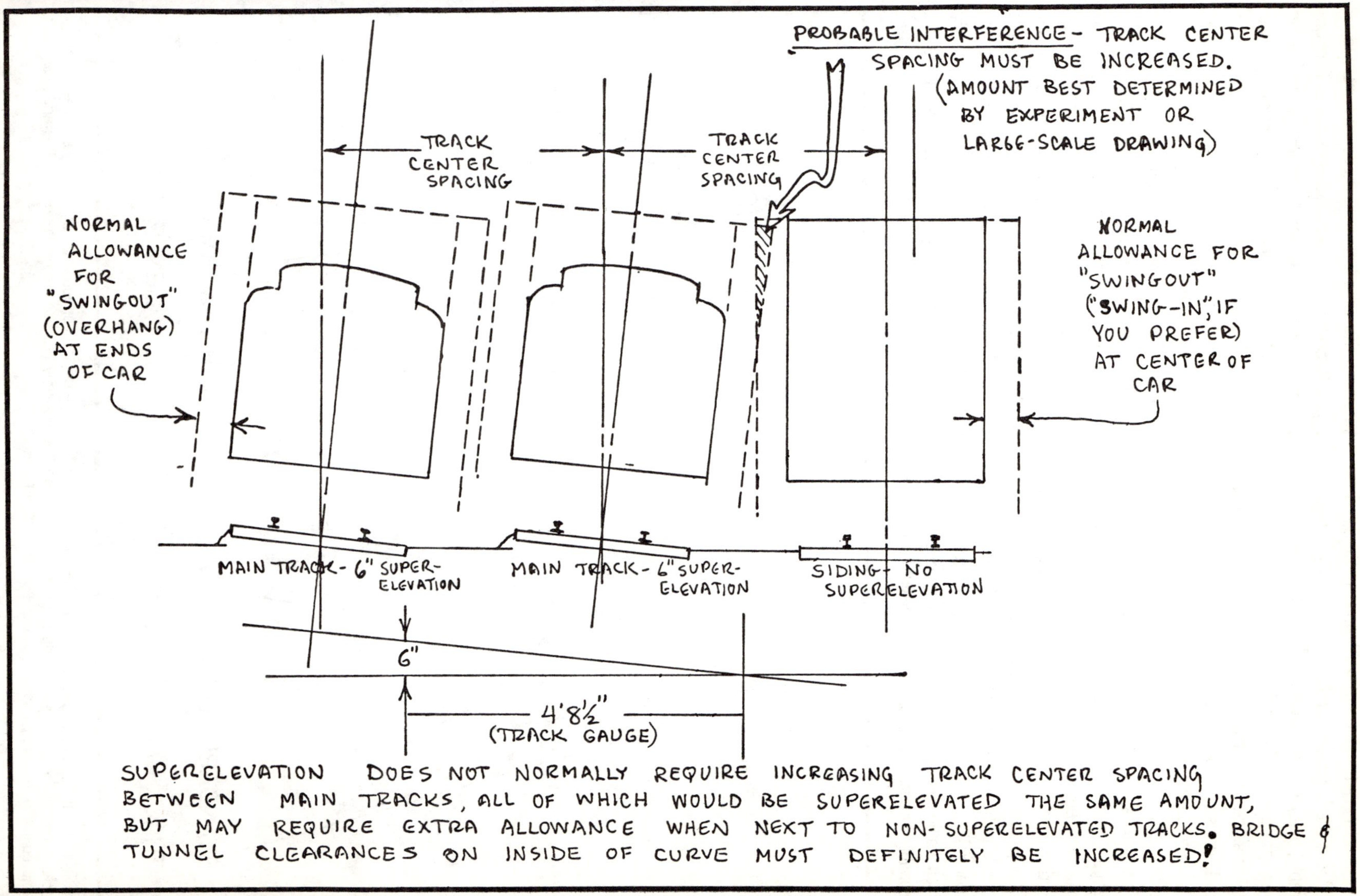

Fig. 1-3. Allowing room for superelevated curves.

tracks on a grade can be used. Doubling the grade reduces the locomotive's hauling capacity considerably, from 20 cars down to 13 in this case where we assume the train has free-rolling, needle-axle, Delrin side-frame trucks. Figure 1-9 shows what grade does to hauling capacity, in a general way. The exact effect varies all over the lot, depending on the scale of the model, the type and lubrication of the trucks, the curvature, exact wheel tread and flange contour, and other factors. The easier-rolling the equipment, the closer it is to full-scale friction levels, and the greater the effect of any given grade in reducing tonnage. Any engine will be able to haul more cars up a given hill if they're freer-rolling, but the number it could haul on level track would increase even more. In practice, you'll probably find your railroad's results will lie somewhere in the area between those two curves on Fig. 1-9. Some trucks achieve even lower friction, but most modelers find it necessary to *add* some drag to get satisfactory automatic coupler performance with such trucks.

As the third grade in Fig. 1-8 shows, it's often necessary to keep the steeper grade but use the grade-splitting technique to let the tracks cross each other within a shorter distance. Getting the track arrangement you want in the space available is usually more of a problem than getting enough engine power to move trains of the length you want to run. But grade 4 illustrates a somewhat curious point: when a grade gets short in comparison to the length of a train, its effect is greatly reduced. This is why full-scale railroaders find it easy to elevate one line over another, even where

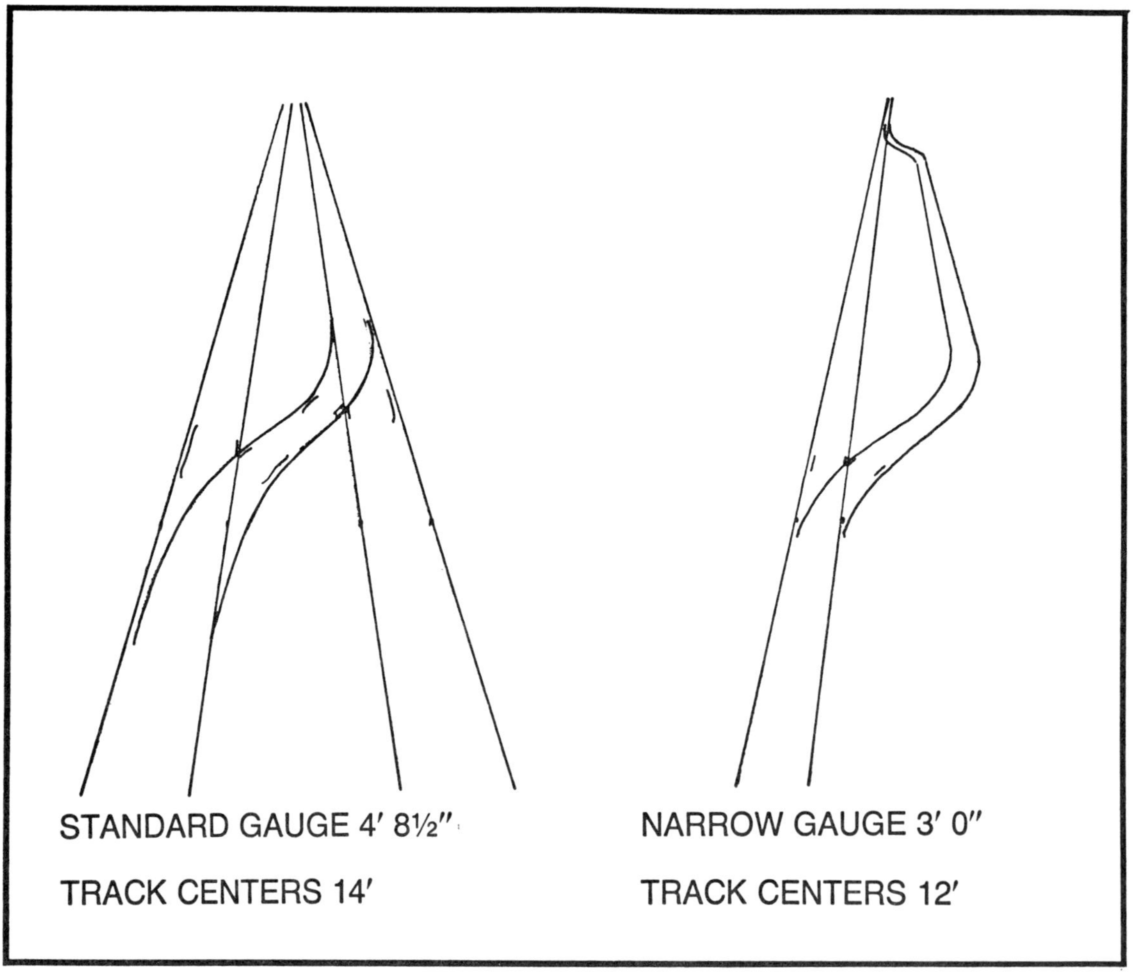

Fig. 1-4. Making sure narrow gauge looks narrow. A good deal of the distinctiveness and attractiveness of narrow gauge trackage comes from its slender appearance in contrast to the relatively wide space between main line and side track, captured in the model by retaining the ample track-center spacing.

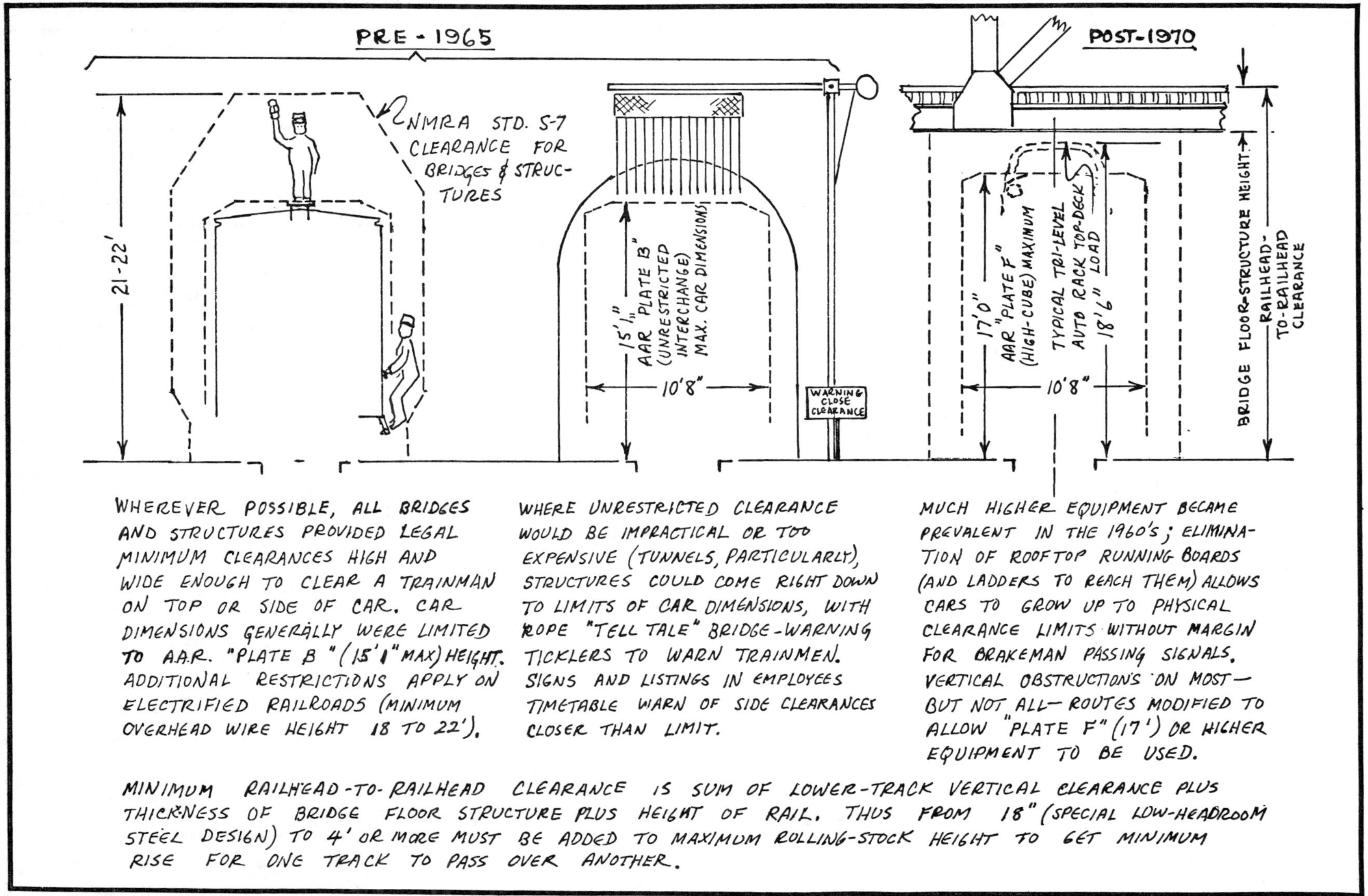

Fig. 1-5. Prototype clearances.

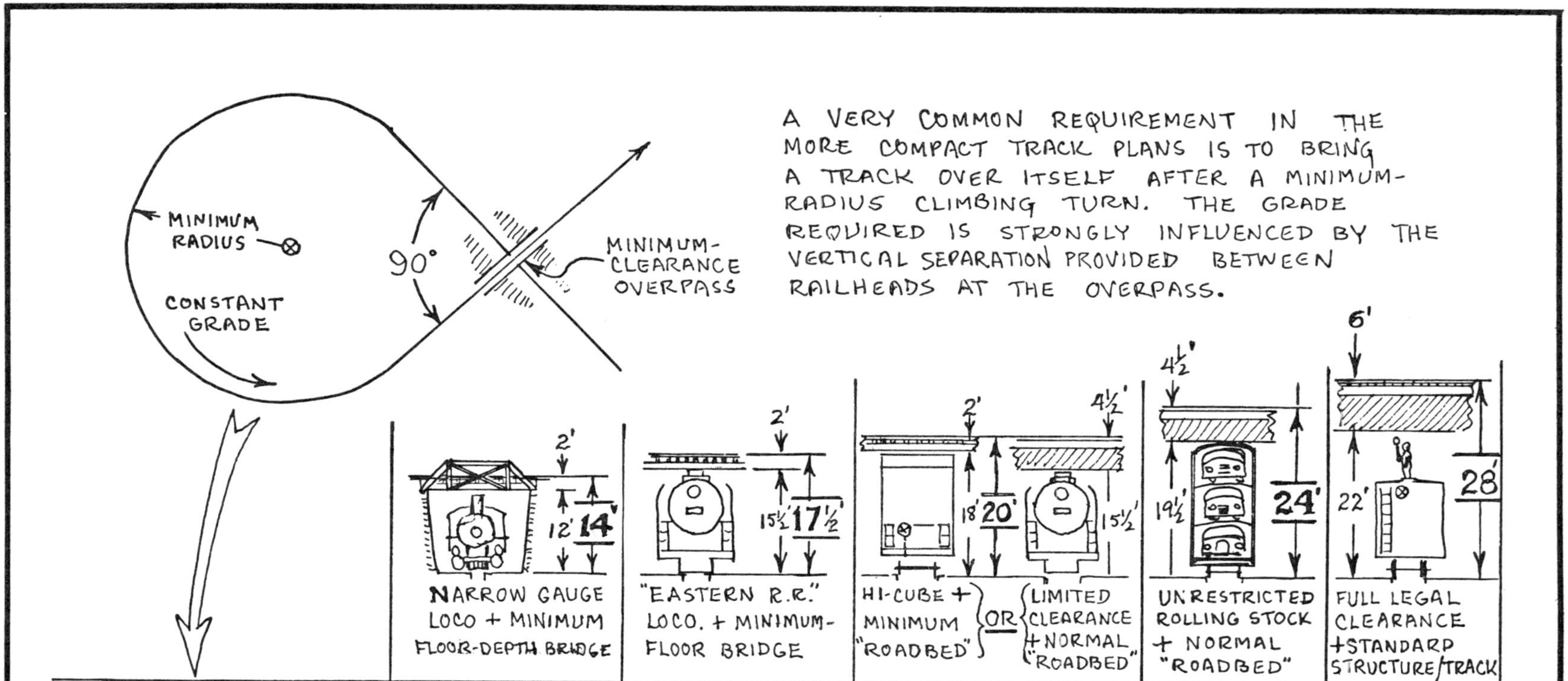

	NARROW GAUGE LOCO + MINIMUM FLOOR-DEPTH BRIDGE	"EASTERN R.R." LOCO. + MINIMUM-FLOOR BRIDGE	HI-CUBE + MINIMUM "ROADBED" OR LIMITED CLEARANCE + NORMAL "ROADBED"	UNRESTRICTED ROLLING STOCK + NORMAL "ROADBED"	FULL LEGAL CLEARANCE + STANDARD STRUCTURE/TRACK
SHARP CURVES	1.6%	2.0%	2.3%	2.7%	3.2%
CONVENTIONAL CURVES	1.2%	1.5	1.7	2.0	2.4
BROAD CURVES	0.9%	1.2	1.4	1.6	1.9
SUPER-BROAD CURVES	0.75%	1.0	1.1	1.4	1.6

Fig. 1-6. What vertical clearance means to your locomotives.

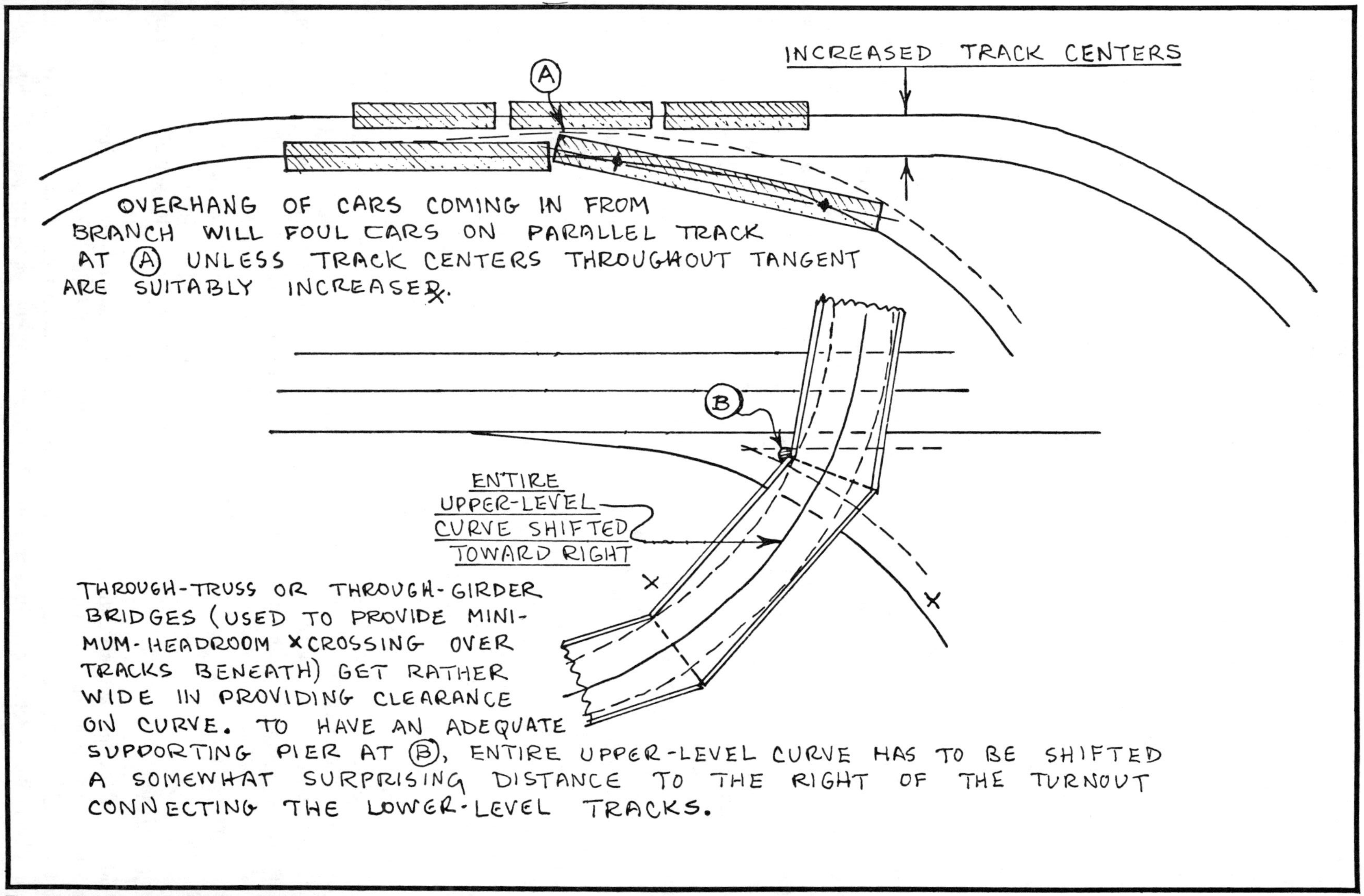

Fig. 1-7. Sneaky close-clearance situations.

trains are heavy. Their trains, averaging 70 cars and the better part of a mile in length, will be starting down the other side before the caboose has approached the beginning of the grade. If your railroad uses enough motive power to run 30 or 40-car trains, you'll find, similarly, that fairly steep but short grades aren't much of a problem.

To accurately *model* a mountain railroad is the second reason for including grades on a layout. Here we *want* the train to slow down, grunt and perhaps need a bigger engine or a pusher to get over the hill. Since our trains are almost always very short in comparison to their prototypes, we at least come closer in modeling a mountain-crossing line where their tonnage is limited, too.

A second look at Fig. 1-9 will show that copying the grade of your favorite railroad's worst mountain trackage won't affect operations in anywhere near the same way. A one percent grade will chop level-track tonnage by 80 percent on the prototype; it takes four percent to do the same thing to even a free-rolling model. We wouldn't be running 150-car trains on level divisions anyway, so this doesn't mean that the model should have slopes four times as steep as the hills they're representing, but it definitely is necessary to *exaggerate* prototype grades if you want your railroad to act mountainous!

Track plans in this book include elevation figures that are usually the minimum necessary to provide proper clearance between levels. In many cases these result in grades which will let any trains that will fit on the layout run up hill and down dale without much strain. Where the track plan is one that would be suitable for representing a more rugged brand of railroading, alternate elevations are suggested, which will give the engines more of a battle. Don't be frightened by grades on the main line as much as three or four percent. They're necessary if the problems of getting traffic over one to two percent grades are to be simulated at all realistically.

VERTICAL CURVES

More trouble from grades in the model comes from vertical kinks in alignment at their juncture with level track than from the steepness of the grades themselves. Determining exactly how large a vertical curve (Fig. 1-10) it takes to stay out of trouble is not nearly as straightforward a matter as it is with horizontal curves. It depends a great deal on such variables as flange height, springing of driver axles on steam locomotives, and exact clearances at a host of potential points of conflict between car and locomotive parts.

Nevertheless, there are a few principles which can be established. Prototype (AAR) standards for freight cars require that, coupled together, they be able to accept a vertical curve of 785 ft. radius. That's a whopping nine feet in HO and sounds as if compliance might make our actual grades a lot steeper than expected from simply figuring the slope from elevation change and length available. The *angles* associated with even steep grades are rather small, though—a 4 percent grade is only a little over 2 degrees—and a 785 ft. radius vertical curve leading into such an incline is only 31 ft. long. On any grade long enough to affect your main-line trains' tonnage ratings (Fig. 1-8), the difference between practical and theoretical grades will be negligible, an increase from 2 to 2.1 percent, for example.

The long-wheelbase example of Fig. 1-10 is extreme, a lanky Santa Fe 5000-class 2-10-4 with its enormous 74 in. drivers and long overhang meeting a sudden 4 percent grade, but it does point out the problems. Two rules pretty well cover the matter, however:

1. *Make all changes in grade on straight track.* This means, in particular, that no change in grade should occur anywhere in a turnout.

2. *Make all changes in grade on a single piece of track supporting structure* (plywood or wood). Figure 1-11 illustrates this point. This isn't strictly a matter of track planning, of course, but it's a rather positive way of insuring that proper vertical curves are used without going to the trouble of calculating them and showing them in detail on the layout drawings. The stiffness of these materials in practical thicknesses is such that they will insure a smooth curve of adequate gentleness to avoid most problems.

Track plans in this book give the theoretical grade on main-track inclines; but on short rises, in industrial trackage for example where the vertical curves represent a significant part of the length of

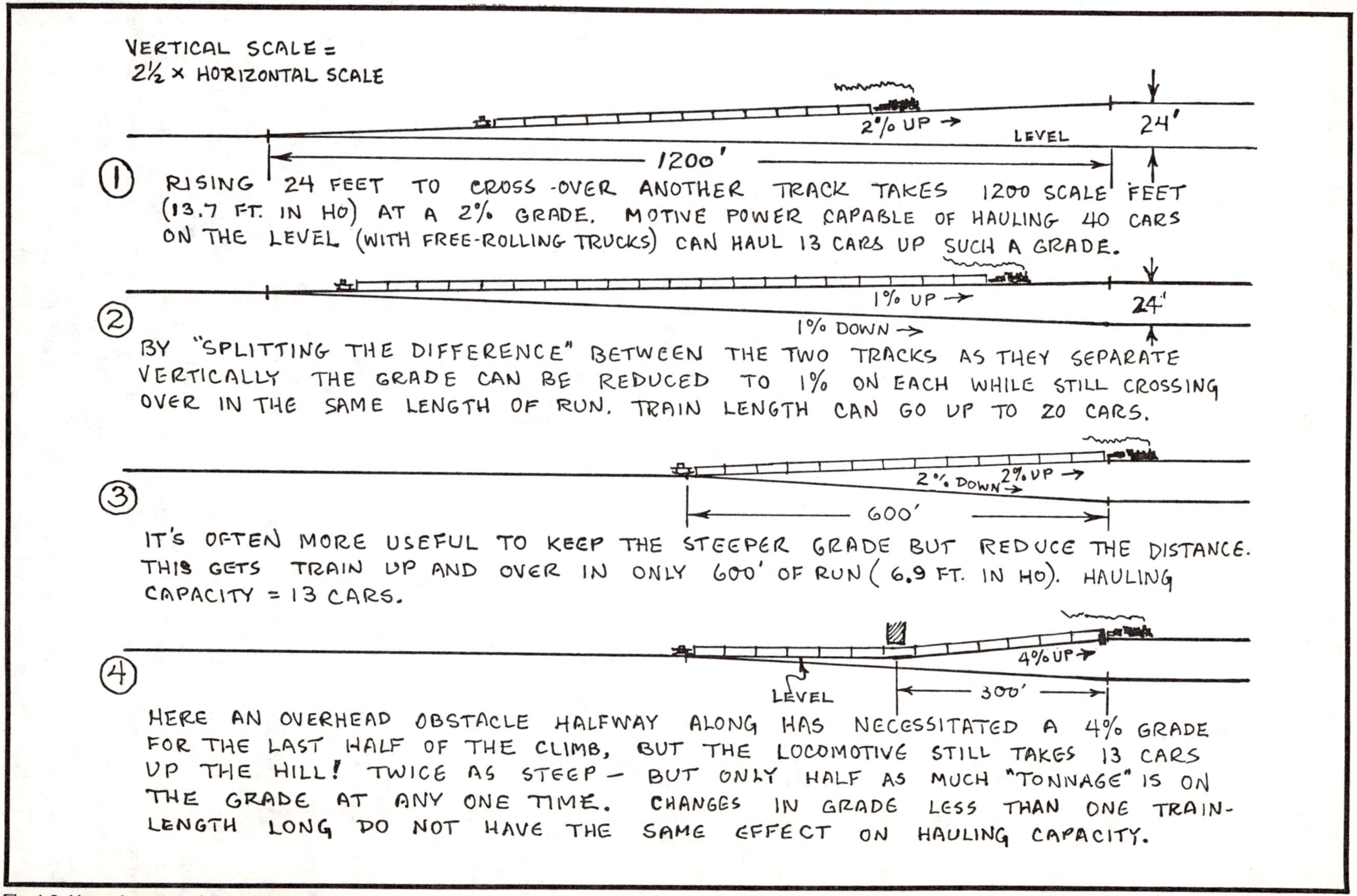

Fig. 1-8. Up and over grades and their effects.

the slope, an adjustment has been made to be sure that the grade figure is conservative.

TRACKWORK

As any kid finds out the day after Christmas, it's a dull railroad that has only an oval of track. Extending the main line into another room and around some more corners postpones the dullness, but switching trains and cars from one track to another is really the name of the game in railroading, prototype or model. Without the basic device for interconnecting tracks, trains would be confined to fixed-consist, round and 'round or back and forth movements—not much good for producing useful transportation. One of the main reasons that there are so few monorail systems is the lack of any simple scheme for "bending the rail" to change the routing or let cars be added or subtracted from the trains.

In conventional railroading—no problem! The key device is what the American civil engineer calls a *turnout* (Fig. 1-12), a set of moving points which divert the wheels from one track to another pair of rails plus a frog/guard rail arrangement that lets the flanged wheels cross over one running rail so that the second track can go its own way, completely clear of its mate. In British practice, the whole affair is referred to as a set of *points* while on the American railroad the trainmen and the operating and signaling departments always talk about it as a *switch*. Technically, the switch is just the moving-part element of the turnout. And that, of course, is what the trainman or tower operator actually shifts when he "throws the switch" by hand on the spot or remotely by power-actuated switch machine.

TURNOUTS

Figure 1-12 also defines the meaning of the *Number* of the frog, which is used to measure the angle at which the rails cross at the frog. This also measures the sharpness of the curve which a train encounters in passing through the diverging route at the turnout and therefore the speed allowed.

A No. 6 turnout in prototype practice is a rather sharply-curved one, used mostly in yards where speed would be limited to 10 mph or less. At a main-line junction where trains are routed to various destinations, you'll find turnouts with switch *points* as long as 45 ft. and No. 20 frogs through which trains can curve smoothly at 50 mph or so. The 150 ft. *lead* or length of a No. 20 is out of the question for model use, but most track plans do use different-number turnouts to match different rolling stock and speed situations.

The basic switch-point and frog elements of the turnout are combined in dozens of different ways to meet the hundreds of routing patterns which must be fitted into the space available. There are even places where tracks from three directions cross each other at a single point! Figure 1-13 reviews some of the more common trackwork items which have been given specific names. In particular, note the difference between a *crossover* and a *crossing*.

Much of the variety in trackwork comes from the need to accomplish the required routings within the space available, especially in passenger-terminal and industrial areas in city locations. The fascinating double-slip switch with its 12 moving points is only the equivalent of two simple turnouts so far as the number of routings it permits (four), but the extra complication may be acceptable if there just isn't room to cross over several parallel approach tracks before reaching the end of the station platforms. The lap turnout needs an extra frog but is standard for use in classification yards where a large number of tracks must feed from a single pair of rails coming over the top of the hump and fan out in as short a space as possible.

Turnout Geometry

Figure 1-14 shows the two principle classes of simple turnout—*curved-frog* and *conventional*. The supply department of a railroad isn't any happier than a hobby shop dealer to have to stock dozens of different turnouts or turnout kits, so the use of a straight frog which will fit either left-hand or right-hand applications is normal. It also is easier for the wheels to pass smoothly through a frog if they're not subjected to curved-track side forces at the same time, so conventional practice introduces a short tangent section through the frog on the diverging track. Switch points are usually straight rather than curved, and a slight kink in the

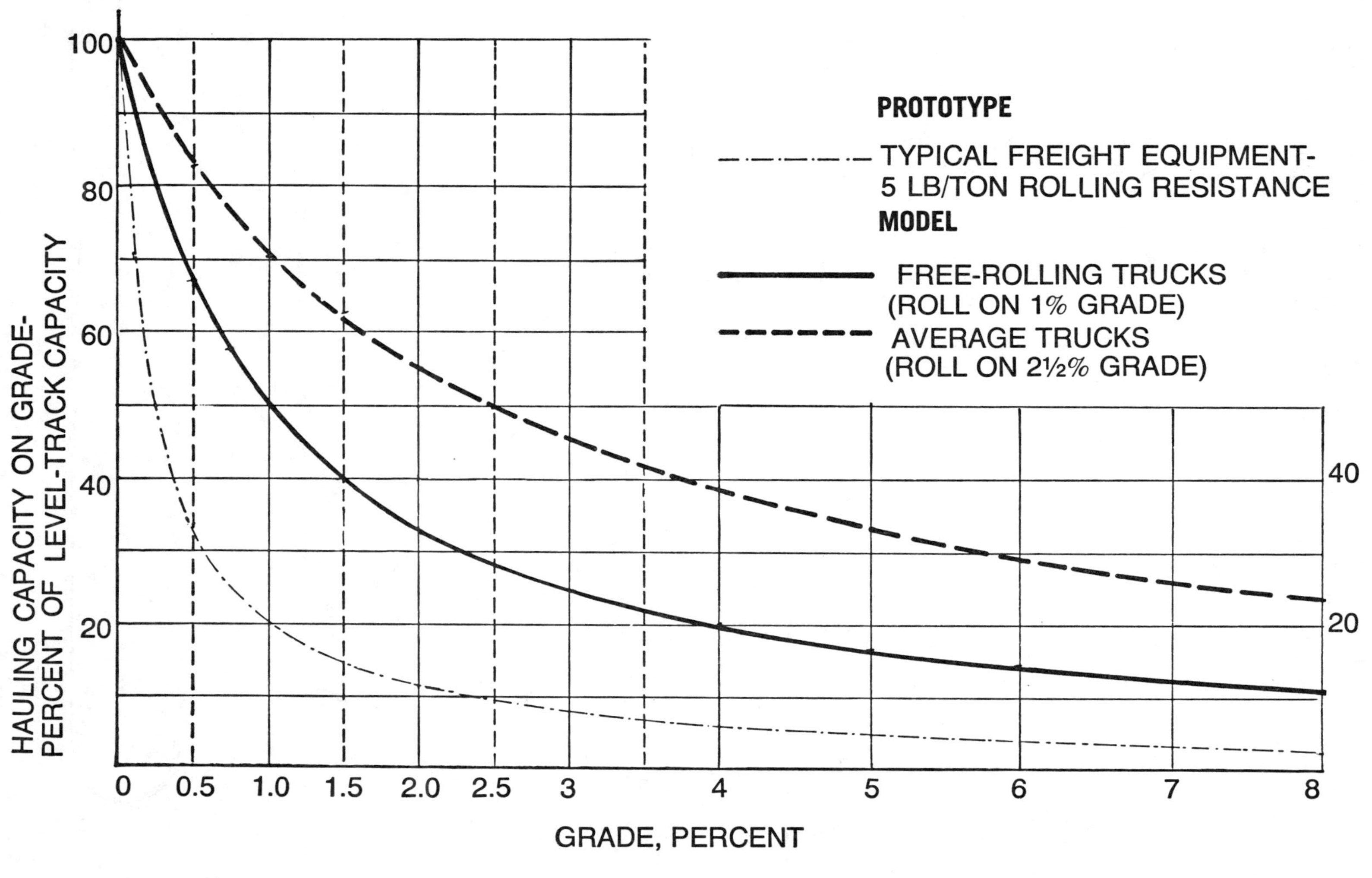

Fig. 1-9. What grade does to hauling capacity.

curved stock rail (Fig. 1-12) is used to make the point shorter and more rugged than it would be if planed down to a fine point. With the relatively gentle curvature of prototype turnouts, usually No. 8 and up, the difference is very small.

When you get down to the almost street-car-like curves sometimes needed in modeling, the smooth radius of the curved-frog turnout may become necessary and worthwhile. Several commercial versions are available. Even in a curved-frog unit, however, there must be an allowance for joining to the next section of track, and this short straight section (Fig. 1-15) must be taken into account in substituting such a turnout for circular sections of curved track. Plans in this book provide such allowances in those areas where these compact turnouts must be used.

How Sharp Is the Curve?

What we really need to know about turnouts is how their curvature reacts with our rolling stock. This is the same general relationship explored in the discussion on selecting suitable minimum radius standards for a track plan. In the case of conventional (straight-frog) turnouts, the diverging leg is actually a series of angles, tangents and curves which is rather messy to contemplate. However, as Fig. 1-14 shows, the conventional turnout's path can be represented satisfactorily by an *equivalent-radius* circular curve joining the connecting trackage ahead of and beyond the turnout itself. The important thing to notice about this curve is that it begins a short distance *ahead* of the toe of the switch points.

As the train passes through the turnout in the facing-point direction (toward the frog), it first continues on a straight course. At the switch points it is forced to make a sudden slight turn but then relaxes again as it travels along the straight switchpoint section. The closure rail is more sharply curved and the wheels are forced to catch up

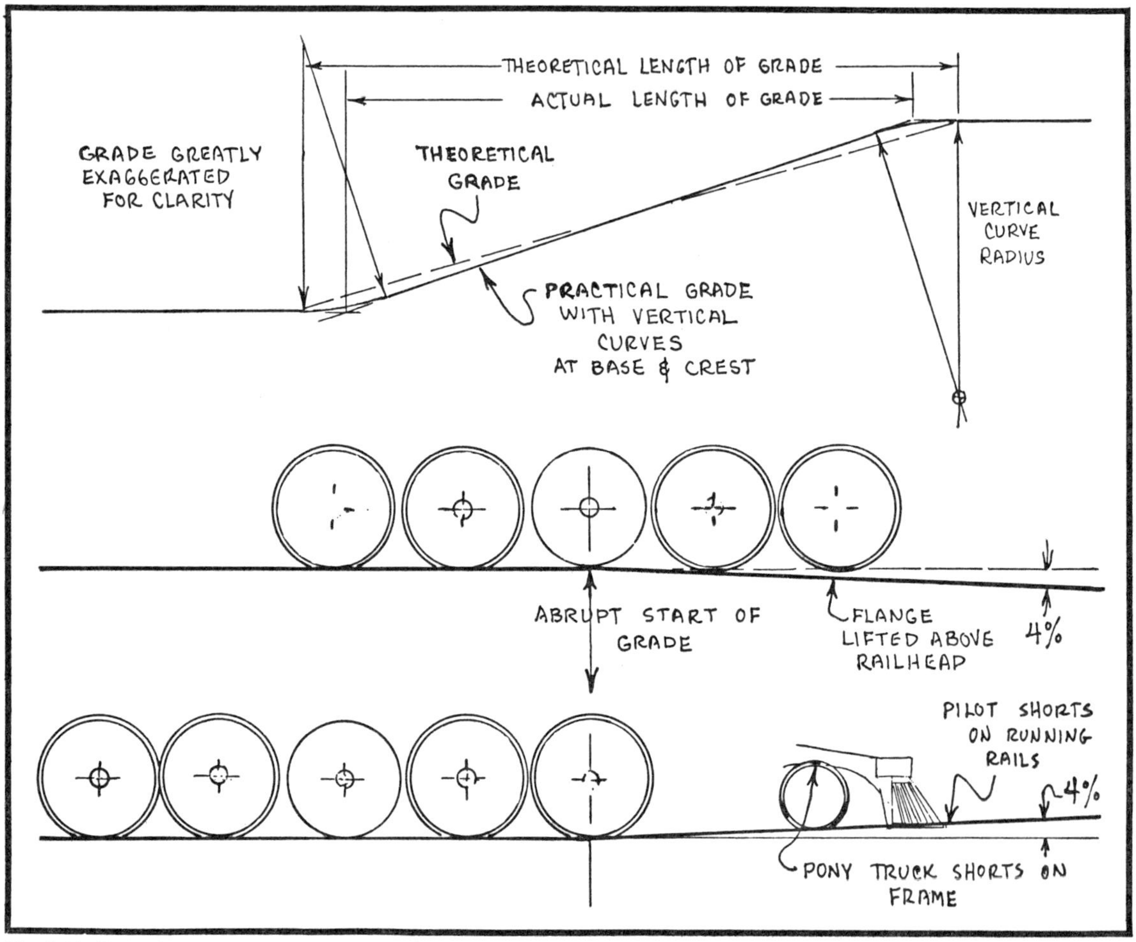

Fig. 1-10. Start-of-grade hazards—concave and convex.

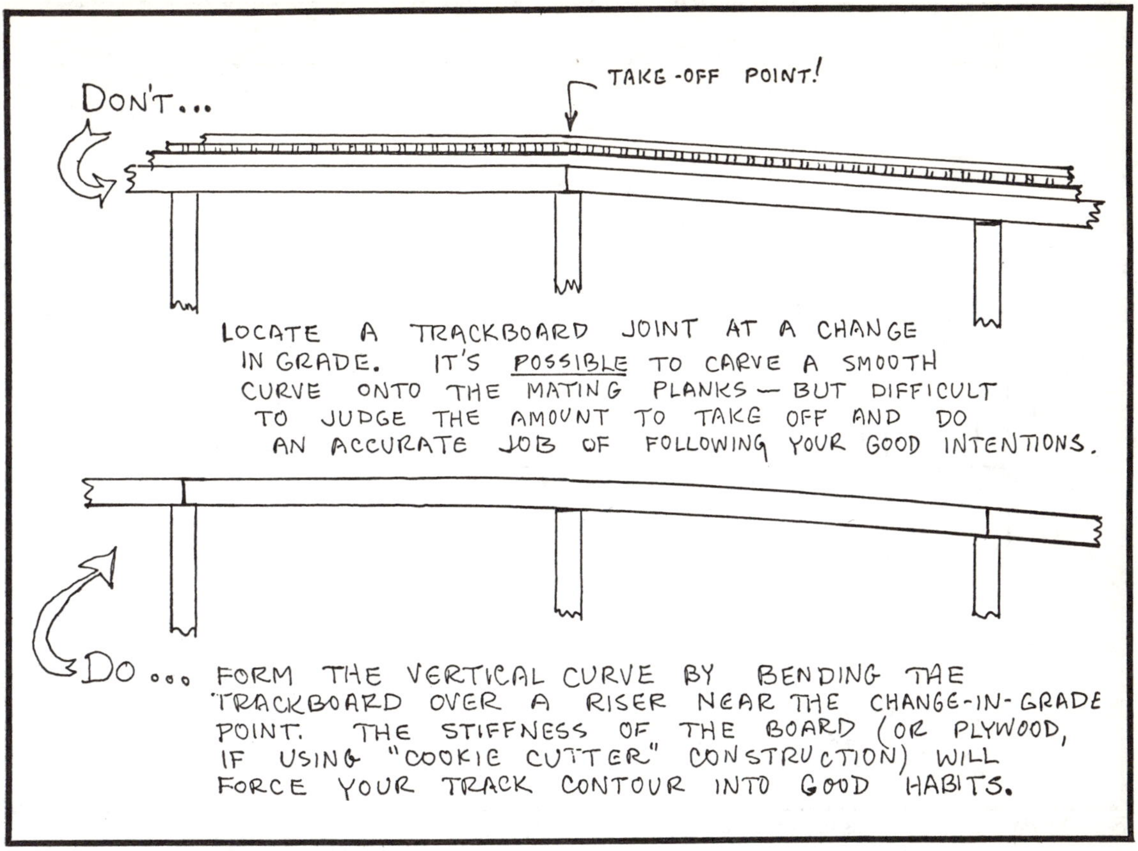

Fig. 1-11. Insuring a smooth vertical curve.

with the equivalent-radius curve. This is the most sharply curved part of the turnout and is the section that governs how long a rigid locomotive wheelbase may be without binding. Through the frog there is another tangent where things ease up again. At the end of all this, the angle through which the train has turned and the sidewise offset from the tangent in front of the turnout is exactly the same as if it has passed around a smooth circular curve of the equivalent radius.

From the standpoints of coupler swing and appearance of long cars and locomotives taking the turnout the hard way, the equivalent radius can be compared directly with an ordinary curve *of the same sharpness*.

Table 1-5 lists some of the conventional numbered turnouts usable in model railroading interspersed with curved-frog and other commercially available configurations of interest, for N, HO, S and O scales and standard 4 ft. 8½ in. gauge. They're listed in approximate order of decreasing sharpness of curvature, with equivalent and closure-rail radius values where available.

Before selecting a turnout that's best for use with the class of curvature typical of a track plan, one other matter should be given some consideration. That's the *S-curve* effect, probably the single largest cause of unsatisfactory tracking associated with track plan design. As Fig. 1-16 points out, the coupler swing required to accommodate two back-to-back curves is almost twice that encountered in going from tangent to curve. A tangent about the length of the longest piece of rolling stock using the track should separate reverse curves if this plague is to be avoided.

In many cases it's possible to revise the detailed alignment of common track arrangements so as to get away from S-curve problems and still not lose space, as indicated in Fig. 1-16. However, a crossover between two parallel tracks automatically contains an S curve, and there are two remedies. You can increase track-center spacing or use longer (larger equivalent radius) turnouts. Both fixes increase the length of the crossover, but any one that can't successfully take the trains from one track to the other is certainly no bargain.

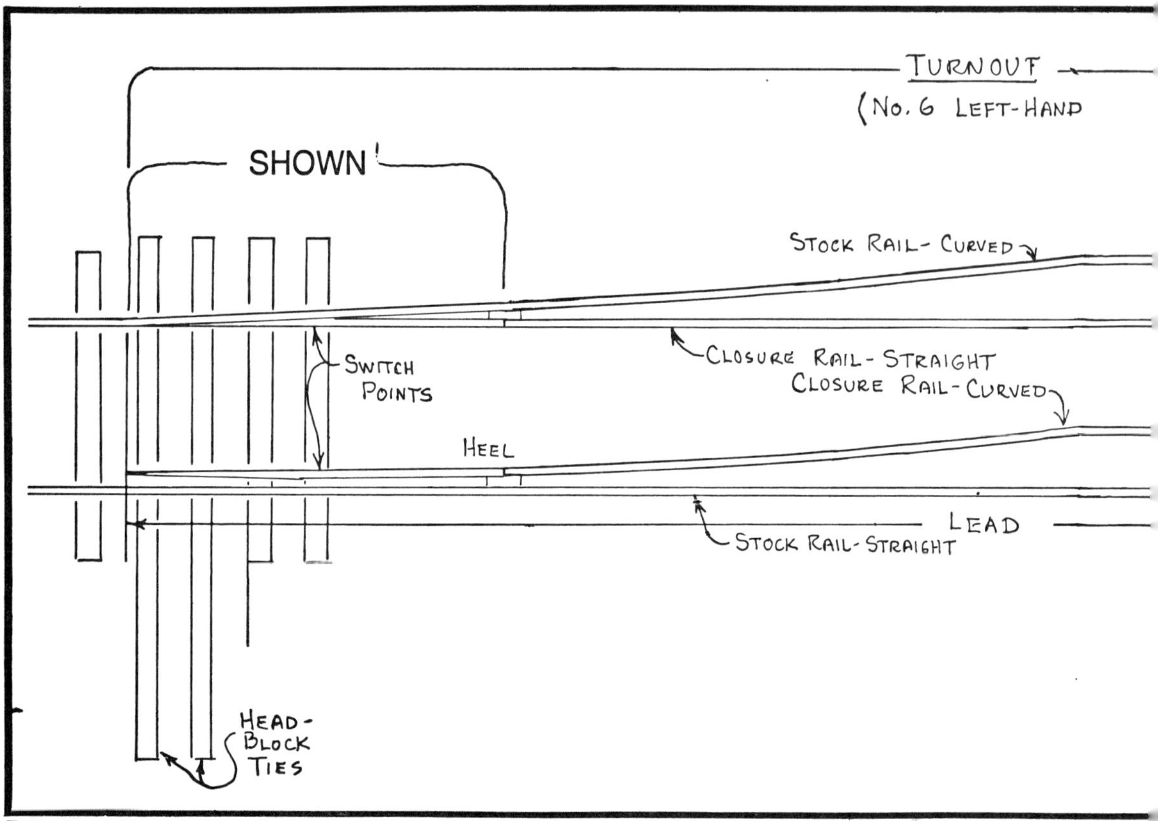

Fig. 1-12. Parts and proportions for turnouts.

While the effect of a crossover between straight tracks isn't as severe as that of the reverse bend between two long curves, it is usually desirable to establish a separate, one-size-longer minimum standard for turnouts in crossovers as compared to single turnouts.

LADDER TRACKS

A good proportion of the turnouts on any railroad will be found grouped together on *ladder tracks*—the key route giving access to all the parallel body tracks in a yard. Yards always have two faults, at least so far as the yardmaster is concerned. They don't have enough tracks to sort cars out into all the classifications desired, and they don't hold enough cars. Things are a little better in the model; if it gets too bad, we can always pick up some of the cars and put 'em on a shelf! Nevertheless, it's almost always desirable to pack as much car storage capacity into the space as possible. Usually, the problem is more a lack of length than a lack of available width. Before there are enough tracks, we come to the end of the plywood or the end of the basement.

As Fig. 1-17 shows, the choice of turnout angle becomes very significant in a ladder track. All yards in these examples are of equal length overall, from the points of the first turnout to the ends of the stub tracks. We hate to buy or build a turnout for a really short track, so here we've arbitrarily said that each body track must be long enough to hold at least four 40-ft. freight cars. With No. 6 turnouts and fairly widely-spaced tracks (17½ scale feet on centers), we can have only three tracks, with a capacity of 15 cars beyond the clearance points as seen in Fig. 1-17A.

Closing up the spacing to a prototypical 14 ft., as permitted by using reliable automatic couplers, buys us another track and almost 50 percent more storage capacity in Fig. 1-17B. Using shorter No. 4½ turnouts (Fig. 1-17C) is even more effective in boosting flexibility and capacity, but we notice that there is quite a severe S-curve effect in entering the first body track. The two turnouts in effect are like a crossover. A railroad-like remedy for this too-tight wiggle (Fig. 1-17D) is to increase the track spacing between the through track and the first body track. It's considered highly desirable to

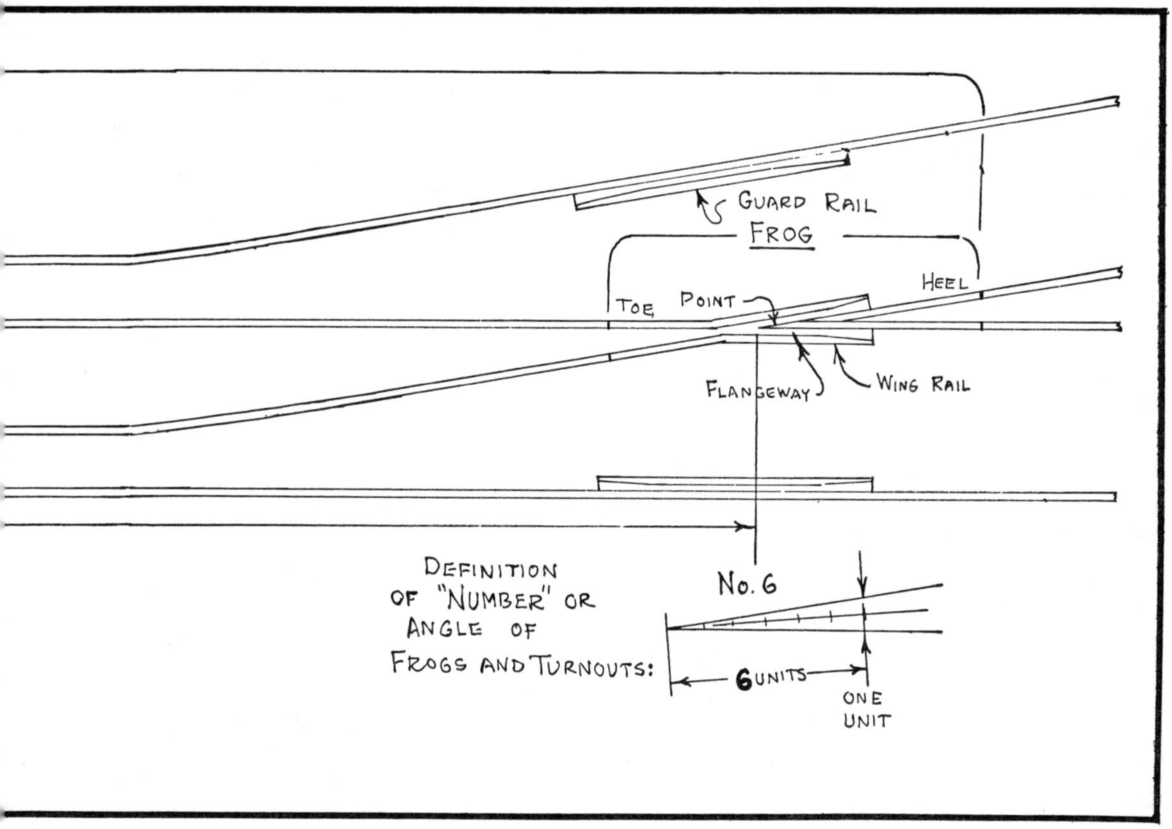

improve safety by allowing some extra room between a "fast" track and areas where cars are standing and personnel must be coupling up air hoses, making inspections and so on. Most of the track plans in this book use this approach to reliable switching. We lose only a couple of cars in average capacity in this case. The exact number of cars per track, of course, depends on whether their different lengths add up to just enough for the track or come out just a bit too long to let that last one squeeze into the clear.

Special Ladder Arrangements

Figure 1-18 shows some of the more exotic arrangements for using yard space more efficiently. The simple ladder is always perferred in the prototype *if there's room* because the switchmen can reach all the switchstands without crossing over the ladder track. Visibility is also much better for the engine crew, making it easier to switch cars smoothly and safely.

There is sometimes a corresponding problem with our model yards when we go to a *compound ladder* as in Fig. 1-18E. There may be interference from the oversize power switch machines in the smaller gauges. Safety is no problem, though, and the increase in capacity is really amazing when you go to the double-ladder arrangements of Fig. 1-18 F and G.

Other Space Savers

The double ladder arrangements would be even more potent in putting more cars in the same-length space by starting out with a *lap turnout* (Fig. 1-13), though it is somewhat unusual to route through traffic over the extra frogs of such a special piece of trackwork.

The one specialty item that often becomes an attractive modeling subject in its own right is the intricate *double slip switch*, which uses up to 12 moving points to accomplish the same thing in the way of routing versatility that two ordinary turnouts can do with one third that number. The space-saving justifying such complexity is usually found in the approaches to passenger stations in center-city locations; one or two of these "puzzle switches" do a lot to give the proper flavor to any model of such terminal throat trackage.

European railway civil engineers apparently find the double slip irresistable, using them extensively even where space isn't so critical and only industrial or other trackage is involved. As a result, double slips (usually of rigid-frog design and sharp angle) are mass-produced and available in the smaller gauges, so some of the track plans in this book make use of them at locations where they are also appropriate for North American use. Operation through double slips is not likely to be as smooth or completely reliable as through more gently curved conventional trackwork, so they should be located where they are accessible for maintenance and adjustment. But they are such interesting items that you would want to put them up front where they can be seen in any case.

TURNOUTS ON CURVES

The most important space-saver is the turnout on a curve. In prototype practice the engineer is careful to limit their use to situations where the main track takes the outer, less sharply curved route; but since his curves are usually gentle enough that the turnout can still be built using standard straight frogs and points, there is no strong prejudice against them. With our sharper curves it's usually necessary to design them to curved-frog and curved-point standards in order to take full advantage of their smooth-curve possibilities, but with equal care in installation the resulting operation can be about as reliable as with ordinary lefts and rights.

Figure 1-19 shows how important the absence of a straight section can be in adding a turnout without ballooning the space required.

Table 1-5. Equivalent Radii For Common Turnouts.

TURNOUT	TYPE	FROG NO.	FROG ANGLE	N		HO		S		O	
				Rcr (in.)	Req (in.)	Rcr (in.)	Req (in.)	Rcr (in.)	Req (in.)	Rcr (in.)	Req (in.)
TRIX N 7⅝" RAD.	CURVED FROG	(3¼)	(17½°)	7⅝	7⅝	—	(14)	—	(19)	—	(25)
ATLAS O	CURVED-FROG	(3⅛)	(18⅓°)	—	(7¼)	—	(13¼)	—	(18)	24	24
ATLAS HO "SNAP SWITCH"	CURVED-FROG	(3¾)	(15°)	—	(9¾)	—	18	—	(24)	—	(33)
TRIX N 13" RADIUS	CURVED-FROG	(3¾)	(15°)	13	13	—	(24)	—	(33)	—	(44)
NO. 4	CONV. STRAIGHT-FROG	4	14¼°	9	15¾	15	29	22½	40	30	53
ATLAS N "STANDARD"	CURVED-FROG	(3¾)	(15°)	19	19	—	(35)	—	(47)	—	(63)
ATLAS HO "No. 4"	CONV. STRAIGHT FROG	4½	12½°	(12)	(19½)	22	36	—	(49)	(40)	(65)
No. 5	"	5	11.4°	14	24	26	44	39	60	52	80
No. 6	"	6	9.5°	24	30	43	56	62	77	83	102
No. 8	"	8	7.15°	37	60	67	110	99	150	132	200

RADIUS VALUES IN PARENTHESIS APPROXIMATE AND FOR REFERENCE ONLY.

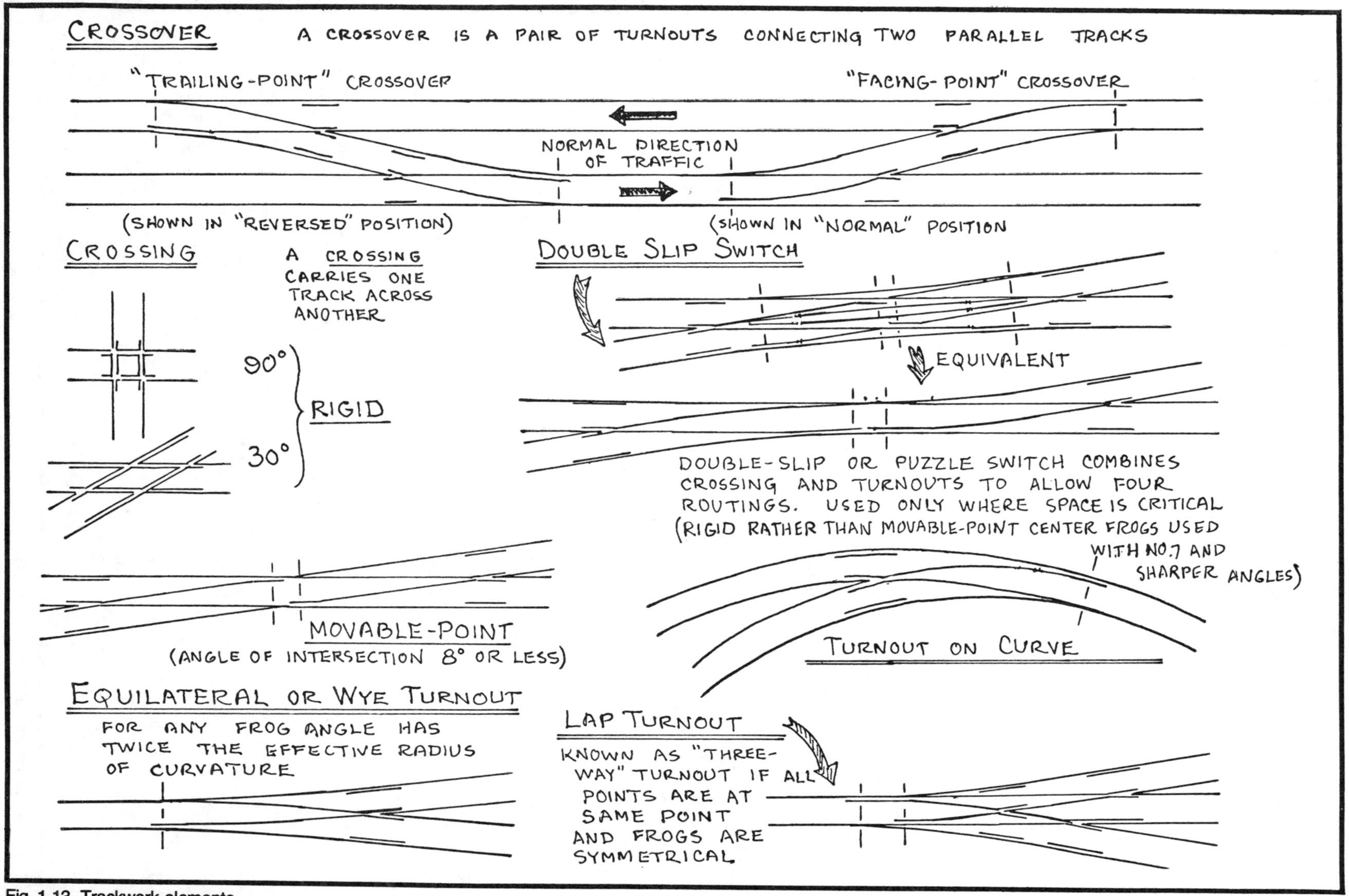

Fig. 1-13. Trackwork elements.

Now that curved turnouts are available in at least one combination of conventional sharp radii, there is little reason to steer clear of them. Several of the track plans in this book use them. Where more liberal curve standards are in use, hand-laid or custom-built turnouts are likely to be required, but

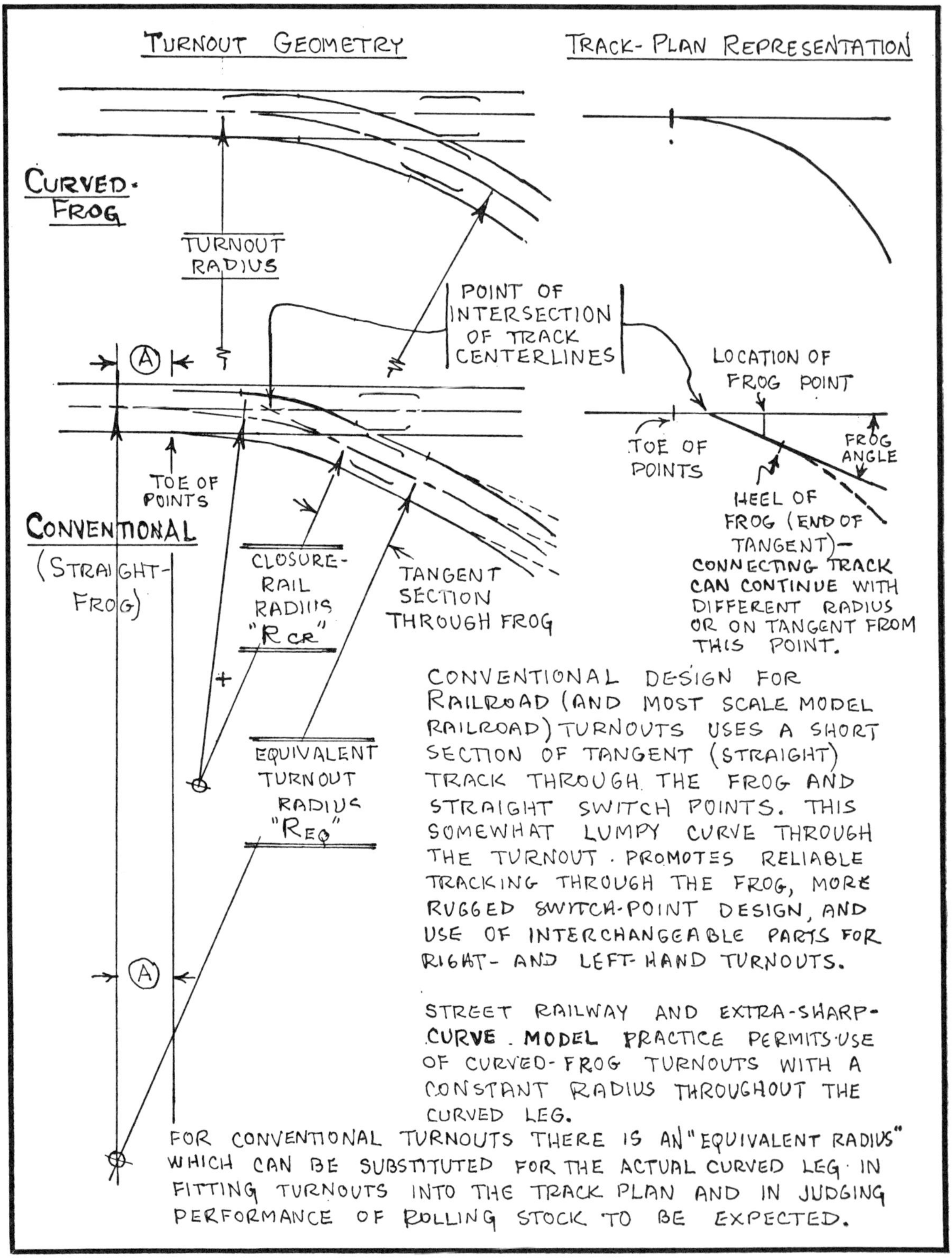

Fig. 1-14. Curved-frog and conventional turnouts.

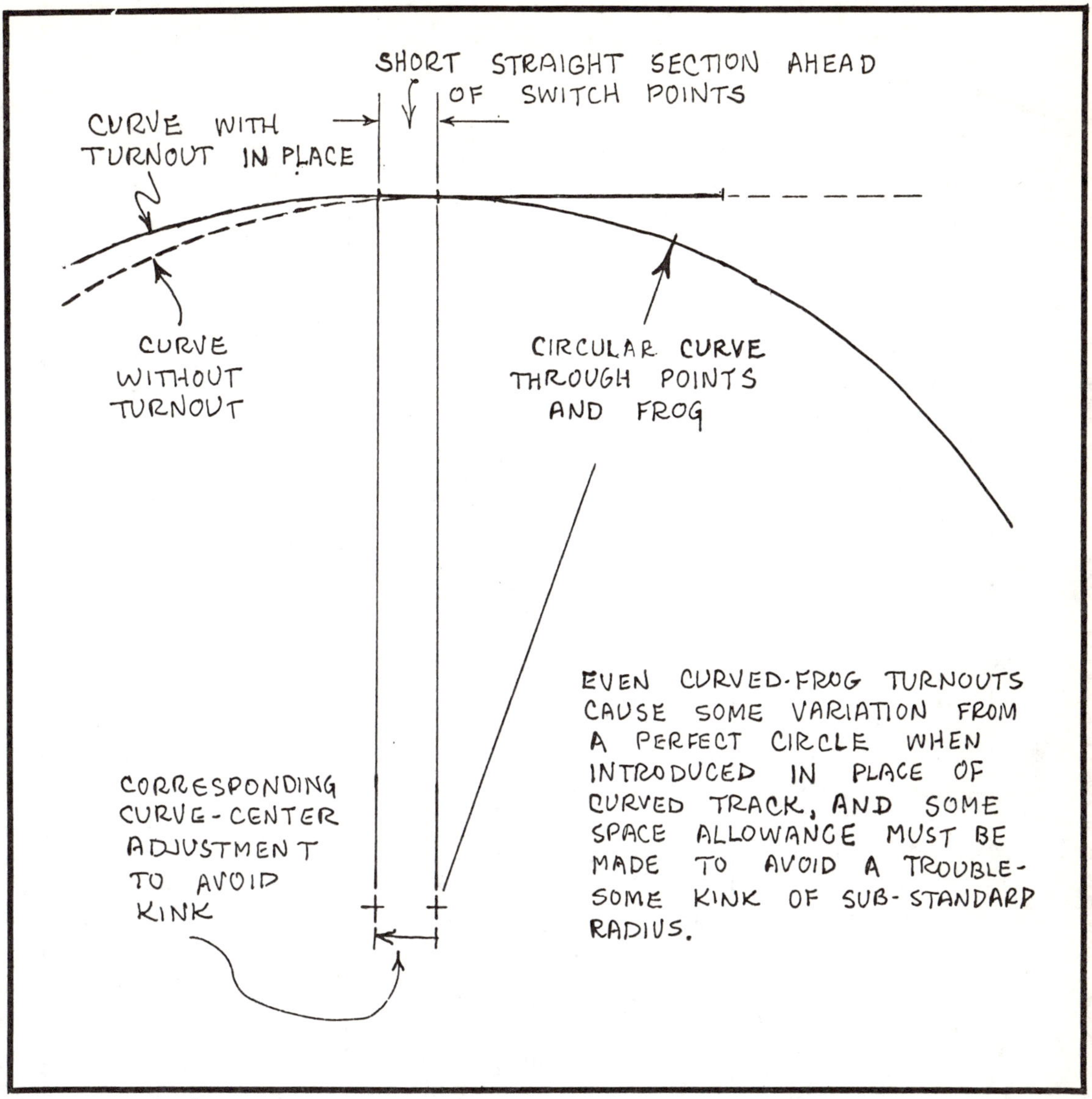

Fig. 1-15. Curved-frog turnouts aren't completely curved.

the design and building of turnouts on a curve has been covered frequently in various publications. It's no more difficult than building a standard equivalent, so they're also called for in some locations on these larger track plans.

The frog angle in a turnout on a curve has no direct relationship to the sharpness of curvature of the two routes involved, so we identify them by their two equivalent radii.

Wye or Equilateral Turnouts

A special case of the turnout on a curve is one in which the two branches curve away from each other at equal degrees of curvature. Unlike all others, these *wye* or equilateral turnouts permit equal speeds via either route, so they're used where double track merges into single track or where two important lines diverge. As Fig. 1-13 shows, for any given frog angle the curvature is only half as severe as with a standard turnout. In model practice we usually take advantage of this to save space. We can run fairly long cars and "stiff" locomotives through very short turnouts, such as a No. 3 wye, with a lead (point-to-frog distance) of only about 3½ in. in HO. The space saving in a wye track for turning equipment around is also impressive, but there is a possible S-curve problem that must be guarded against, as cautioned in Fig. 1-20.

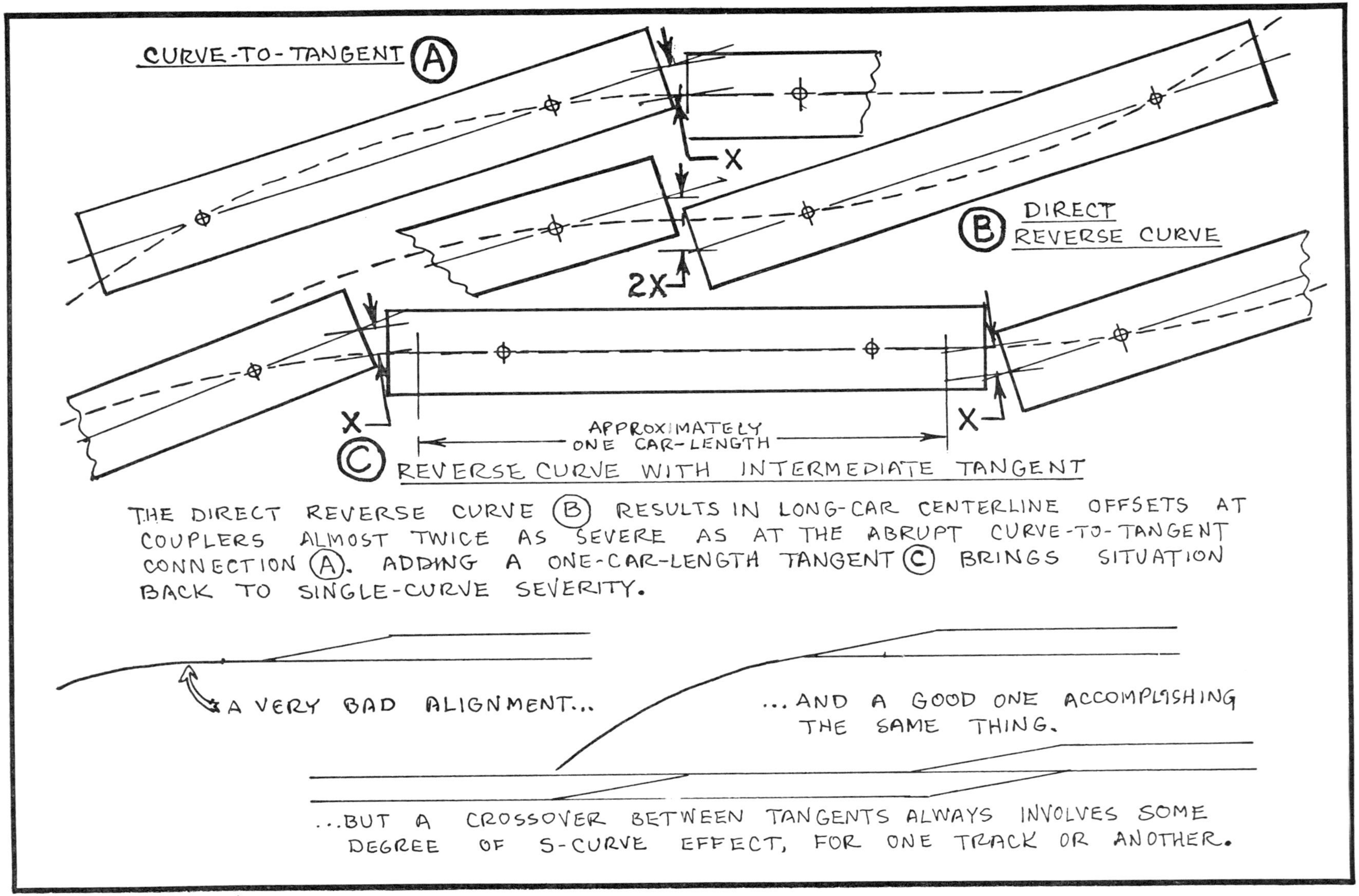

Fig. 1-16. The S-curve at work.

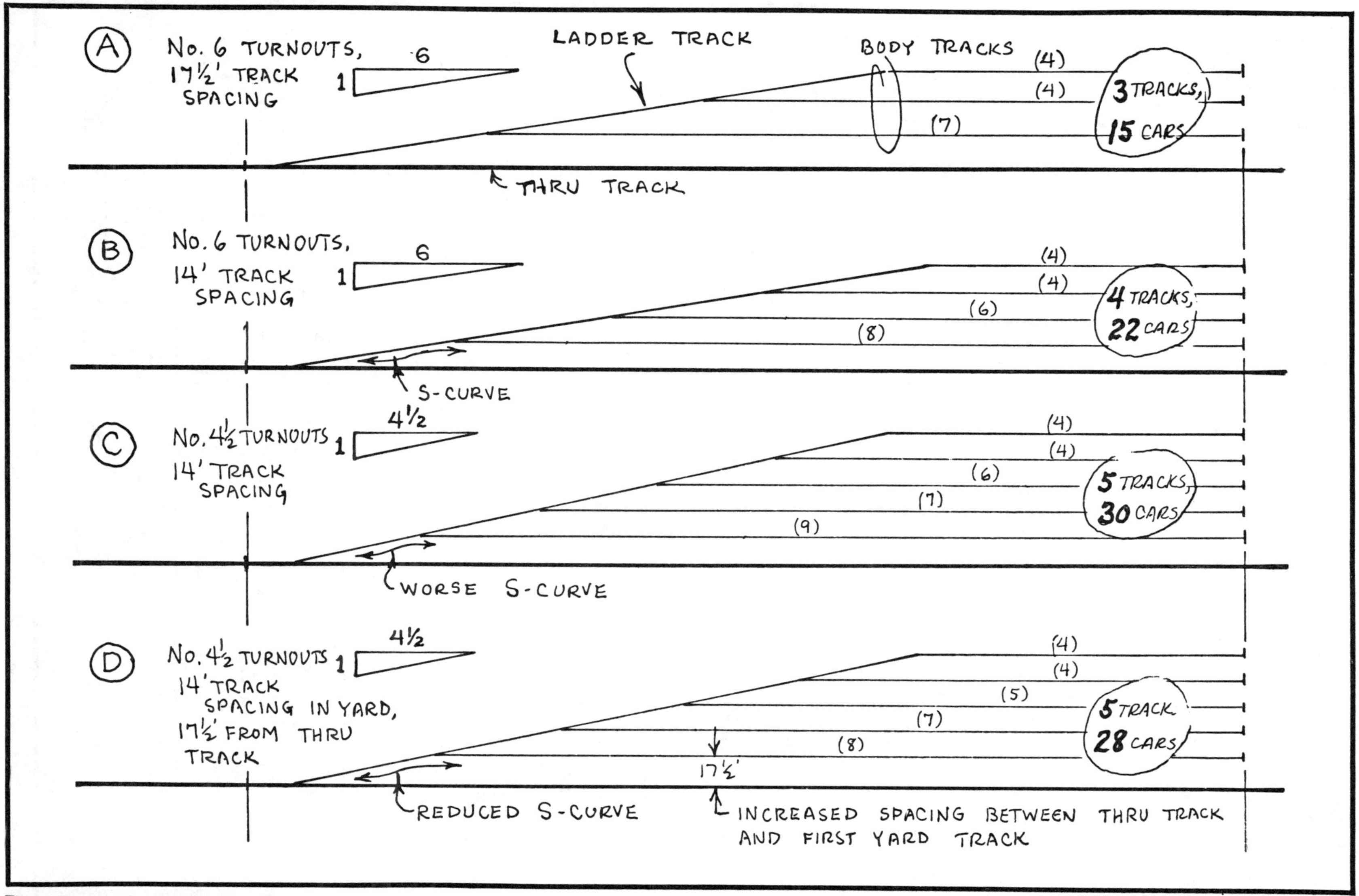

Fig. 1-17. Ladder tracks and yard capacity.

Turnout Standards

Table 1-6 gives recommended turnouts for general use with trackage built to the various classes of curvature. These are for steam railroad layouts with rolling stock suitable for the indicated sharpness of curve. A separate, more liberal standard is given for turnouts in crossovers because of the S-curve effect. For hand-laid or custom-built trackwork, these turnout recommendations can be used as given.

Two requirements have been observed in these selections. The closure-rail radius (R_{cr}) is *at least as large* as the basic curve radius. This insures that any long-wheelbase locomotives and car trucks which can run satisfactorily on the curved track won't bind up right in the turnout. Most straight-frog turnouts also have a short-radius bend right at the points, but this is ordinarily no more severe than the curve between the heel of the point and the start of the frog tangent.

The equivalent radius of the turnout as a whole (R_{eq}) is at least *50 percent larger* than the minimum radius. This insures that the *appearance* of the train running through the curved leg of the turnout is somewhat better than on the minimum-radius curve and that coupler-swing and clearance problems will not occur at single turnouts. Running through a turnout with its necessary roughness and discontinuities at points and frog is a somewhat traumatic experience for the train at best, so it's well to be sure that it is not also being asked to flex its backbone to the limit at the same time.

Nevertheless, the resulting standards allow for shorter turnouts than you will find recom-

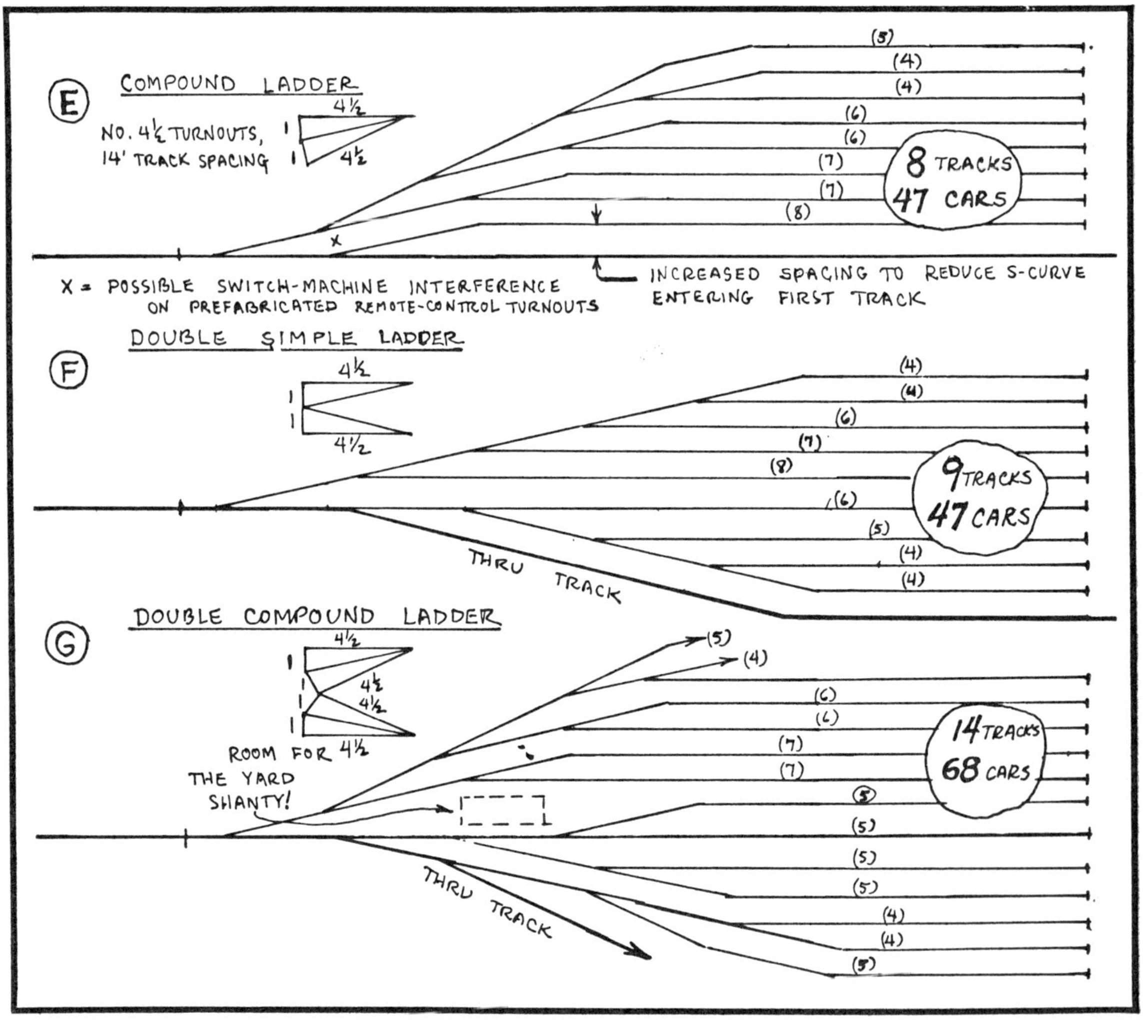

Fig. 1-18. More tracks with special ladders.

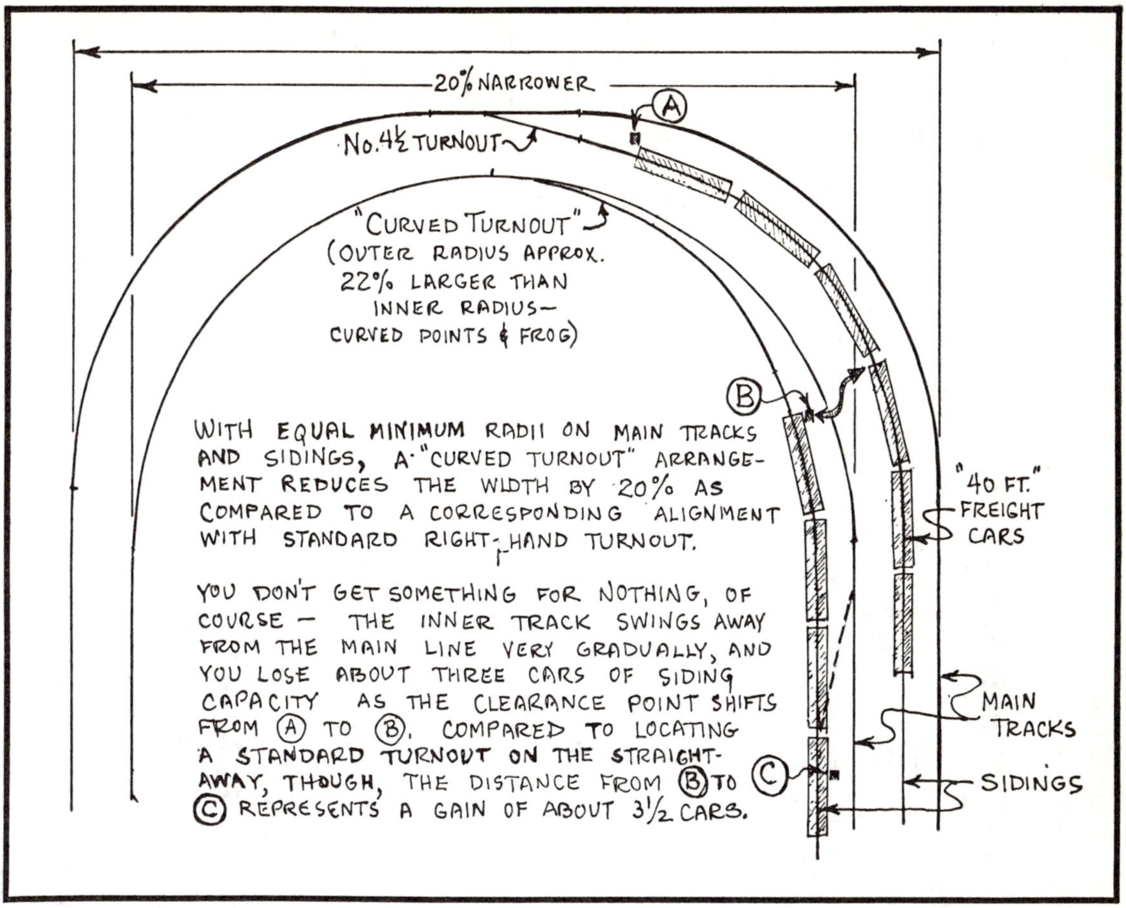

Fig. 1-19. Space saving with turnouts on curves.

mended in some quarters. Once you get above a curvature that's a comfortable match with your minimum radius, additional turnout length is a complete waste of room that can ruin the operating possibilities of any layout built in something less than unlimited space! Since this last condition covers just about all layouts built this side of heaven, it's very difficult to justify any flat rule calling for "nothing shorter than a No. 8." Trains *do* look nicer running through a No. 8 than a No. 6, but when they are going to have to run around a super-broad curve *which is three times as sharp* in the next couple of feet, the difference quickly gets lost.

The Easement Effect

With turnouts of the standard recommended, there is actually an appearance bonus when entering a curve from a tangent via the switch. As Fig. 1-21 shows, you can get the equivalent of a nice easement without even realizing it! This is taken advantage of in many of the plans throughout this book, which in general allow for easements or their equivalent on most main-track curves.

N AND HO TURNOUT RECOMMENDATIONS

Thinking in terms of prototype curvature figures takes some getting used to, so for the two most prevalent gauges Table 1-7 and Table 1-8 translate suggested standards directly into model terms. In N gauge, particularly, the variety of prefabricated turnouts is somewhat limited, so the standards have been modified to conform to those components that are most readily available at this time. It is certainly possible that other lines and additional items in existing brands will become available.

As time goes on and more modelers gain confidence in their skill, the practice of building turnouts from scratch in the smallest gauges will increase. In the meantime, N and HO plans in this book allow room for commercially-available turnouts and other trackwork except where indicated.

Table 1-6. Recommended Turnouts, General.

CURVATURE CLASS	MIN. RADIUS, FT. (PROTOTYPE)	RECOMMENDED STANDARD TURNOUT					
		BASIC			CROSSOVERS		
		TURNOUT NO.	Rcr	Requiv.	TURNOUT NO.	Rcr	Requiv.
EXTRA SHARP	95-110 (TYPICAL)	MATCHING CURVED-FROG	95-130	95-130	No. 4†	109	210
SHARP	130	No. 4½	159	261	No. 5	159	319
CONVENTIONAL	175	No. 5	188	319	No. 5#	188	319
BROAD	220	No. 6*	312	406	No. 6	312	406
SUPER-BROAD	260	No. 6	312	406	No. 8	486	798

* NO. 5 IN FREIGHT YARDS, WITH WIDENED FIRST-TRACK SPACING (FIG. 1-22).

0† CURVED-FROG TURNOUTS PRODUCE VERY SEVERE REVERSE-CURVE EFFECTS IN CROSSOVERS.

\# NO. 6 MAY BE JUSTIFIED IN PASSENGER TERMINALS IF 85 FT. CARS USED (NOT RECOMMENDED BUT POSSIBLE ON CONVENTIONALRADIUS LAYOUT)

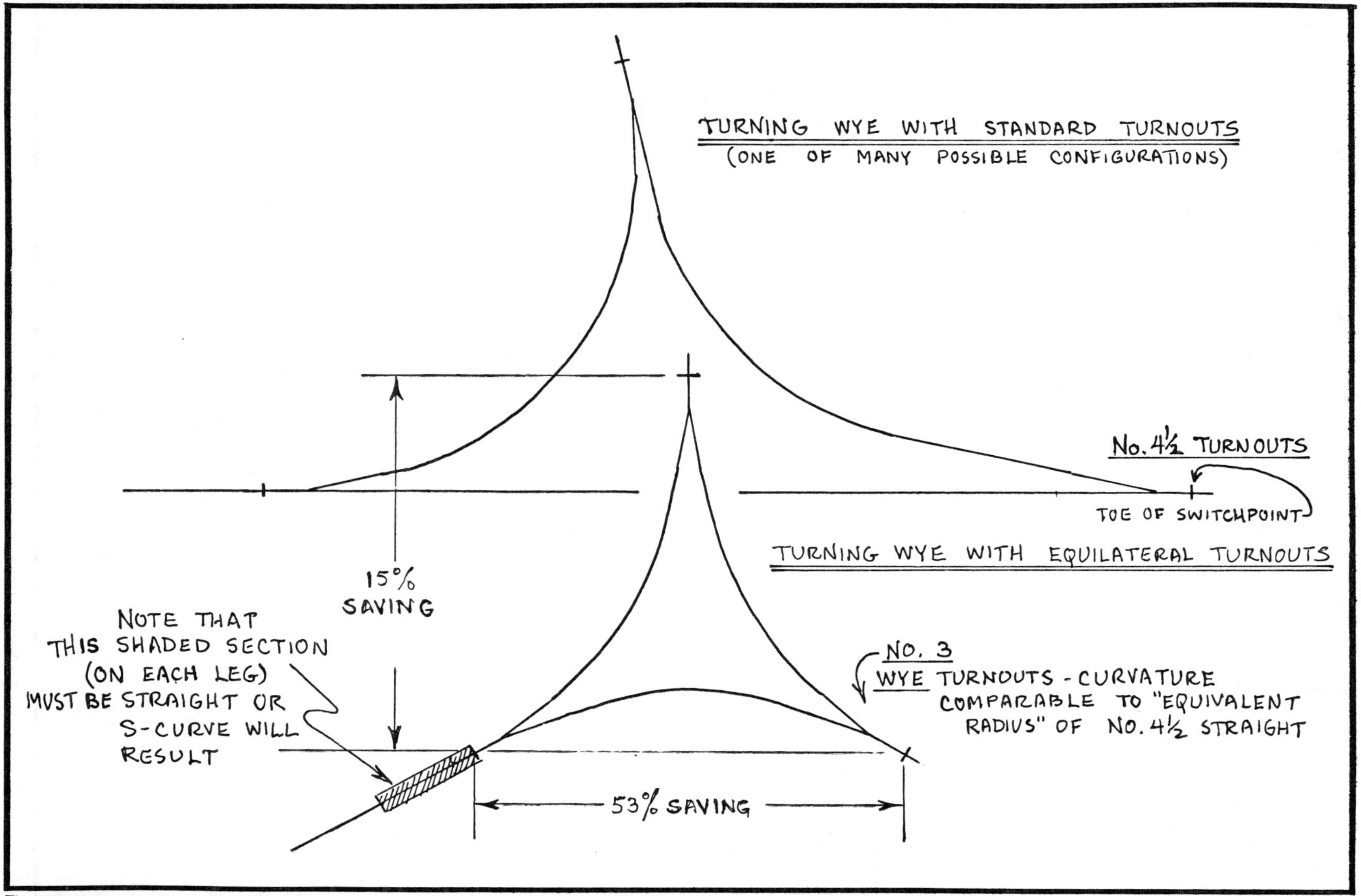

Fig. 1-20. Why wye turnouts are great for wyes.

Spacewise, you can always do better building your own, so this is conversvative.

As Fig. 1-22 explains, frog angles don't equate to the same curvatures in narrow gauge turnouts. Similar relationships exist between 0 and On3. Narrow-gauge and dual-gauge trackwork called for in plans in this book takes these relationships into account.

MINIMUM ISN'T THE MAXIMUM!

All this talk about the minimum radius and the sharpest turnout shouldn't obscure the fact that the best plans do *not* use one standard everywhere on the layout. Even though all rolling stock must be selected and adjusted so it can make it around and through these tight points, it will always look and run better under easier conditions. As Fig. 1-23 illustrates, there are some points where the minimum definitely shouldn't be used and places where it doesn't cost anything to spread out and go first class!

HAND-LAID, PRE-FAB OR SECTIONAL TRACK?

Any track plan can be duplicated with hand-laid track and trackwork, so there can be no geometry problems should you choose to go that route. A plan directly adaptable to assembly from sectional track is considerably constrained and will inevitably require a somewhat larger area to accommodate the same track arrangement. On a simple layout the difference is hardly noticeable; but as more junctions, crossings and multiple main tracks are added, the facts that concentric curves are not exactly parallel and that turnout locations must be adjusted to match track sections take their toll.

Sectional track has some advantages, however. It allows use of the track itself in laying out the railroad. A trial assembly quickly finds any goofs and the track becomes a template for locating the roadbed, building supporting framework and identifying possible minor changes in the interest of appearance, compatibility with scenery and structures, etc. For a given level of care in

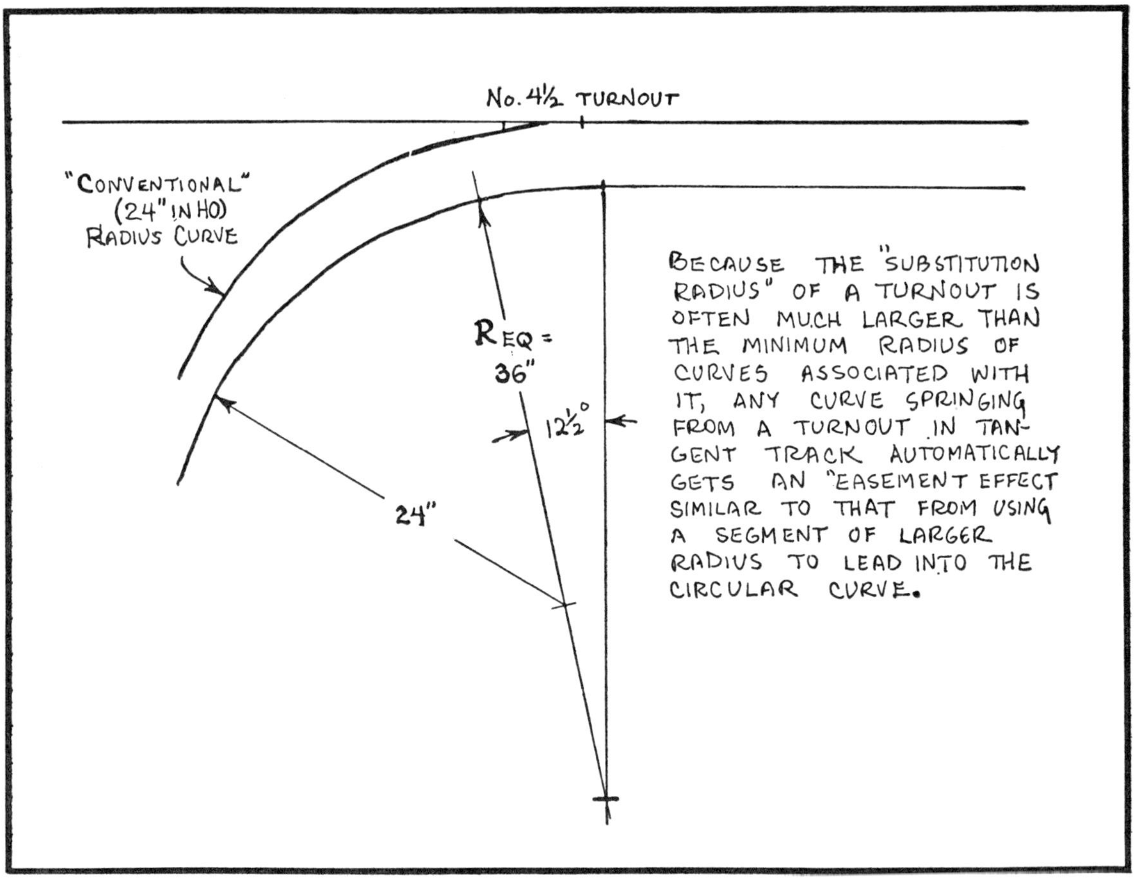

Fig. 1-21. The subconscious easement.

Table 1-7. Turnout Selection N Gauge.

CURVATURE CLASS	MIN. RADIUS (IN.)	BASIC			CROSSOVERS		
		TURNOUT	Rcr	Req	TURNOUT	Rcr	Req
EXTRA SHARP	7⅝	7⅝″ R. CURVED-FROG (TRIX 7⅝″R)	7⅝	7⅝	13″ R. CURVED FROG (TRIX 13″)	13	13
SHARP	9¾	13″R CURVED-FROG (TRIX 13″)	13	13	19″ R CURVED-FROG (ATLAS "STANDARD")	19	19
CONVENTIONAL	13	19″ R CURVED-* FROG (ATLAS "STANDARD")	19	19	19″ R. CURVED; FROG (ATLAS "STANDARD")	19	19
BROAD	16	19″ R. CURVED-* FROG (ATLAS "STANDARD")	19	19	No. 6 (ATLAS)	24	30
SUPER-BROAD	19	No. 6 (ATLAS)*	24	30	NO. 6 (ATLAS)	24	30

* PECO 32″/18″ TURNOUT ON CURVE A HIGHLY USEFUL ALTERNATE WHERE APPLICABLE

Table 1-8. Turnout Selection HO Gauge.

CURVATURE CLASS	MIN. RADIUS (IN.)	BASIC			CROSSOVERS		
		TURNOUT	Rcr	Req	TURNOUT	Rcr	Req
EXTRA-SHARP	15″	18″R CURVED-FROG (ATLAS "SNAP")	18	18	No. 4½ (ATLAS "NO. 4")	22	36
SHARP	18″	NO. 4½ % (ATLAS "NO. 4")	22	36	NO. 4½ * (ATLAS "NO. 4")	22	36
CONVENTIONAL	24″	NO. 4½ * (ATLAS "NO. 4")	22	36	NO. 6 †	43	56
BROAD	30″	NO. 6 @	43	56	NO. 6	43	56
SUPER-BROAD	36″	NO. 6	43	56	NO. 8#	67	110

* NO. 5 IS PREFERRED ALTERNATE IF HAND-BUILT; NO. 4½ A BIT TIGHT

† NO. 5 IS PREFERRED ALTERNATE—NO. 6 VERY WASTEFUL.

@ NO. 6 TURNOUTS ON NO. 5 ANGLE IN FREIGHT-YARD LADDERS (FIG. 1-22)

PRIMARILY FOR APPEARANCE. USE NO. 6'S IN CONNECTION WITH ANY DOUBLE-SLIP SWITCHES TO ALLOW USE OF RIGID CENTER FROGS.

% 22″/18″ "CURVED TURNOUT" ALTERNATE—FOR ALL USES ON SHARP-CLASS TRACKAGE AND SECONDARY TRACKAGE ON WIDER-RADIUS TERRITORY.

construction, it is more likely to result in *smooth curves* on accurate radius and in *straight tangents. It is possible* to lay lumpy curves with sectional track, but the kinks are more obvious and likely to be adjusted before things are nailed down.

Under its various trade names, flexible track in long, two foot or more, sections is widely available, with rail sections and crossties matching trackwork components and sectional track. Once you bend it, of course, the ends of the rails go out of square and some way of cutting them to match becomes necessary, not a major investment when spread over the construction of the whole railroad. Curving the track to any reasonable radius is easy, but it is necessary to use a template or trammel to generate a satisfactorily accurate, smooth curve when you're working near the minimum radius. Locomotives take a dim view of a curve whose *average* radius is correct but achieved via alternating kinks and tangents. Overcome these minor hurdles and flexible track has many advantages:

- Track goes where the plan wants it to, rather than vice versa. Multiple tracks can have exactly the radii needed to provide proper track center spacing throughout. Angles between track segments are not limited to specific 10 or 15° increments.
- Broad and sweeping curves are possible. Almost every track plan has room for at least one sweeping curve of almost prototypical gentleness on which trains will have a beautifully authentic appearance.
- The number of rail joints is greatly reduced. Just as railroading has moved toward continuous-welded rail once its technology was perfected, reducing the number of joints in the model improves operation and reliability both mechanically and electrically.

These are important enough reasons to make the use of flexible track, at least at some points, a definite first choice for most layouts. The discussion accompanying each track plan in this book indicates whether or not it assumes the use of flexible track. Point where modifications are pos-

DUAL-GAUGE TURNOUTS ARE FASCINATING MODELS IN THEIR OWN RIGHT, WITH SEVEN DISTINCT VARIETIES POSSIBLE, DEPENDING UPON WHETHER BOTH NARROW- AND STANDARD-GAUGE TRACKS OR ONLY ONE OR THE OTHER CAN TAKE EITHER ROUTE.

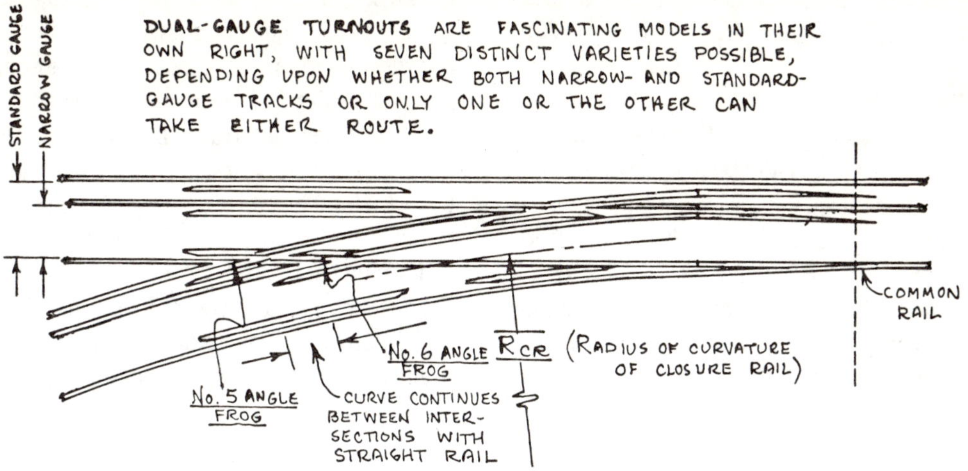

⇩R_{CR} / FROG ANGLE ⇨	No. 4	No. 5	No. 6	No. 8	No. 10
HO	15"	26"	43"	67"	117"
HOn3	9"	16"	27"	42"	75"

BECAUSE OF ITS SHORTER CLOSURE RAILS, A NARROW-GAUGE TURNOUT WITH THE SAME FROG ANGLE HAS A CONSIDERABLY SHARPER CLOSURE-RAIL RADIUS THAN ITS STANDARD-GAUGE COUNTERPART. TYPICALLY, THERE'S ABOUT ONE FROG NO.'S DIFFERENCE BETWEEN HO AND HOn3 FOR COMPARABLY-SHARP TURNOUTS. THE SMALLER NARROW-GAUGE ROLLING STOCK, OF COURSE, USUALLY WILL OPERATE WELL AND LOOK GOOD ON SHARPER CURVES THAN STANDARD GAUGE EQUIPMENT BUILT TO THE SAME SCALE.

Fig. 1-22. Dual gauge, narrow gauge turnouts.

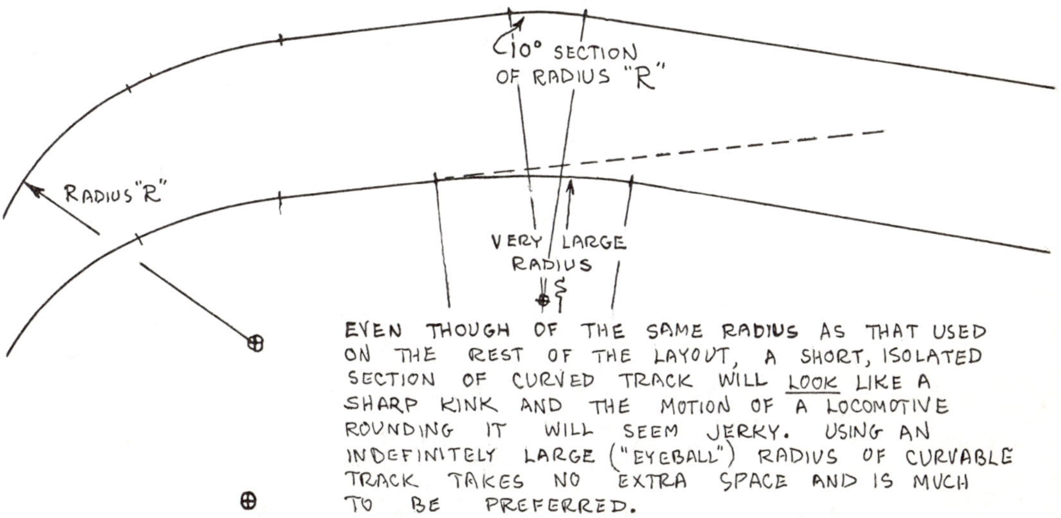

EVEN THOUGH OF THE SAME RADIUS AS THAT USED ON THE REST OF THE LAYOUT, A SHORT, ISOLATED SECTION OF CURVED TRACK WILL LOOK LIKE A SHARP KINK AND THE MOTION OF A LOCOMOTIVE ROUNDING IT WILL SEEM JERKY. USING AN INDEFINITELY LARGE ("EYEBALL") RADIUS OF CURVABLE TRACK TAKES NO EXTRA SPACE AND IS MUCH TO BE PREFERRED.

THIS IS ALSO A GOOD PLACE FOR A LONGER-THAN-NORMAL TURNOUT (E.G. NO. 8), SINCE IT WON'T CAUSE SPACE PROBLEMS ELSEWHERE IN THE TRACK PLAN.

Fig. 1-23. One point where sectional track is out of place.

sible by its use are indicated on some of the sectional-compatible plans.

CROSSINGS

Building a crossing from rail is relatively easy in the larger scales. In HO standard gauge crossings are manufactured in a variety of angles ranging from 12½ to 90 degrees, and it has been no problem to arrange all HO plans so that only available angles are called for. In some cases, it may be necessary to crop off the approach track on one or more legs of the crossing to let it fit with adjacent trackwork, but this should be no problem.

In N scale, building a crossing from scratch is considerably more of a challenge, although the relatively wider flangeway tolerances and coarser wheel contours let trains bounce through less-than-perfect trackwork more reliably than you'd expect. Unfortunately, at present the selection of crossing angles available in N is extremely limited and somewhat unpredictable in the United States. Track plans in this book call only for 30 and 90 degree crossings (sometimes requiring cropping to fit) in plans primarily intended for this gauge.

2

Types of Model Railroad Layouts

What *one* characteristic really describes a particular model railroad? Ask half a dozen active modelers to describe their layouts with one term, and chances are you'll get six unrelated answers:

"It's a lumbering line."

"Just a simple out-and-back, but I'm adding a branch."

"I'm modeling a Gay Nineties narrow gauge."

"It's a doughnut lift-up that fits in our one-car garage."

"We're building it on a chunk of plywood that sits on the pool table."

"Mostly a model of South Baltimore with lots of dockside trackage."

What its business is, the pattern of its train movements, its historical period, where it's located in your home, where you stand to run it, how it's constructed, what it emphasizes scenically—all are essential characteristics. The variety itself shows how many angles there are to the hobby and also says a lot about why things need never go stale, why no two pikes are the same, and why it's worth taking a little time to decide which track plan is best *for you* as a starting point.

WHAT TYPE OF RAILROAD ARE YOU MODELING?

Railroads have always come in all sizes and flavors. And just when it seems as if everything will be swallowed up into some Conrail conglomerate with no individuality, we find that dozens of independent short lines are springing up to handle branchline, tourist or industry traffic, often in weird and wonderful ways. That's great for the modeler seeking variety, though not really essential since we always can invent our own composite company, big-time or the reverse and, in fact, most do. It's more fun to get off the dime and start building than it is to stew around trying to fit the various kinds of railroading into neat boxes, but Table 2-1 lists a few types to stimulate your imagination. For each, some of its characteristics are mentioned along with aspects that tend to make it relatively easy or challenging. The challenging ones will just take more space and time, perhaps to model.

Few prototype railroads of any size are limited to one of the categories in Table 2-1. Most will have main lines *and* branches, some with a mix of traffic and others dominated by one commodity. Industrial or commuter operations are likely to occur in some territories. Patterning your railroad after the Illinois Central Gulf or Boston and Maine still leaves lots of options open. Model railroads likewise often attempt to include more than one type. In most cases, though, space limitations are such that concentrating on no more than two categories will result in a lot more realistic situation than a more scatter-shot approach.

All but the largest track plans in this book can be recognized as favoring one or two classes of traffic in making the best use of the area available; you can relate them to particular prototype railroads yourself. There have been a lot of "Grand Central, Chicago and Indian Gulch" railroads attempted in a 4 × 8 ft. space in the past, and there will undoutedly be many more in the future, but we really ought to do better!

THE PERIOD RAILROAD

From a track-plan standpoint, it's often possible to change the historical era represented by a model railroad by simply substituting rolling stock and perhaps making a few changes in the engine terminal servicing trackage if crossing the great divide between all-steam and all-diesel. Going farther back in time may still only require switching some buildings. Uproot a supermarket in favor of a row of storefront shops and locate the O.K. Corral and Livery Stable where the oil company's Gas and Go later dominated the scene.

As we mentioned in the discussion of vertical clearances, operating post-1960 freight cars means providing a few scale feet more headroom, but the extra height doesn't spoil the scene for the relatively low boxcars of the 1900-1930 era. Go back to the Civil War, Gay 'Nineties period, though, and engines and cars were enough smaller that adjusting curve radii, track centers, roundhouse stall lengths and so on may allow a worthwhile increase in the amount of railroading per square foot. Figure 3-2 and Fig. 4-2 are two examples of short-train railroads on which the compactness of earlier-era standard-gauge equipment would represent an attractive alternative to the bigger trains of later years.

The *stub-switch* turnout of this period (Fig. 2-1) is of limited commercial availability and doesn't save space in comparison to the later *split point* design we're accustomed to, but it's easy to build and is the single most obvious trackwork trademark of the earlier era. *Light rail*, now generally available thanks to the great narrow-gauge boom, is another hallmark, perhaps requiring hand-laid track but not otherwise affecting the track plan.

CHOOSING A SCHEMATIC

From the standpoint of how the trains move, the *schematic* is the thing that tells the story. A large part of model railroading is the creation of an illusion, so it naturally follows that most track plans are somewhere between mildly and utterly confusing. The desire to get a lot of track and motion into a little area frequently leads to the "bowl of spaghetti" effect (Fig. 2-2), which is tough enough to follow. Then the next stage of development calls for covering up enough of the track to restore a reasonably uncrowded appearance to the sections of *main line* left exposed.

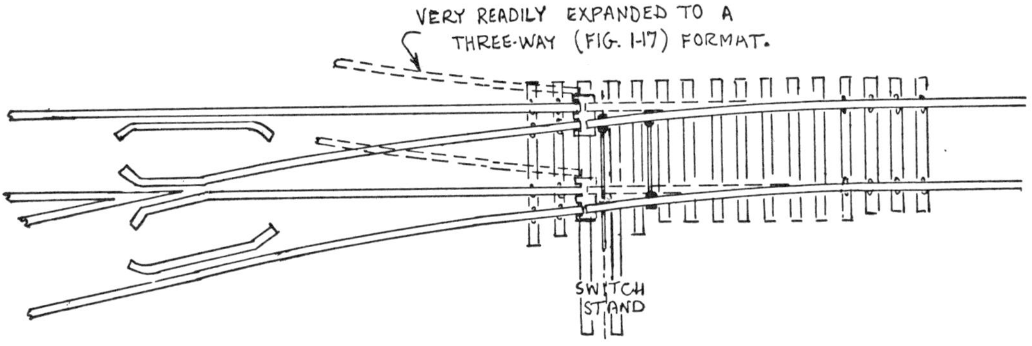

THE STUB-SWITCH TURNOUT, IN WHICH THE TRAINMAN LITERALLY "BENDS THE IRON" TO DIRECT THE WHEELS TO ONE ROUTE OR THE OTHER, WAS STANDARD FROM THE PIONEERING RAILROAD ERA UNTIL THE "SPLIT-POINT" SWITCH REPLACED IT IN THE 1875-1900 PERIOD — WITH SOME SPECIMENS SURVIVING ON SECONDARY LINES WELL INTO THE TWENTIETH CENTURY, PARTICULARLY WHERE THEIR SELF-CLEARING CHARACTERISTIC IN HEAVY SNOWFALLS WAS ATTRACTIVE. LESS DESIRABLE WAS THE ASSURANCE OF DERAILMENT IN TRAILING THROUGH A MISPLACED SWITCH AND THE BATTERING OF THE RAILS AT THE OPEN JOINT UNDER EVEN MODERATELY HEAVY TRAFFIC.

Fig. 2-1. The stub-switch turnout.

Table 2-1. How Accommodating Are Railroads to Our Needs?

RAILROAD TYPE	TYPICAL TRACKAGE	TYPICAL ROLLING STOCK	NICE-TO-MODEL ASPECTS	CHALLENGES
A GENERAL-TRAFFIC MAIN LINE-THROUGH/LOCAL FREIGHT, PASSENGER	SINGLE-OR DOUBLE-TRACK MAIN, LARGE YARDS	UP-TO-DATE, HEAVY	REAL (LONG!) TRAINS; ROLLING STOCK VARIETY (INCL. BIGGIES) JUST LIKE A HOBBY SHOP	HARD TO CONDENSE INTO AVERAGE-SIZE SPACE
B BRANCH OR SHORT LINE-FREIGHT AND SECONDARY PASSENGER	SINGLE MAIN TRACK, OFTEN CROOKED & LIGHT	HAND-ME-DOWN MOTIVE POWER, OLD OR UP-TO-DATE FGT. CARS	SHORT, INTERESTING TRAINS; LINES COME IN ALL SIZES & SETTINGS.	LIMITED NO. OF TRAINS, SIMPLE TRACKAGE
C SINGLE-COMMODITY RAILROAD OR BRANCH-TIMBER, COAL, ORE	SINGLE TRACK, MOUNTAINOUS (NARROW GAUGE A NATURAL)	TO SUIT FREIGHT, OFTEN COMPACT, UP-TO-DATE OR EXPERIENCED	ALREADY BENT TO FIT THE SPACE; STEEP GRADES JUSTIFY HEAVY MOTIVE POWER	LIMITED NO. & VARIETY OF TRAINS; EMPTY/LOADED CONDITION OBVIOUS
D INDUSTRIAL OR SWITCHING RAILROAD-PORT, STEEL, CHEMICAL PLANT, ETC.	NO "MAIN LINE" AS SUCH, SMALL "YARDS"	SMALL LOCOS, SPECIAL-PURPOSE FREIGHT CARS	ULTRA-COMPACT, COMPLEX TRACKAGE; VERTICAL "SCENERY" SAVES SPACE	LOTS OF "NON-R.R." STRUCTURES TO BUILD, LIMITED "TRAIN" OPERATIONS
E COMMUTER/PASSENGER "CORRIDOR"/HEAVY-RAIL RAPID-TRANSIT LINES	MULTIPLE-TRACK MAIN LINE; JUNCTIONS; COMPLEX TERMINALS	PUSH-PULL OR MULTIPLE-UNIT ELECTRIC TRAINS MAIN-LINE PASSENGER	LOTS OF TRAINS (JUST LIKE A MODEL R.R.) IN CROWDED, URBAN SETTINGS	LIMITED VARIETY OF CONSISTS & TRAFFIC; LONG CARS
F TRACTION: INTERURBAN, STREET-RAILWAY ("LIGHT RAIL VEHICLE" ROUTE THESE DAYS)	SINGLE-OR DOUBLE-TRACK ROUTES, STREET OR PRIVATE RIGHT-OF-WAY	SINGLE-UNIT OR SHORT M.U. PASSENGER; TROLLEY FREIGHT	EASILY-CONTROLLED DENSE TRAFFIC, SHORT CARS. EXTREMELY COMPACT "MODEL STYLE" TRACKAGE	MANY HAVE TO LEARN TO LIKE "TRACTION" EQUIPMENT & OPERATIONS

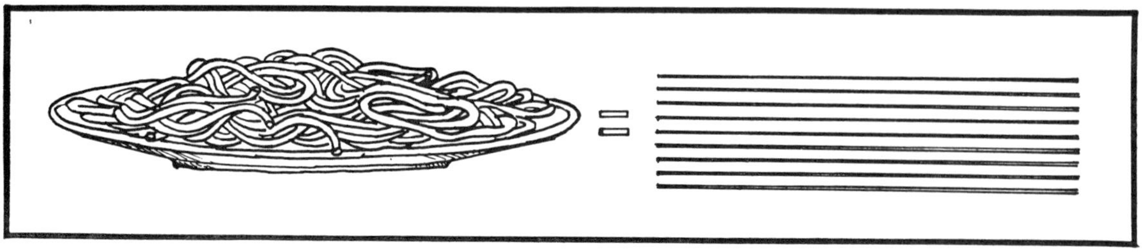

Fig. 2-2. A complex mess turns out to be simple when reduced to its schematic.

To pick a suitable plan, though, you need to know what's going on. A complex mess may actually turn out to be very simple when reduced to its schematic, and our spaghetti platter if literally followed in a track plan wouldn't really let the trains get up much speed. Suitably interconnecting the strands, however, is the basis of most track plans, including some of the best. The name of the game is finding the basic hook-up that lets the trains run in realistic fashion. All plans in this book, except those which are so uncluttered or simple that the pattern of operation is completely obvious, include a schematic diagram of the principal trackage. Despite the best efforts of two generations of doodlers, there are only a few basic arrangements. No one type is best for all sizes of layout or operating preferences, but some are a lot better than others. Let's take a look at the principal varieties and their strong and weak points.

Point-to-Point

The objective of a railroad is to provide transportation from one location to another, so the most authentic model would seem to be one that's laid out in the same way as in Fig. 2-3A. The main line will always be disappointingly short, so it's usual to fold it up to fit (Fig. 2-3B). In actuality, the line may often cross over itself in the process. This doesn't affect the schematic, of course, but is best disguised with suitable scenic tricks since it doesn't often make sense in the real world.

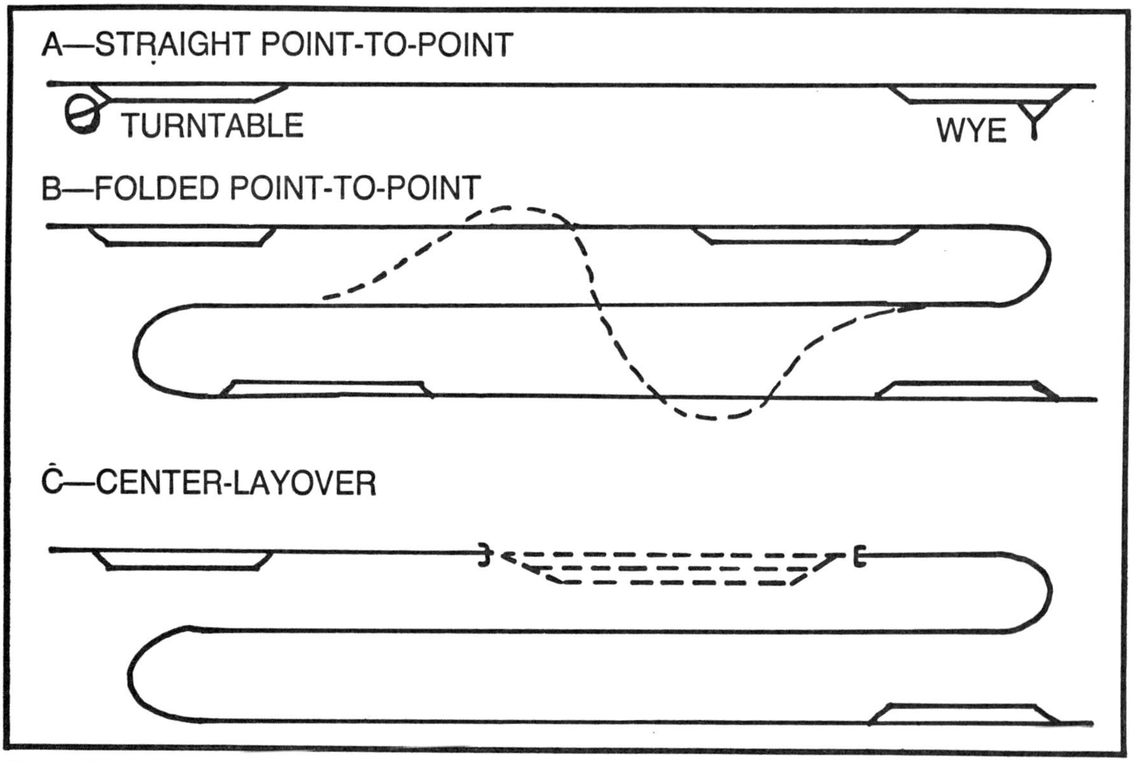

Fig. 2-3. Point-to-point track plan schematics. Straight point-to-point (A); folded point-to-point (B); center-layover (C).

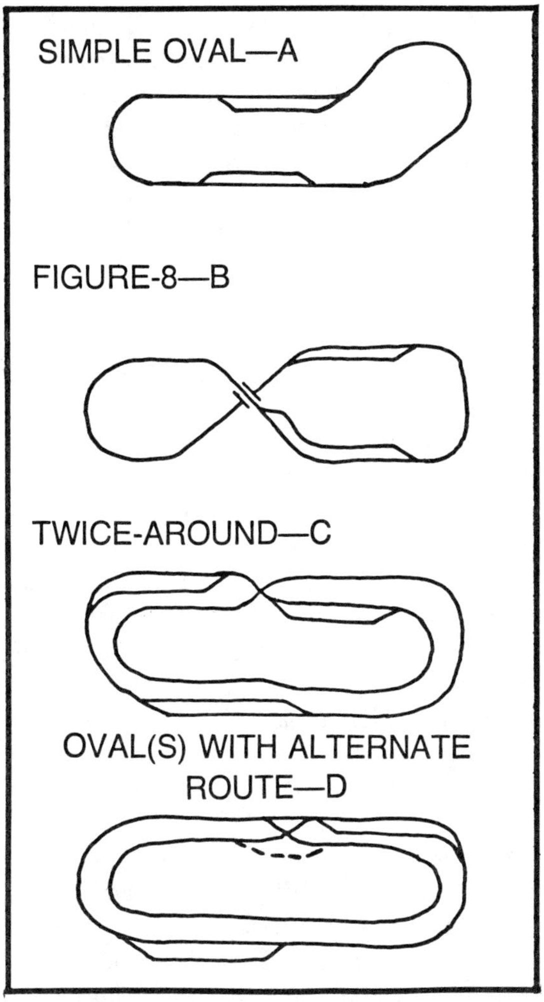

Fig. 2-4. Continuous track plans. Simple oval (A); figure-8 (B); twice-around (C); oval with alternate route (D).

At the end of the line there has to be some way to turn the trains for their return. On an electrified commuter line running only multiple-unit trains, or on its diesel equivalent using only present-day push-pull consists, the track can simply end at a platform. All other lines will need something more—a *runaround* track to let the locomotive get back on the front end, and a turntable or *wye* track if the motive power is not equally at home running in reverse. The key requirement defining the schematic as a *point-to-point* is that there is no way to turn the entire train around in a continuous forward movement.

If your interest is in branch or short-line railroading and your primary operating enjoyment is in switching, the point-to-point can be a good choice, particularly for a fairly large layout. By definition, there have to be *two* terminals; and unless there are extensive traffic sources along the line, they both must have about the same train-handling capacity. Everything starting at one end will eventually arrive at the other. No subterfuges—what heads west will have to come east on its next trip, and to get from A to Z you must go through all the stations in between in proper order.

On the smaller layout the main problem that shows up with the point-to-point is the very small ratio of out-on-the-road running to terminal switching time. No sooner is a train ready to leave than it's coming into the other yard, ready to be broken up again. If most of the trains are local freights and there are lots of intermediate industry tracks, the trip over the line may become an adequate interlude between periods of yard work, but this implies a railroad of more than minimum proportions.

Center-Layover Railroading

If your interest lies more in modeling big-time operations, the difficulty with the point-to-point format is that all its action is out in the open. Most trains which you have assembled will reach the other destination so quickly, even if they do encounter some delays in meeting opposing traffic on single track, that the effect of a trip across the limitless prairie or over the Appalachians or even from Oakland to San Jose is hard to achieve.

A tremendous improvement is the *center-layover* pike (Fig. 2-3C) with one or more hidden passing tracks somewhere in the middle of the route. Now a train can leave its western terminal, disappear on its long run across the desert, and only reach its next terminal after a time which can easily seem like tomorrow morning. If it's a drag or local, some faster trains may pass it en route and come into the east-end yard a realistic hour or two ahead of its schedule. During these kill-time periods, the difference is that the train is out of sight, where your imagination is free to picture it as continuing its progress, rather than sitting there growing cobwebs right where everybody can see what a disorganized railroad this is.

Continuous Track Plan Schematics

By far the most common track plan, on the other hand, is some form of the 'round and 'round or *continuous* schematic. The Christmas-tree simple oval (Fig. 2-4A) has the basic advantage of the continuous scheme. The main line is indefinitely long so far as unattended running of a train is concerned. Double-track it and two can keep rolling until the gears give out. Provide passing sidings on single track and you, as the dispatcher, can arrange meets all evenings without having to wait for a yard crew to make up new trains.

A slight variation, which doesn't really alter the schematic unless the crossing is at grade, greatly increasing the visual variety is the figure-8 (Fig. 2-4B). Seen from one side of the layout, the same train can appear to be going in opposite directions at different times.

Flop one half of the figure-8 inside the other and you have the *twice-around* (Fig. 2-4C), with its double-length route in about the same space. It takes some extra bends and artful scenery to separate the two laps enough to make this incipient bowl of spaghetti *look* like a longer, end-to-end-connected, line of single track, but those are the basic ideas behind all deliberate deceptions aimed at something approaching an adequately long route.

Alternate Routes

Add a couple of switches and a connecting track by-passing one lap of the twice-around and the scheme collapses into the *alternate-route* plan (Fig. 2-4D). This isn't necessarily a move in the right direction, since we have cut the length of the trip in half; but it is the basis of the *convertible* schematics discussed later on, if it's done right. Once you've made it possible to get back to go with only one lap, you may as well add a second connection from A to B and create, in effect, two separate ovals. For any layout where running two trains continuously for exhibition purposes is a desired capability, this alternative routing is useful. Some of the track plans in this book incorporate such a feature, usually with some gimmicks to make things look at least somewhat legitimate.

It's easy to get carried away and run tracks around the space three times (Fig. 2-5A) or go completely wild and create a pretzel (Fig. 2-5B). Railroads properly going from one city to another don't go crossing over themselves in the process at all, let alone doing it repeatedly, but some industrial or switching railroads actually can end up with such arrangements. Therefore, there are two in this book, with proper excuses for their lack of a singleminded, straightforward main line suggested by the structures and secondary trackage included in the complete plan. Otherwise, such confused schematics represent a questionable way to go.

Reversing Tracks

Unless your motive power is a Shay, with its rather uninterestingly cylinderless left side, allowing a view of the other side of the same train isn't likely to be an important track-plan goal. Nevertheless, the capability for reversing the direction of an orbiting train is highly desirable. It lets you switch from having opposing trains meeting each other at passing tracks to a series of following-train movements. This brings in the opportunity for moving the faster train past its slower predecessor, a maneuver that doesn't have to be made every trip but can be even more challenging to pull off with a minimum of delay.

The schematic in Fig. 2-6A adds a *single reversing connection* to the simple oval, which of course requires mastering the moderately mysterious matter of two-rail reversing-section wiring. That has been covered so thoroughly in the many books and articles concerned with model railroad electrical matters that it needn't be discussed here. Some track plans in this book as a reminder identify non-obvious reversing-section situations where they occur but omit any details of handling them, since that should be worked out in connection with the particular system of electrical control adopted for the railroad as a whole.

The single reversing connection can be more tantalizing than satisfying when used on a simple-oval schematic. All trains quickly end up running in the direction favored by the reversing track, and the only way to easily get back to bi-directional operation is to back a train through the connection. Therefore, it's more common to work in a second reversing track, opposite to the first (Fig. 2-6B). The result is a far more versatile system. Like all plans based on the simple oval, it favors main line train running rather than switching and terminal operations.

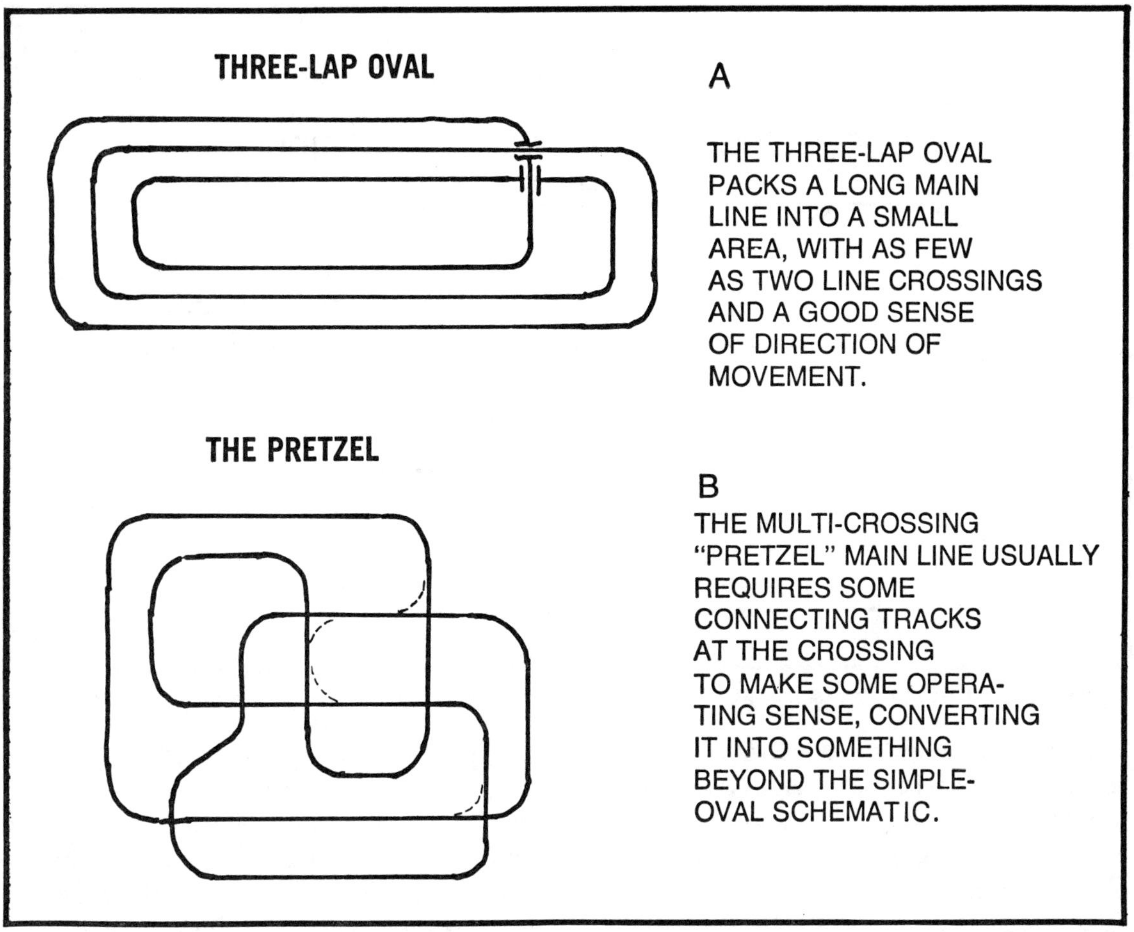

Fig. 2-5. The oval gone wild. Three-lap oval (A); the pretzel (B).

When the reversing-track idea is applied to an oval that has been expanded, twisted and wrapped around into something more appealing than the basic racetrack, the opportunities for confusion in identifying reversing connections are considerable. What looks like an oval with double reversing connections may very well turn out to be an oval with alternate route. Both of the connections turn out to be alternate routes, interesting perhaps but incapable of doing any train-turning. Another slightly different-looking arrangement may turn out to provide two reversing connections which unfortunately duplicate each other's function, leaving no way to get back from clockwise running on the outer track. What's needed, of course, is a second connection between points A and B rather than C and D (Fig. 2-7), not much different in appearance but a lot more effective in operation.

There are times when a connection that is *not* a reversing section is what's wanted. The only way to be sure of what you have is to run trains around the plan mentally, drawing little arrows as you go if things are the least bit complex, and see where they come out. These auxiliary tracks, being somewhat phoney in most cases, should at least do what we need them to!

Semi-Point-to-Point Schematics

A reversing loop gets a train turned around and heading back in a hurry. Since the chief deficiency of the point-to-point railroad model is too much time turning trains, why not combine the two into a hybrid? The result is the *point-to-loop* schematic (Fig. 2-8A) which is an excellent compromise. It's compact and realistic to use space inside the loop for hidden layover trackage, letting trains return to the terminal in a sequence different from the one in which they left.

Expanding the loop until it makes up most of the main line results in the *out-and-back* plan (Fig.

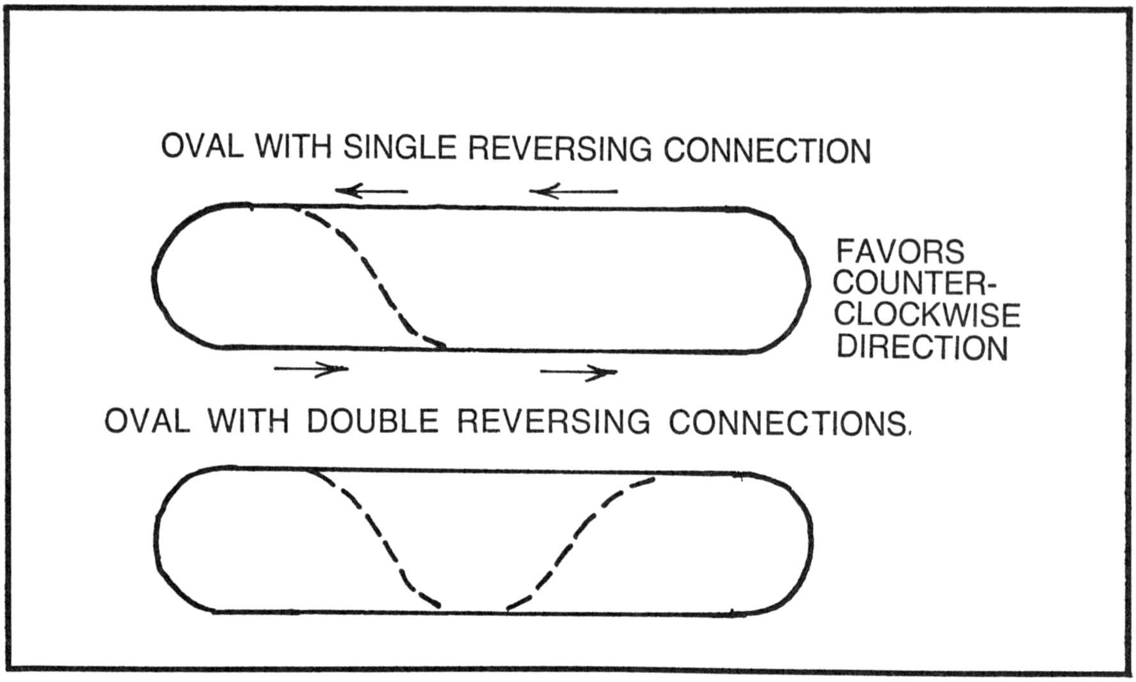

Fig. 2-6. Ovals with reversing tracks. Oval with single reversing connection (A); oval with double reversing connections (B).

2-8B) a varient which sometimes fits the space better if an around-the-room railroad is the objective. Schematically things are the same if the terminal is physically inside the loop, and this alternative packages neatly into a rectangular area in the smallest gauges. The out-and-back swings the balance back a little bit toward the point-to-point so far as switching vs. running is concerned. Every train that leaves the terminal returns after passing over the main-line trackage once, whereas it covers much of the line twice in a similar excursion over a point-to-loop road of the same size.

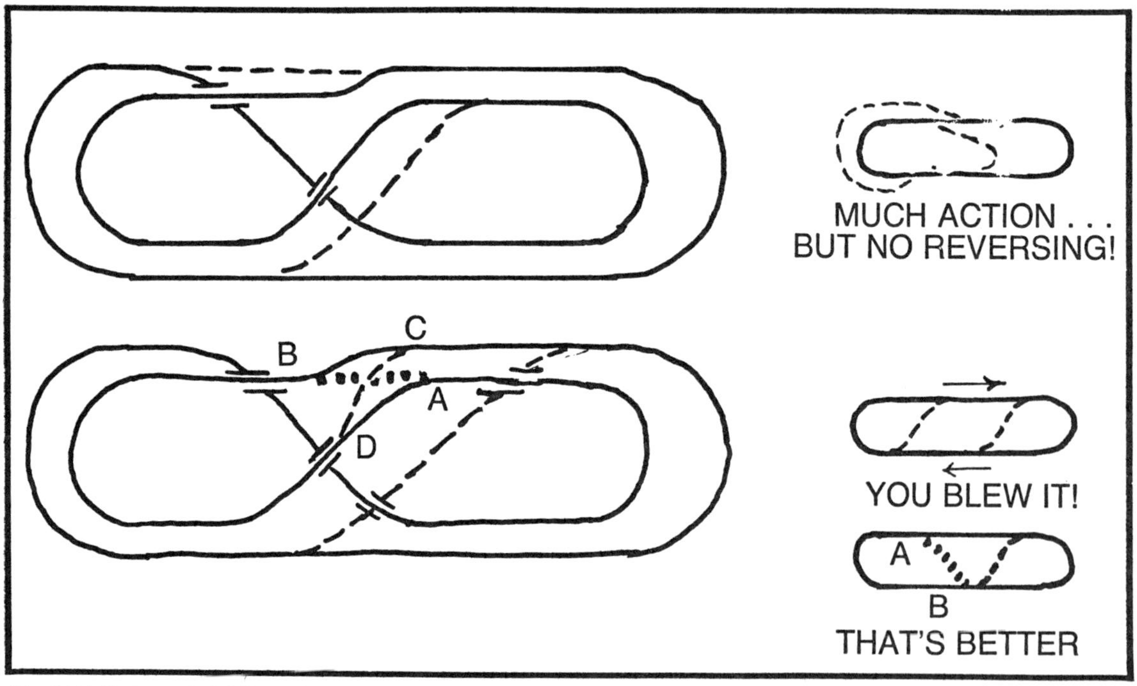

Fig. 2-7. What type is it? Oval with alternate route (top); oval with single reversing connection (bottom).

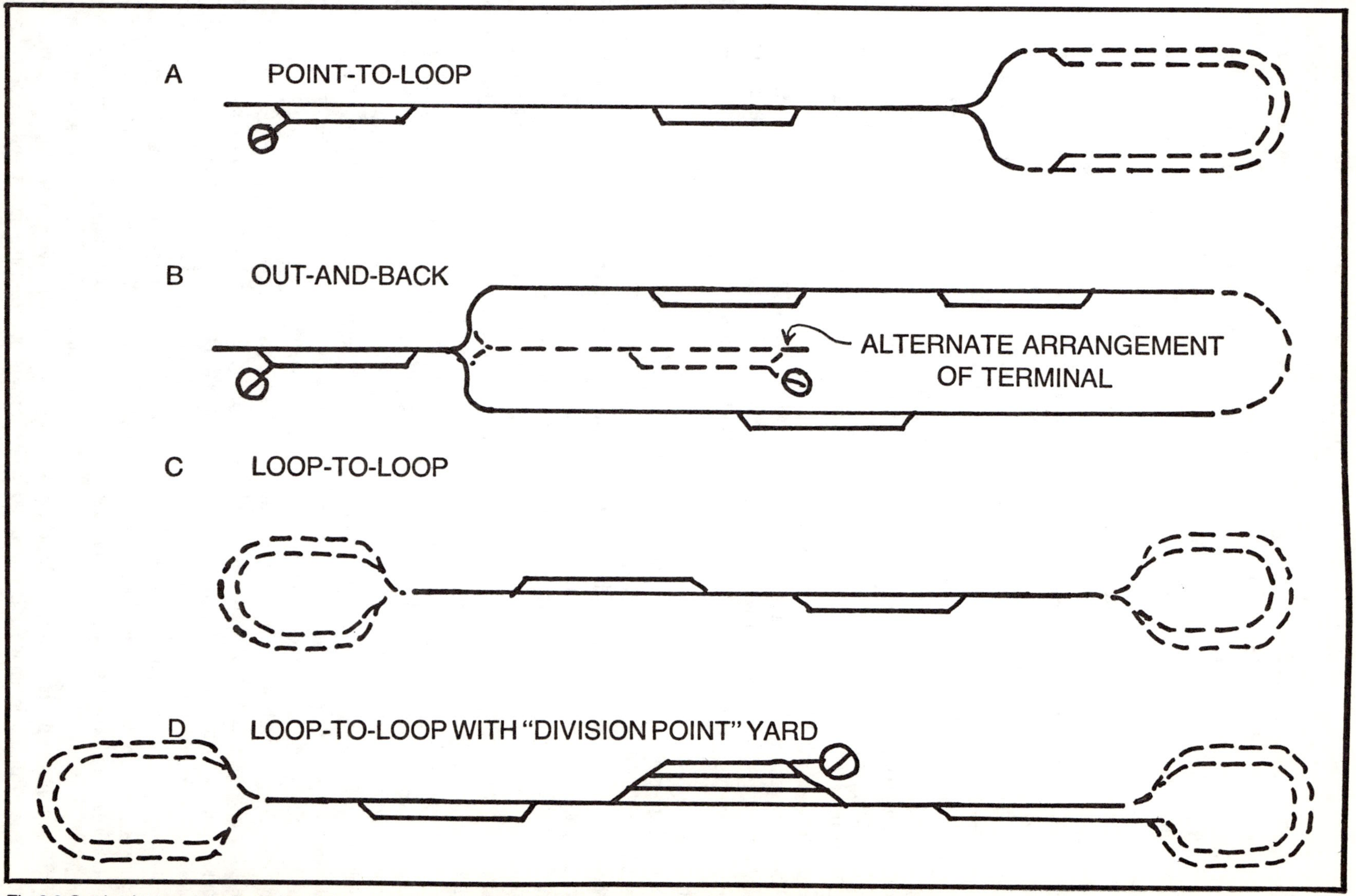

Fig. 2-8. Semi-point-to-point schematics. Point-to-loop (A); out-and-back (B); loop-to-loop (C); loop-to-loop with division point| yard (D).

Loop-to-Loop

Figure 2-8C extends the quick-turn-around feature to both ends of the line, so it's never necessary to turn a train around just to keep things moving, even though the traffic pattern is point-to-point. If a yard is located along the main line, it becomes an intermediate rather than a terminating installation, just like the hundreds of division point yards spaced along all through rail routes. Since all medium and larger model railroads patterned after general traffic railroads are likely to include as big a yard as space permits, being able to make do perfectly well with a single such yard is an important benefit of the *loop-to-loop*. In line with most division points in the real world which are also important traffic sources, this yard can not only serve to forward some through trains but serves as an originating or terminating point as well (Fig. 2-8D), so the full spectrum of functions can be represented. All in all, the loop-to-loop is probably the best arrangement available for the larger layout attempting to portray heavy-duty railroading, except for one picky little point.

The Dogbones

Running a train around a loop and back onto the main line in the opposite direction still requires reverse-switch operation each trip, so the *dogbone* arrangements of Fig. 2-9 have always been popular. Schematically they're just a simple oval, stretched and squeezed in the middle but still a continuous 'round and 'round route though disguised to look like things are moving to and fro.

The *narrow-shank dogbone* (Fig. 2-9A) pushes the two tracks so close together that they represent a double-track main line. The ends are usually partially or completely hidden and may include layover tracks. This schematic *looks* and acts like the loop-to-loop; and once you put a crossover anywhere along the main line, you've created an electrical reversing loop. It provides unlimited traffic density without *requiring* changes in train consist, while providing the appearance of movement from one point to another and back. In its larger versions, the narrow-shank dogbone usually includes hidden layover sidings at one or both ends.

Those knobs at the end of the dogbone are fixed in size by the minimum main-line radius so they're usually the main space-eaters, and efficient design often calls for stacking them one above the other. The double-track shank can then be wrapped around the rest of the area quite freely, until the basic scheme is properly unrecognizable.

Most railroad routes in the United States and Canada, including most of the Western main lines, are single track. To represent these in your basement the *single-side dogbone* is a good alternative (Fig. 2-9B). This schematic is essentially just a big oval. If there's room enough to make the railroad look and act bigger than it is, the second side of the dogbone is separated from its companion and hidden, with its passing tracks serving as concealed layover points. The end loops can then come out into the open, and we have a considerably longer visible main line.

The single-side dogbone bears the same relationship to its double-shanked cousin as single-track railroading does to operation over double track. Its traffic-handling capacity is less, though not a great deal less if Centralized Traffic Control (CTC) signaling and dispatcher-operated switches are provided, but train-for-train it's a lot more interesting.

The Open-Top Problem. In the model we have another little problem with the double-track dogbone if we're attempting to represent a railroad that handles a lot of traffic in open-top cars, hoppers, gondolas or flats. Typically the loaded cars are headed one way, the empties the other, as lumber, ore, coal or whatever goes to its destination in city, power plant or port and the essential supply of cars for loading is replenished by a corresponding stream of returning traffic. A working mine at one end of your railroad and an equally genuine car dumper at the other, along with judicious weighting to keep the empties on the track, will keep everything sincere, but the time and repetitive effort it takes to follow this approach faithfully is too much for most of us.

The result is usually a string of loads traveling back and forth on the double-track railroad. It looks as if equally-large power plants at each end of the line insisted on drawing their supplies from mines unfortunately distant in precisely opposite directions, or as if *none* of the coal, ore or whatever was of acceptable quality and *all* of it was

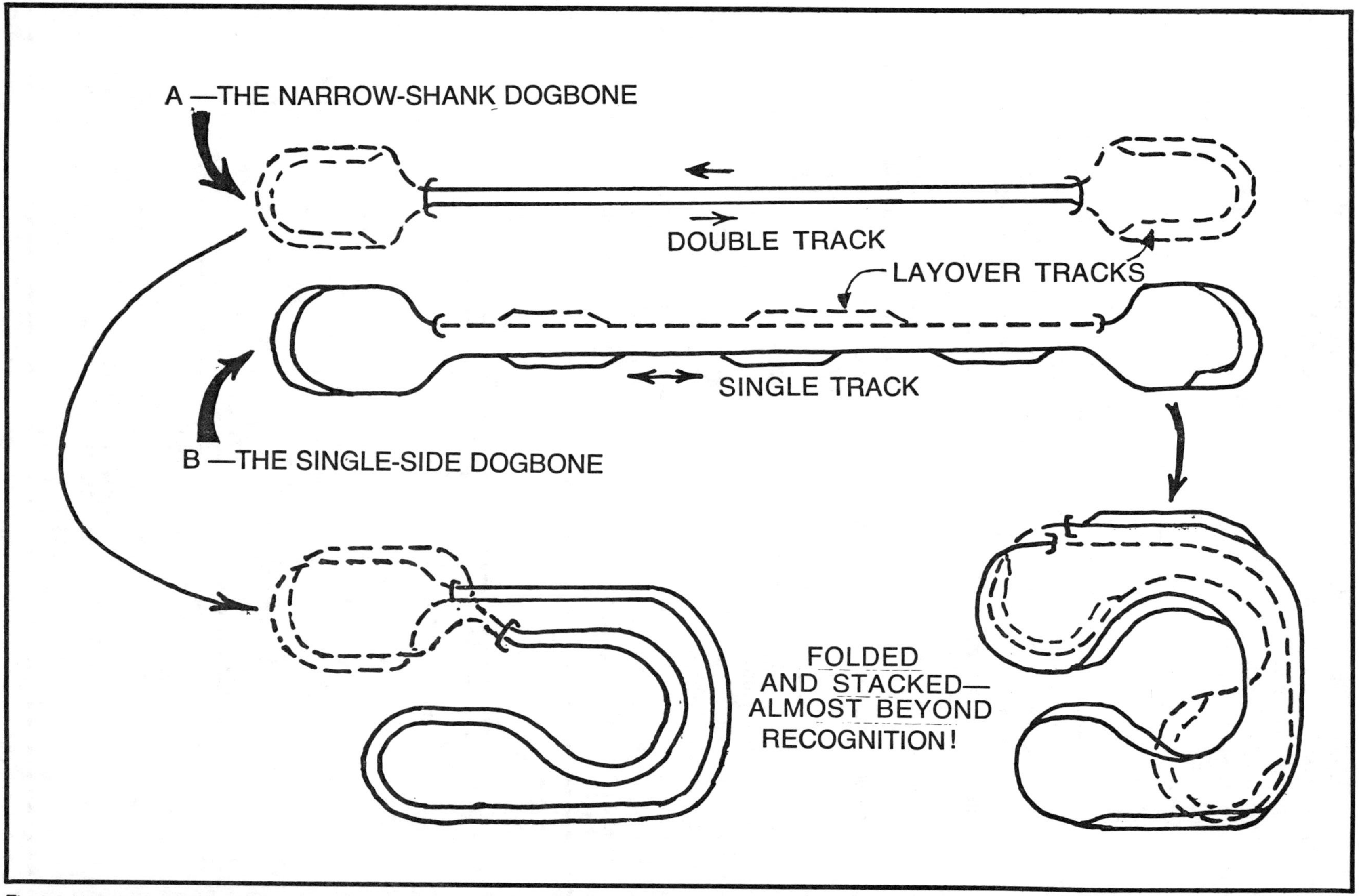

Fig. 2-9. Variations on the oval. The narrow-shank dogbone (A); the single-side dogbone (B).

rejected and sent back by a hard-nosed purchasing agent. With covered hoppers of grain, or boxcars and reefers of merchandise or perishables, which conceal their empty or loaded status, there's no problem; the open-top movements are subject to kindly comments.

The single-sided dogbone also has no problem with the hopper-car traffic—you can have a train of empties and a train of loads. Running one clockwise and its mate counter-clockwise, with the return trips out of sight, clears up the situation maybe even to the point where a determined train-watcher will begin to check car numbers. Most railroads handling a lot of exposed loads have both double- and single-track routes. This difference might tip the balance in favor of picking a single-track section as the prototype and the single-side dogbone as the method of modeling it.

The Empty/Load Illusion. Figure 2-10 shows another approach, as applied to the narrow-shank dogbone but generally useable with any schematic. In our contorted layouts it's not at all uncommon for tracks representing opposite ends of the main line to be physically close to each other, so the surreptitious, beind-the-scenes scheme for giving the illusion of an unlimited supply from forest or mine and equally unlimited and rapid consumption at the other end of the pipeline-on-wheels isn't hard to build into many track plans.

COMBINATION SCHEMATICS

Running tracks wherever they'll fit and interconnecting them wherever they cross with no rhyme or reason results in a model railroad whose purposeless pattern of operation loses interest rapidly; therefore, designing around a single basic schematic leads to more railroading fun, now and in the long run. Many of the best track plans, though, including some of the smaller ones, are based on a combination of the types discussed above.

In particular, it's possible to add a branch to most continuous schematics without adding much if any to the space required. The entirely different pattern of operation adds immeasurably to the pike's enjoyment potential. There's a "run trains when you feel like it" flavor to a *stub-end branch* that usually contrasts pleasantly with the more structured, and sometimes deliberately frantic, pattern of main-line running.

Figure 2-11A combines a stub terminal, which can represent a branch or one end of a main line, with a simple oval. Trains originating on the branch enter the main line at a junction feeding

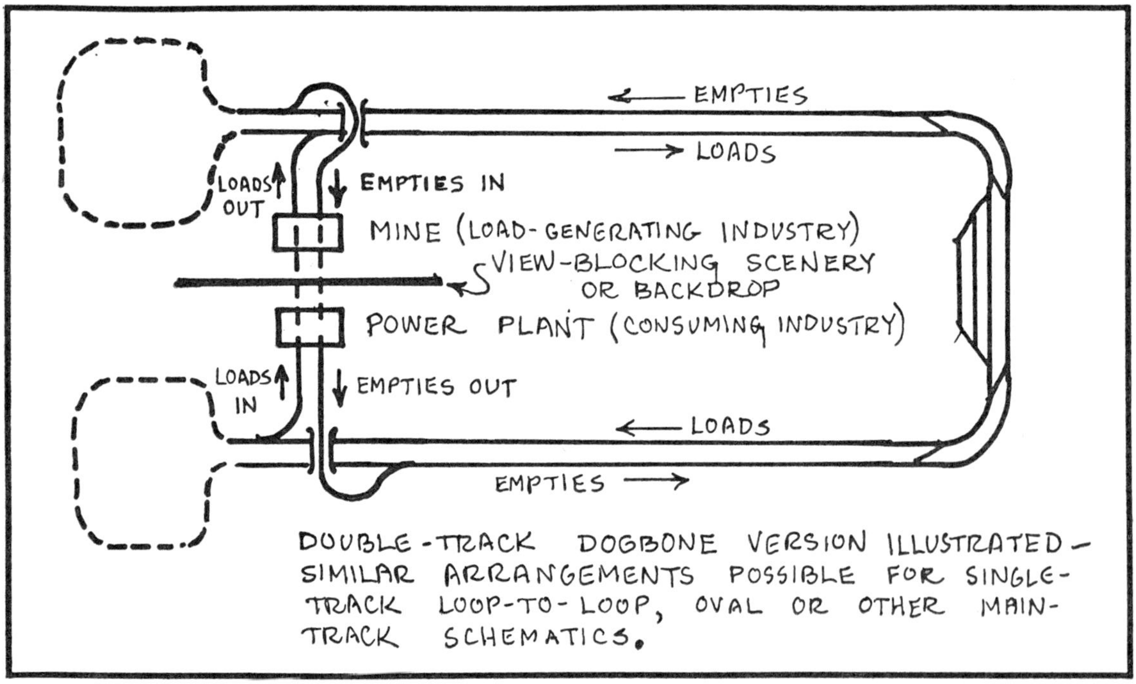

Fig. 2-10. Frustrating the "empties-loads" nit-pickers.

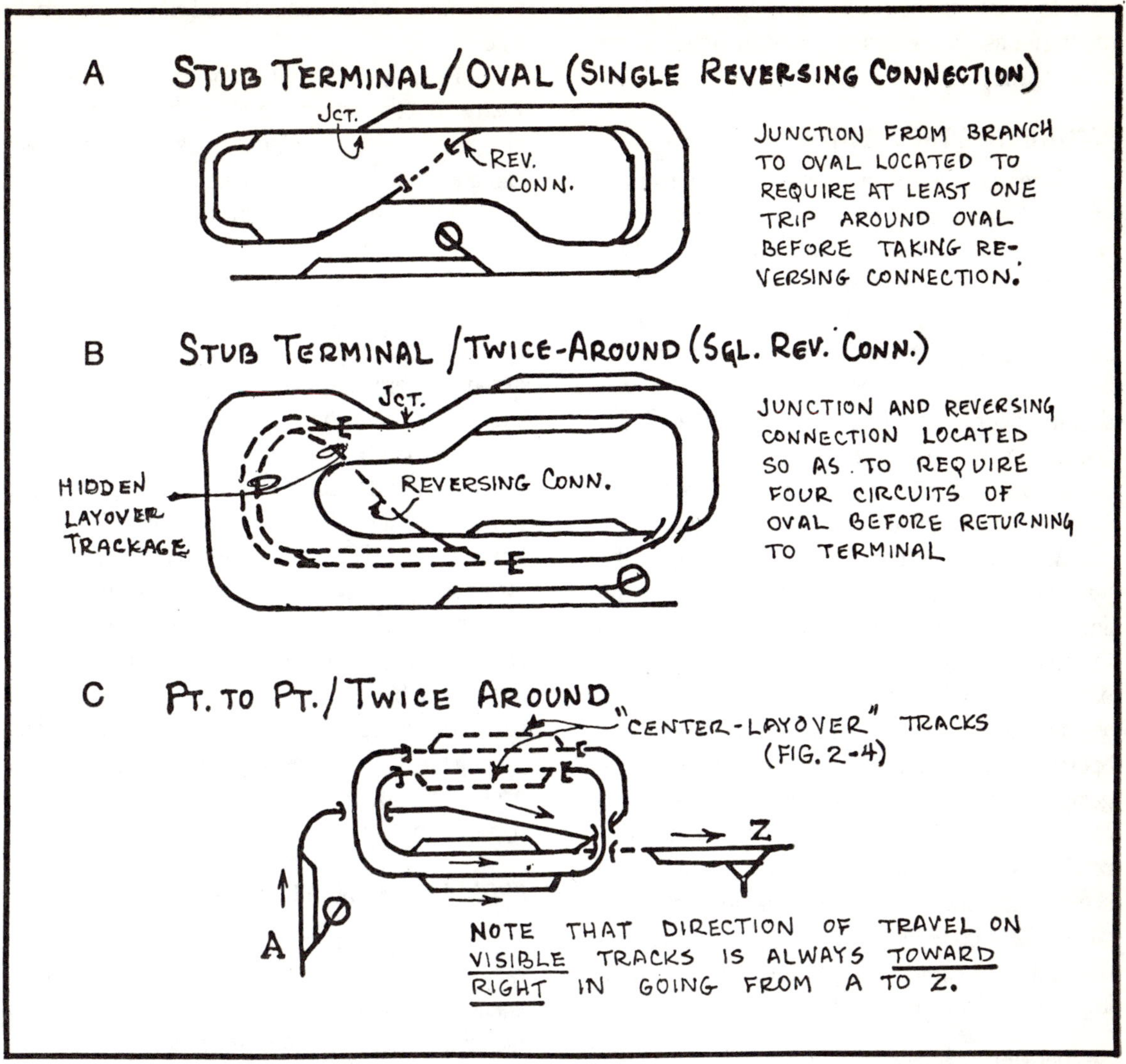

Fig. 2-11. Combination schematics. Stub terminal/oval, single reversing connection (A); stub terminal/twice-around, single reversing connection (B); point-to-point twice-around (C).

them into the counter-clockwise traffic flow around the continuous oval. After any appropriate number of orbits they can take the reversing connection, which can well be arranged as a hidden layover, and emerge headed for home.

Figure 2-11B is similar, but with a slightly more spacious twice-around main line. In this case, judicious placement of junction and reversing-connection switches *requires* a fairly long journey, and this minimum mileage trip runs up its distance without repeated travel over the same trackage in the same direction.

Both of these examples need only a single reversing connection, since trains will always end up headed for the branch terminal and its facilities, whatever they are, for turning them around. Since reversing connections are usually rather artificial additions, not really typical of for-real trackage, this is a point in favor of the stub-terminal scheme in comparison to the double-reversing oval plan. All in all, for small to medium-size pikes, the combination of a continuous oval with a single branch and terminal represents an almost ideal use of the space to provide versatile operation with balanced switching and train-running opportunities.

Figure 2-11C, combining two stub terminals with a twice-around continuous segment, leans more in the direction of terminal switching. It's really a development of the center-layover scheme, but trades some of the sincerity of the point-to-point for the ability to have a train keep moving for as many miles as you want in the course of its journey.

ACCENTUATING THE POSITIVE

Schematics aren't supposed to be concerned with the *positioning* of tracks, but rather with the ways in which they are connected to each other and what that means in terms of route the trains can and cannot take. The hiding of a track and the suitability this creates for its use as a layover point has already been interjected into these schematics; however, in this point-to-point twice-around combination we've gone a step farther to illustrate another weapon in the battle for more convincing illusions of reasonable railroad operations.

Most of the travel in the journey from the terminal at A to its counterpart at the far end of the line at Z takes place in roughly circular fashion on the continuous section of the plan, so for a good part of the trip the train is traveling in a direction *opposite* to its objective. This tends to confuse operator and spectator alike, not only as to what's going on but as to which train it is—the westbound or the eastbound? By hiding most of this apparently backward movement and arranging the scene so that the parts exposed to view are those where the locomotive is pointing in the general direction of its goal, the situation can be much improved, at no cost in space.

CONVERTIBLE SCHEMATIC PLANS

Not only is each model railroader different in his relative interest in turning 'em on and watching 'em roll vs. taking 'em apart and switching 'em around, but what he wants most to do on his railroad varies from year to year, day to day and even hour to hour on the same evening. Running the railroad with a crew experienced in keeping several trains moving and ready to try something new and different calls for a track plan with a variety of obstacles. Showing the results of years of construction to the casual visitor doesn't need tricky maneuvers to be impressive, but rather an operating scheme that lets one or two trains keep moving smoothly and reliably without taking so much concentration that the proprietor has to be a poor host. Solo running, to see how a new creation performs or just to relax, should also be uncomplicated.

In general, providing for such a shift is a matter of converting one of the more labor intensive arrangements, single-track, point-to-point and the like, toward unopposed, continuous train movements, sometimes irreverently referred to as "idiot loop" running. As Fig. 2-12 shows, this can be a matter of a few strategically-located cut-off tracks. Provided that these by-passes are thought of during the basic design of the plan, including them is usually a simple matter, but one that can pay handsome dividends in keeping it fun.

Conversely, with those invitations to just running the little choo-choos constantly at hand, how do you keep the grown men from staying in kindergarten? Taking out a section or two of track is the for-sure way of doing it. Disguising the cut-off as a pair of back-to-back industry spurs or an interchange connection between two different lines, to be blocked off by setting out some freight cars on them is a less brutal approach. Either way, putting two different railroads in the same space by adding a pair of turnouts and two feet of track is an opportunity to be grabbed.

PROGRESSIVE PIKE PLANNING

You can't start on Dec. 15 and get much of a railroad running for Christmas, but it can be equally devastating to start on a project roughly the size of the Panama Canal in such a way that there won't even be a motorboat ride until the whole thing is completely cut through. There are some plans, usually ones more suited to the advanced modeler, which can only be built as a pre-engineered whole in such a sequence that operating possibilities are limited until some final segments on the top layer tie the whole main line together. Many pikes, however, can be built efficiently in stages, with fun-and-games possibilities commensurate with the area covered almost from the beginning.

Figure 2-13 illustrates such a two-stage set of schematics. An additional twist is the chance to veer off in one of two rather different directions based on experience! The first-stage railroad is small enough for apartment modeling, but it includes the mix of continuous running and terminal

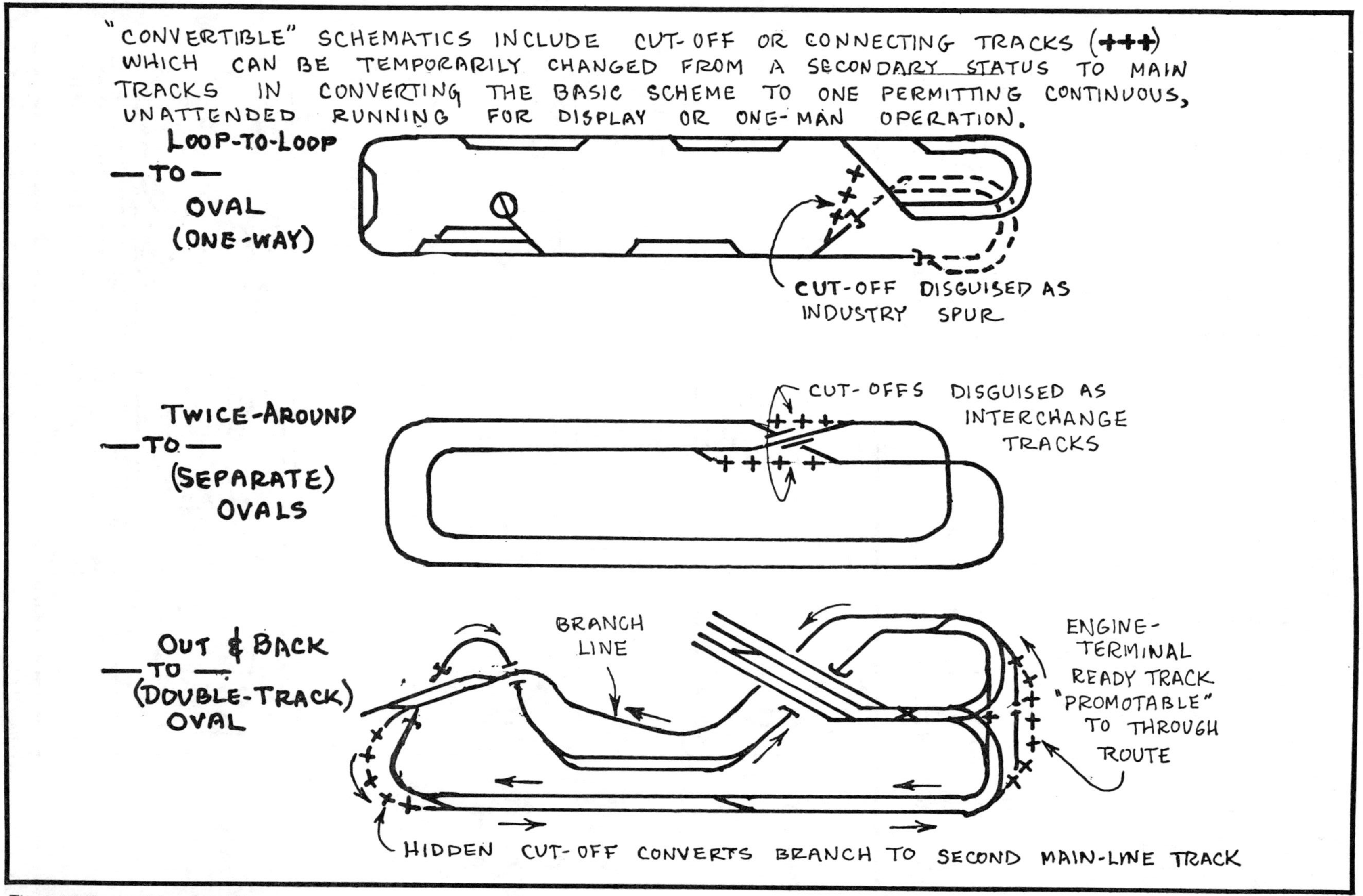

Fig. 2-12. Convertible schematics.

switching of short consists which makes a combination schematic of this type an ideal starter plan. If you find yourself running trains on the main line most of the time, and making many saw-by meets because you can't resist tacking on too many cars to fit into those short passing tracks, your second-stage choice should be one like version B. Double-track main lines, for a railroad of any given size, can handle longer trains and more of them without frustration.

On the other hand, should first-stage experience demonstrate a preference for tinkering around in the little yard and arranging things out on the line so that trains meet each other with well-timed precision, version B retains its single-track main line, extending it to a more worthy length and accommodating somewhat longer trains, and becomes the preferred plan for taking advantage of the broadened horizons that come with more space. In either case, much of the trackage of the first stage remains in place—timewise, planning ahead does beat starting over! Track plans in Figs. 4-3, 4-4 and 4-6 are examples of this approach.

DOUBLE-TRACK VS. SINGLE

Basic schematics are concerned with the *routes* trains may take rather than with *how many tracks* are provided on each line, so most are worked out showing a single line. Passing tracks or double track presumably can be added later without changing the basic pattern. On large pikes this is generally true. For small ones, the difference

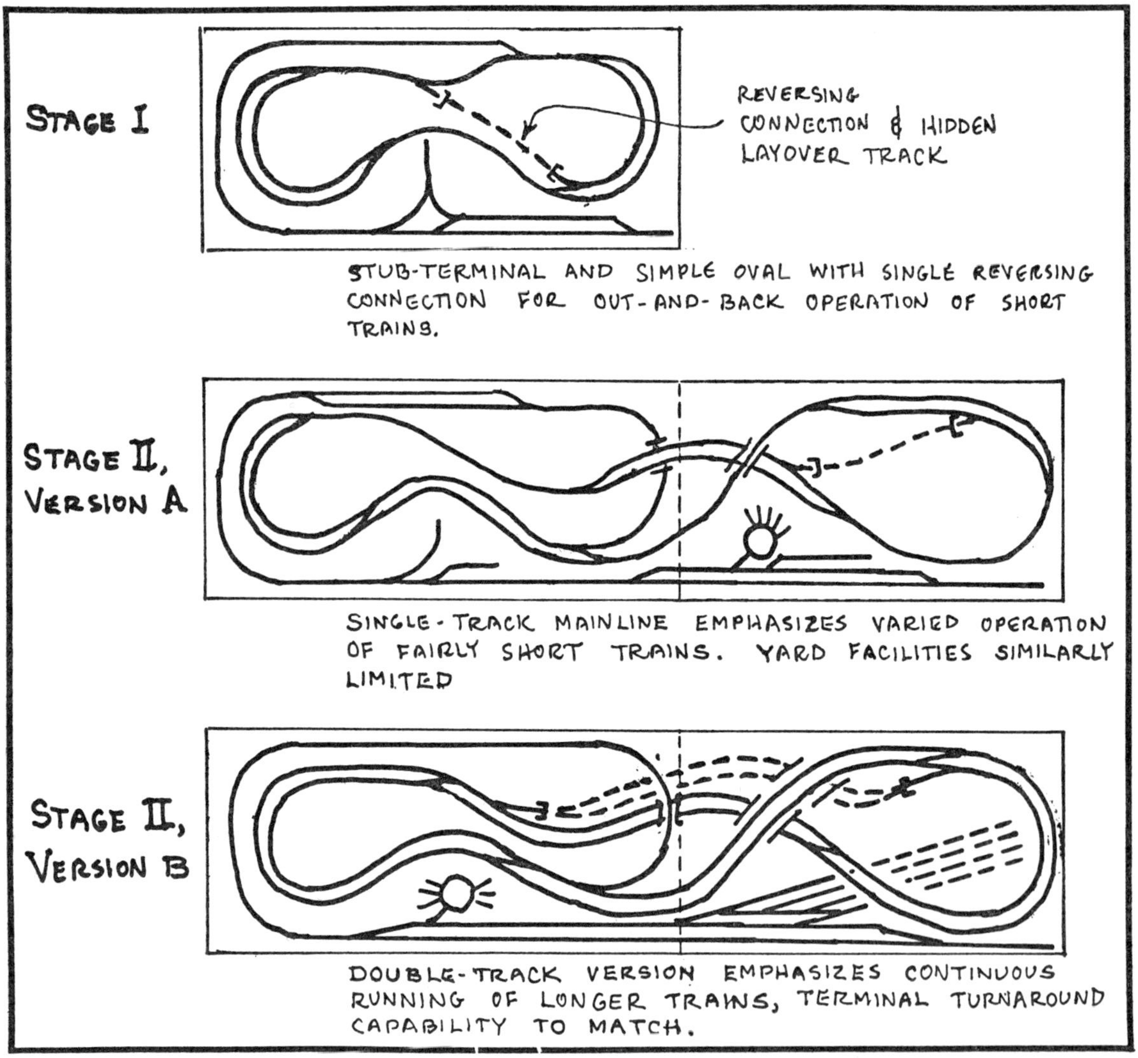

Fig. 2-13. Progressive track plans.

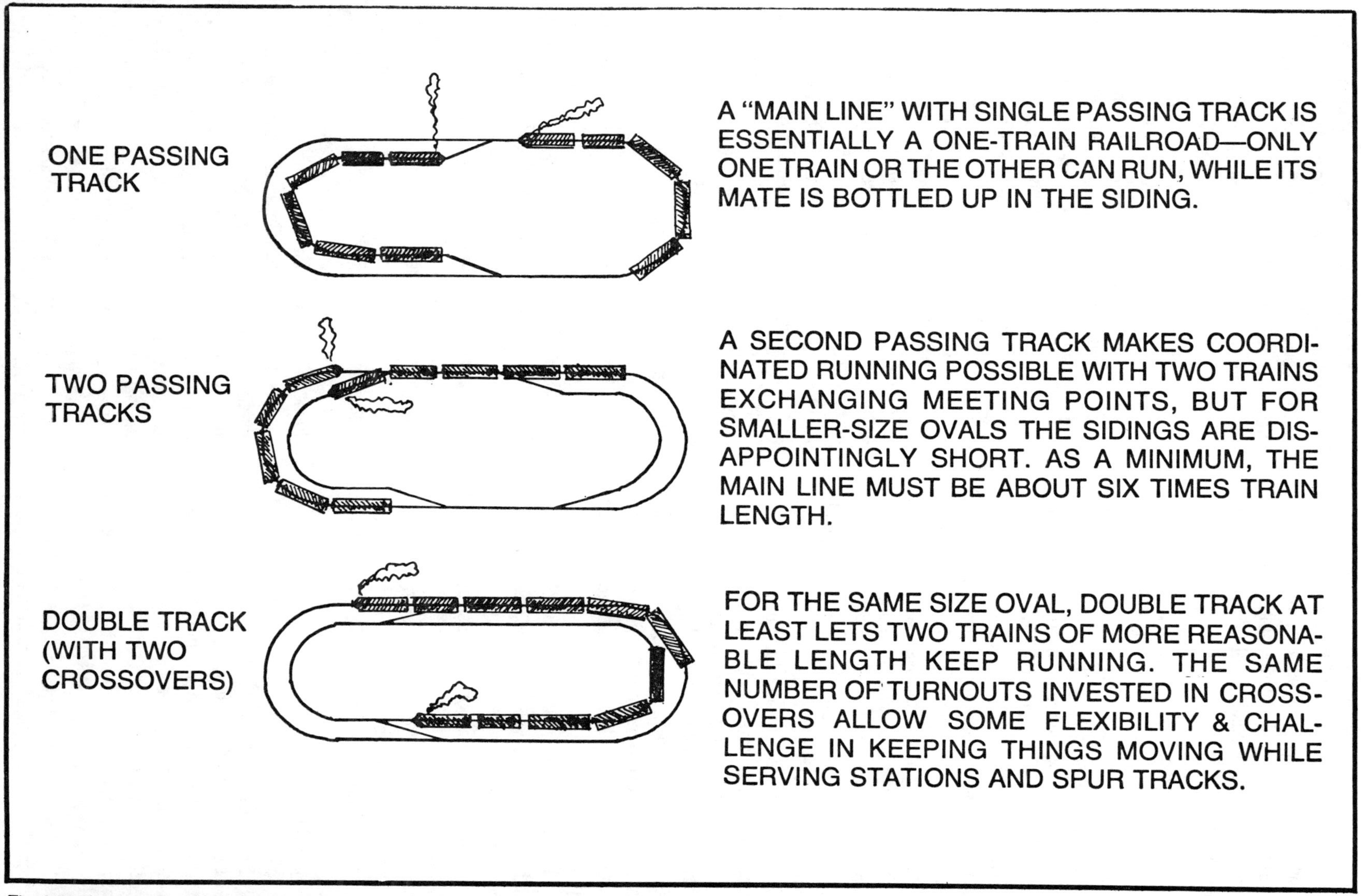

Fig. 2-14. Single track may be too big.

between one track and two is vital, and it's not in the direction you might think! Figure 2-14 points out why there is a lower limit to the size of a single-track line capable of meaningful two-train operation. This can make double track the more practical choice.

HOW IS IT BUILT?

By and large, model railroads are built using tools, materials and fabrication techniques basically intended for some more fundamental function such as building houses and apartments to keep the wind, rain, heat and cold away from model railroaders and their families. After all plywood never would have reached its present state of development just because it's a vital ingredient of most layouts, and it's often essential to have some non-enjoyable work around the house to justify buying a saber saw.

Accepting these subsidies from the outside world does mean that *the way the track is supported* has quite a bit to do with selecting the most practical track plan. The details of converting a drawing of an arrangement of curves, tangents, turnouts and grades into a solidly-supported right of way are not covered in this book. Books such as Paul Mallery's "Trackwork Handbook" and the Atlas Tool Company's series in N and HO gauges will help you.

For the purpose of helping you select a track plan best in turn with your situation, we will take a quick look at the main methods of layout construction and their trade-offs between ease and speed of assembly on the one hand and flexibility in accommodating any track and scenery arrangement on the other. Suitable construction methods for each plan in this book are indicated in the write-up accompanying it; here's what we mean by the terms used.

TABLETOP CONSTRUCTION

Once you get tired of trying to keep the sections of track together, and lint out of the car axles, on the rug and go out after a piece of plywood on which to fasten down your basic train-set oval, you've reinvented this fundamental system of layout construction. As Fig. 2-15 illustrates, the only basic characteristic of the tabletop is that it's flat, horizontal and stiff enough to remain so throughout the life of the railroad. There are various ways to provide these qualities, with the choice depending on the cost, convenience and weight of providing a surface of required shape and size.

Most of the acceptable types of tabletop construction depend on plywood, either as the entire structure in the case of some smaller layouts or as the rigid surface stiffened by a framework below. No other material provides as good a combination of properties as plywood, though we may wince at the price sometimes. Track cannot be spiked *directly* onto standard (fir) plywood. It's just too hard and its grain has too strong an opinion as to which way the spikes should shift if they do succeed in penetrating the surface, but with suitable subroadbed materials between it and the ties we have a good combination of characteristics. For appearance's sake the track should be raised somewhat above the surface in any case. Softer sheet building materials (Homasote) are not stiff enough unless so thoroughly braced as to defeat the purpose of using them, while hard particle board compositions are disastrously unstable under even moderate loads over a period of time.

The Standard-Size Syndrome

Plywood and other building materials come in standard 4 × 8 foot sheets, so it's no coincidence that there are probably as many HO railroads of that size as all others put together. Four by eight isn't a bad size because it is about the largest rectangle that can be wrestled up apartment stairways, stood verically against a wall, and otherwise handled with some degree of ease and comfort. It's just that some shapes of more or less equivalent size may accommodate significantly better track arrangements; some of these alternatives will be found in this book, for your consideration.

A track plan 5 ft. 8 in. long is infinitely more useful than one just a few percent bigger if under-the-bed storage is what it takes to make anything other than armchair railroading compatible with a particular apartment, so some other sizes have special advantages reflected in the examples presented. For HO, availability of plywood just six inches wider than the standard (4½ × 5 foot pairs for making official size table-tennis tops) opens up some worthwhile possibilities.

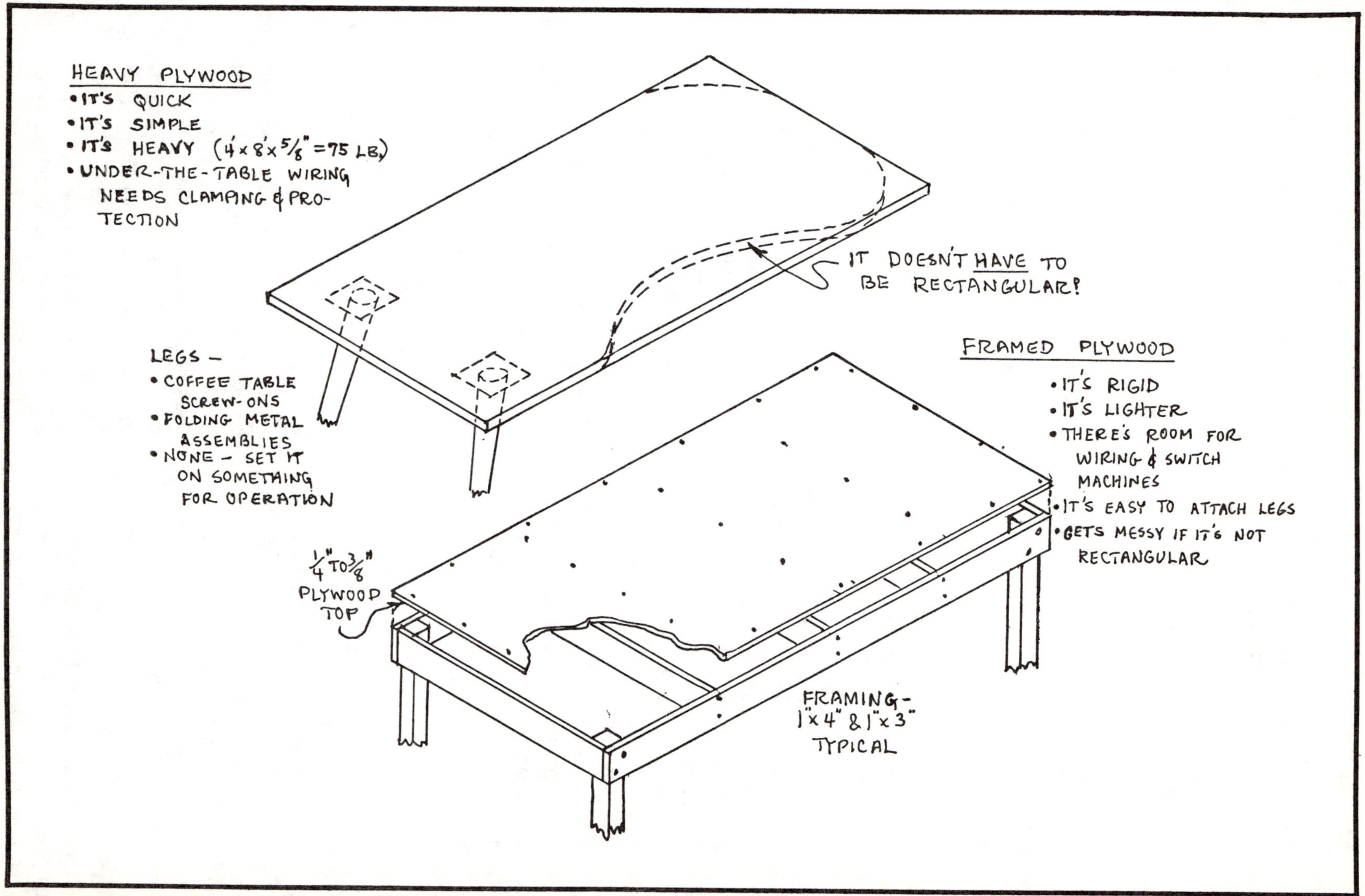

Fig. 2-15. Flat top railroading.

Railroading on the Flat

Trains don't like to go up and down hill, so wherever the terrain permits a railroad main line is a pretty level thing. It's thus not at all unreasonable to plan a model railroad to lie comfortably and conveniently on a surface level as a tabletop, and many of those in this book have nothing but grade crossings between their tracks. Since some cars will roll away on anything more than a 0.5 percent grade, a flat railroad is a good choice if you want the most in switching possibilities, using automatic couplers, in the space available.

Up-And-Over Railroads

The sight of trains crossing over each other is interesting in its own right. Wherever the lay of the land is at all favorable, railroads avoid grade crossings with each other, so there are thousands of such scenes in real life. The quickest way to add this to an otherwise flat railroad is to climb up and over with the sets of graduated-height plastic piers commercially available. They're designed to support sectional track, which is stiff enough in the smaller gauges to hold up the trains despite lack of the massive bridge structure that it would take in the prototype. This isn't too unrealistic unless you look at and think about it, in which case it can look pretty awful. Providing some reasonable-depth girders between piers or filling in around them to represent an embankment is not much trouble, so this out-of-the-box approach to two-level railroading is still the easy way from a structural standpoint.

The pier approach to elevating some of the trackage is extremely restrictive to the track plan, though. It's awkward to locate turnouts anywhere on the line once it starts up the slope, and the grade-reducing technique of getting half the overhead clearance by depressing the level of the lower track (Fig. 1-8) won't work. There are a couple of examples of by-the-piers second levels in this book, but ascending via the prefabricated props won't work in other multi-level plans.

Open Grid Construction

The most flexible, adaptable system for supporting the track on layouts with trackage at many different levels is the *open grid* scheme illustrated in Fig. 2-16. Not only can the rails go anywhere at any desired grade, but the scenery can descend below track level wherever it should and in the extreme, all the way to the floor! Over the years various worthwhile tricks of the trade have been learned the hard way. Reading up on the subject is worthwhile, even though it's easy to get the basic idea from such a simple example as that shown. It's possible, for example, to plan the structure so that none of the screws are covered up by track or scenery and future modifications can be made with a minimum of agony and disruption.

Most larger layouts use some form of open grid construction over most of their area, where open-country scenery is appropriate and tracks are continually rising or falling at various rates. Yard and terminal areas, though, are still likely to be built on plywood attached directly to the benchwork grid.

A special form of open grid construction uses a deformed-plywood surface to carry tracks up and down grade smoothly; it accomplishes the smooth vertical-curve contouring called for back in Fig. 1-11 with a high degree of assurance and has become popular enough to have a well-established name.

Cookie-Cutter Construction

Figure 2-17 illustrates this hybrid between solid top and open grid approaches, with its track supported by plywood applied in large chunks supported and bent into shape by risers attached to a rigid grid. The plywood sheet is slit between track locations which will be at different elevations or slopes, using the full-scale plan laid out on its surface as a guide. The grid is designed to provide support at the proper intervals, usually on a rectangular pattern.

As already mentioned, the strong point of the cookie-cutter is the smooth vertical curves it insures at points where the grade changes. The bi-directional stiffness of the plywood virtually guarantees that track will not have vertical kinks severe enough to cause operating problems or a haphazard "toonerville" appearance. Special inserts are needed where one route crosses over another; the usual cookie-cutter top is a practically solid surface, but holes can be left open at points

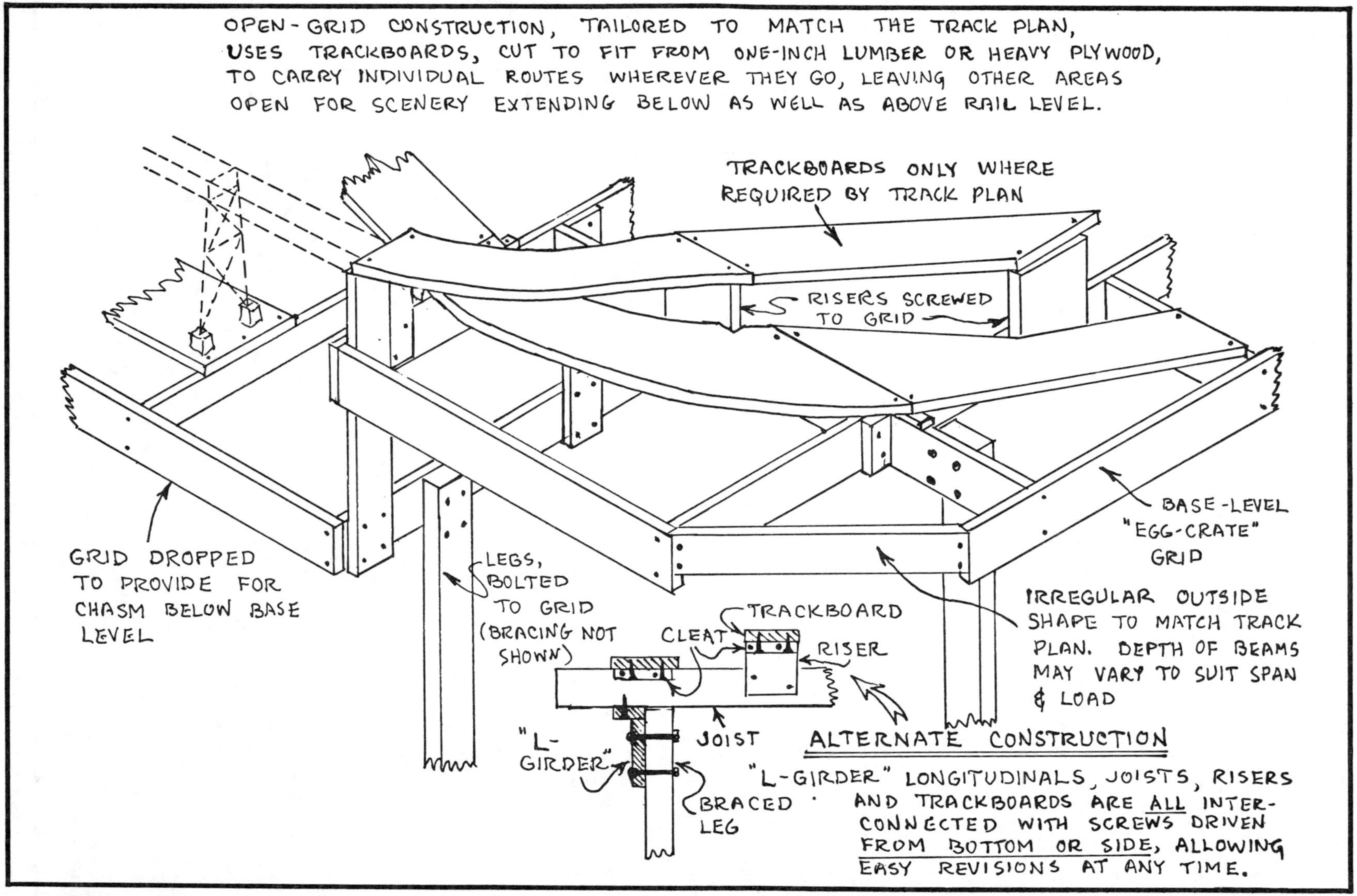

Fig. 2-16. Open grid framing.

where access is needed or where below-grade scenery is appropriate.

Once it's designed properly, the cookie-cutter foundation goes together easily and rapidly. The catch is that considerable planning is required to locate the grid members so as to provide the best combination of support and flexibility and to figure out exact elevations to come up with the desired grades and clearances between levels. The end result is ideally light, strong and stable. Study of some of the detailed construction articles for specific track plans in magazines and books, which include detailed parts diagrams and assembly-sequence recommendations, will reveal such cookie-cutter tricks as are not already obvious once you grasp the basically simple idea of this form of construction. Building your railroad this way gets off to what seems like a slow start but finishes up with a rush, with a smooth and solid roadway that makes track laying a pleasure.

If a track plan contains many, many places where one track crosses over another, the cookie-cutter scheme becomes more laborious than ordinary open grid construction. Such plans are identified in the track-plan chapters in this book. On these plans, though, it's still a good idea to work in an area of slit-plywood trackboard at points where there are several changes in grade in the vicinity of turnouts.

One Caution! Without going further into the matter of tabletop materials, it is important to point out the desirability of sticking with larger-gauge standards of rigidity when working in N scale. The tiny locomotives, even though powerful with their almost solid metal construction, are still light. Even a five-unit diesel probably wouldn't bend a two-foot span of quarter-inch plywood enough for you to see the movement. It's a temptation to go with such thinner materials, but it's not the weight of the trains that cause bending, sagging or warping to be troublesome, it's such strains as lifting the whole railroad, leaning on it to fasten scenery in place, and not getting risers set at exactly the right elevations that really can get things out of shape. The important thing is that in N scale the same wiggle that would be almost invisible with larger-scale trains makes the little ones look as if they're wallowing over the waves. Half-inch plywood is none too thick and can be notched down to one or two of the top plies where clearance below is important.

LAYOUT CONFIGURATIONS

We all have somewhat different ideas as to which of the many aspects of model railroading are

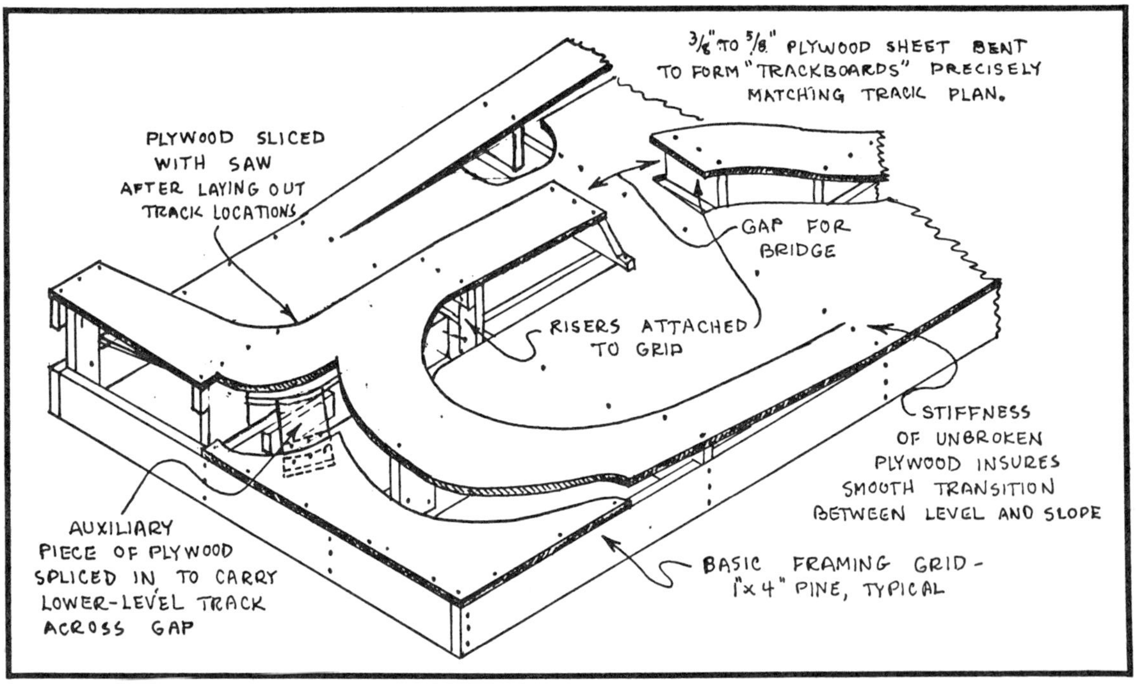

Fig. 2-17. Cookie-cutter construction.

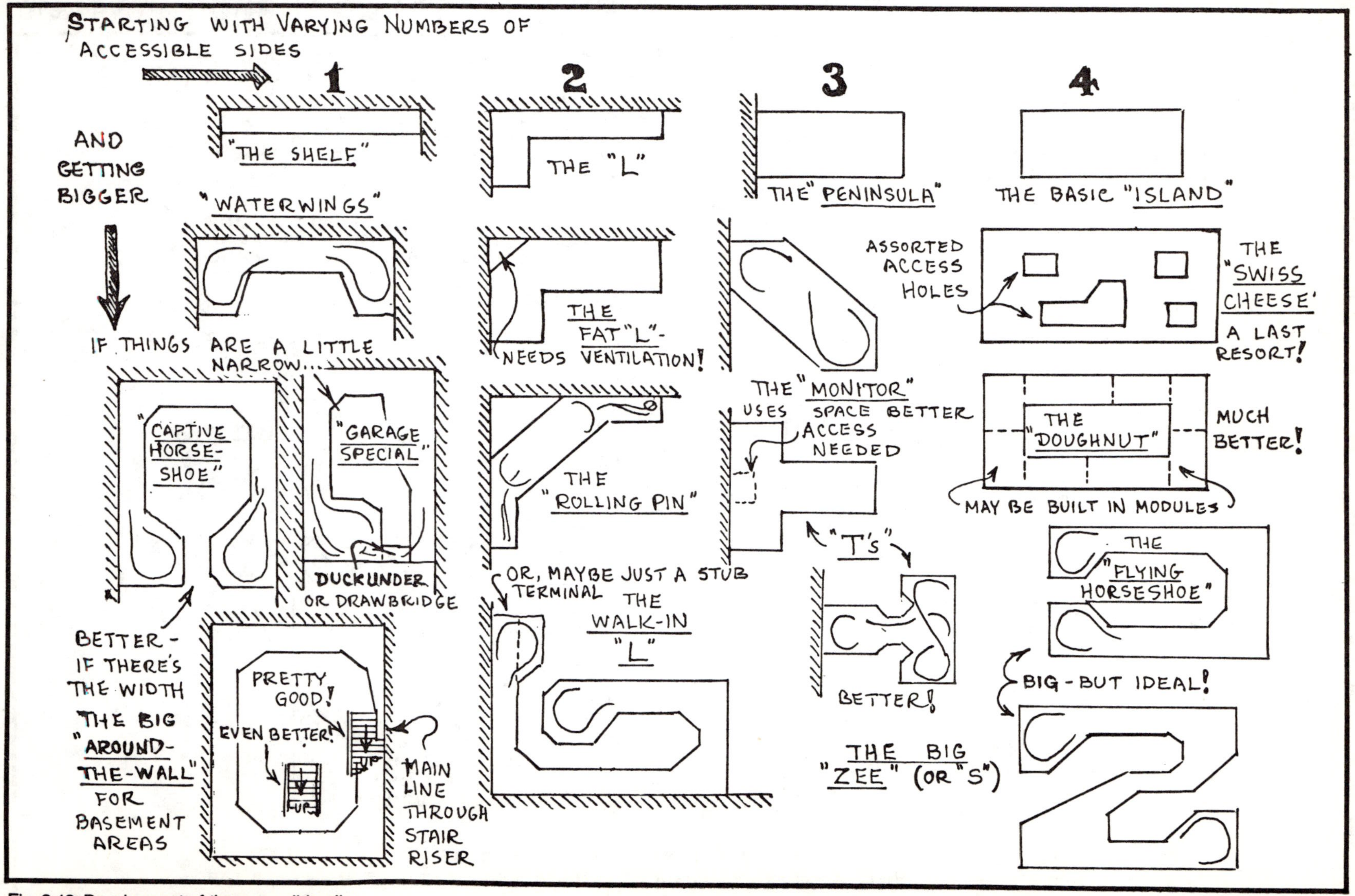

Fig. 2-18. Development of the accessible pike.

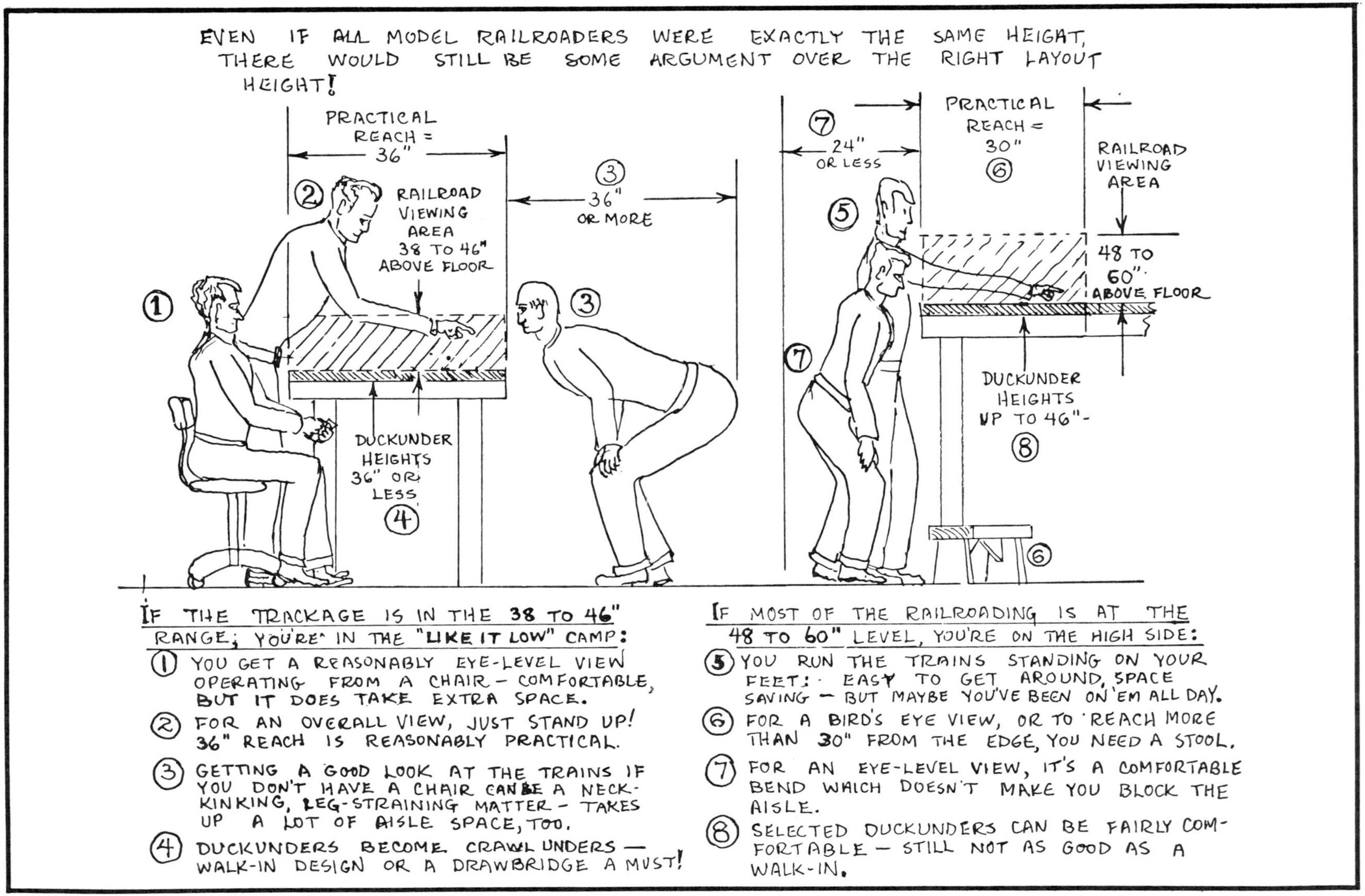

Fig. 2-19. Build it low or build it high?

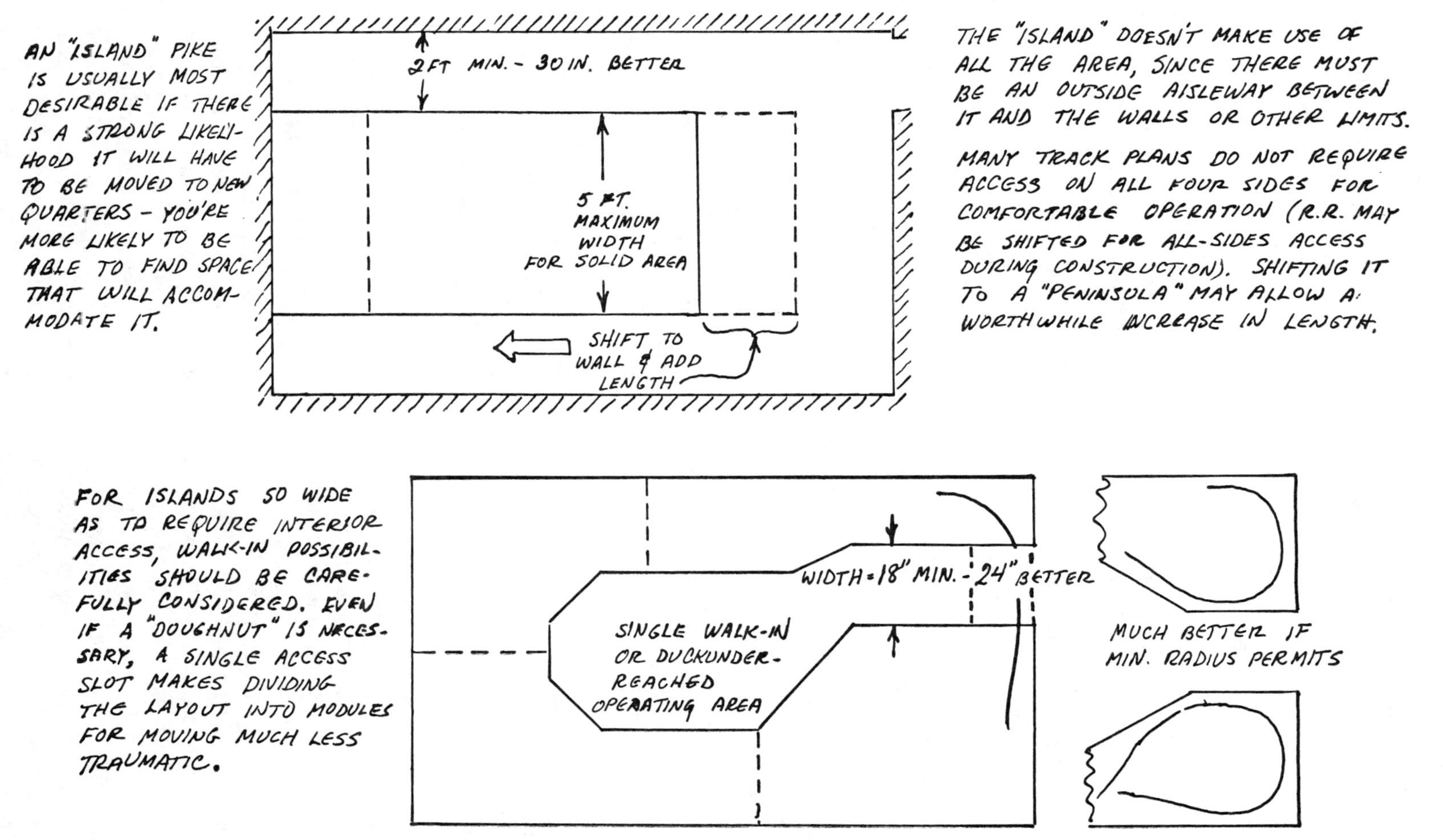

Fig. 2-20. Island track plans.

most important, and there have been many jokes over the years about the fellow who really gets his biggest thrills from watching the little lights chase each other around the control panel. He can just hook the bulbs (LED's in this modern era) to a microcomputer and do away with the bulk and nuisance of the trains!

For most of us, though, trains are to build, to run and to watch. For anything in the way of model railroading beyond putting finished models on the shelf or mantelpiece, that means track: a layout you can build to the point of satisfying operation in a reasonable length of time; trackwork, power and controls that let the trains run realistically and *stay on the track*; and, a final item without which the others don't do much for you, lighting and a place to stand so you can see the railroad work.

There's one common ingredient that's important to all the above—*access*! In the smallest layouts, it's only a problem when something gets stuck under a bridge or the high-power filament in the bridge lamp that lights the whole railroad burns out, but on average to large pikes it can be the difference between pain and joy in construction, operation, maintenance and enjoyment. If you can't get close enough to install, locate, adjust, re-rail, and see the detail on the trains, the layout isn't doing its job.

Finding places to build a railroad despite a forest of obstacles ranging from chimneys and hot-water heaters to scarcities of two-bedroom apartments or supportive family members is something the determined empire builder must do for himself, but even where the space is relatively abundant the *shape* of the track plan is worthy of a great deal of thought. Filling up the area with track, even if it lets the trains run through a variety of schedules as authentic as you could imagine within so confined a space, isn't the whole story. People-planning is just as important!

If you're the only person involved, it's still a lot nicer to be able to see the intricate stairways on the rear of the coal tipple without using a mirror. Being able to adjust the key switch to the return loop from a stand-up aisle is safer and easier than having to work from a ladder temporarily extending between a cabinet-top and a window-well. On multi-operator pikes, simultaneous, unimpeded flow of visitors, yard operators and road engineers may be harder to come by than a long, interesting main line.

We've come a long way from a simple choice between solid island or around-the-room shapes. Figure 2-18 traces some of the ways a pike might expand, starting with small shelf or table layouts with varying numbers of inaccessible sides. As a model railroad fills more and more of the space available, maintaining the enjoyment of its area requires more and more ingenuity. You get too much far-away, unreachable middle in proportion to the useful area up front as a simple rectangular island or narrow L expands.

Some remedies are good, some others, exemplified by the Swiss cheese with its collection of access holes reached only by painful crawling, simply don't accomplish the purpose of confirming that model railroading is fun. The smaller layouts are usually at least semi-portable, so it may be possible to move one face against a wall when it turns out that working space at the opposite side is worth more than infrequently required access in that area. The bigger the pike, the more built-in it's likely to become, so reasonable foresight backed up by fairly accurate surveys of the railroad's potential homeland can be as vital as checking doorway size is to our boat-building friends. Unfortunately, personal experience seems to be the only really effective teacher when it comes to getting a feel for duckunders. Some of us, particularly during our younger years, can zip back and forth through a 42-inch-high opening a dozen times a night without feeling it, while to others a 48-incher is enough of an obstacle to inspire drastic measures in seeking a 100 percent walk-in plan.

HOW HIGH IS HIGH ENOUGH?

Track elevations in most plans in this book are given in inches above a base height or datum, usually the lowest level point on the main line. You can thus set this sea level at any distance above the floor, or below the ceiling or overhead joists to locate the railroad at the right height for your situation. Ceilings are usually level and therefore often much more dependable than floors as a working reference for a fairly large pike. But how high *is*

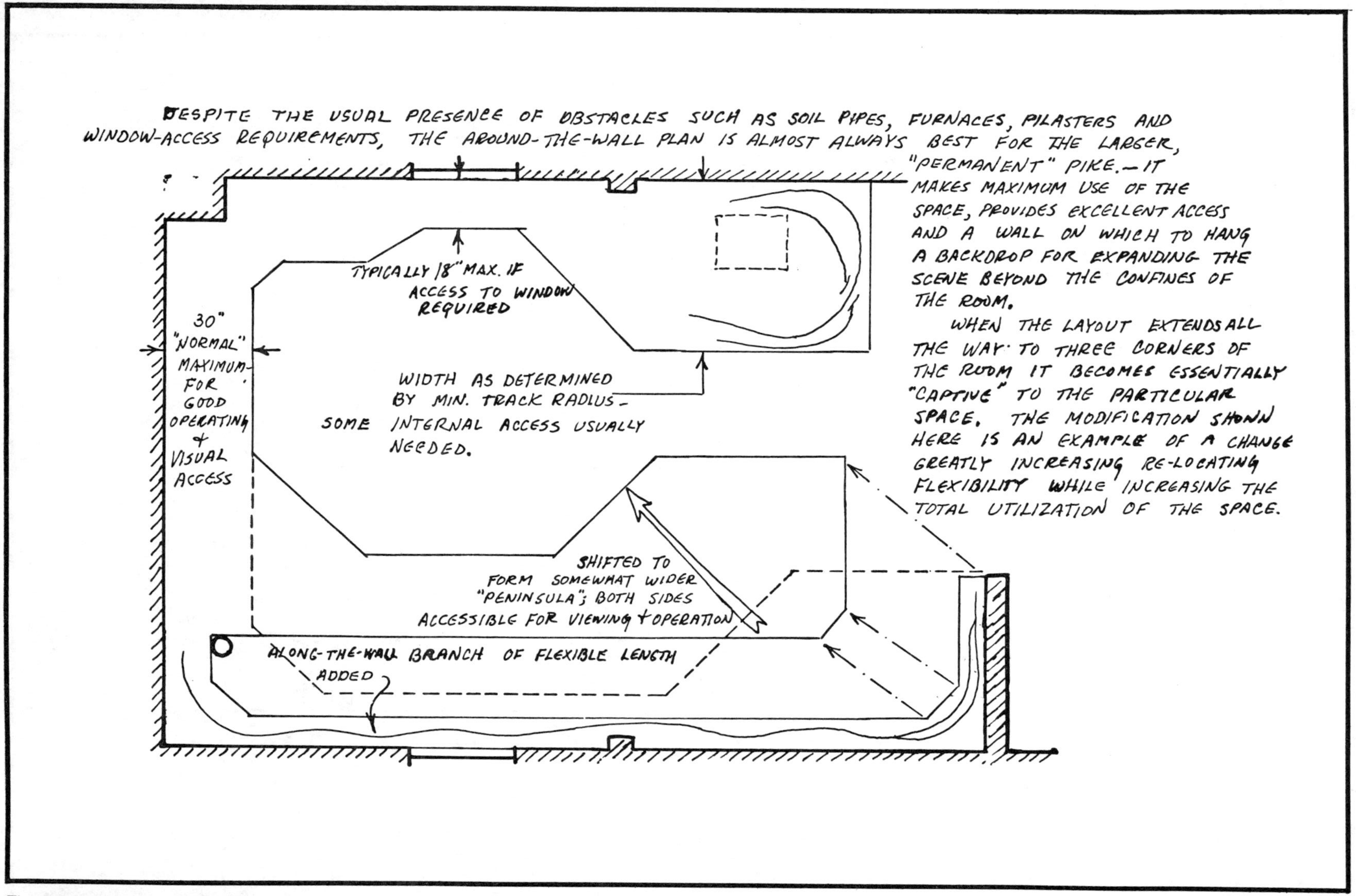

Fig. 2-21. Along-the-wall layouts.

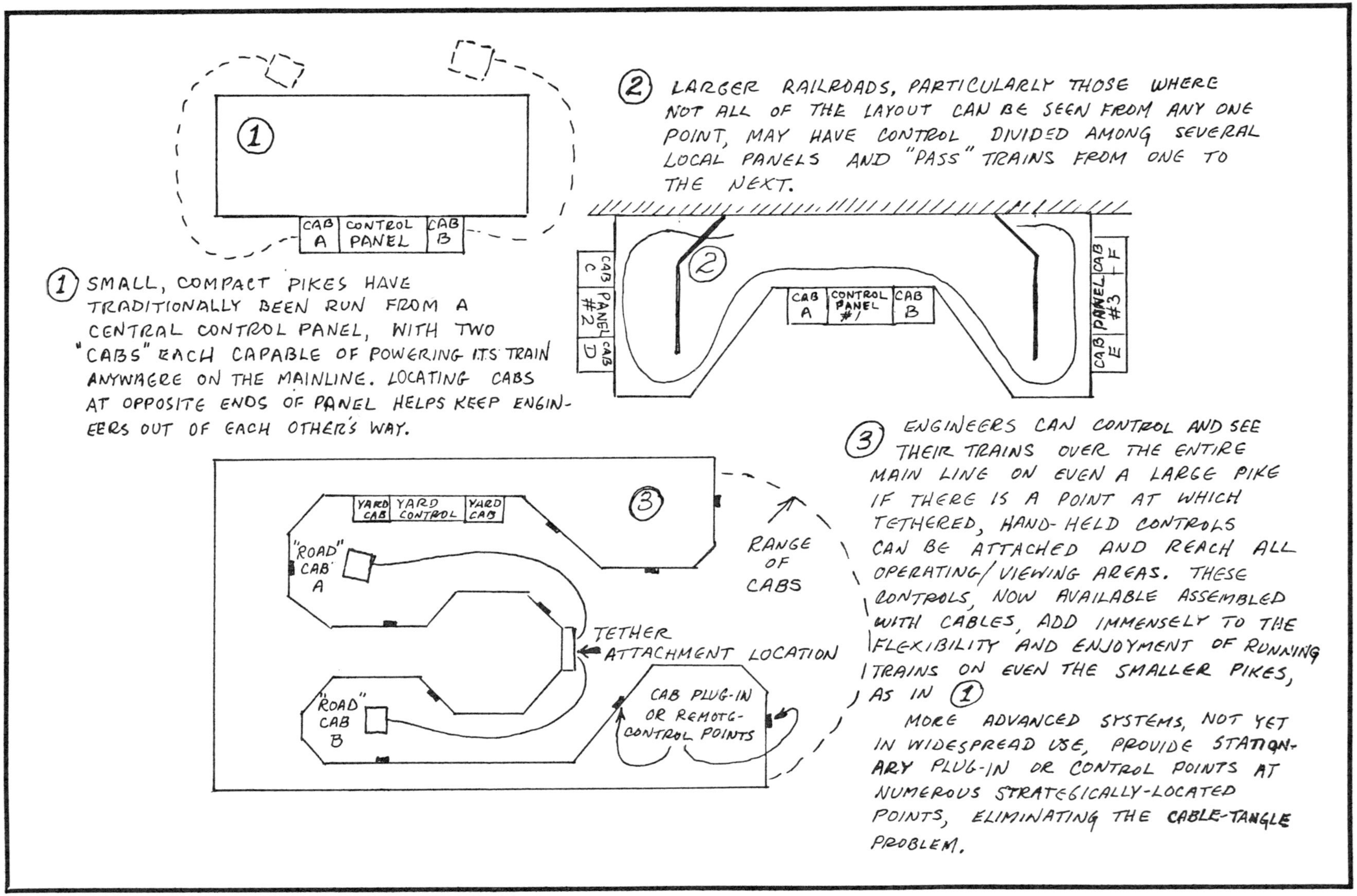

Fig. 2-22. Electrical control flexibility.

that? This is one of the more controversial issues in model railroading.

Figure 2-19 illustrates a source of the difference of opinion. It is generally agreed that looking at the trains close to eye level makes everything more realistic. Most of us prefer to stand at trackside and watch the *sides* of locomotive and cars roll by, rather than seeing mostly roof details on whatever it is that's roaring underneath a vantage point on an overpass or bluff. Where there are several tracks full of cars, as in a yard, of course, you'll scramble for that some topside view instead of settling for a detailed look at the one on Track 1.

There are two ways, though, for positioning your eyeball beside the trains. Those who favor building the railroad at about 42 inches above the floor point out that running the trains from a castered chair gives a nice view of the trains, and you can simply stand up to get the big picture or each way into the interior to build, rerail or whatever. The high-layout believers like to, or at least are satisfied to, run and watch the trains standing up, which does get rid of the clutter of chairs. To get a topside vista or reach more than 30 inches from the edge they need some low step-stools parked at various points on the premises.

Many of the larger track plans make a partial adjustment automatically. Yards are typically at the lowest level of the layout, where you'd like to be able to see over the first few tracks, while any mountains on the main line bring trains out on the road up closer to eye level. Smaller railroads, such as those which can be supported on four to eight legs, don't really force a permanent height decision. You can put them on high legs to start with, making under-the-table work a little more comfortable, and then saw them off later if you find you'd like to sit down for serious train running, or jack the whole thing up if you find yourself scrunching down too much of the time.

If your pike involves tunneling through a stairway, as in some around-the-way basement empires, it's a doubly good idea to visit some other model railroads, club and individual, before getting out the saw and chisel.

In any case, it is especially important that N-scale railroads provide for comfortable eye-level viewing. The tiny trains will gradually grow bigger in your mind if you give them a chance by looking at them from as close up as your eyesight will allow.

While it's handy to pin names on some of the more time-honored pike shapes, and Figs. 2-20 and 2-21 give some of the general virtues and vices of the two major classes, several of the plans in this book and many of the best model railroads already in being, defy being tagged with any simple description. If it fits your situation, that's good, so the comments on the standard shapes are intended more as a stimulus to your imagination in using unpromising spaces and as a reminder of the importance of being able to get to and look at your handiwork *comfortably*.

ELECTRICAL CONTROLS AND THE TRACK PLAN

You miss a great deal of the fun if you're tied to a single stationary control point when running the trains, so the traditional systems in Fig. 2-22 are rapidly being supplemented with walk-around cabs, usually controls or controls plus miniaturized power supplies attached via cable tether to the control panel. Being able to see the same layout from so many more angles while in control of your locomotive is almost like adding several additional pieces of railroad in the same area, so most of the track plans in this book have been planned with walk-around control possibilities in mind; the new cab units make walk-in railroads doubly desirable.

3

Track Plans for Small Layouts

Good things come in small packages, and the finest modeling is often associated with those compact pikes that leave time for the proprietor to go the whole way in detailing track, structures, scenery and rolling stock. For those whose ultimate goal is a larger railroad, the *starter* track plan that provides hands-on experience you can get in no other way is usually within the 4 × 8 ft. dimensions or equivalent 32 sq. ft. we've arbitrarily picked as the upper limit for this chapter's layouts.

CHARACTER PROFILES

Included with each plan is a diagram giving some feel for its character. For instance, whether it puts track ahead of scenery or vice versa, how well it's likely to fit into typical spaces available for model railroading, and how quick and easy its construction, using commercially-available items and materials where applicable, is likely to be. Figure 3-1 shows how to read the profile and expands a bit on some of the plus factors contributing to each bar. There's some element of "for its size" present in the ratings. A big railroad rated high on *ease of construction* will still take more time to build than an equally-rated 3 × 5-footer.

If you're looking for a plan that will have you running lots of trains in a hurry, a profile that's *concave on the right* (Figs. 3-4, 3-5) indicates a candidate. On the other hand, if you're more interested in taking impressive pictures in a year or two of trains rolling gracefully through spectacular scenery, you'll do better to look closely at one with a *convex* contour, (Fig. 3-14 or 3-22).

LET'S GET STARTED

Figure 3-2 shows a two-train single-track operation with some industry switching. This layout is primarily a way to get early experience in model railroading and serves as a guide in developing plans for a larger or more sophisticated layout which can emphasize those aspects you find most interesting.

There's ample room for scenery and structures. Trackwork and tabletop materials are all reusable in a second layout with little waste even though the track plan itself is not particularly adaptable to modification or direct add-on.

Size: 4 × 6 ft.
Gauge: HO
Curvature standards: sharp
Schematic: oval with passing tracks and spurs
Recommended construction: flat top
Trackwork options: Uses only available trackwork elements, including sectional curves

THE IMPROVED OVAL

Figure 3-3 shows an improved oval layout with long trains moving over a double-track oval. This is main-line railroading with no surprises and an emphasis on reasonable appearance. There's a

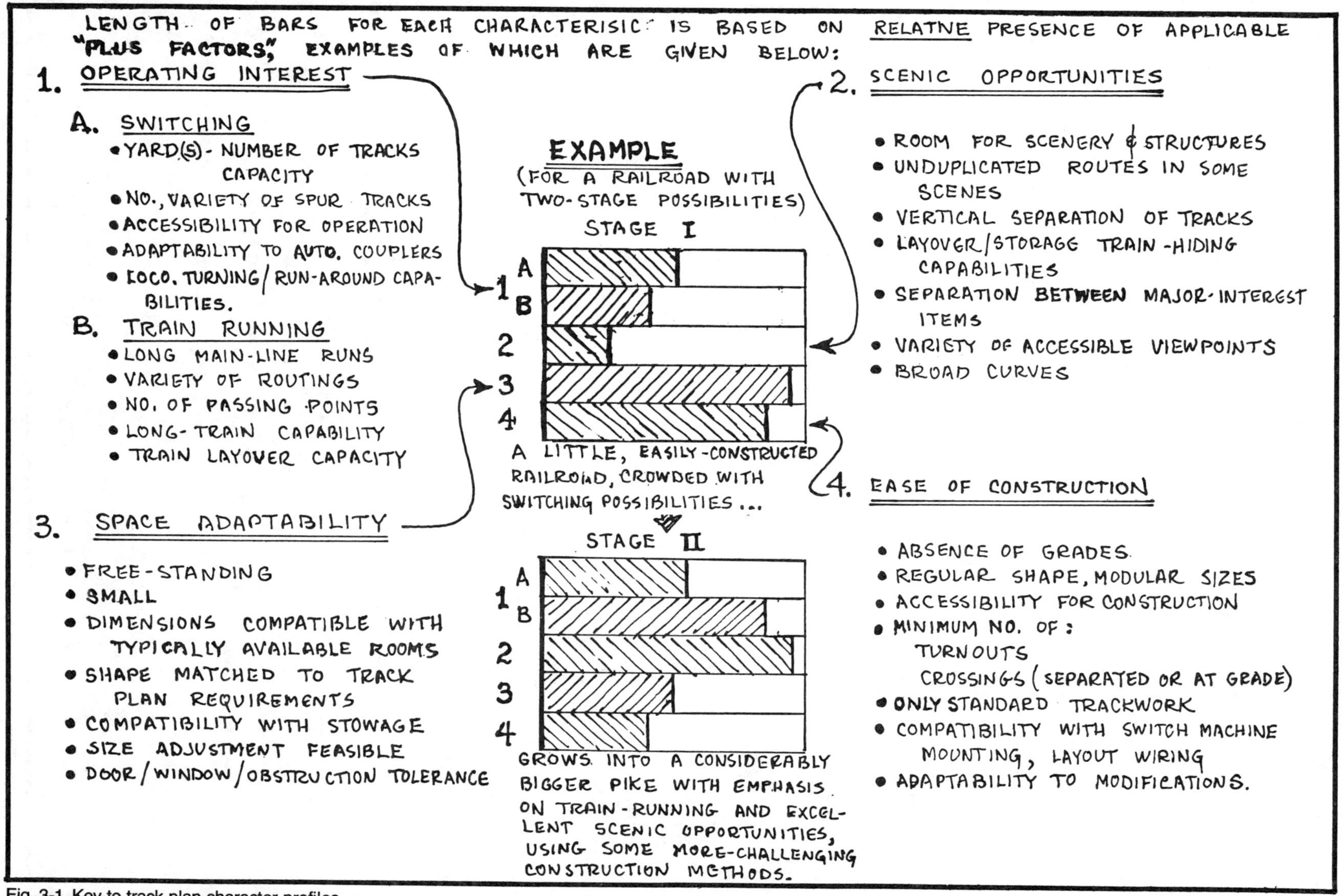

Fig. 3-1. Key to track plan character profiles.

large and efficient yard and passenger station, with some main-line crossover maneuvers to let trains enter and leave without snarling up the traffic.

In the future the number of yard tracks could be easily increased or decreased. Plus there's room for a large engine terminal and several additional industry spurs. Full realization of the scenic possibilites depends on providing for some below-track areas, but ample space is available.

Size: 3½ × 7 ft. island or peninsula

Gauge: N

Curvature standards: conventional

Schematic: multiple-track oval

Recommended construction: flat top

Trackwork options: all trackwork items standard; sectional track useable for all curves except some sweeping bends introduced for appearance reasons—curvable recommended; easements provided for

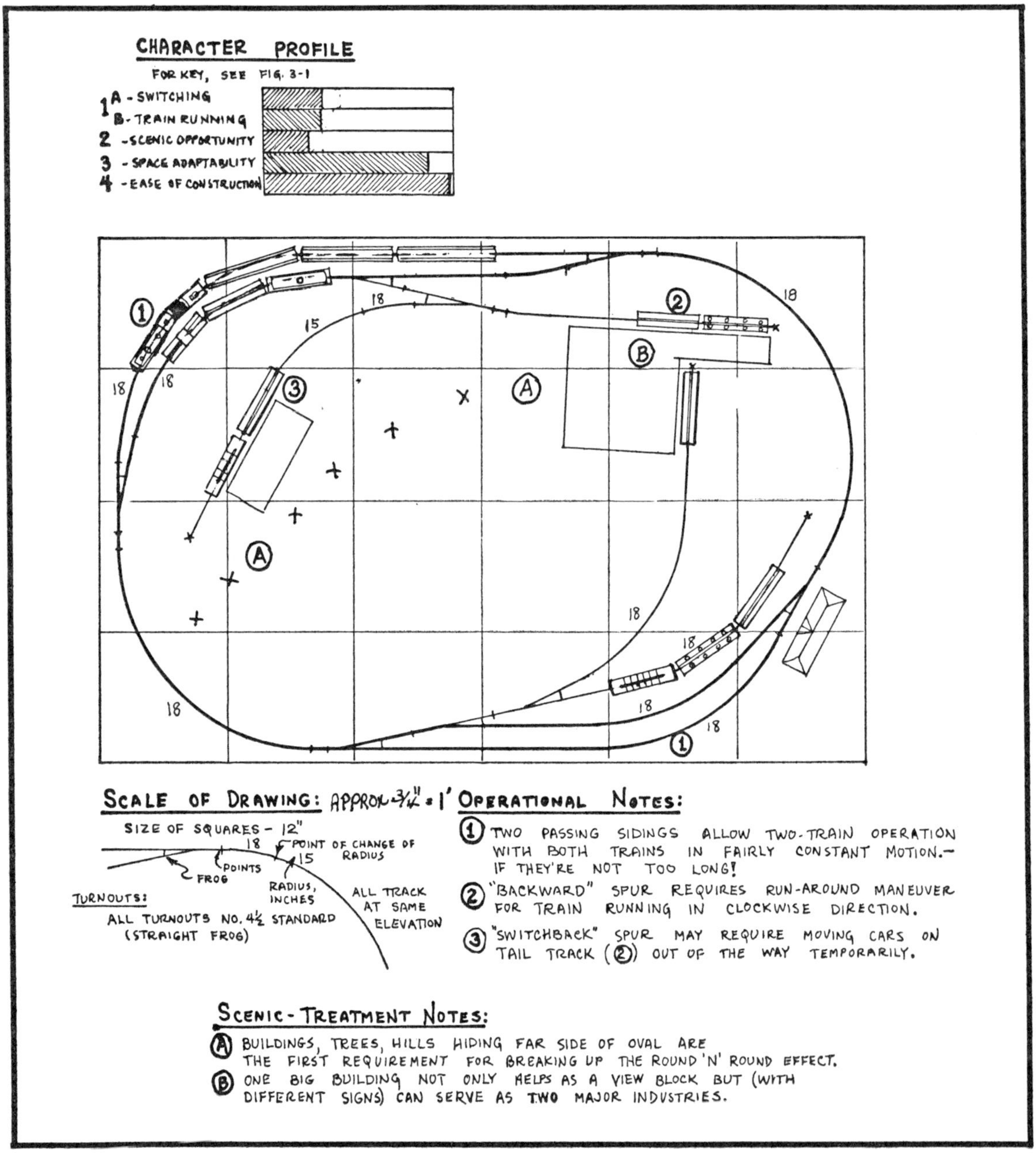

Fig. 3-2. Let's Get Started track plan for HO gauge.

THE LITTLE BIG TIME

This layout (Fig. 3-4) goes all out to keep two fairly long trains moving in minimum space, with the flavor of multiple-track big time railroading. Trains can be terminated, turned, rebuilt in the little *yard*, with moderate effect on continuing main-line traffic if you plan ahead.

This is primarily a starter railroad, but the trackage will be useable on a later, larger pike. There's reasonable freedom for adding and rearranging industry trackage here.

Size: 4 × 8 ft. island or peninsula
Gauge: HO
Curvature standards: sharp
Schematic: multiple-track oval
Recommended construction: flat top
Track work options: all trackwork items standard; sectional track useable for curves, but curvable recommended for exactly parallel two and three-track sections

THE PRAIRIE DIVISION POINT

This layout (Fig. 3-5) represents a typical *division point* on a single-track railroad across the prairies, where through trains pause for crew change and to set off and receive cars from local freight trains working out of the terminal in both directions. This plan emphasizes yard capacity, classification of cars without fouling main track, and twice-around main line with three points at which trains may meet or pass each other. Passing tracks accommodate 12 to 14-car freight trains.

This plan can very readily be built as a *cookie-cutter* with an overpass substituted for the crossing, greatly enhancing the scenic-treatment opportunities and allowing the addition of more industry spurs before the whole affair gets too crowded in appearance.

Size: 3 ft × 6 ft. 8 in.
Gauge: N
Curvature standards: sharp
Schematic: twice-around
Recommended construction: flat top—may be built on a standard 36-in. wide flush door, providing rigidity and light weight at minimum cost
Trackwork options: uses available trackwork elements; curvable track recommended, with most curves larger than minimum for better appearance; optional industrial spur-track locations

SHELF-STYLE SWITCHING LAYOUTS

Where space is extremely limited and portability a must, the shelf-style switching railroad can provide hours of enjoyable operation after a brief period of construction. Not to be overlooked are the scenic opportunities. Since such industrial areas in real life are crowded, with extremely sharp curves not too much different from those in the model and agile little locomotives handling a few cars at a time, the entire scene can achieve a degree of realism difficult to equal in main-line modeling. The number and variety of structures in two or three city blocks are sufficient to provide modeling fodder for years of painstaking building, while their vertical dimensions give you all the excuse you need to carry the background well above eye level within the horizontal space of a few scale feet.

Industrial spurs can and do run off in all directions. For crowding the maximum operating fun into a typical along-the-wall space, the following general principles are worth incorporating into such a track plan. In other respects, all sorts of changes can be made to suit particular industries, track components you may happen to have on hand, or personal whims. It's hard to come up with something too wild to be unreasonable!

Switchbacks

The main track can be arranged so that moving from one corner of the shelf to its opposite takes two or three switchback movements covering most of the length of the layout. It'll never act like a transcontinental run, but the effect of accomplishing considerable transportation within a few square feet can be impressive.

Short Tail Tracks

The whole thing is further converted into a switching puzzle by the requirement that cars be worked past each switchback in small groups, perhaps one at a time in the extreme. If the tail track is also a freight delivery point at times, the extra moves in setting a partially-unloaded car out

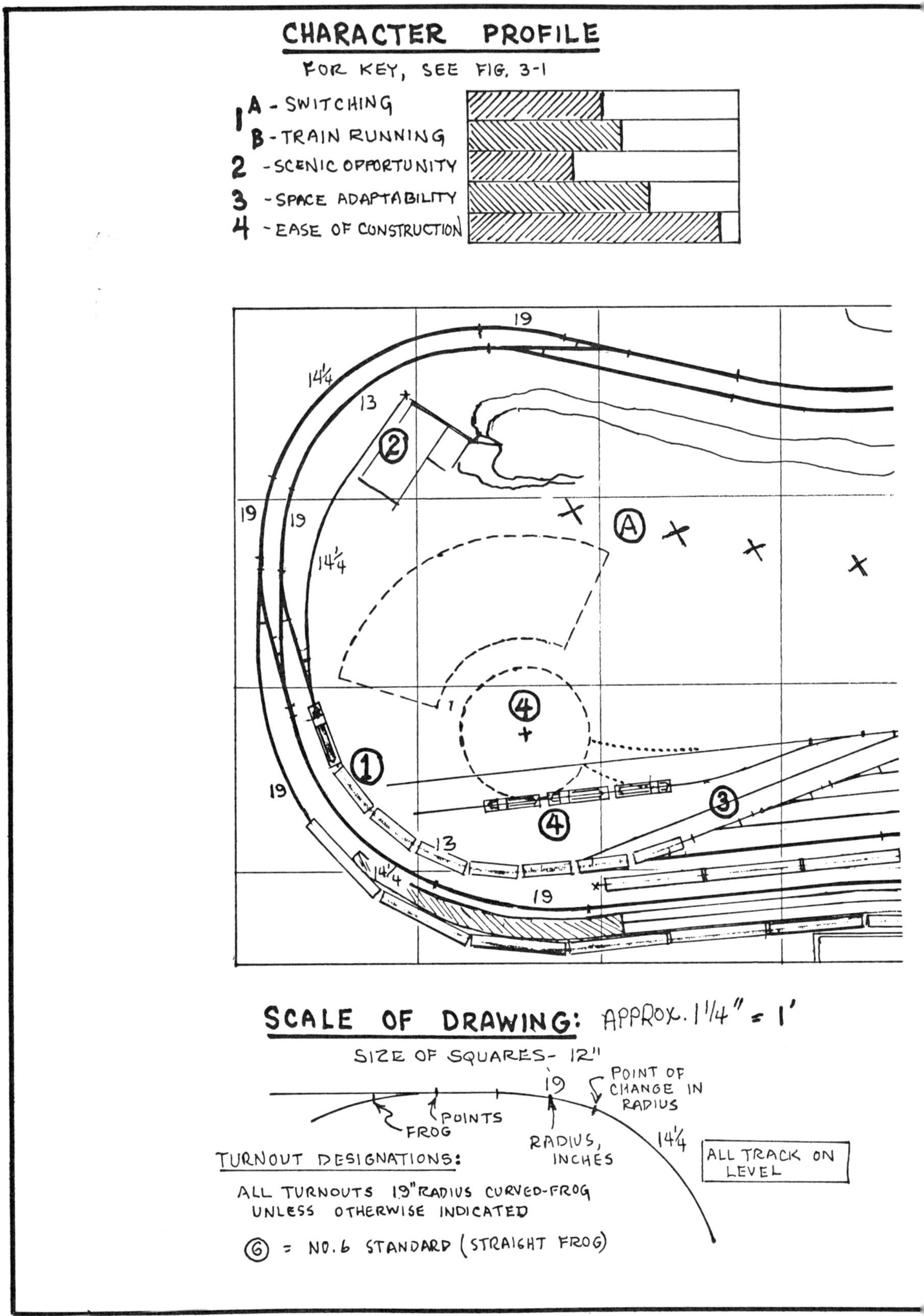

Fig. 3-3. The Improved Oval track plan for N gauge.

OPERATIONAL NOTES:

1. THIRD MAIN TRACK SERVES AS YARD SWITCHING LEAD & AS RECEIVING OR DEPARTURE TRACK FOR FREIGHTS IN EITHER DIRECTION.
2. SPUR TO INDUSTRY ALSO SERVES AS EXTENDED SWITCHING LEAD WHEN NECESSARY
3. CABOOSE AND RUN-AROUND TRACK PARALLELS YARD LADDER TRACK. NUMBER OF YARD TRACKS MAY BE VARIED FROM THREE TO SIX OR MORE.
4. DIESEL SERVICE TRACKS. ROOM AVAILABLE FOR GOOD-SIZED (100 FT. TURNTABLE, 120 FT. STALLS) STEAM ENGINE HOUSE OR DIESEL SHOP.

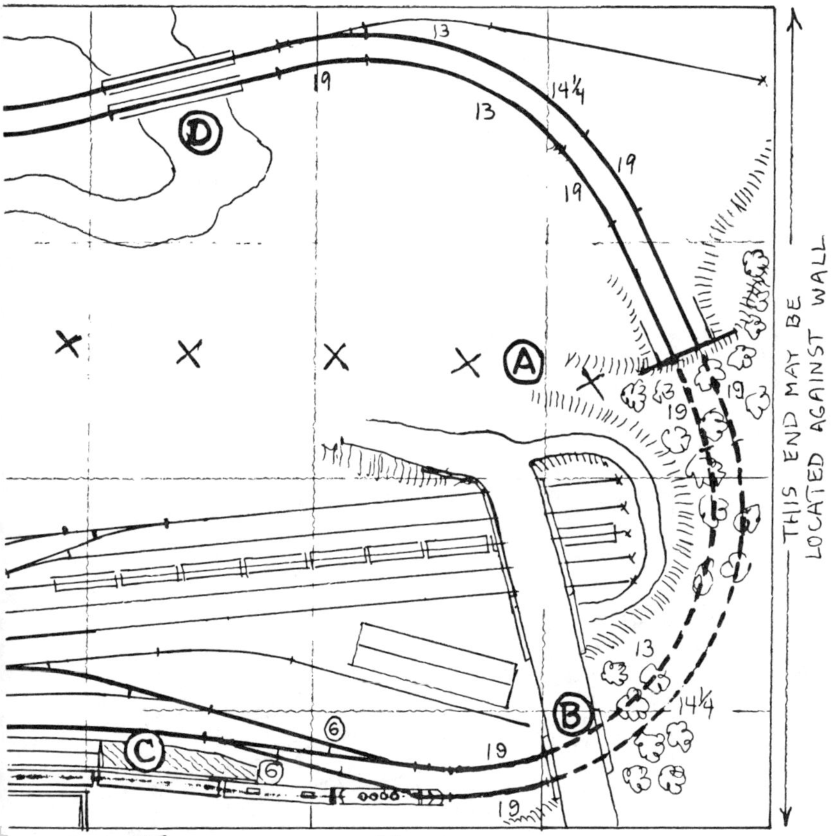

CENIC-TREATMENT NOTES:

(A) VIEW-BLOCK ESSENTIAL TO BREAK UP 'ROUND 'N' 'ROUND EFFECT, INCREASE APPARENT SIZE OF LAYOUT.

(B) OVERPASS USED TO HELP MAIN TRACKS DISAPPEAR QUIETLY — ESPECIALLY IF IN FLAT-COUNTRY SETTING WHERE NUMBER OF TUNNELS IS TO BE MINIMIZED.

(C) PASSENGER STATION ON SWEEPING "EYEBALL" CURVE PROVIDES NICE VIEW OF TRAINS, PLATFORM LONG ENOUGH FOR 8 TO 10-CAR TRAINS.

(D) EXTRA EFFORT OF LOWERING WATER SURFACE (BY CUTTING PLYWOOD AND DROPPING IT BELOW REST OF PLATFORM) CAN GREATLY ENHANCE SETTING OF THIS REALISTICALLY-CURVED SECTION OF MAIN LINE.

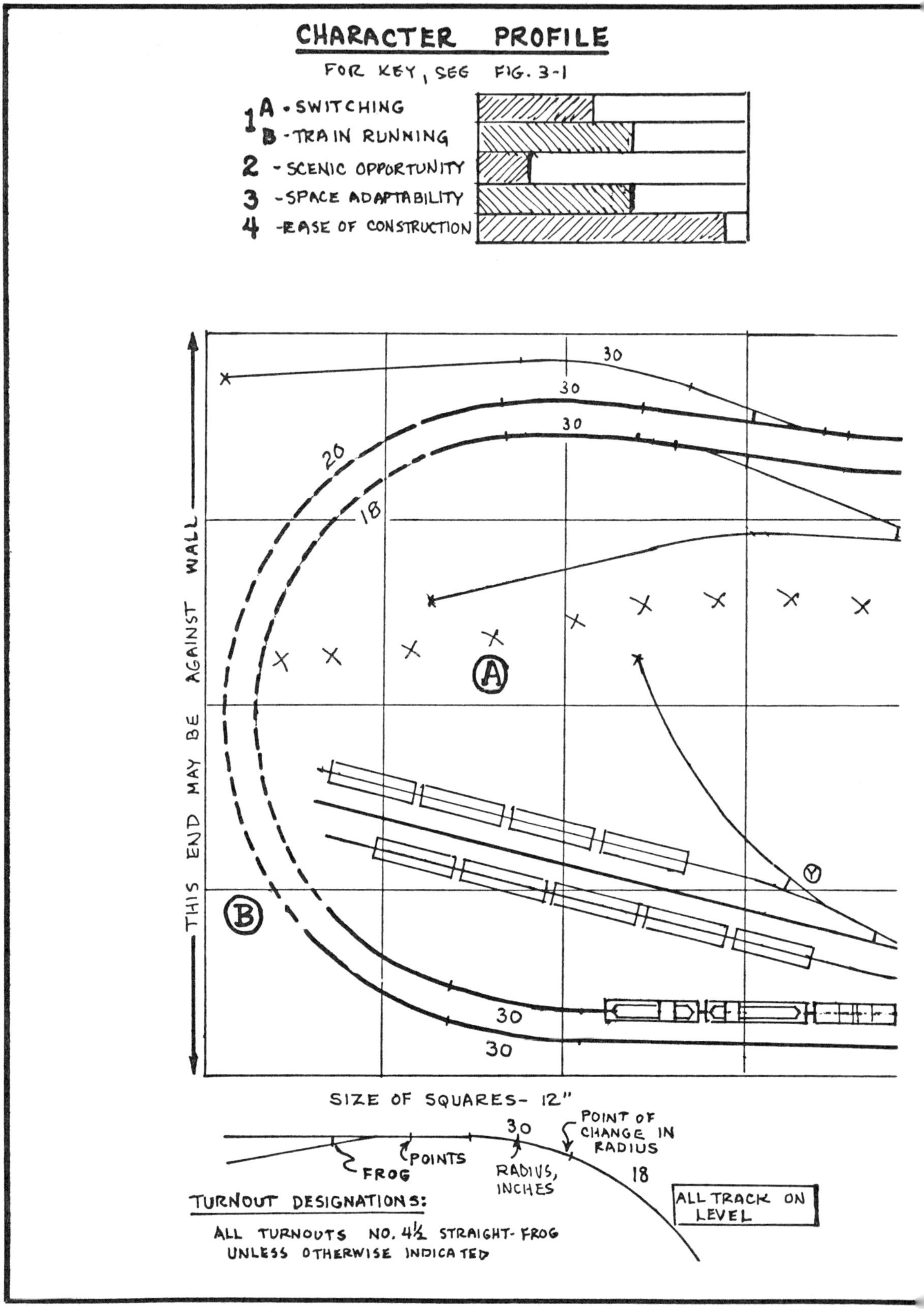

Fig. 3-4. The Little Big Time track plan for HO gauge.

OPERATIONAL NOTES:

(1) DOUBLE TRACK MAIN LINE, NORMAL DIRECTION OF TRAFFIC RIGHT HAND. SHARP CURVES, BUT EASEMENTS AT START OF PRINCIPAL CURVES TO IMPROVE APPEARANCE OF 65 FT. CARS.

(2) TRIPLE TRACK SECTION FOR PASSING MANEUVERS – INNER TRACK ALSO SERVES AS SWITCHING LEAD FOR "YARD."

(3) YARD WORKED BY SWITCH ENGINE TO MINIMIZE INTERFERENCE WITH RIGHT-HAND MAIN LINE TRAFFIC – IF RAILROAD BUILT AS MIRROR IMAGE OF THAT SHOWN, ROAD ENGINE CAN SWITCH YARD DIRECTLY.

(4) SMALL (65 FT.) TURNTABLE FOR LOCAL FGT. OR OTHER SHORT LOCOS

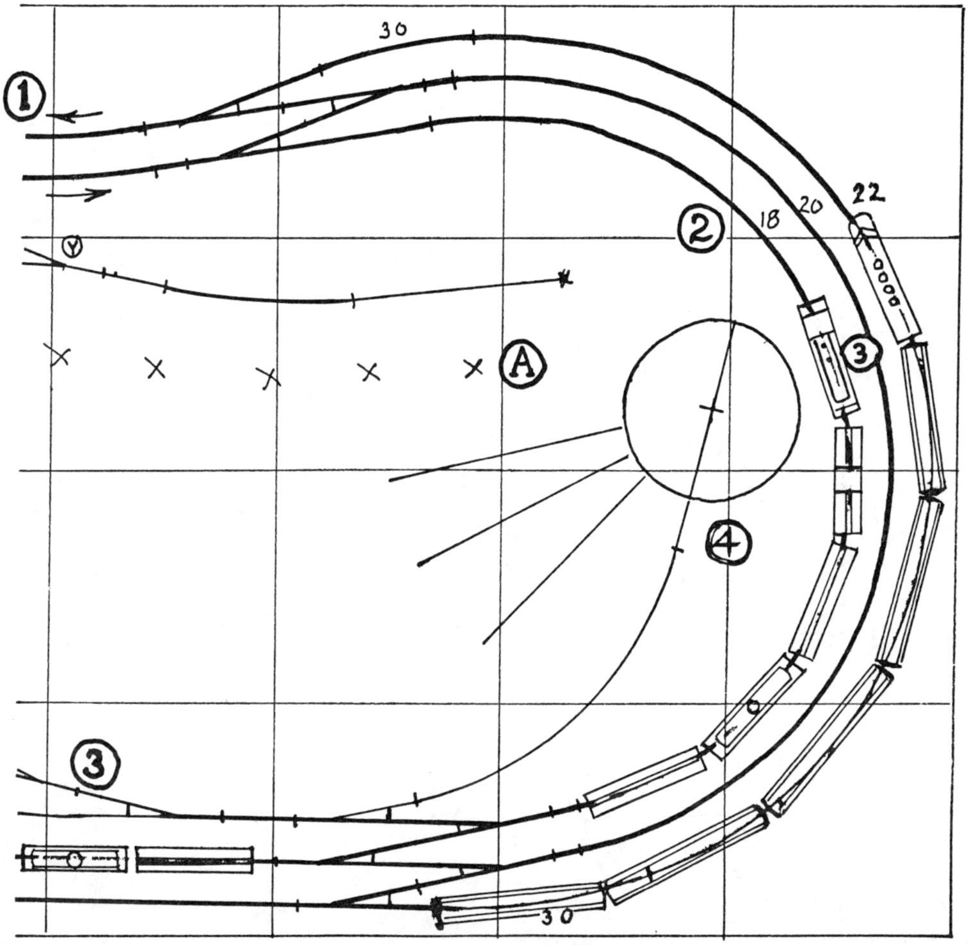

SCENIC TREATMENT NOTES:

(A) VIEW-BLOCK DESPERATELY NEEDED TO BREAK UP ROUND AND ROUND EFFECT – HILL OR BUILDINGS TO SUIT RURAL OR URBAN TREATMENT.

(B) TRACK HIDING (WITHOUT SOMETHING OBVIOUS LIKE A TUNNEL, IF POSSIBLE) WILL HELP INCREASE APPARENT SIZE OF LAYOUT, LENGTH OF TOO-SHORT MAIN LINE

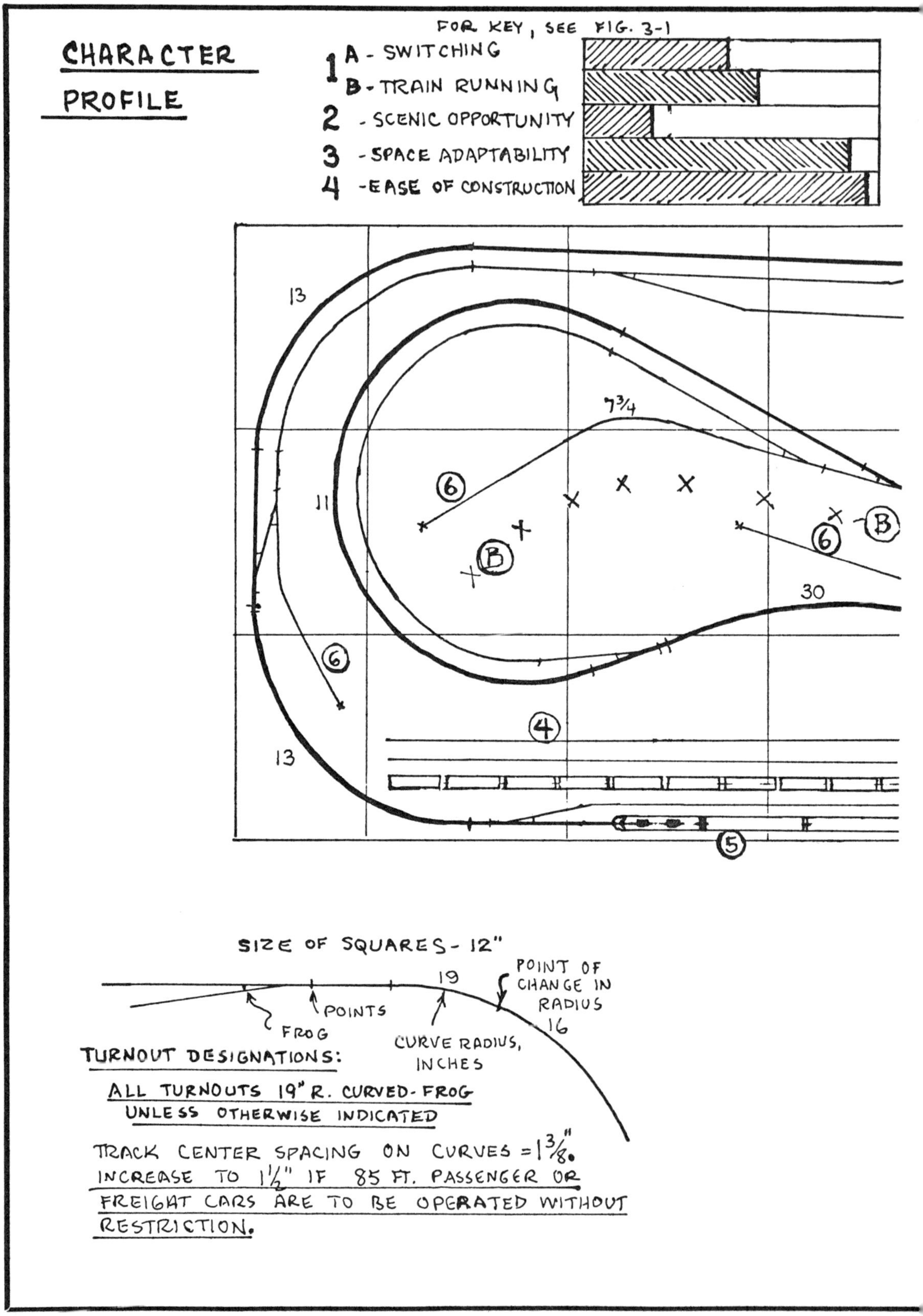

Fig. 3-5. The Prairie Division Point track plan for N gauge.

SCHEMATIC

ALL TRACK AT SINGLE LEVEL

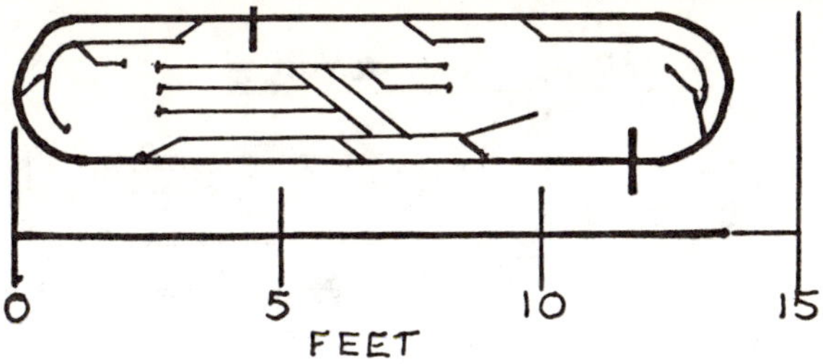

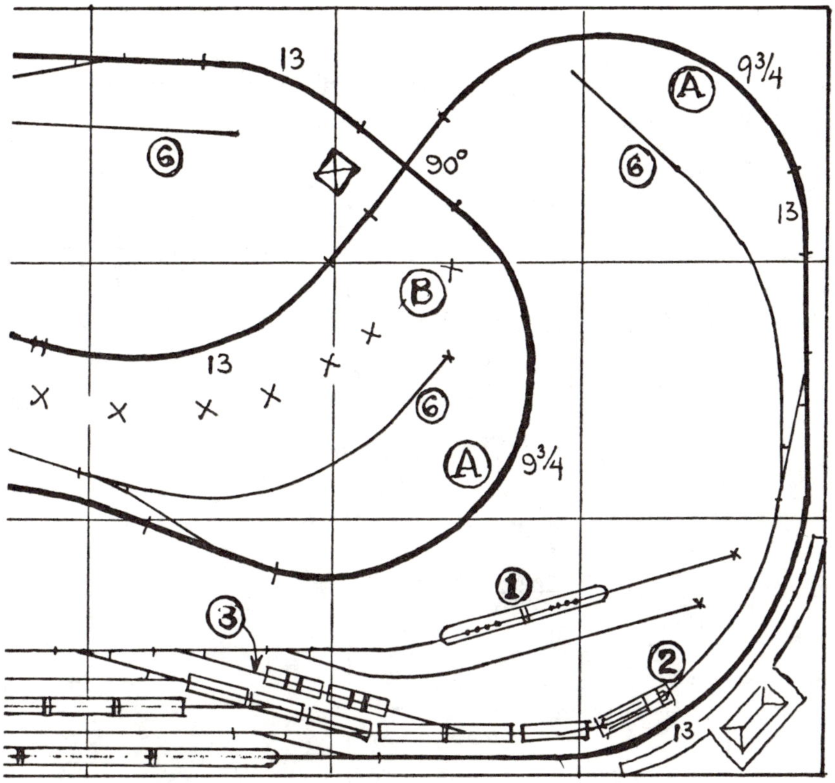

OPERATIONAL NOTES:

① LOCO SERVICING - FUELING TRACKS

② MODERATE- RADIUS TRACK SERVES AS SWITCHING LEAD FOR YARD AND MAKE-UP TRACK FOR LONG TRAINS, AVOIDING TYING UP THE MAIN LINE.

③ CABOOSE TRACK

④ CLASSIFICATION TRACKS FOR SORTING CARS BY DESTINATION — CAPACITY APPROX. 32 40-FT. CARS

⑤ SHORT TRAINS MAY MEET OR PASS OPPOSING TRAFFIC AT THIS POINT, AS WELL AS AT FULL-LENGTH PASSING TRACKS ON "MAIN LINE."

⑥ SPUR TRACKS FACE IN BOTH DIRECTIONS, REQUIRING LOCAL FREIGHT CREWS TO MAKE NUMEROUS "RUN AROUND" MOVEMENTS.

SCENIC TREATMENT NOTES:

Ⓐ SHARPEST CURVES SHOULD BE HIDDEN - IN CUTS, BEHIND TREES AND STRUCTURES—TO MINIMIZE EFFECT ON APPEARANCE OF TRAINS.

Ⓑ "VIEW BLOCK" HIGH ENOUGH TO CONCEAL TRAINS ON FAR SIDE WILL REDUCE OBVIOUS "ROUND 'N' ROUND" EFFECT. CANDIDATES: RIVER BLUFFS, STEEP-WALLED QUARRIES OR GRAVEL PITS, LARGE INDUSTRIAL STRUCTURES.

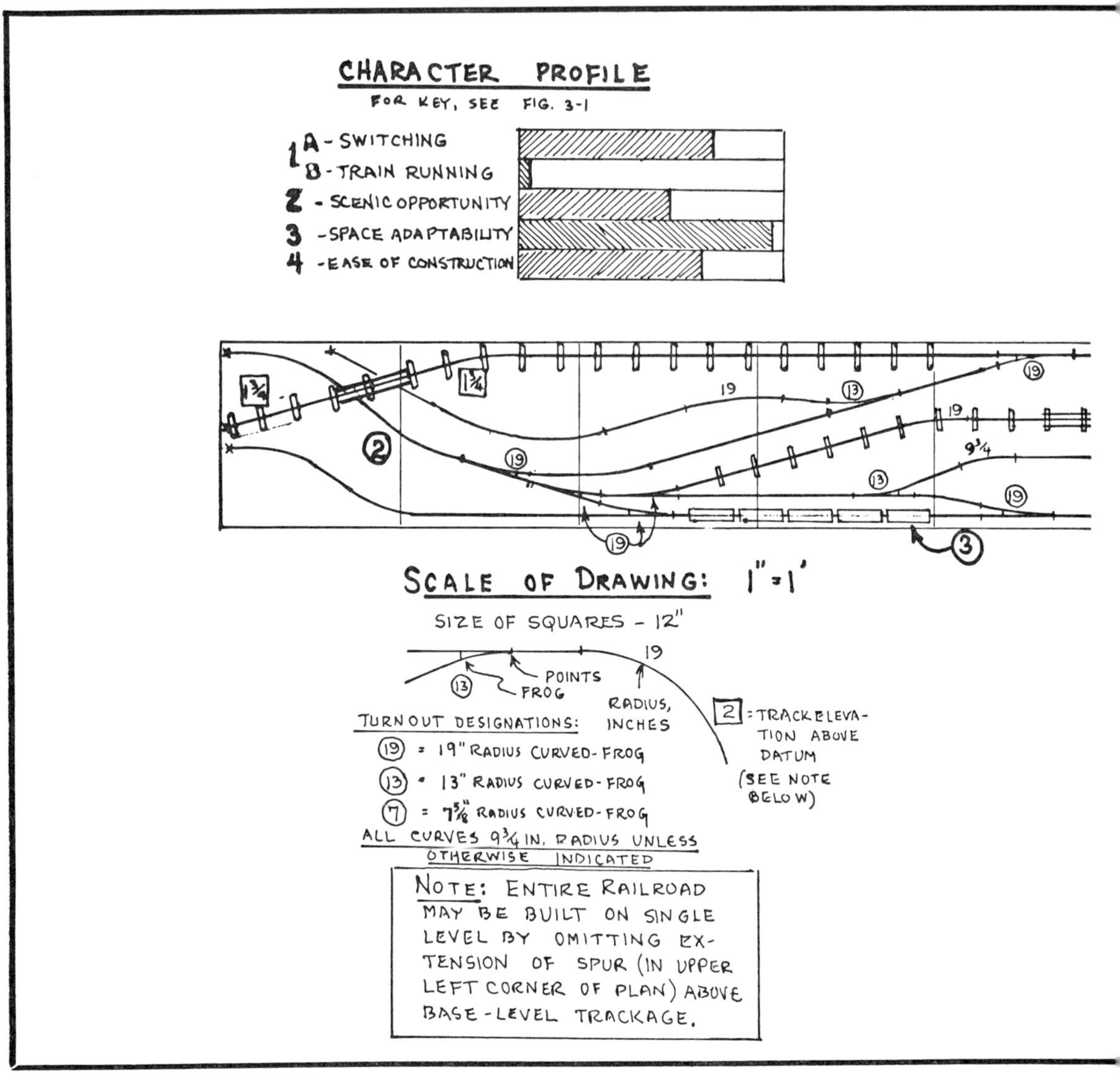

Fig. 3-6. Constricted Connecting Railroad track plan for N gauge.

of the way and re-spotting it later adds to the fun. Plan ahead, or tie yourself in knots!

Run-Around Tracks

Each layout needs at least one point at which the switcher can run around cars which must be worked in and out of spurs facing in the "wrong" direction. For a realistically challenging situation, though, there should usually be only one or two such run-around tracks—and they're typically not long enough to do the whole job in one maneuver!

Turning Facilities

Switchers run forward and backward with equal ease, of course, but some loads of freight can be unloaded only from one side or one end of the car and Murphy's law says that they will arrive in the destination yard wrong end to and need to be turned around before spotting. A wye or turntable thus adds a note of completeness to the spectrum of authentic operations.

Stiff Grades

To keep cars from rolling away, tracks where cars are set out should be level or at not more than 0.5 percent slope. In between, grades up to 6 percent are used to reach upper-level unloading facilities, descend to dock levels, or whatever—with the short cuts that are handled, the tough little switchers can overcome otherwise unthinkable slopes.

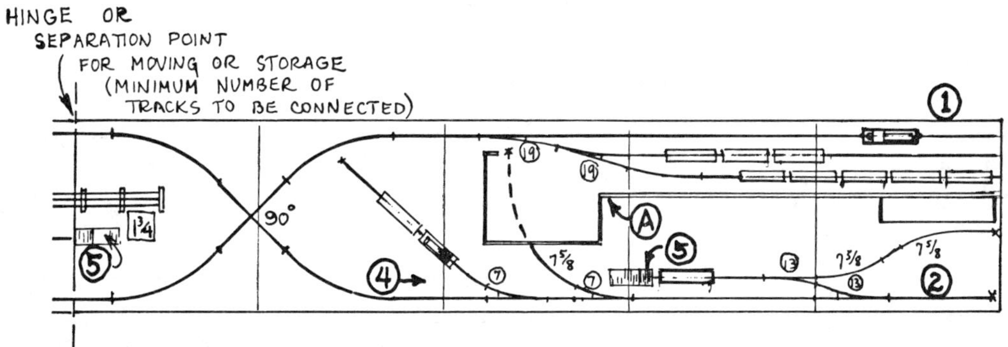

OPERATIONAL NOTES:

(1) "FIDDLE YARD" - INTERCHANGE WITH CLASS I RAILROADS. RERAILERS ON EACH TRACK RECOMMENDED.

(2) TAIL TRACKS - VARYING (BUT ALWAYS TOO SMALL) CAPACITY.

(3) RUN-AROUND TRACK SERVING ENTIRE AREA - SMART CREWS LEAVE HERE WITH ALL CARS ON PROPER END OF LOCOMOTIVE.

(4) TRACKAGE BEYOND THIS POINT INCLUDES "EXTRA SHARP" SPURS - SOME ENGINES MAY BE RESTRICTED, THUS JUSTIFYING USE OF SECOND SWITCHING CREW TO WORK THIS AREA WITH SMALLER LOCOMOTIVE.

(5) END-LOADING RAMPS - PLAN AHEAD, CORRECT END OF CAR MUST BE AT RAMP WHEN SPOTTED!

SCENIC-TREATMENT NOTES

(A) "FIDDLE YARD" HIDDEN BY BUILDINGS, TRACKS ACCESSIBLE FROM END OR ABOVE FOR INSERTING/REMOVING CARS.

Fiddle Yards

The supply of freight cars almost always greatly exceeds the trackage available, and that's good! Just as in real life, the cars on the property at any one time are a sampl ng drawn from the pool of 2 million on the railroad system of North America. Come back next week and the cast of characters wil have changed completely. British model railroaders, typically even more space-cramped with their basementless homes, long ago invented the *fiddle yard* as the bridge between the layout in the flesh and the railways of the tight little isle. This is a hidden yard where the cars (more properly called *wagons* over there) are surreptitiously "fiddled" front track to shelf and vice versa, by giant-hand action.

An essential part of the shelf-style switching layout, therefore, is an *interchange point*, preferably hidden, connecting with the outside world. On the larger versions, there can be more than one, with the little switching road serving as a connecting link between various Class I lines. Providing rerailing devices on the fiddle-yard tracks is a good idea, particularly in the smaller gauges. It cuts down on wear and tear on the rolling stock as well as on aggravation on the "0-5-0 switcher" doing the aerial interchange.

CONSTRICTED CONNECTING RAILROAD

This layout (Fig. 3-6) is another "switchman's nightmare," with a fair-sized fiddle yard for more variety in rolling stock on line at any moment.

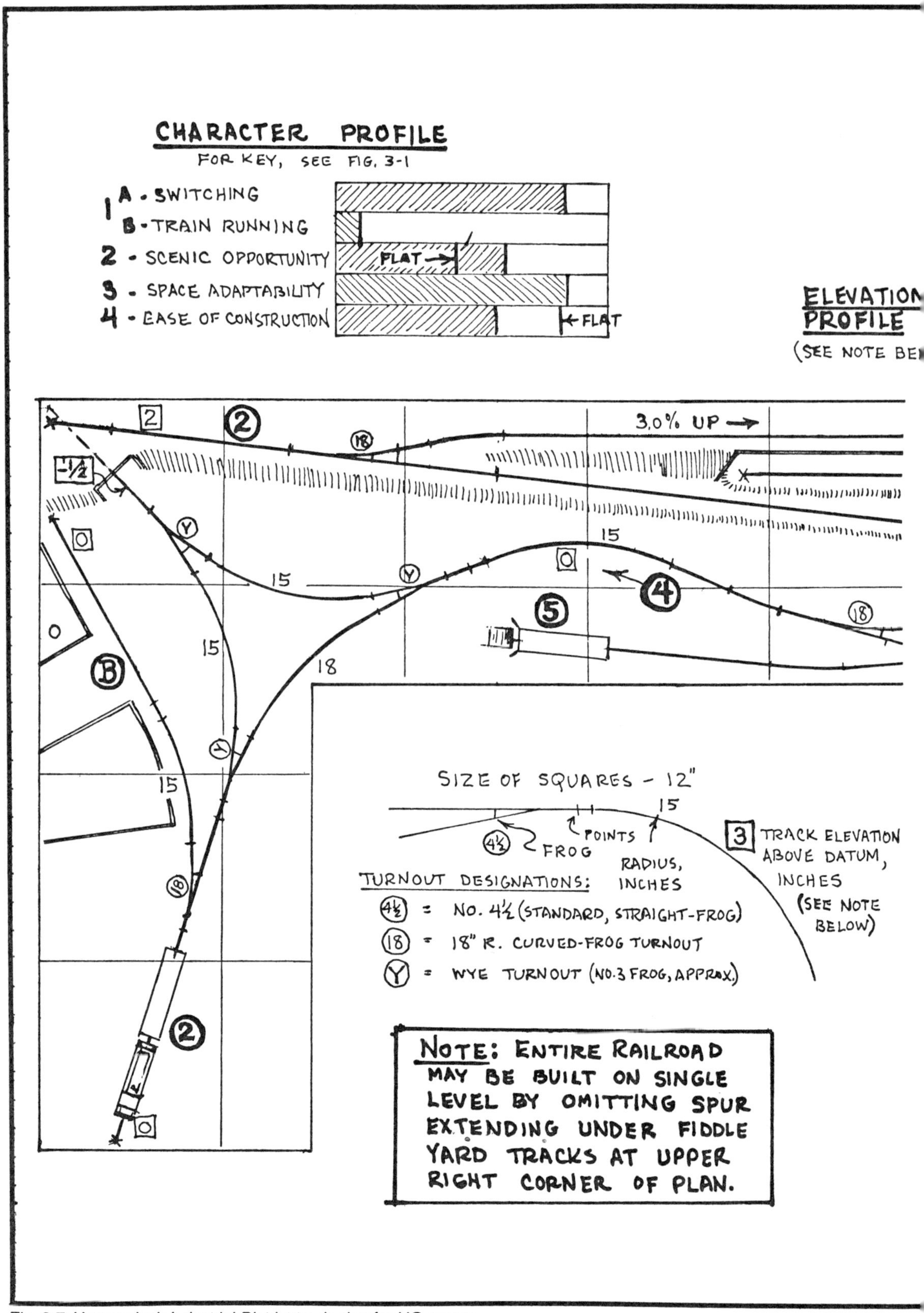

Fig. 3-7. Hammerlock Industrial District track plan for HO gauge.

SCHEMATIC

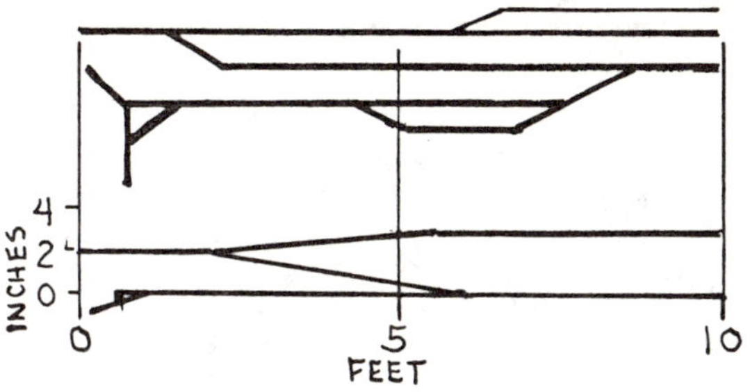

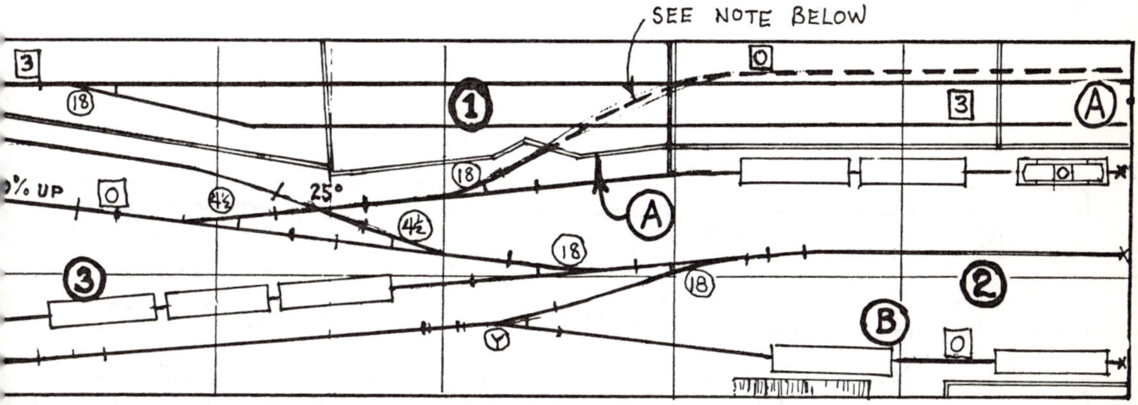

OPERATIONAL NOTES:

1. "FIDDLE YARD" - INTERCHANGE WITH THE OUTSIDE WORLD. RERAILERS ON EACH TRACK RECOMMENDED.
2. TAIL TRACKS - ONE-OR TWO-CAR PLUS ENGINE CAPACITY.
3. RUN-AROUND TRACK - ESSENTIAL FOR SERVING THREE SPURS CONNECTED IN "BACKWARD" DIRECTION.
4. TRACKAGE BEYOND THIS POINT TO "EXTRA SHARP" STANDARDS - SOME LOCOMOTIVES MAY BE RESTRICTED, THUS REQUIRING PASSING CARS TO SECOND CREW FOR DELIVERY OR TURNING ON WYE.
5. END-LOADING RAMP - MAY REQUIRE TURNING CARS FOR UNLOADING.

SCENIC-TREATMENT NOTES

(A) "FIDDLE YARD" HIDDEN BY BUILDING FLATS, ACCESSIBLE FROM END FOR INSERTING/ REMOVING CARS.

(B) SERVING MORE THAN ONE INDUSTRY PER SPUR FURTHER COMPLICATES SWITCHING!

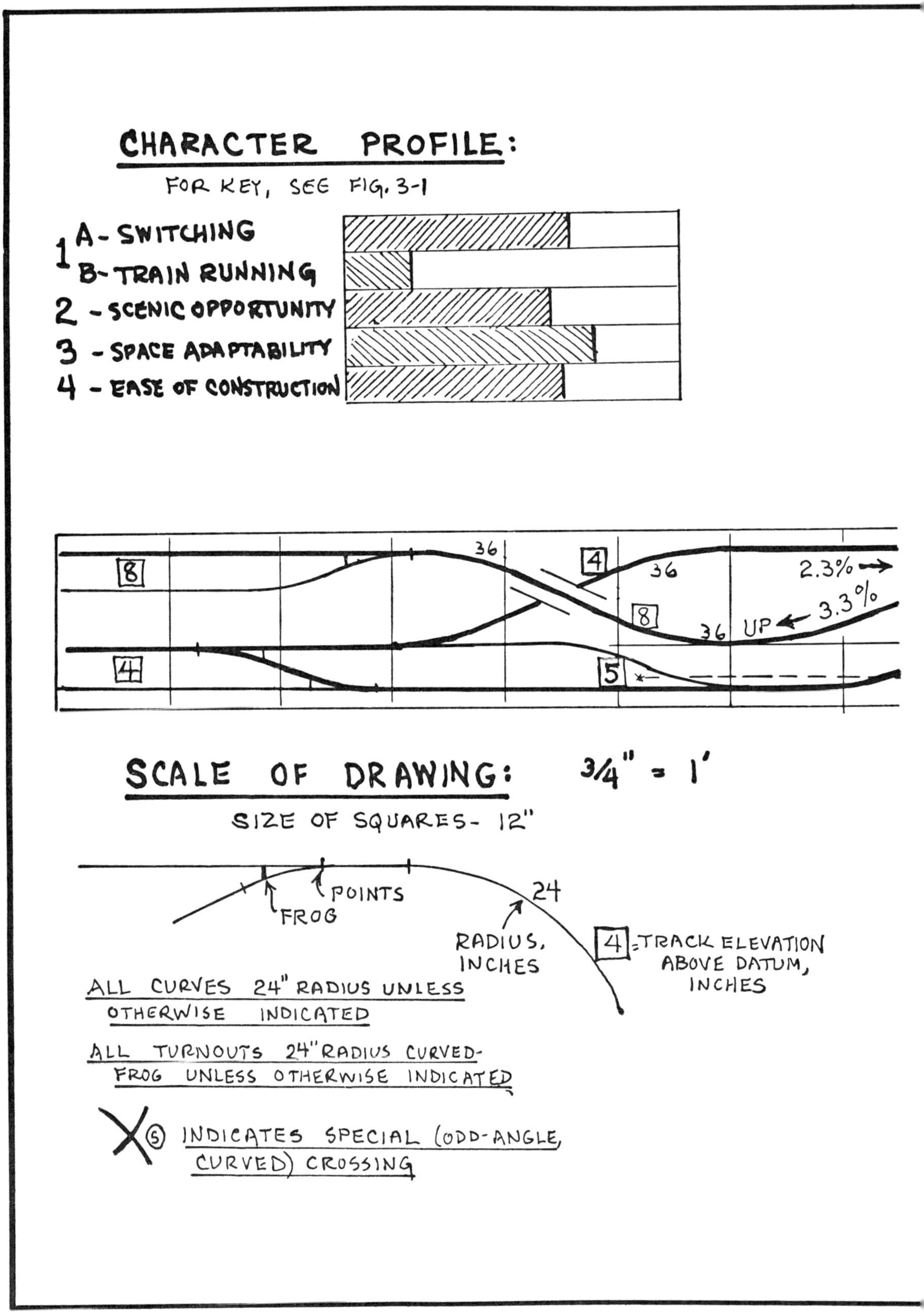

Fig. 3-8. Big Scale in a Small Package track plan for 0 gauge.

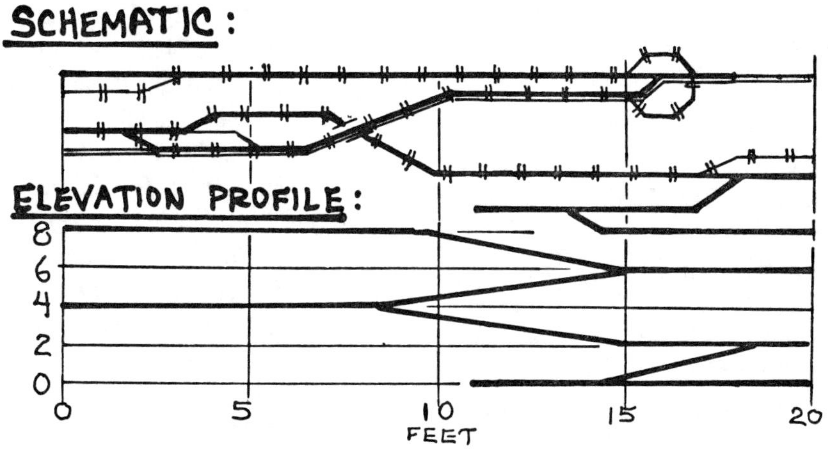
SCHEMATIC:
ELEVATION PROFILE:
8
6
4
2
0
0
5
10
15
20
FEET

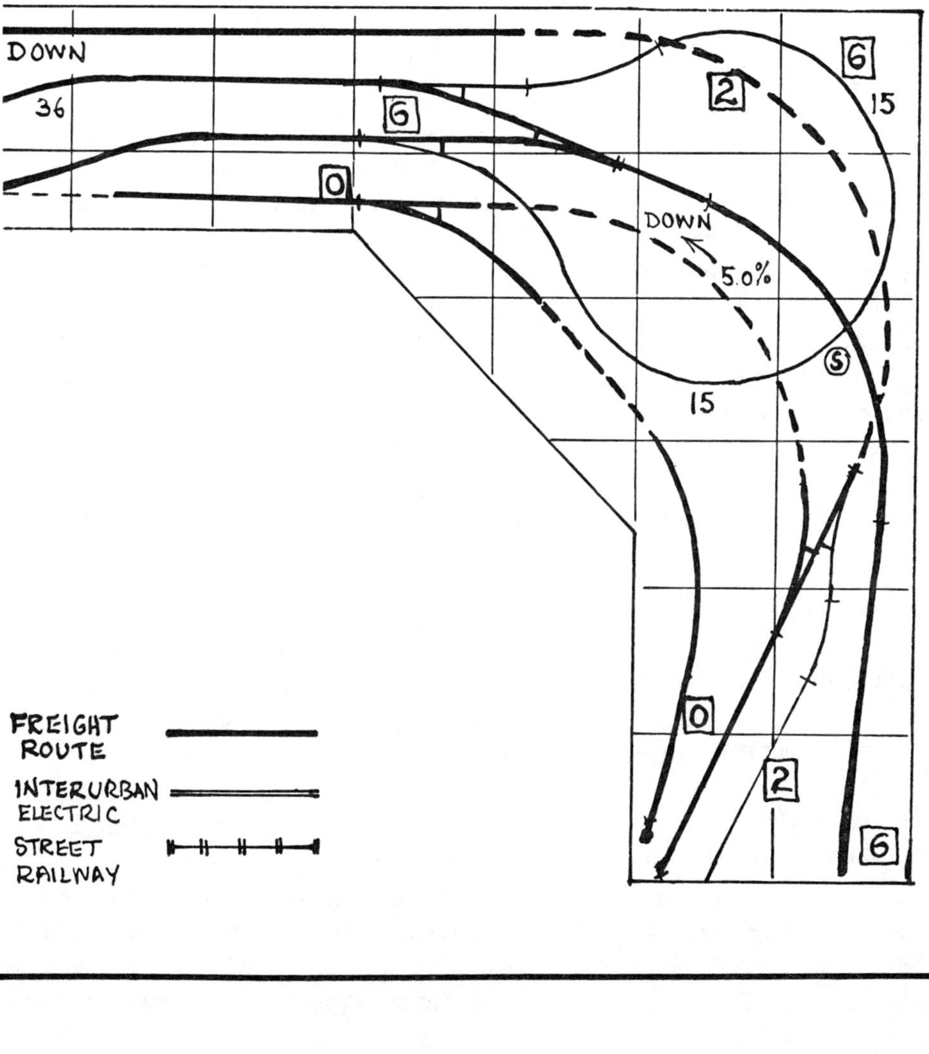
DOWN
36
6
2
6
15
0
DOWN
5.0%
S
15
0
2
6
FREIGHT ROUTE
INTERURBAN ELECTRIC
STREET RAILWAY

You could add extra length up to 16 ft., with corresponding increase in the number and variety of spur tracks, without exceeding handling and storage capacity if operating space is available. Sections may be joined at 90 degrees with simple track revision, converting long railroad into L-shaped one more compatible with a small room.

Size: 13½ in. × 10 ft.
Gauge: N
Curvature Standards: sharp and extra sharp
Schematic: switching railroad with switchback main line
Recommended construction: flat top on plank, hinged for storage and transportation; note that 1 × 14 in. shelving is widest commonly available and is 13¼ in. wide; plastic pier sets for elevated spurs
Trackwork options: uses only available trackwork elements; hand-laid trackwork would allow inserting some additional trackage

HAMMERLOCK INDUSTRIAL DISTRICT

This plan (Fig. 3-7) features a one or two-engine "switchman's nightmare" serving numerous industries via awkwardly-connected spurs, steep grades and extra-short tail tracks. The wye for turning cars is so short-tailed that the engine must set out a car, and retrieve it from other leg.

Additional spurs can be worked into this space. Shelf-width can be increased if space permits without exceeding a comfortable reaching or viewing distance.

Size: 4 × 10 L-shaped shelf 1½ ft. wide
Gauge: HO
Curvature standards: sharp and extra sharp
Schematic: switching railroad with wye; switchback main line
Recommended construction: cookie-cutter; may be built as flat top with minor track revisions

Trackwork options: as shown, uses only available trackwork elements; hand-laid trackwork would allow squeezing in additional spurs.

BIG SCALE IN A SMALL PACKAGE

This layout (Fig. 3-8) has steam-railroad-interchange freight cars combined with street railway and electronic interurban service to compress a variety of operations into a small area by virtue of the 24 inch radius they can negotiate, thus bringing the detail and mass of 0 scale within small-layout limits.

One ultra-sharp loop lets a local streetcar get a longer run before having to reverse its trolley pole and complete its trip in reverse motion (Fig. 3-9). Modest grades for such an operation should be increased to provide more liberal vertical clearances if genuine overhead-wire current distribution is to be used.

This line's future is most likely to be tied to its inclusion as an adjunct to a larger, future 0 scale railroad, readily adaptable to any connecting room or hallway area.

Size: 6 × 14 ft. L, 1½ ft. wide shelf legs (32 sq. ft.)
Gauge: 0
Curvature standards: extra sharp
Schematic: switchback point-to-point
Recommended construction: cookie-cutter
Trackwork options: standard extra sharp curved-frog turnouts, with one special (optional) crossing to be constructed; sectional or curvable track as desired

TWICE AROUND, TWO WAYS

This twice-around main line (Fig. 3-10) allows *three* short passing tracks for greatly increased variety in single-track operation with up to three short trains. There's very limited industrial development, with no provision for terminating or originating trains other than running engine around consist, as a result of allowing a little more room between the two laps of track in the interest of more reasonable scenicking and easements on some of the sharp curves.

The flat top version can represent the first stage of development if care is taken not to fasten plywood flat top to supporting grid with screws located underneath track. Plywood can then be slit with saber saw and railroad reconstituted in the more scenically-adaptable cookie-cutter version.

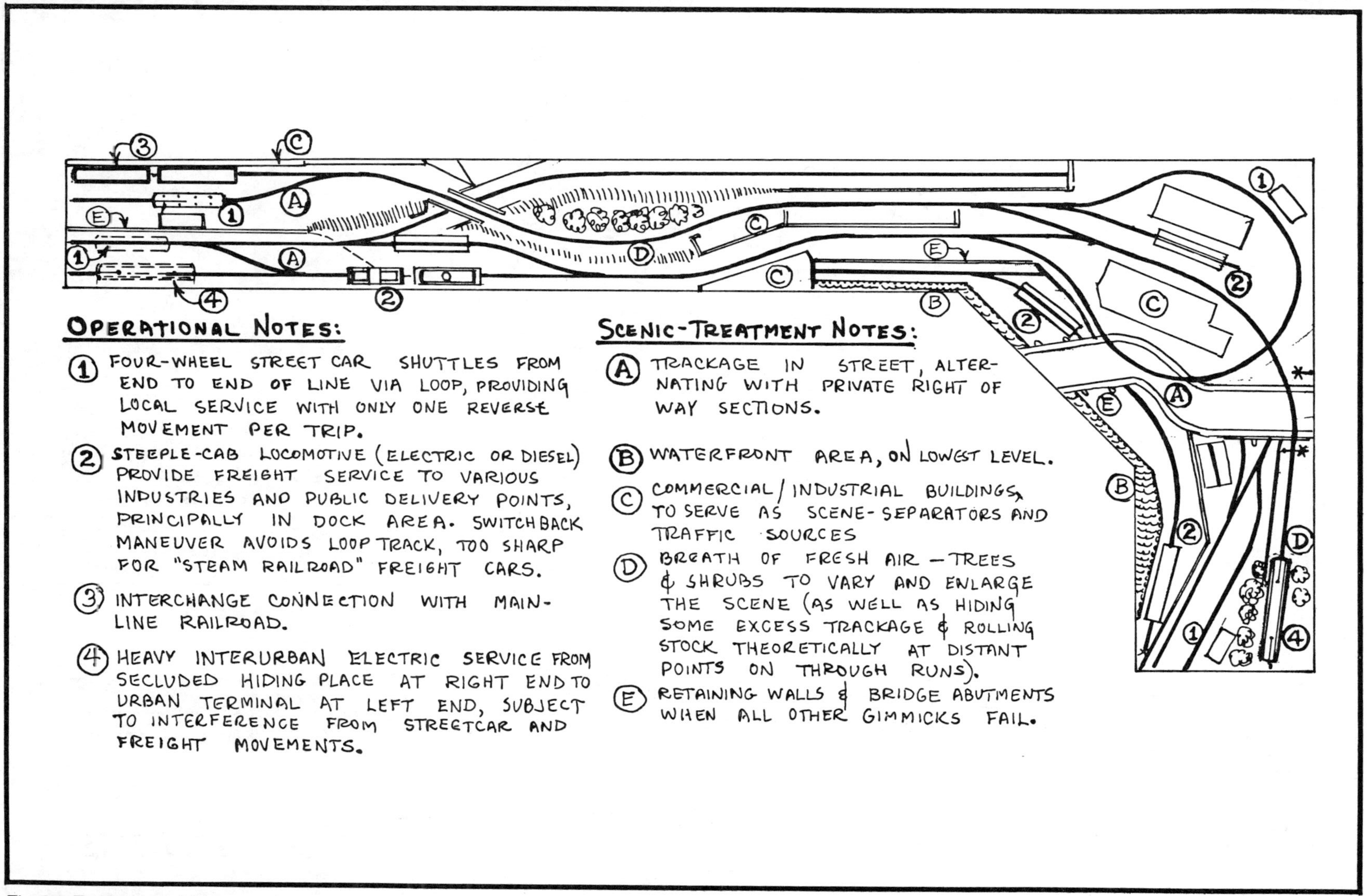

Fig. 3-9. Top-level trackage.

CHARACTER PROFILES:

FOR KEY, SEE FIG. 3-1

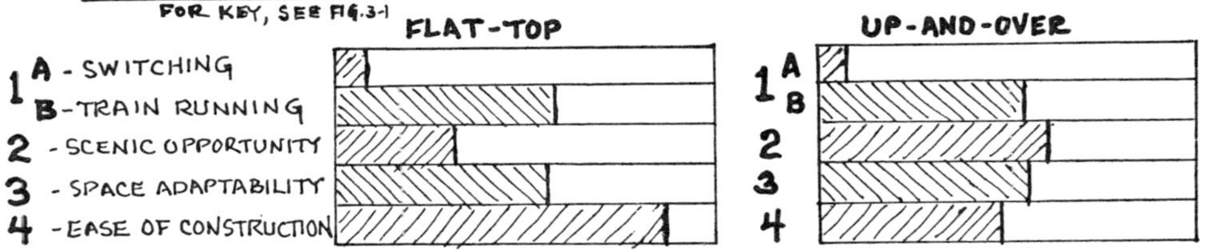

SCHEMATIC:

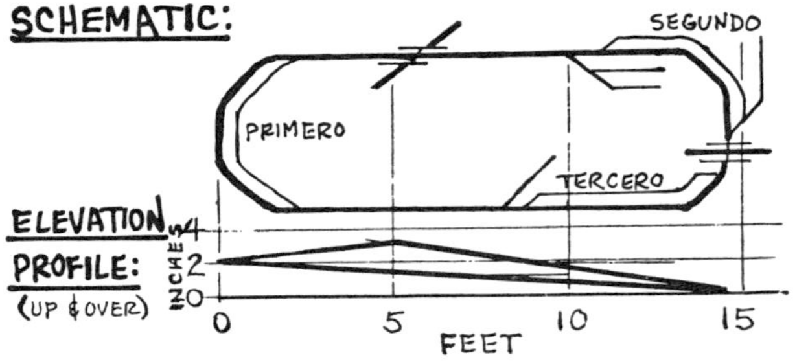

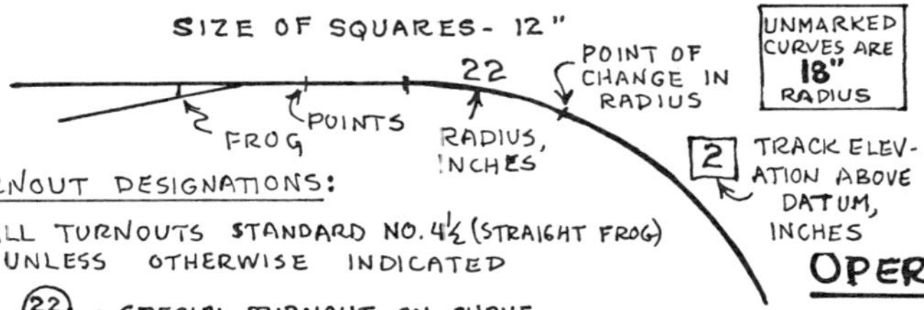

TURNOUT DESIGNATIONS:

ALL TURNOUTS STANDARD NO. 4½ (STRAIGHT FROG) UNLESS OTHERWISE INDICATED

(22/18) = SPECIAL TURNOUT ON CURVE (22 & 18" RADII)

OPERATIONAL NOTES:

① DIFFICULT RAMP LOCATION ON CURVED SPURS MAKES AUTOMATIC UNCOUPLING UNLIKELY — USE OF UNCOUPLING TOOL RECOMMENDED.

② SHORT TRAIN MAY MAKE HIDDEN LAYOVER IN TUNNEL — BUT DON'T FORGET IT'S THERE!

③ ACCESS TO TURNOUT FROM OPEN SIDE OF "MOUNTAIN".

④ PUTTING THE SHORT TRAIN THROUGH THE PASSING TRACK MAY ALLOW A NORMAL MEET — BUT SOME TRAINS THAT CLEAR IN PRIMERO SIDING WILL HAVE TO SAW BY AT SEGUNDO OR TERCERO. FORTY-FOOT FREIGHT CARS SHOWN.

SCENIC-TREATMENT NOTES:

Ⓐ HIGHEST AND WOODSIEST POINT ON THE RAILROAD, TO LET TRACKS DISAPPEAR INTO DEEP, CURVED CUT.

Ⓑ GRAVEL PITS ARE GREAT — FOR COMPACT, VERTICAL-FACE SCENERY AND A SOURCE OF TRAFFIC AS WELL.

Ⓒ A STREAM BED TO SEPARATE THE PARALLEL TRACKS OF THE TWICE-AROUND

Ⓓ CLIMBING AROUND THE SHOULDER OF THE HILL AND OVER THE GULLY VIA CURVED TRESTLE — IT ALMOST SEEMS PLAUSIBLE!

Ⓔ TWO CLOSELY-SPACED TRACKS AT ABOUT THE SAME LEVEL - ONLY THING TO DO IS HIDE ONE OF THEM IN A TUNNEL...

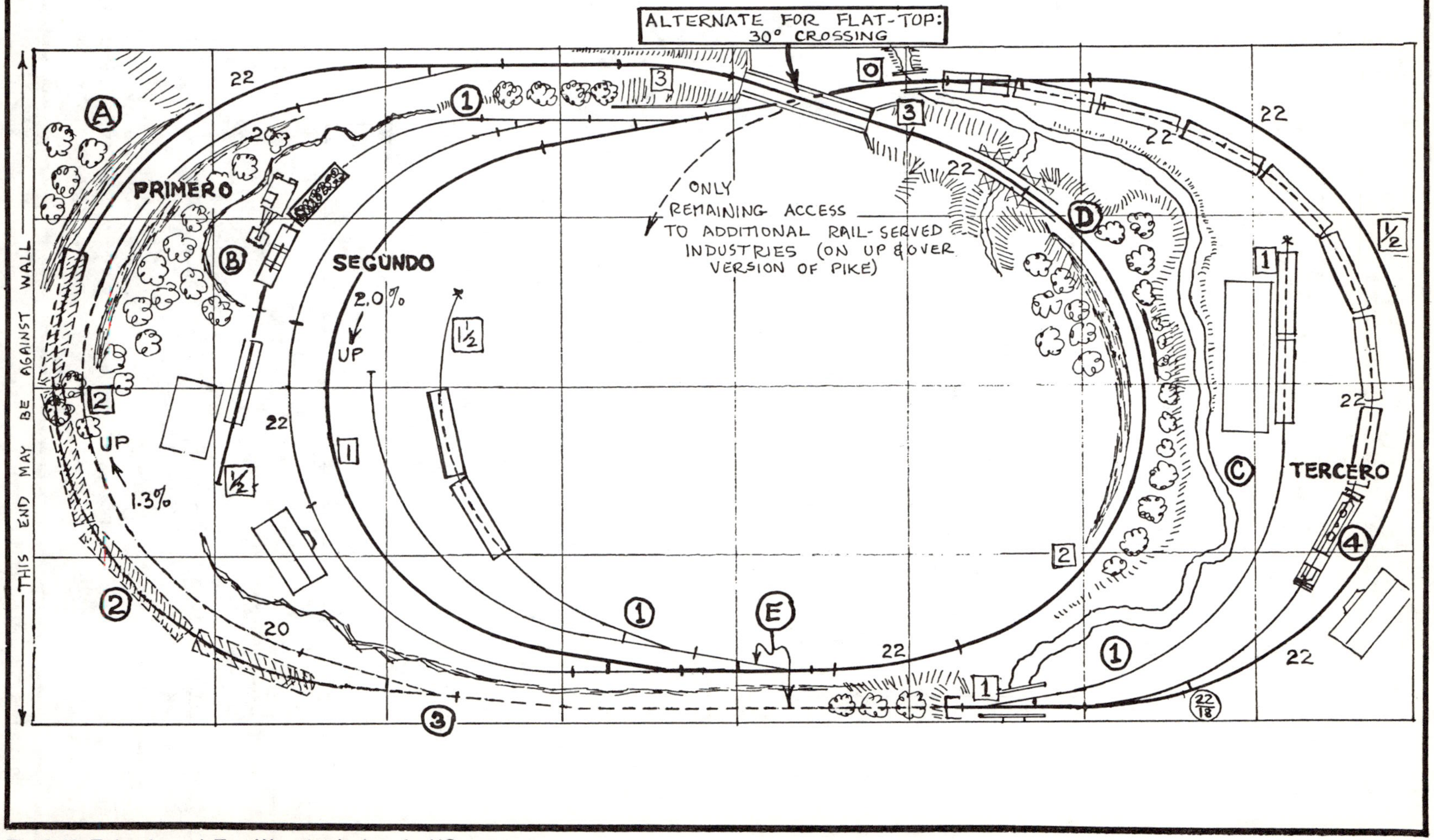

Fig. 3-10. Twice Around, Two Ways track plans for HO gauge.

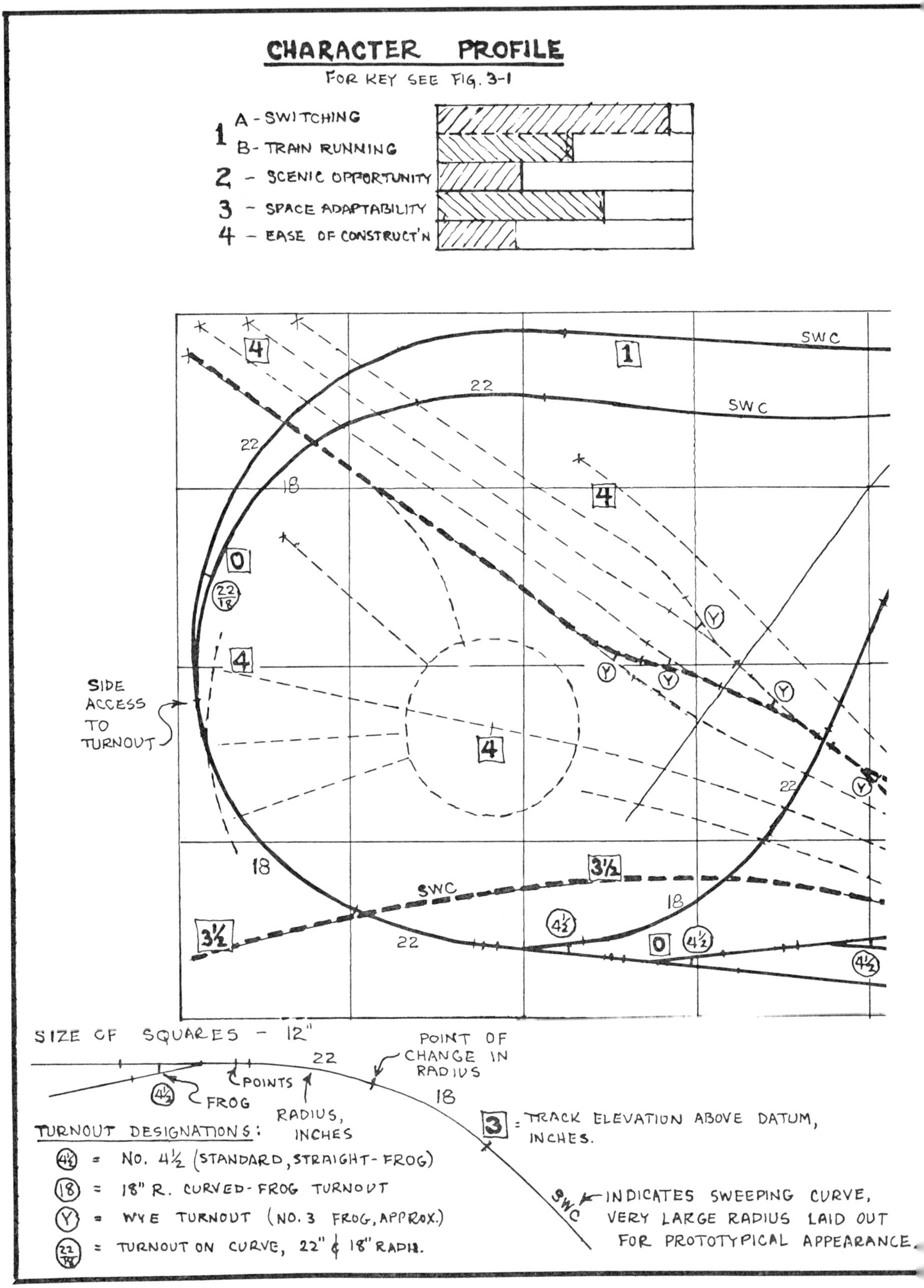

Fig. 3-11. The Iron Ranger track plan for HO gauge.

SCHEMATIC

ELEVATION PROFILE

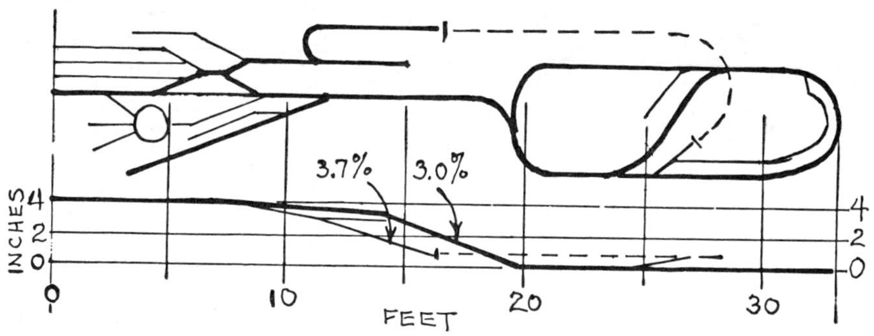

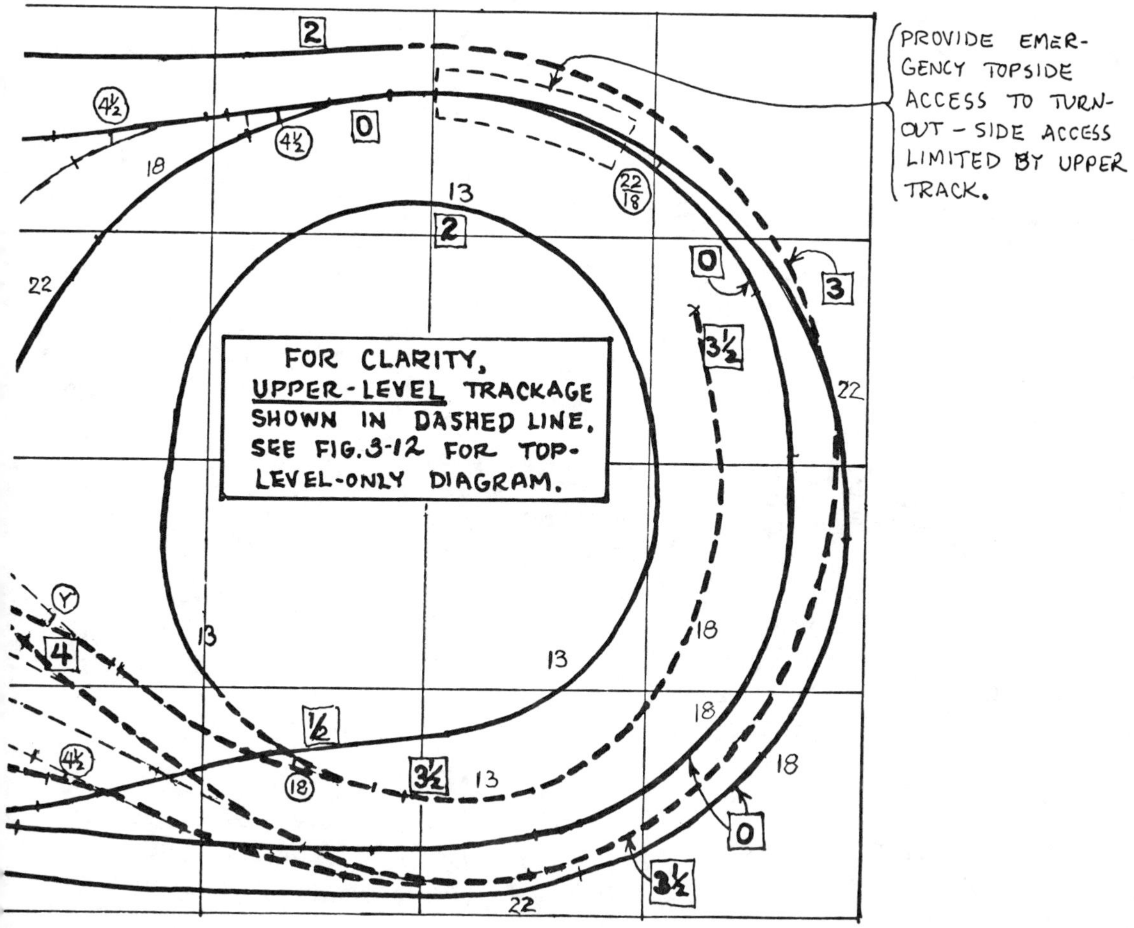

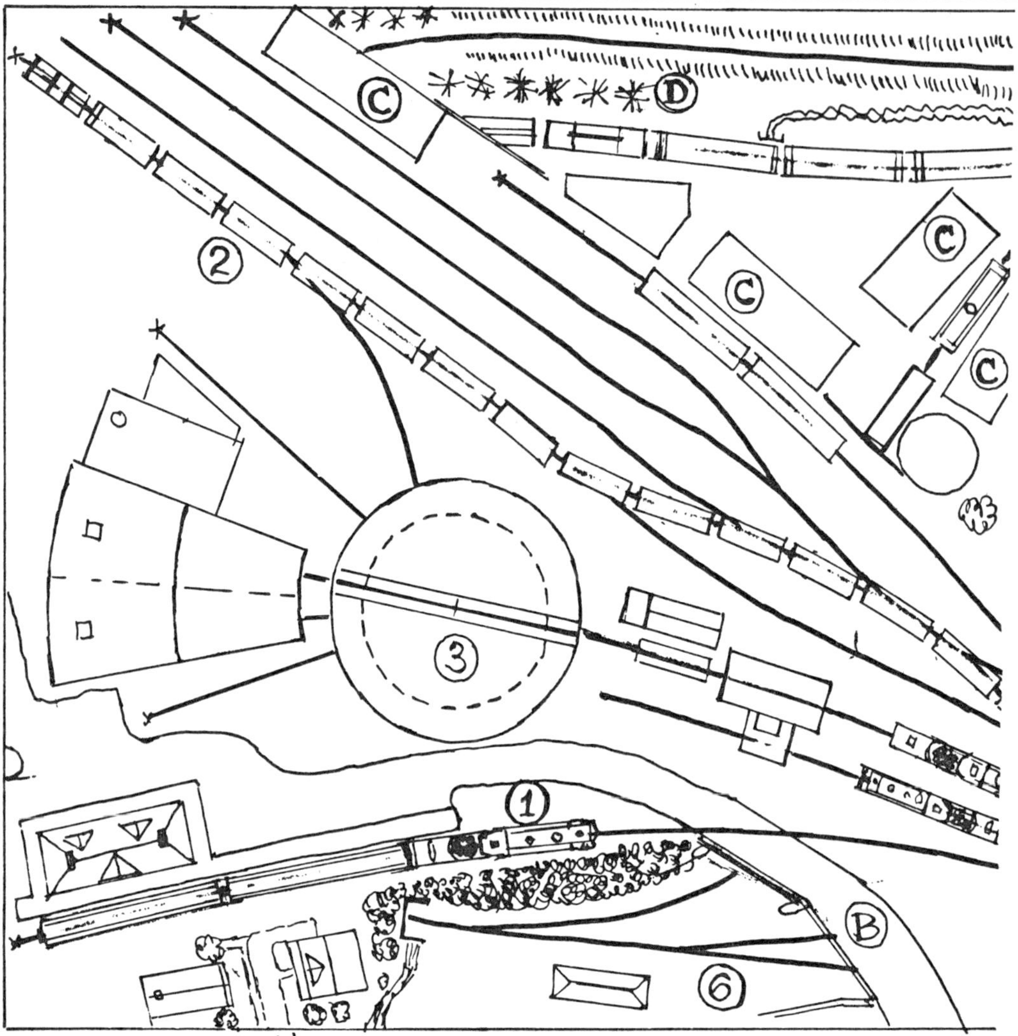

OPERATIONAL NOTES:

1. LOCAL PASSENGER TRAIN - UP TO 65-70 FT. CARS
2. LOADED ORE TRAIN ASSEMBLED IN YARD FOR DOWN-HILL TRIP. FIFTEEN ORE JIMMIES ACCOMMODATED.
3. TURNTABLE LENGTH TO SUIT LARGEST ROAD POWER— 87 FT. TABLE ILLUSTRATED (FOR SMALL 2-6-6-2).
4. LOCAL FREIGHT WITH GEEP — SERVES TRAFFIC OTHER THAN ORE.
5. MINING CO. SWITCHERS TAKE EMPTIES FROM YARD TO PIT & RETURN WITH LOADS, VIA SWITCHBACK. CARS/TRIP GOVERNED BY LENGTH OF TAIL TRACK OR TONNAGE RATING OF LOCOMOTIVE UPHILL WITH LOADS.
6. ROAD ORE TRAIN EXCHANGES LOAD FOR EMPTIES AT THIS "INTERCHANGE" CONNECTION.

Fig. 3-12. Top-level view.

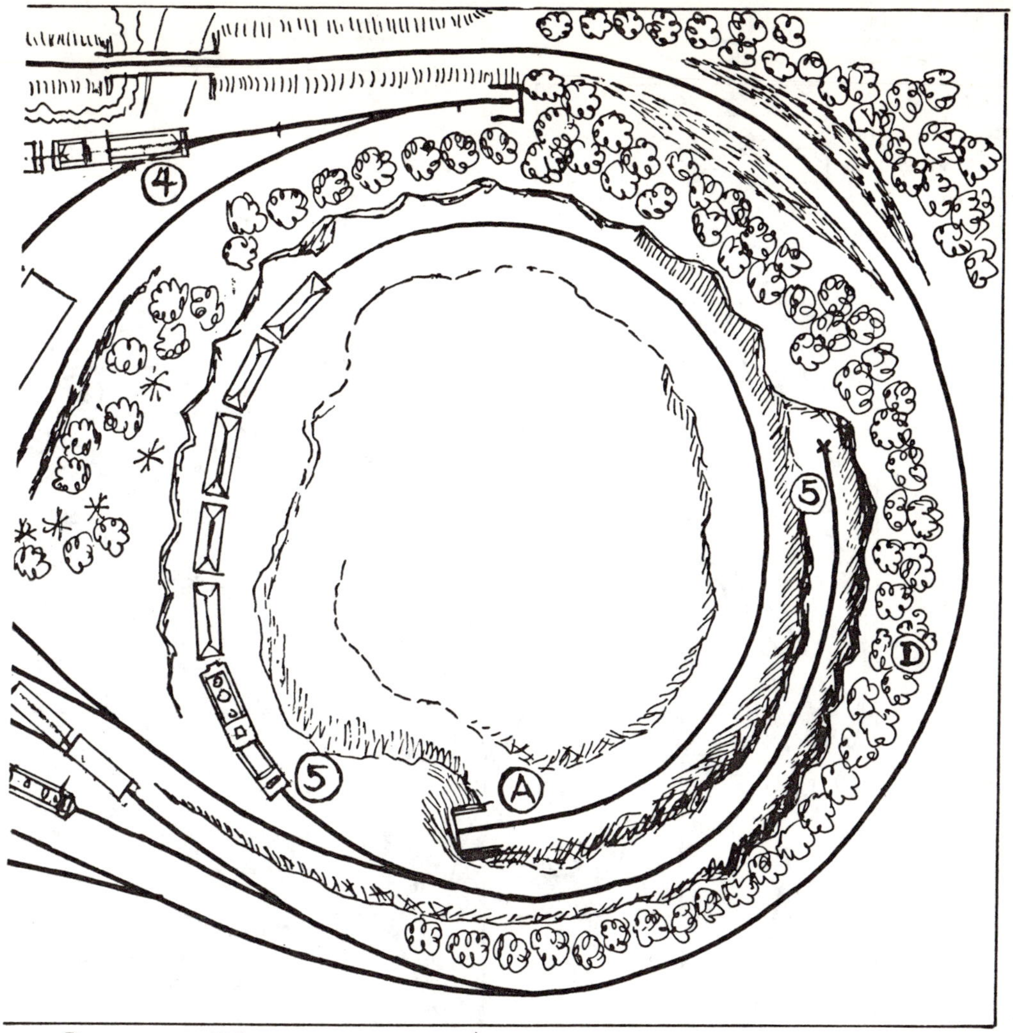

SCENIC-TREATMENT NOTES:

(A) OPEN-PIT MINE - SPIRAL TRACK IN "INACTIVE" BUT VISIBLE PIT LEADS THROUGH TUNNEL TO OUT-OF-SIGHT "ACTIVE" PIT WHERE CARS (PRESUMABLY) ARE LOADED.

(B) HIGHWAY OVERPASS USED TO LET LOWER-LEVEL TRACKS DISAPPEAR WITHOUT ANOTHER TUNNEL (WE ALREADY HAVE TOO MANY PORTALS TO BE REALISTIC).

(C) HIGH INDUSTRIAL BUILDINGS ARRANGED TO SEPARATE "YARD" AND "MAIN LINE" (LOWER LEVEL) SCENES, LET SOME TRACKS DISAPPEAR QUIETLY. SAME BUILDING LABELED DIFFERENTLY ON OPPOSITE SIDES. TO HELP ILLUSION.

(D) TREES USED TO SEPARATE MINE PIT SCENICALLY FROM BRANCH LINE, & INCREASE APPARENT DEPTH OF PIT, HELP LET MAIN LINE SNEAK AWAY UNDER YARD.

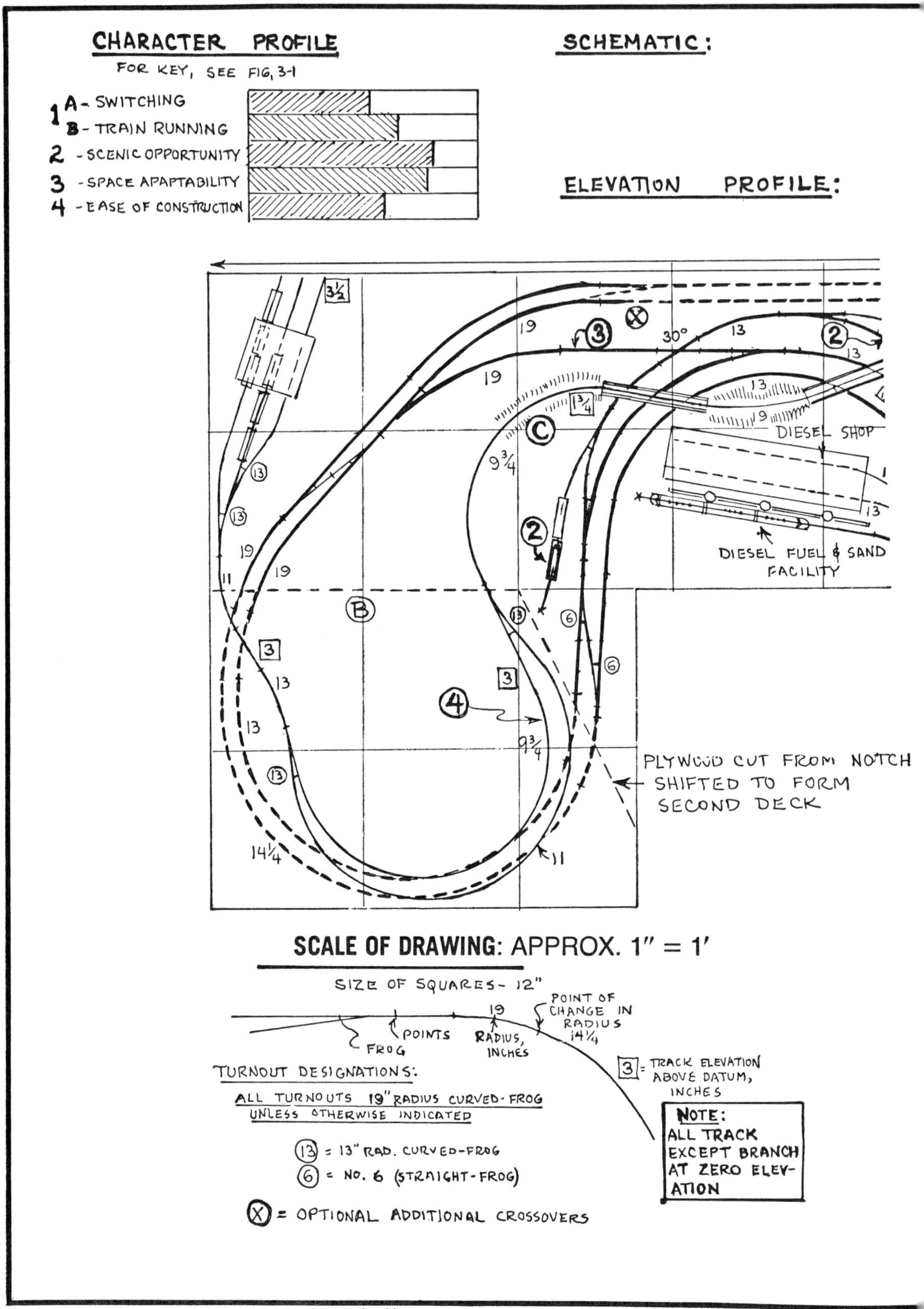

Fig. 3-13. The Accessible Waterwings track plan for N gauge.

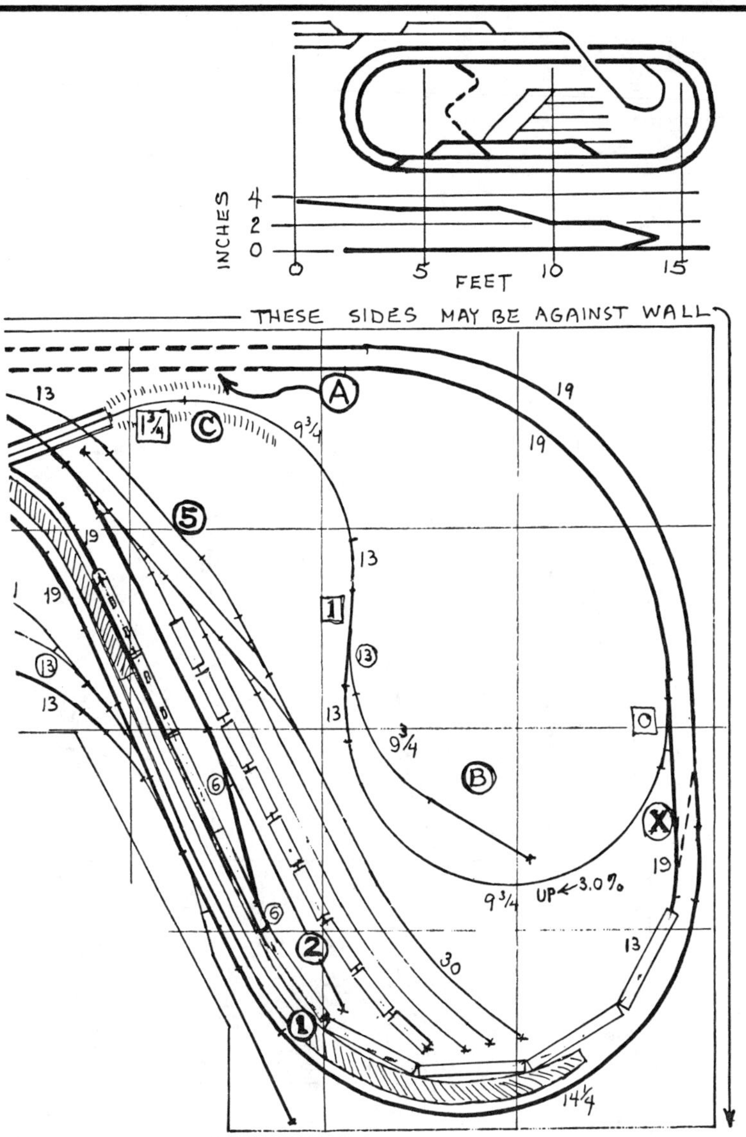

OPERATIONAL NOTES:

1. BETWEEN-MAIN-LINES PASSENGER STATION PLATFORM LONG ENOUGH FOR 8-TO 10-CAR TRAINS.
2. YARD SWITCHING LEAD CLEAR OF MAIN LINES. STUB TRACKS HOLD SWITCHER WHILE TRAINS ARE LEAVING OR ENTERING MAIN LINE.
3. RETURN CUT-OFF (ONE DIRECTION ONLY) ALLOWS "OUT AND BACK" OPERATION FROM MAIN YARD
4. RUN-AROUND TRACK SO BRANCH-LINE TRAIN CAN SERVE MAJOR MINE AND MAKE TRIP IN BOTH DIRECTIONS WITH ENGINE AHEAD OF CARS— BRANCH LONG ENOUGH TO JUSTIFY SUCH AN OPERATION.
5. CABOOSE & RUN-AROUND TRACKS FOR YARD VERSATILITY

SCENIC-TREATMENT NOTES:

- (A) TRACKS HIDDEN BEHIND LOW EMBANKMENTS, BUILDING FLATS, ETC., BUT OPEN FOR ACCESS FROM ABOVE.
- (B) INDUSTRIAL DEVELOPMENT AREAS— EASY RAIL ACCESS BY MAIN OR BRANCH LINE!
- (C) BRANCH LINE MAY BE CARRIED BY COMMERCIAL PIER SETS OR COOKIE-CUTTER CONSTRUCTION.

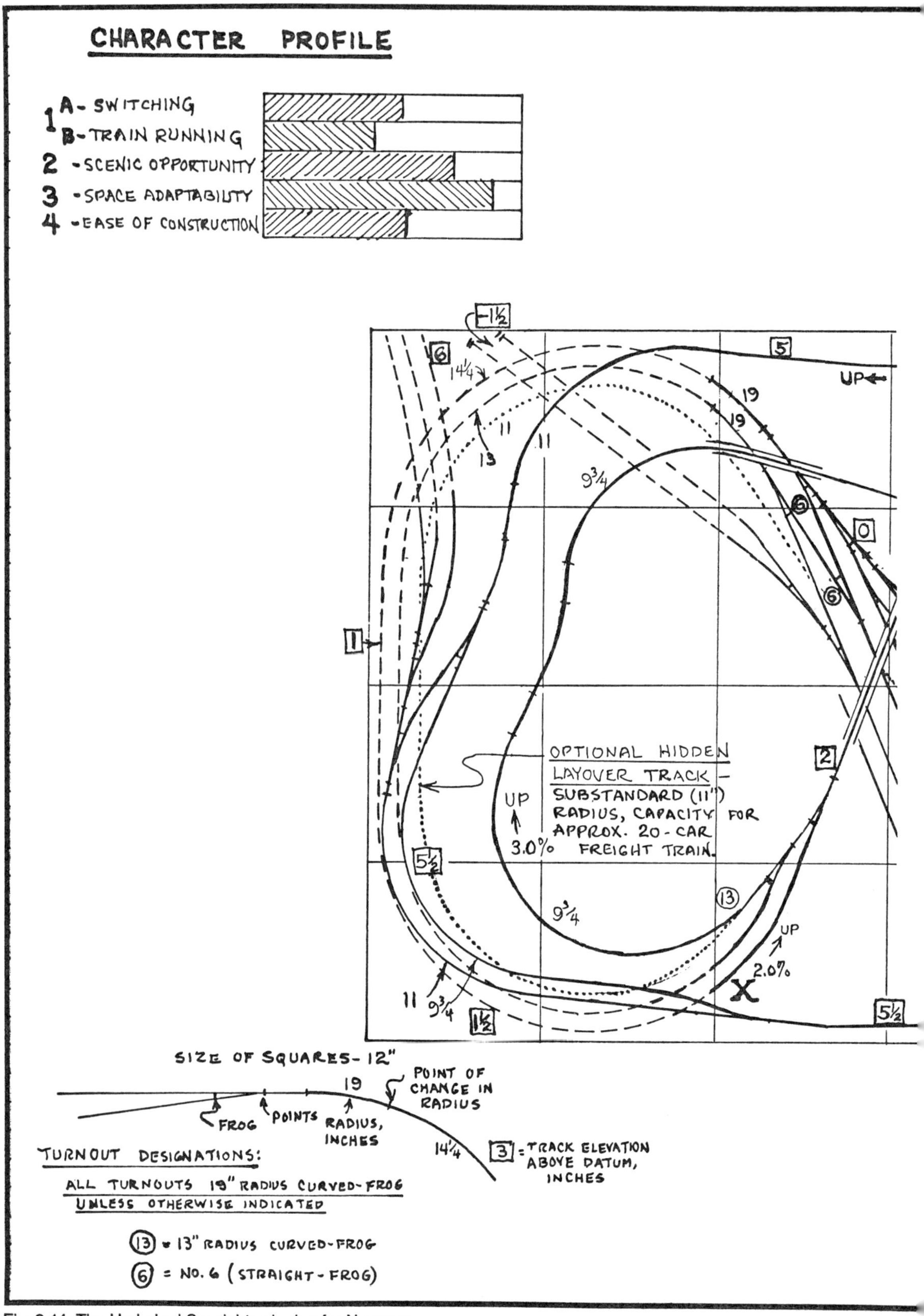

Fig. 3-14. The Underbed Special track plan for N gauge.

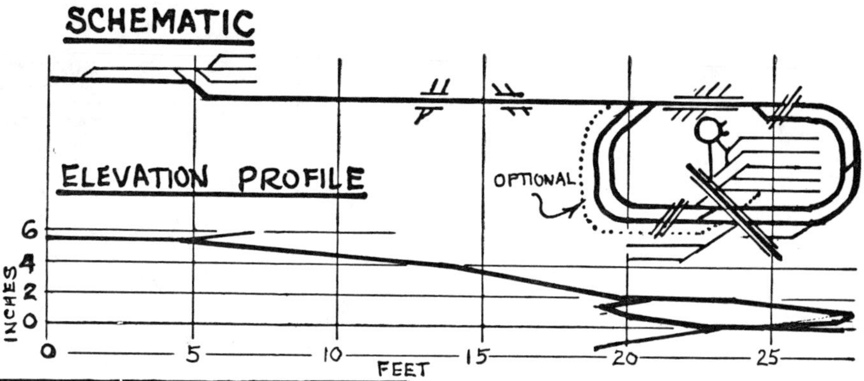

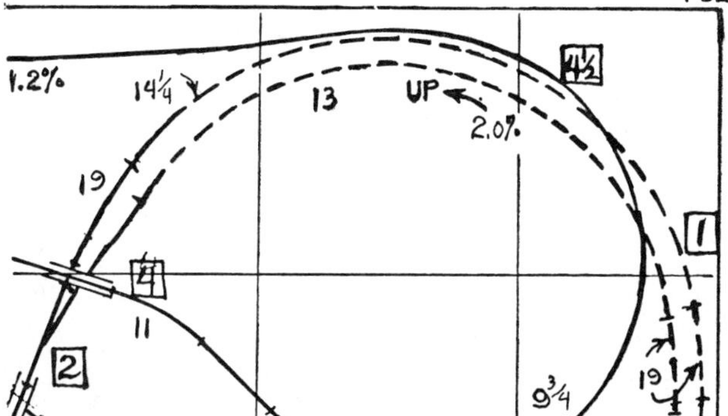

NOTE: OPTIONAL CROSSOVER TO PROVIDE SHORT RUN-AROUND TRACK FOR YARD.

X - REVERSING CONNECTION TERMINII (OPTIONAL - APPROX. 5% DOWNGRADE).

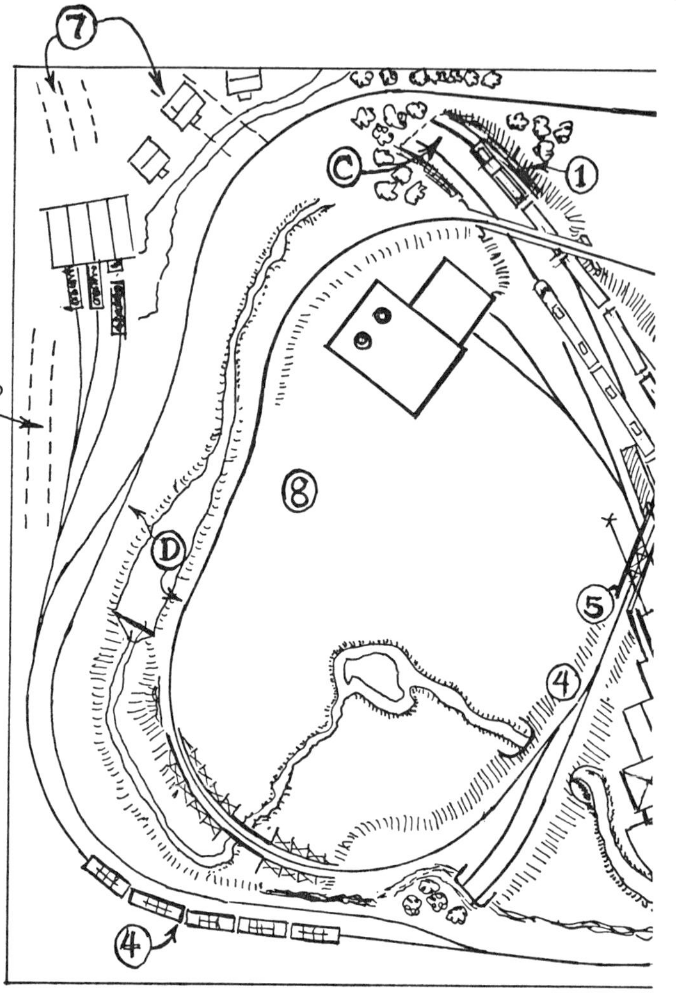

OPERATIONAL NOTES:

1. SECOND MAIN TRACK SERVES AS SWITCHING LEAD FOR YARD WHEN NECESSARY.
2. MODERATELY LONG PASSENGER PLATFORM, WITH SET-OUT TRACK AT STATION FOR HEAD-END CARS, SLEEPERS OR DINERS.
3. HIDDEN SECTION OF MAIN LINES SERVES AS LAY-OVER TRACKAGE TO INCREASE OPERATING FLEX-IBILITY, GIVE SOME SENSE OF LONGER RUNS.
4. RUN-AROUND & STORAGE TRACK NEAR END OF LONG BRANCH LINE. BRANCH JUNCTION AT SOME DISTANCE FROM YARD.
5. SINGLE-TRACK BRIDGE "BOTTLENECK" IN OTHERWISE DOUBLE TRACK MAIN LINE.
6. ENGINE TERMINAL - STEAM, DIESEL OR COMBINATION AS APPROPRIATE. ROOM FOR 100 FT. TURNTABLE
7. MINE / POWERPLANT COMBINATION FOR EMPTY / LOAD ONE-DIRECTION MOVEMENT — CARS MAY BE "FIDDLED" BETWEEN ADJACENT LOADING / DUMPING TRACKS, ACCESSIBLE FROM OUTER ENDS.

Fig. 3-15. Top-level view only.

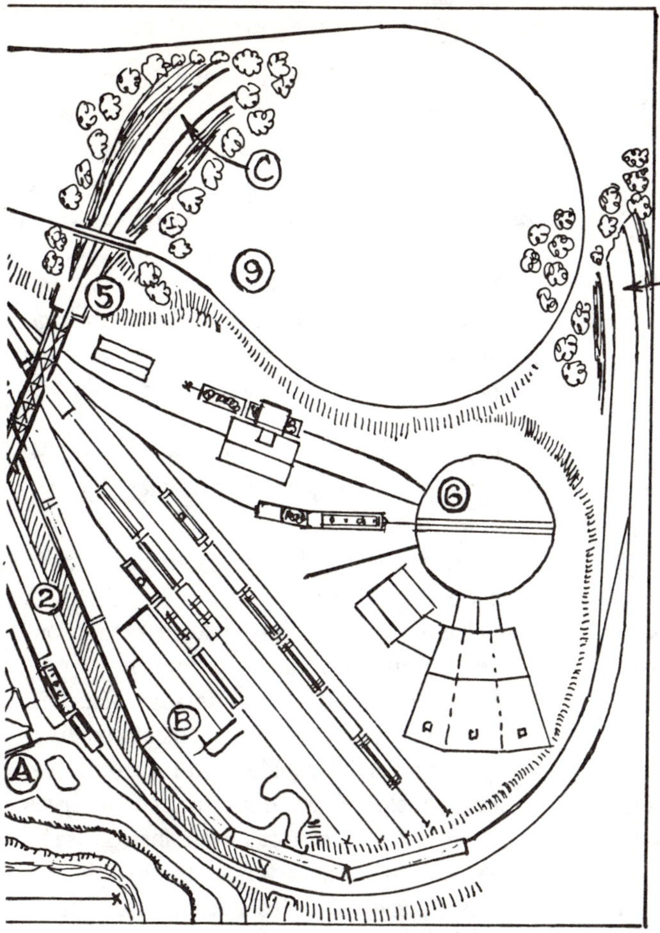

SCENIC-TREATMENT NOTES:

(A) PASSENGER STATION - COMPACT, PICTURESQUE LOCATION

(B) ROOM FOR FREIGHT STATION AND PUBLIC DELIVERY ("TEAM") TRACK.

(C) TRACKS DISAPPEAR INCONSPICUOUSLY INTO DEEP CUTS, IF POSSIBLE, TO MINIMIZE NUMBER OF TUNNEL PORTALS.

(D) STREAM AND DIFFERENCE IN ELEVATION SEPARATES TWO PARALLEL TRACKS OF BRANCH LINE.

---

(8) INDUSTRIAL SITES, WITH RAIL CONNECTION FROM BRANCH OR MAIN LINE.

(9) LUMBER, MINING OR INDUSTRIAL DEVELOPMENT AREA.

Size: 4 × 8 ft. island or peninsula
Gauge: HO
Curvature standards: sharp
Schematic: twice-around continuous, single track
Recommended construction: flat top, cookie-cutter
Trackwork options: standard switches, crossing and most curves; passing track curve at Primero (20 in. radius) may be made by alternating 18 and 20 in. pieces of recommended track; curvable preferred

THE IRON RANGER

This plan (Fig. 3-11) allows operation of 15-car and longer trains in a very restricted space by depicting an ore-hauling railroad using extra-short (24 ft.) *jimmies* for most traffic, with loaded cars always moving downhill on the steep main line. There's limited general freight and local passenger service possibilities, the latter enhanced by easements on the sharp curves. This shows a highly realistic representation of an open-pit mining operation, at the expense of a lot of behind-the-scene switching. The fiction of loading cars from the out-of-sight mine provides an endless source of ore without actually gnawing away at the plaster scenery in the visible mine. For the top-level view see Fig. 3-12.

In a slightly larger area, more of the main line continuous oval could be left exposed, providing a better look at the trains and their over-the-road running, with additional industry tracks and traffic variety. With relatively small road locomotives, a helper engine may be required to get the empties up the grade to the yard, providing additional operating variety.

Size: 4 × 8 ft.
Gauge: HO
Curvature standards: sharp and extra sharp
Schematic: combination stub terminal to continuous oval with single reversing connection and empty-load by-pass connection
Recommended construction: cookie-cutter
Trackwork options: completely compatible with prefabricated trackwork elements, making extensive use of wye turnouts and turnouts on curve; curvable track for extra sharp sections in mine and sweeping curves elsewhere

THE ACCESSIBLE WATERWINGS

This conservatively-designed layout (Fig. 3-13) favors the operation of fairly long trains over a short, double-track *waterwings* oval, with periodic rearrangement of consists in the single large yard. A steeply-graded, crooked branch of reasonable length provides a change of pace.

You can further develop this layout by using the vacant space for additional industry trackage and structures or use open-country scenery matching the conventional-standard main-line trackage.

Size: 4 × 8 ft. with "sit-in" notch for access when two sides are placed against wall
Gauge: N
Curvature standards: conventional (main line); sharp (branch)
Schematic: oval with single reversing connection, multiple-track with branch
Recommended construction: flat top, with pier set for branch (simplest construction) or partial cookie-cutter (preferable, very simple); plywood cut from notch serves as second-deck material for branch-line area
Trackwork options: all trackwork elements standard, with sectional track useable for easemented curves if curvable track not used; additional pair of crossovers between main tracks (at point indicated by X) will add flexibility in run-around moves on double track if fairly short trains are run

THE UNDERBED SPECIAL

This layout (Fig. 3-14) can be stored under a double bed. The figure-eight main line arrangement shortens the plan enough to stay within storage-length limitations.

The extra-long branch can be built with much steeper grades, accentuating scenic possibilities, if railroad stowage doesn't limit height. See Fig. 3-15 for top-level view. A turntable long enough for main-line steam power may be readily adapted from HO gauge (Atlas) mechanism.

Since trains can readily originate or terminate their runs in either direction at the main yard, no reversing connection is shown. If added between points X and X, out and back operation from ladder end of the yard is possible.

You can further develop the plan by adding more industry or higher hills—take your choice!

Size: 4 ft. × 5 ft. 9 in.

Gauge: N

Curvature standards: conventional (main line); sharp (branch)

Schematic: oval with branch

Recommended construction: cookie-cutter

Trackwork options: all trackwork items standard, with sectional track useable for easemented curves if curvable track (recommended) not used; optional additional hidden layover siding highly recommended and should be built as part of original layout as it's difficult to install after upper layers in place

COFFEE TABLE RAILROADS

The advent of smaller and smaller scales in model railroading has naturally opened up tinier and tinier territories as sites for layouts, even desk drawers for executives who want to sneak a little N- or Z-gauge railroading into the office. The glass-topped coffee table, usually built for the railroad, rather than adapted from the furniture-store's stock, is an obvious possibility for the most cramped apartment-bound lifestyle. Nowadays the top may well be cut from a sheet of heavy plastic, making a free-form shape highly practical for anyone with access to some woodworking tools. From a track-plan standpoint, the coffee table situation does call for some novelties in emphasis if the result is to be more than a ship-in-a-bottle stunt and have some real operating possibilities.

Most of the time the railroad should be operable with the transparent top in place, which means that *operating reliability* becomes of paramount importance. A simple derailment, whether from marginal trackwork and rolling stock or from running through a misplaced switch, means calling for the big hook to remove the lid. Most of the railroad operations should therefore involve fixed routings selected by a minimum number of turnouts. The sharp or extra sharp curves needed to keep the coffee table's dimensions compatible with its living-room location must be complemented by modest consists of equipment well adapted to move around the bends without strain and grades which will allow hauling well-weighted, low-center-of-gravity cars.

The railroad will be viewed primarily from above, putting an entirely different slant not only on scenery but on what is a most suitable *suite* of rolling stock. Billboard refrigerator cars will tend to look much alike when most of what you see is roof, whereas the differences between loaded and empty open-tops or between tank cars of various sizes and shapes will assume greater attractiveness and interest.

Intricate and extensive switching will probably mean removing the transparent top, so if there is to be some local freight operation there might as well be enough spur tracks to make a serious operating session worthwhile. With care in track alignment to favor reliable uncoupling and coupling with automatics and ramps, limited under-glass switching may be practical. Reasonable variety in the track space available can come from adding a *side-loading* feature to the little pike in the form of a fiddle yard accessible through the wall of the table structure.

The traditional approach to coffee table railroading is via continuous running of trains whose short consists are appropriate, and there are a couple of such plans in this section. It is possible to do something radically different by taking advantage of some special situations in modern-day railroading.

In any case, the modest area available and the considerable time and outlay in providing the piece of furniture to support and protect the railroad makes fully and intricately detailed scenic treatment both practical and emotionally acceptable. More than most, the coffee table pike can become a little jewel and thoroughly justify the engineering effort and care that goes into a cookie-cutter foundation.

TRADITIONAL COFFEE TABLE RAILROAD

With a single passing point, this is essentially a one-train or one-train-at-a-time operation (Fig.

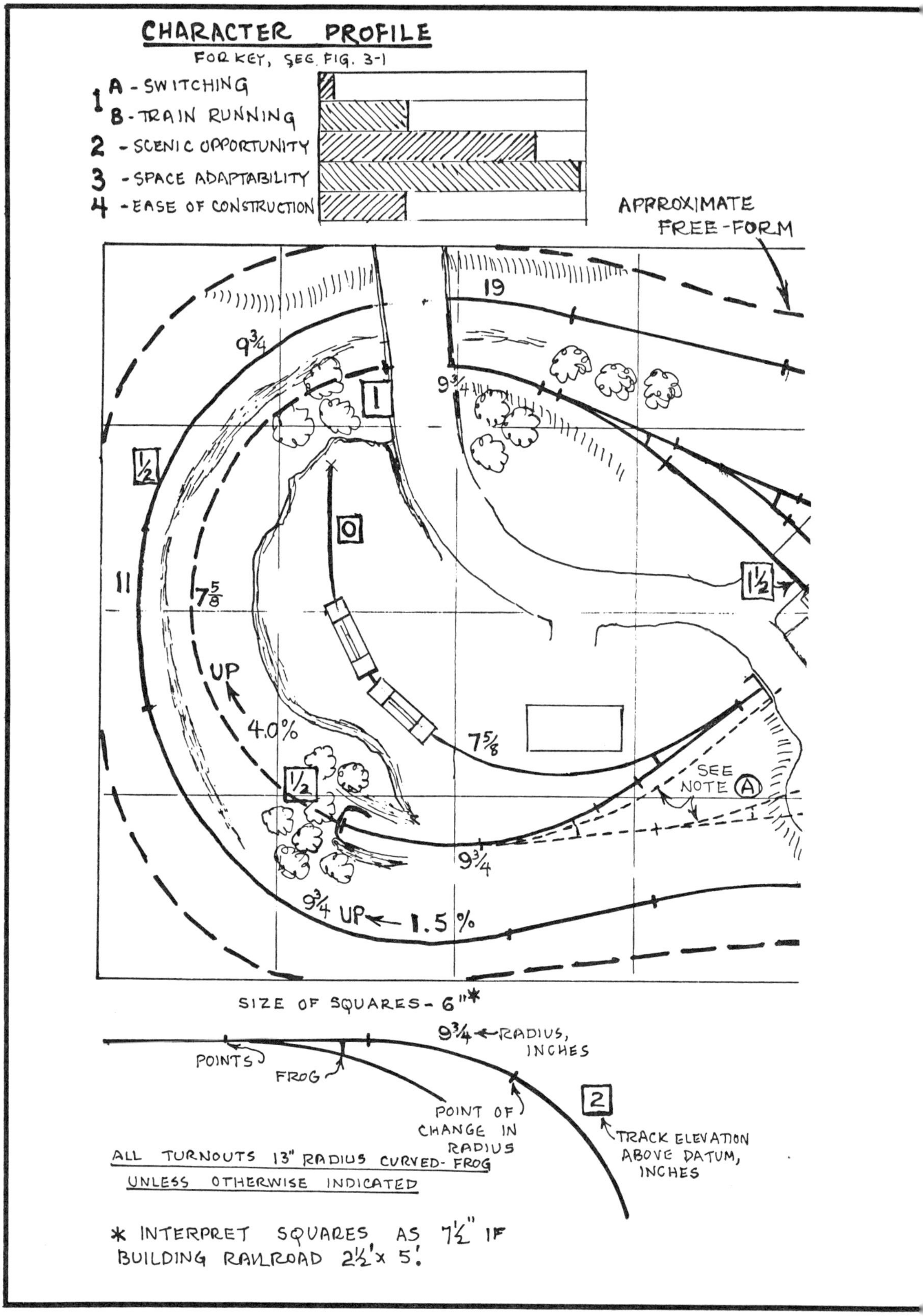

Fig. 3-16. The Traditional Coffee Table Railroad track plan for N gauge.

GENERAL NOTES:

- RAILROAD MAY BE BUILT IN RECTANGULAR 2×4 FT. FORMAT, OR WITH FREE-FORM CONTOUR INDICATED (PLASTIC SIDES & COVER).
- BY INCREASING OUTSIDE DIMENSIONS TO 2½×5 FT., ALL TRACK RADII MAY BE INCREASED BY ONE INCREMENT (7⅝" → 9¾", 9¾" → 11", ETC.), THUS UPGRADING CURVATURE CONTOUR STANDARD TO "SHARP."

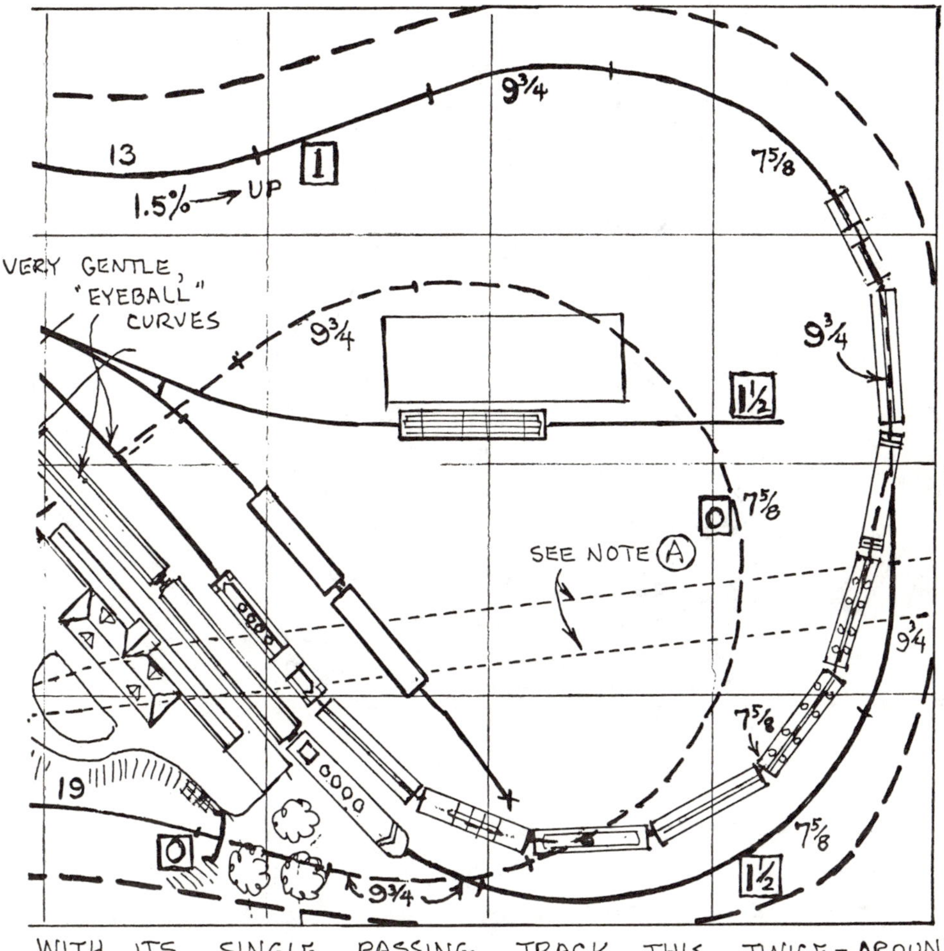

WITH ITS SINGLE PASSING TRACK, THIS TWICE-AROUND RAILROAD IS BASICALLY A ONE-TRAIN-AT-A-TIME OPERATION. BE SURE TO PROVIDE A PASSENGER STATION (OR ITS FREIGHT EQUIVALENT, A POINT WHERE A LOCAL FREIGHT RUN COULD ORIGINATE) NEXT TO THE PASSING SIDING SO THE TRAIN CAN LOOK LOGICAL WHILE AWAITING A CLEAR TRACK!

NOTE (A): OPTIONAL ALIGNMENT AND DOWNHILL, HIDDEN "FIDDLE YARD" WITH ENDS OF TRACK ACCESSIBLE THROUGH SIDE OF COFFEE TABLE — MORE OPERATING VARIETY THROUGH AN EASIER "CHANGE OF CHARACTERS" IN THE ROLLING-STOCK DEPARTMENT.

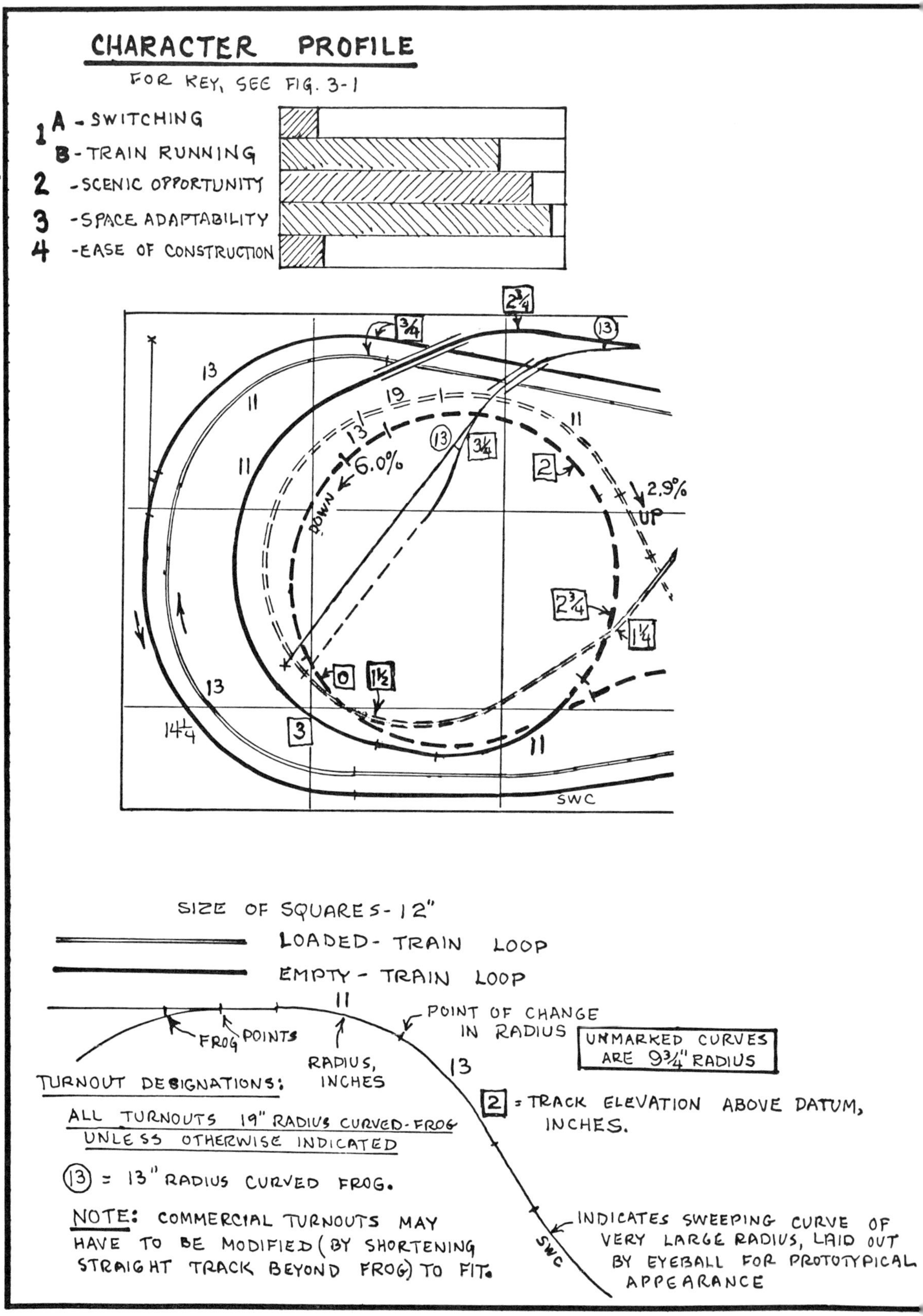

Fig. 3-17. Long Trains for the Coffee Table track plan for N gauge.

SCHEMATICS:

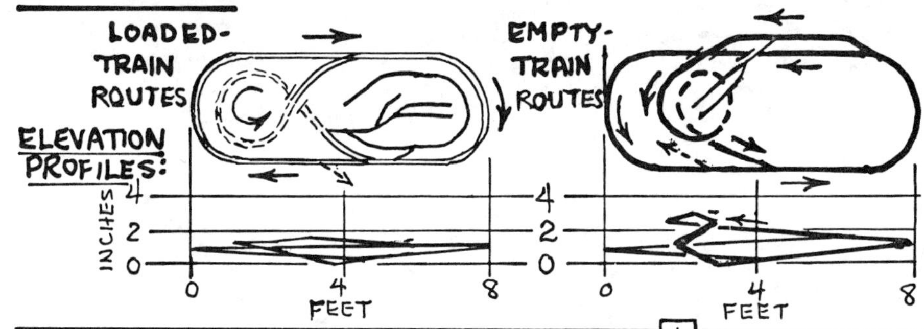

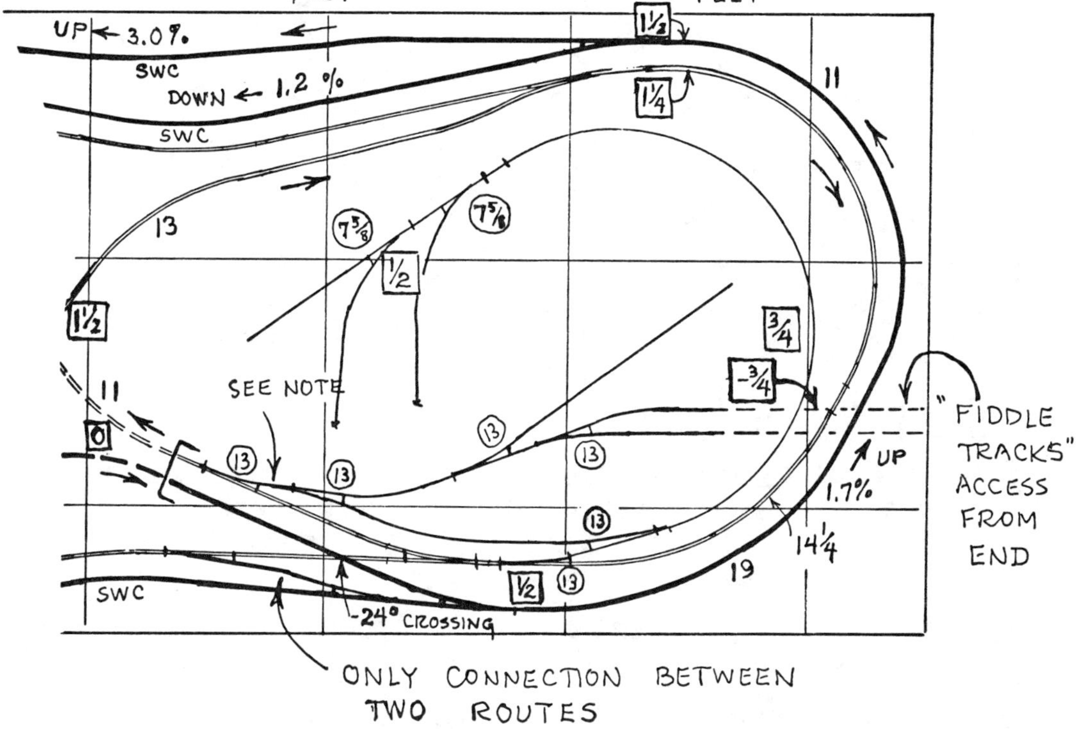

NOTE THAT, DESPITE APPEARANCES, THERE ARE NO ELECTRICAL REVERSING SECTIONS ON THIS LAYOUT — NOR IS IT POSSIBLE TO CHANGE HEADING OF TRAINS OR LOCOMOTIVES EXCEPT BY "GIANT HAND" ACTION.

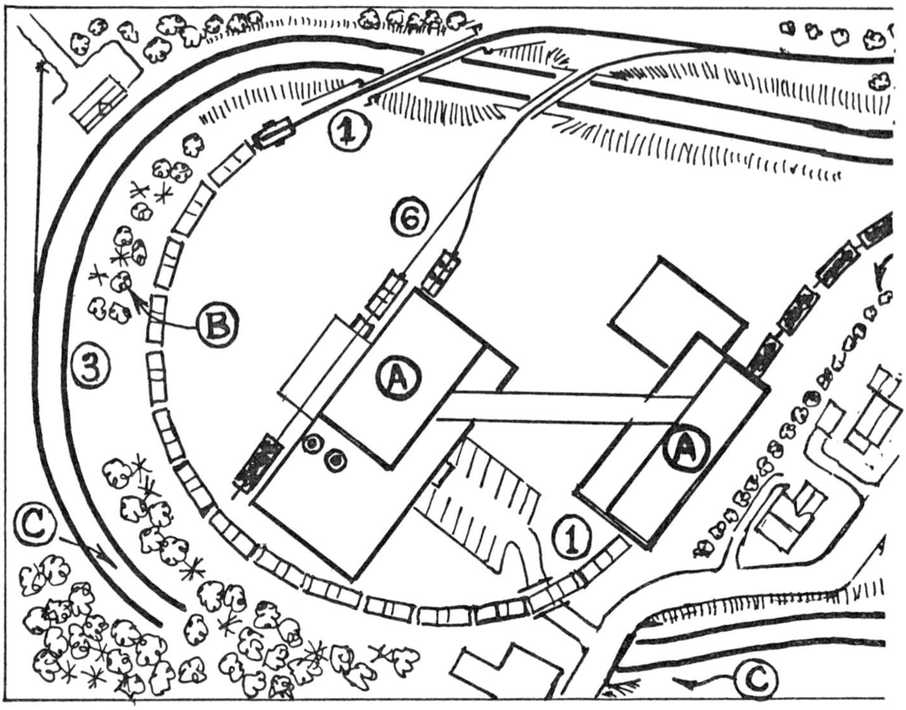

OPERATIONAL NOTES:

(1) TRAIN OF EMPTIES DISAPPEARS INTO PROCESSING PLANT AT STEADY, "LOAD-IN-MOTION" RATE AFTER TRAVELING AROUND BALLOON TRACK FROM FLYOVER MAIN-LINE CONNECTION.

(2) LOADED TRAIN EMERGES FROM PLANT AT SIMILAR PACE, RETURNS TO MAIN LINE VIA DIRECT CONNECTION.

(3) LOADED TRAIN CIRCLES MAIN LINE OVAL AS MANY TIMES AS DESIRED, ON RIGHT-HAND TRACK.

(4) LOADED TRAIN DIVERTED TO "DOCK BRANCH" AT JUNCTION DISAPPEARS, NOT TO BE SEEN AGAIN UNTIL PLANT RECEIVES TRAIN OF EMPTIES AND BEGINS LOADING.

(5) TRAIN OF EMPTIES EMERGES FROM DOCK BRANCH, TO CIRCLE MAIN LINE OVAL AND EVENTUALLY RETURN, VIA BALLOON TRACK, TO LOADING PLANT.

(6) MISCELLANEOUS NON-ORE FREIGHT (BENTONITE FOR PELLETIZING TACONITE, COAL FOR PLANT POWER, ETC.) RECEIVED FROM CONNECTIONS ("FIDDLE YARD") BY LOCAL FREIGHT, TAKEN VIA CROSSOVER & LEFT-HAND TRACK TO PLANT SPURS.

(7) ONLY RUN-AROUND TRACK ON RAILROAD, NEEDED TO SERVE SOME SPURS.

Fig. 3-18. Top-level trackage.

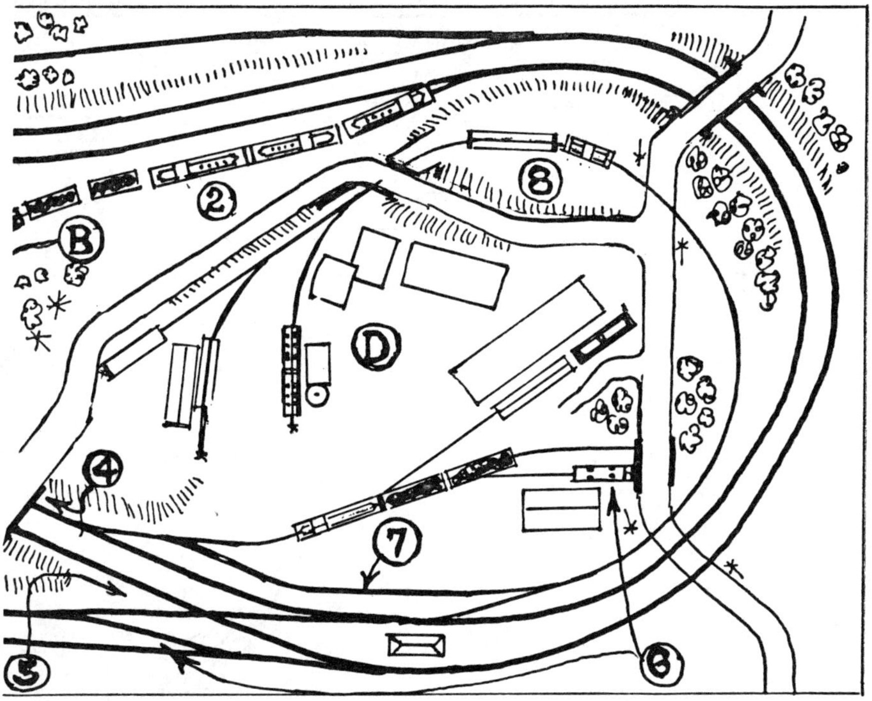

SCENIC-TREATMENT NOTES:

(A) UNIT-TRAIN ORIGINATING OR TERMINATING FACILITY—MINE, PROCESSING PLANT, TRANSHIPMENT TERMINAL, POWER PLANT OR WHATEVER. TACONITE ORE PELLETIZING PLANT SHOWN — IF RECEIVING PLANT, FLIP ENTIRE PLAN (MIRROR IMAGE) TO PRESERVE RIGHT-HAND RUNNING ON MAIN LINES. EASY-GRADE RUN THROUGH PLANT FOR LOADED TRAIN.

(B) "ENVIRONMENTAL BARRIERS" SEPARATING PLANT FROM NEIGHBORS (ALSO HELPS EMPHASIZE BALLOON-TRACK LOOP SERVING PLANT — THE ONE SITUATION WHERE THE TOY-TRAIN LOOP IS FOR REAL AND CAN BE LEFT OUT IN THE OPEN.

(C) USUAL SNEAKY DISAPPEARANCES OF MAIN TRACKS, MADE A LITTLE MORE CHALLENGING BY FACT RAILROAD WILL BE OBSERVED FROM ABOVE.

(D) INDUSTRIAL AREA, TO SUIT TRAFFIC DESIRED IN LOCAL FREIGHT.

---

(8) EXTRA-SHARP TRACKAGE — SMALLER SWITCHER MAY BE REQUIRED (AAH—EXTRA VARIETY!) TO SERVE INDUSTRIAL SPURS IN THIS AREA.

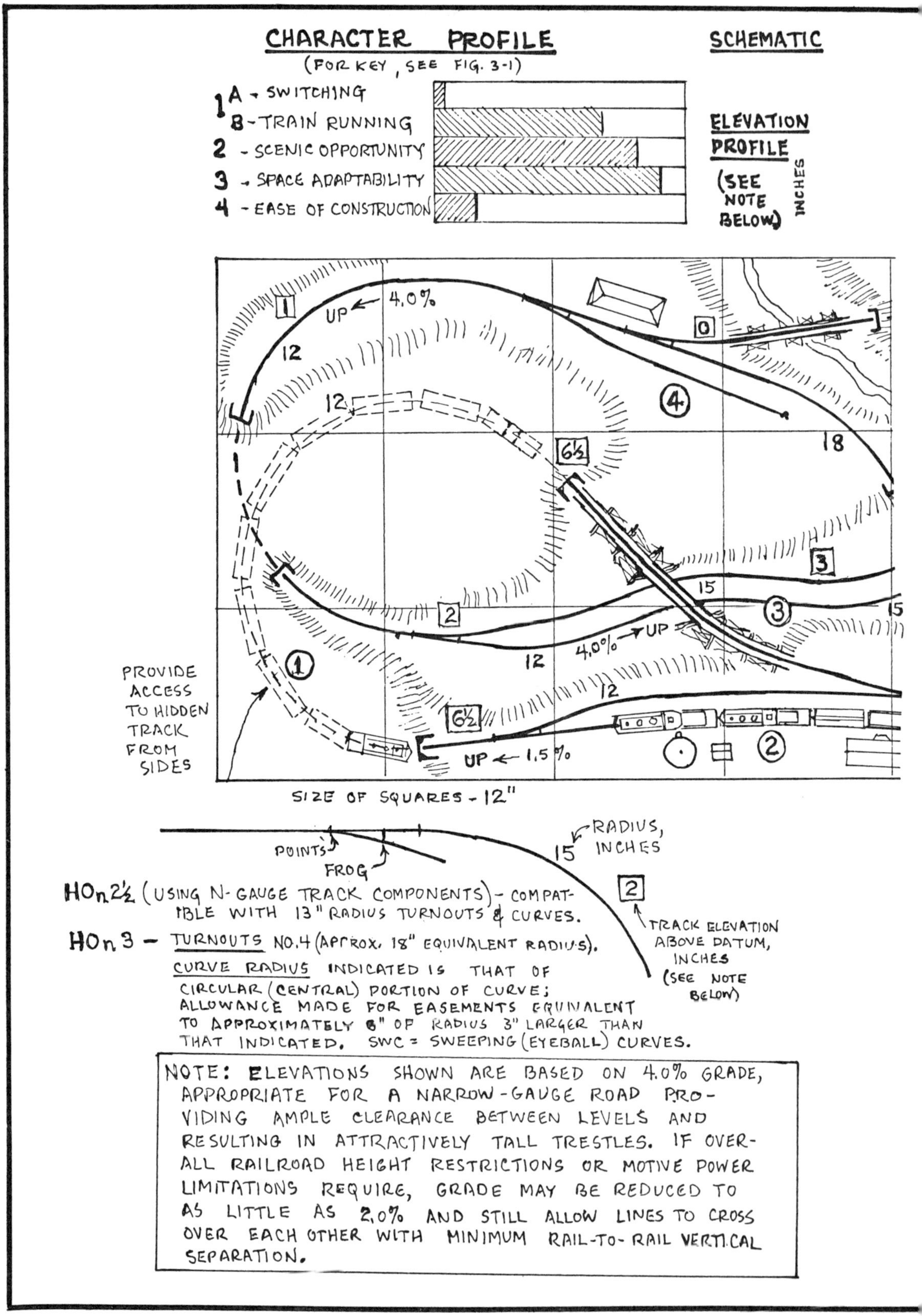

Fig. 3-19. The Coffee Table Upper Limit track plan for HOn3 gauge.

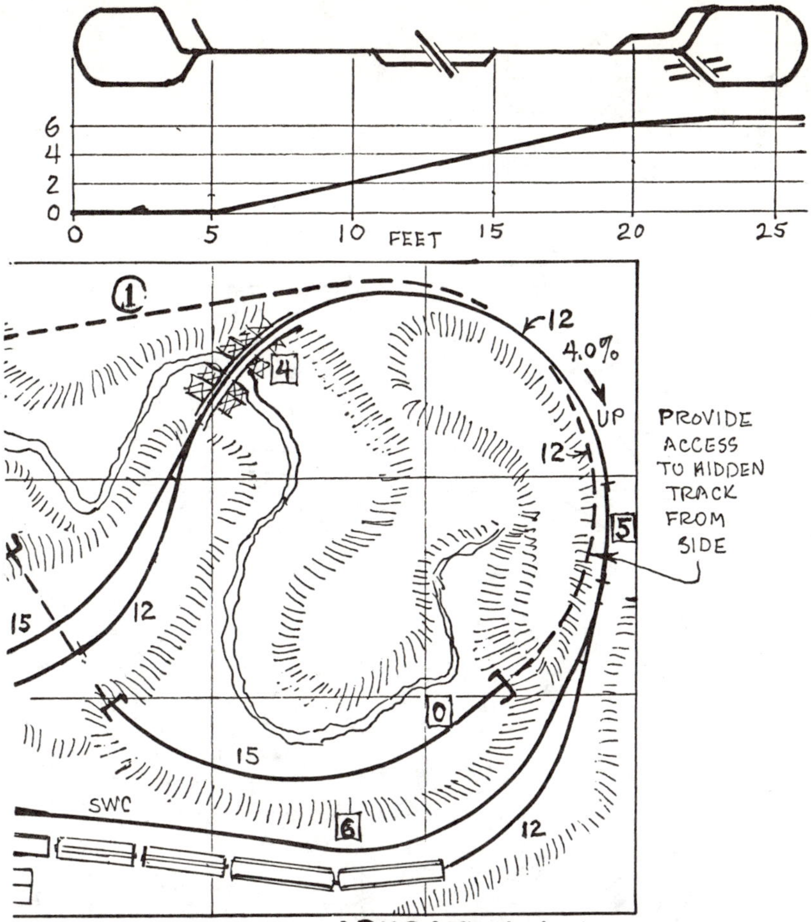

OPERATIONAL NOTES:

1. CONCEALED PORTIONS OF END LOOPS LONG ENOUGH TO HIDE NORMAL-LENGTH TRAINS BETWEEN RUNS, AVOID CROWDED APPEARANCE.
2. DOUBLE-HEADED SIX-CAR MIXED TRAIN — ONE OF THE BEAUTIES OF 4% GRADES ON THE NARROW GAUGE WITH SMALL (2-6-0, 2-8-0) POWER.
3. PASSING TRACK ENOUGH SHORTER THAN ONE AT TOP OF HILL TO CAUSE SOME SAW-BY MEETS.
4. ROOM FOR SOME EXPANSION OF TRACKAGE, TO PROVIDE ENGINE SERVICING, LIVESTOCK LOADING, MINING/LOADING OR OTHER DESIRED FACILITIES.

SCENIC-TREATMENT NOTE:

AS A COFFEE-TABLE RAILROAD, SCENIC CONTOURS SUGGESTED ARE GENERALLY "CONCAVE", FOR VIEWING PRIMARILY FROM ABOVE. IF BUILT AS A MORE CONVENTIONAL PIKE, SET AT A MUCH HIGHER ELEVATION FROM FLOOR LEVEL AND VIEWED FROM THE SIDES, A "CONVEX" APPROACH WITH A CENTRAL RIDGE WOULD BE PREFERABLE.

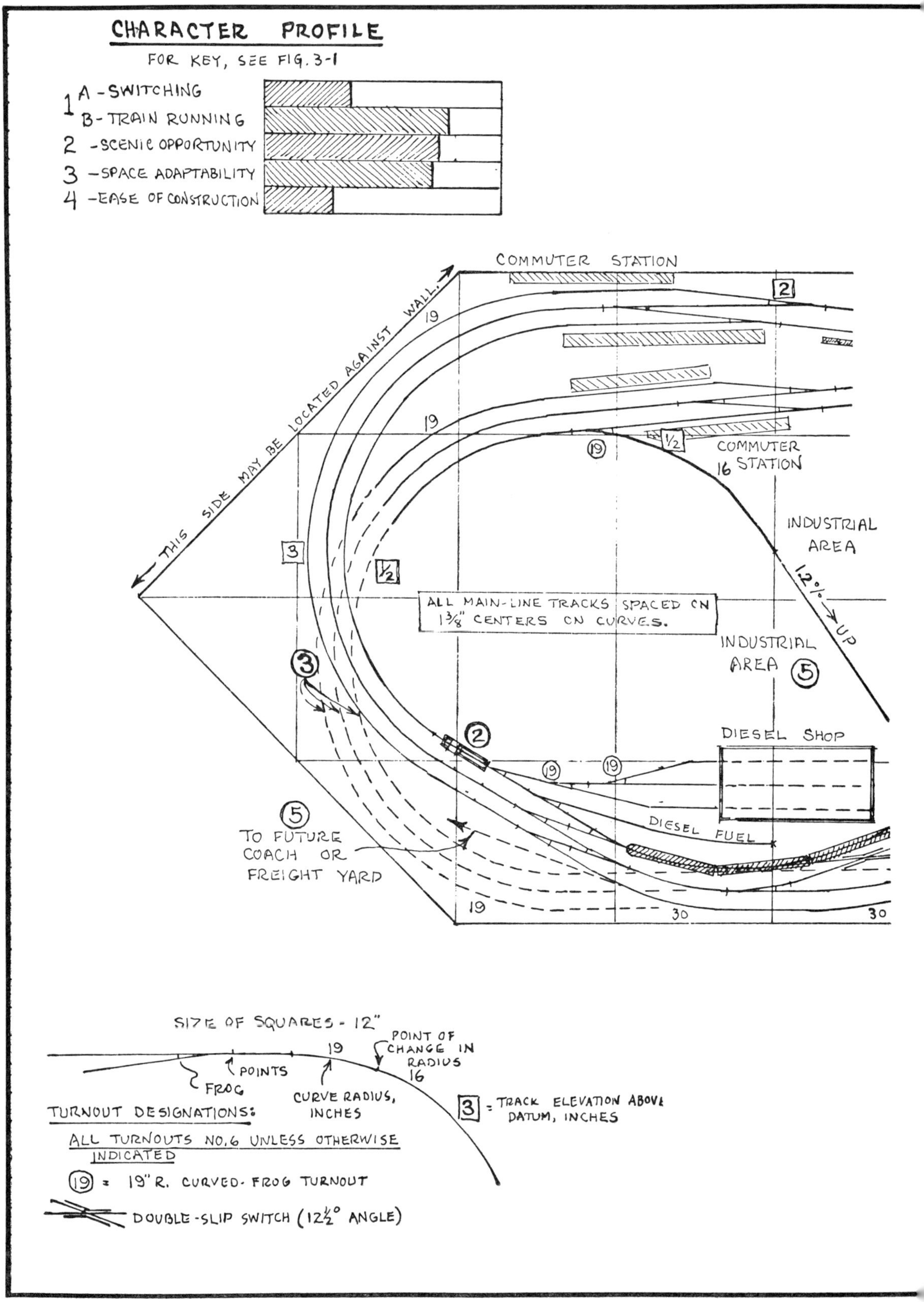

Fig. 3-20. Grand Central Junior track plan for N gauge.

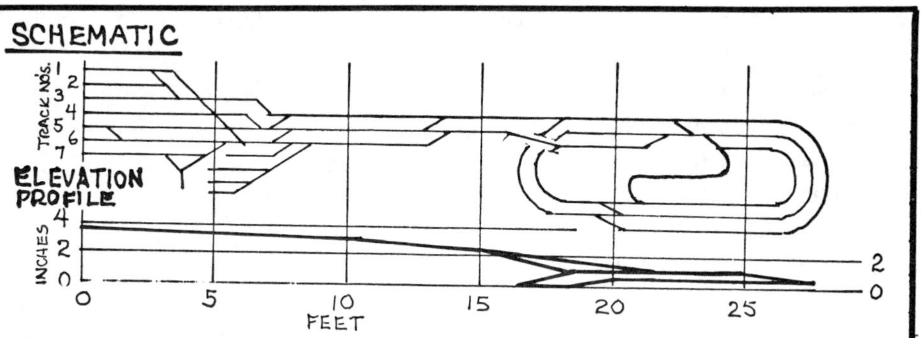

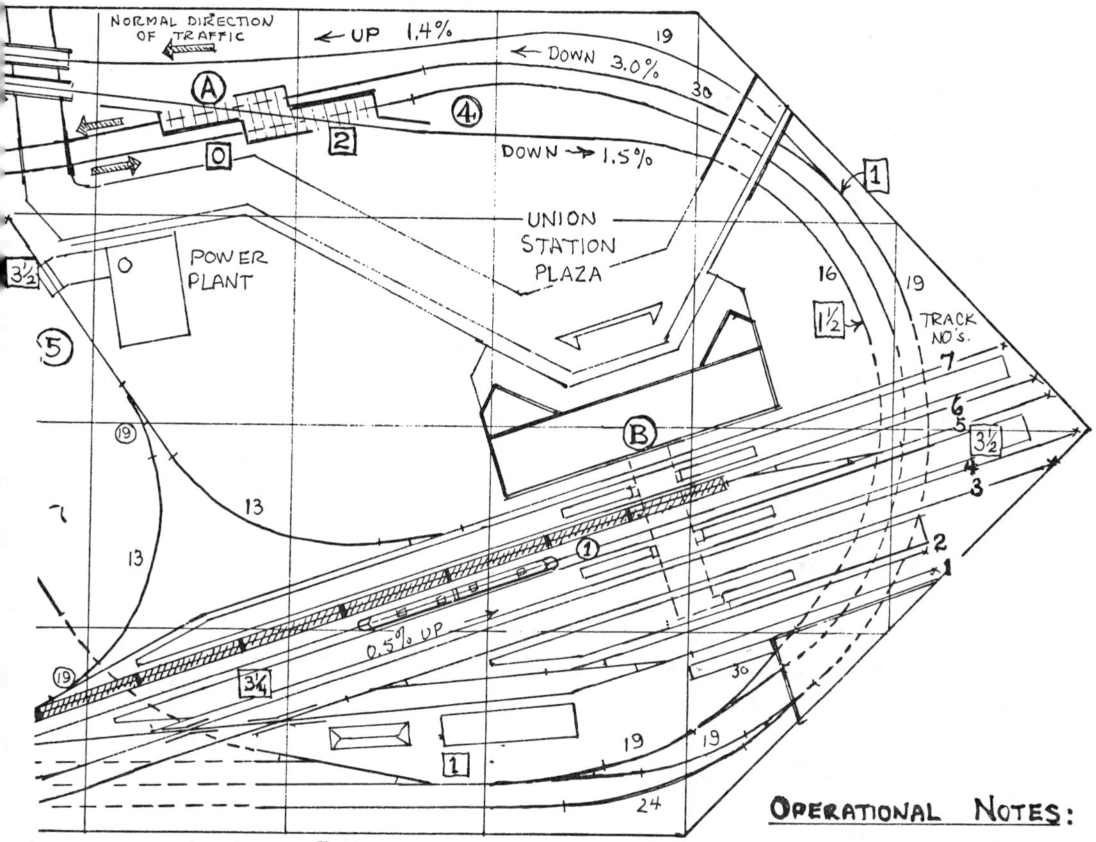

Operational Notes:

① Two-unit road diesel returning to fuel track after cutting off from arriving passenger train (ten 85 ft. cars).

② Switcher ready to push passenger train up to bumping post of track 6, clear crossovers in station throat.

③ Triple-track section of main-line serves to provide out-of sight layover/storage capacity – electrical sub-division to allow two trains/track recommended.

④ "Flying junction" connection between station approach tracks and double-track main; no track crossings at grade.

⑤ Additional freight, switching operations with sharply-curved yard, industrial trackage in these areas when & if desired.

Scenic-Treatment Notes:

Ⓐ "Abutment" bridges carry track over main line at shallow angle.

Ⓑ Subway to station platforms from low-level station preferable to overhead concourse because it leaves trains more visible, but room is available for either.

3-16). But no home is too small to accommodate it and there's room for scenery.

A fiddle yard addition greatly improves the versatility and should be built as part of the original construction if it's desired.

Size: 2 × 4 ft. (alternate 2½ × 5)
Gauge: N
Curvature standards: extra sharp (alternate sharp)
Schematic: twice-around oval
Recommended construction: cookie-cutter
Trackwork options: all trackwork items standard, including sectional-radius curves; one section of next-size-larger radius included at start of all extra sharp curves to provide some degree of easement and improve appearance with too-long rolling stock, which will inevitably be used sooner or later

LONG TRAINS FOR THE COFFEE TABLE

Figure 3-17 synchronizes movements of one empty and one loaded train of open-top cars to create the illusion of loading or unloading unit train as it passes through the plant. Trains can operate continuously over main line ovals between cycles through the plant, with only four turnouts involved. Use of short ore cars allows 25 to 40-car trains. There is minimal local freight and industrial district switching. For a top view see Fig. 3-18.

As an alternative to the industrial district, a plant railroad bringing raw ore from an open-pit mine (as in Fig. 3-11) to the processing plant can be worked in, with extra sharp curves and perhaps an empties-one-way, loads-the-other feature.

Size: 2½ × 6½ ft.
Gauge: N
Curvature standards: sharp and extra sharp
Schematic: two ovals, each with alternate route, arranged as double track with single interconnection
Recommended construction: cookie-cutter
Trackwork options: all trackwork components standard (mixed brands); curves standard except for some sweeping bends; curvable recommended

THE COFFEE TABLE UPPER LIMIT

This relatively long main line (Fig. 3-19) represents a typically mountainous section of a Western narrow-gauge line through sparsely-settled and sparsely-vegetated country. There's light traffic density, with no more than two trains in evidence at any one time.

There is room for a few more side tracks, even a small turntable for the helper engines, but not much more if the uncrowded flavor is to be maintained.

Size: 3 × 7 ft.
Gauge: HOn3 or HOn2½
Curvature standards: sharp (for narrow gauge)
Schematic: loop-to-loop
Recommended construction: cookie-cutter
Trackwork options:
HOn3: compatible with use of curvable prefabricated or hand-laid track and standard No. 4 turnouts (Fig. 1-22)
HOn2½: HO scale running on N-gauge track; compatible, with minor adjustments, with use of 13/14 in. radius sectional track and 13 in. radius curved-frog turnouts; curvable or hand-laid track preferable

GRAND CENTRAL JUNIOR

This plan (Fig. 3-20) shows an all-out emphasis on a realistic representation of a big-city passenger terminal with through and commuter service, primarily with double-ended motive power or trains. There's limited capability (wye) for turning engines. The curvature accommodates full-length passenger equipment attractively. The flying junction with moderate grades provides for heavy-traffic connection between double-track lines.

Size: 4 × 10 ft. "Monitor"—32 square ft.
Gauge: N
Curvature standards: broad and super-broad
Schematic: combination stub terminal to continuous oval with single reversing connection, multiple track
Recommended construction: cookie-cutter; basic shape represents rearrange-

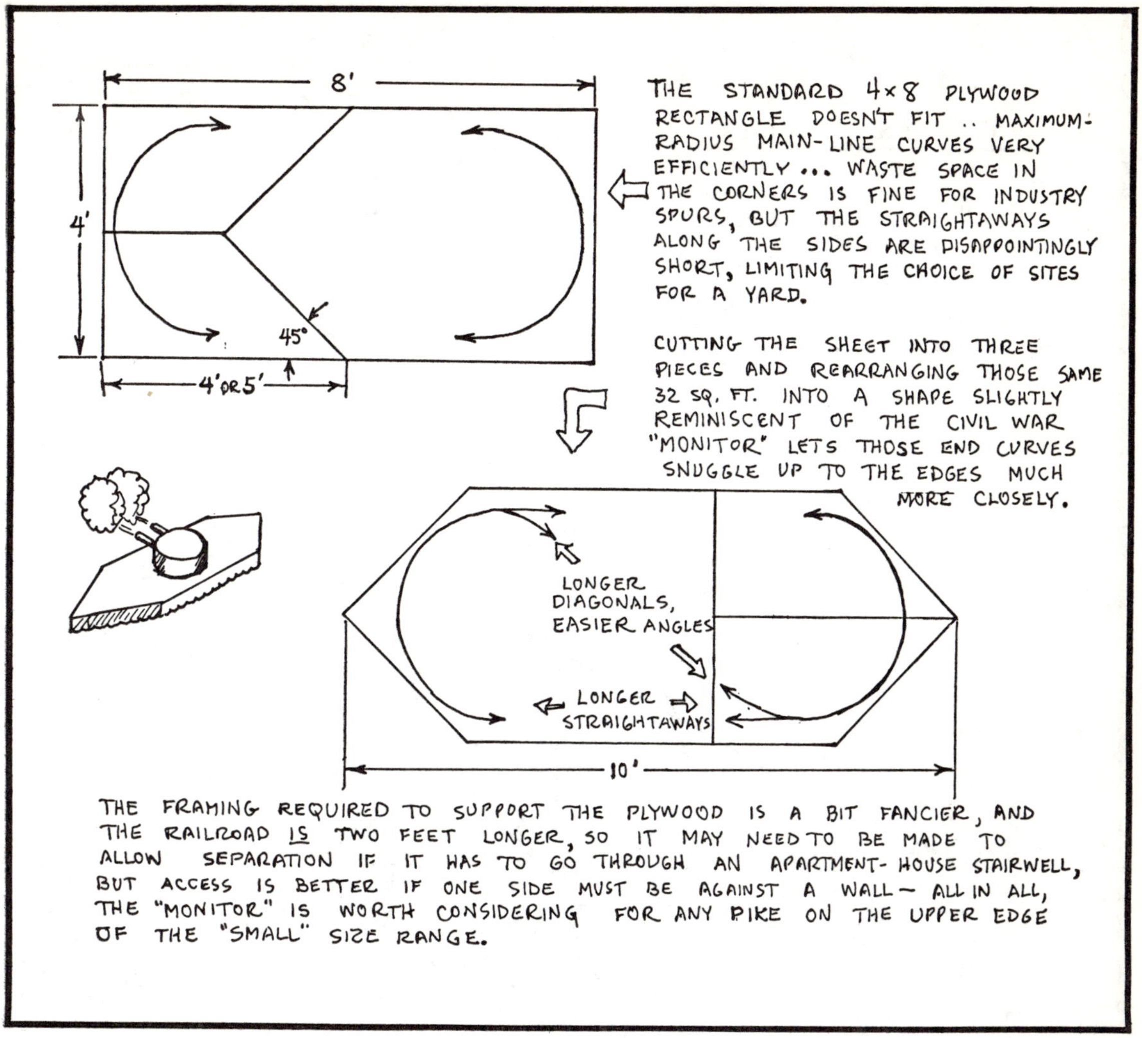

Fig. 3-21. Rearranging those square feet.

ment of standard 4 × 8 plywood sheet to make better use of material in corners (Fig. 3-21)

Trackwork options: all trackwork elements standard; curvable track recommended for multiple-track lines; double slip switches used for realistically compact station throat trackage, on straight-through alignment to minimize any tracking problems; super-broad standards wherever consists of long cars may have to be pushed

CENTENNIAL PEAK BRANCH

This plan (Fig. 3-22) shows a classic narrow-gauge mining railroad in rugged country, with two changes in train consist necessary as grade changes from river grade to long 3 percent climb followed by final 6 percent switchback to the big concentrator, source of most of the line's tonnage. Few trains are long enough to make full use of tractive force of at least two engines, but careful dispatching is required because of the long run between passing points. The curves are adequate for good appearance of any typical narrow gauge freight or passenger rolling stock. The operation is tricky because cars will run away on steep grades if given the slightest opportunity! A top-level view is shown in Fig. 3-23.

Size: 4 × 10 ft. "Monitor"—32 sq. ft.
Gauge: HOn3
Curvature standards: conventional (for narrow gauge)

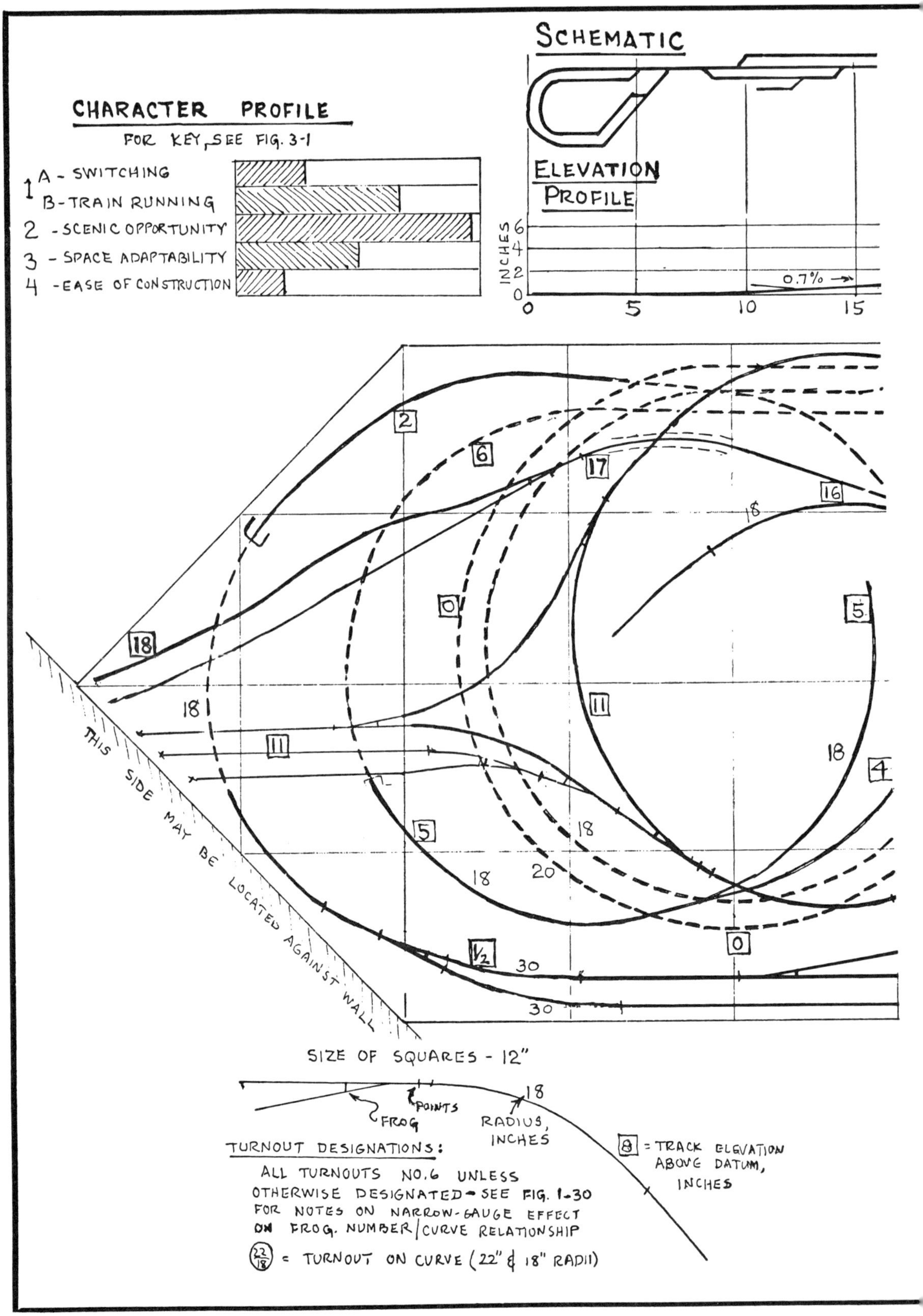

Fig. 3-22. The Centennial Peak Branch track plan for HOn3 gauge.

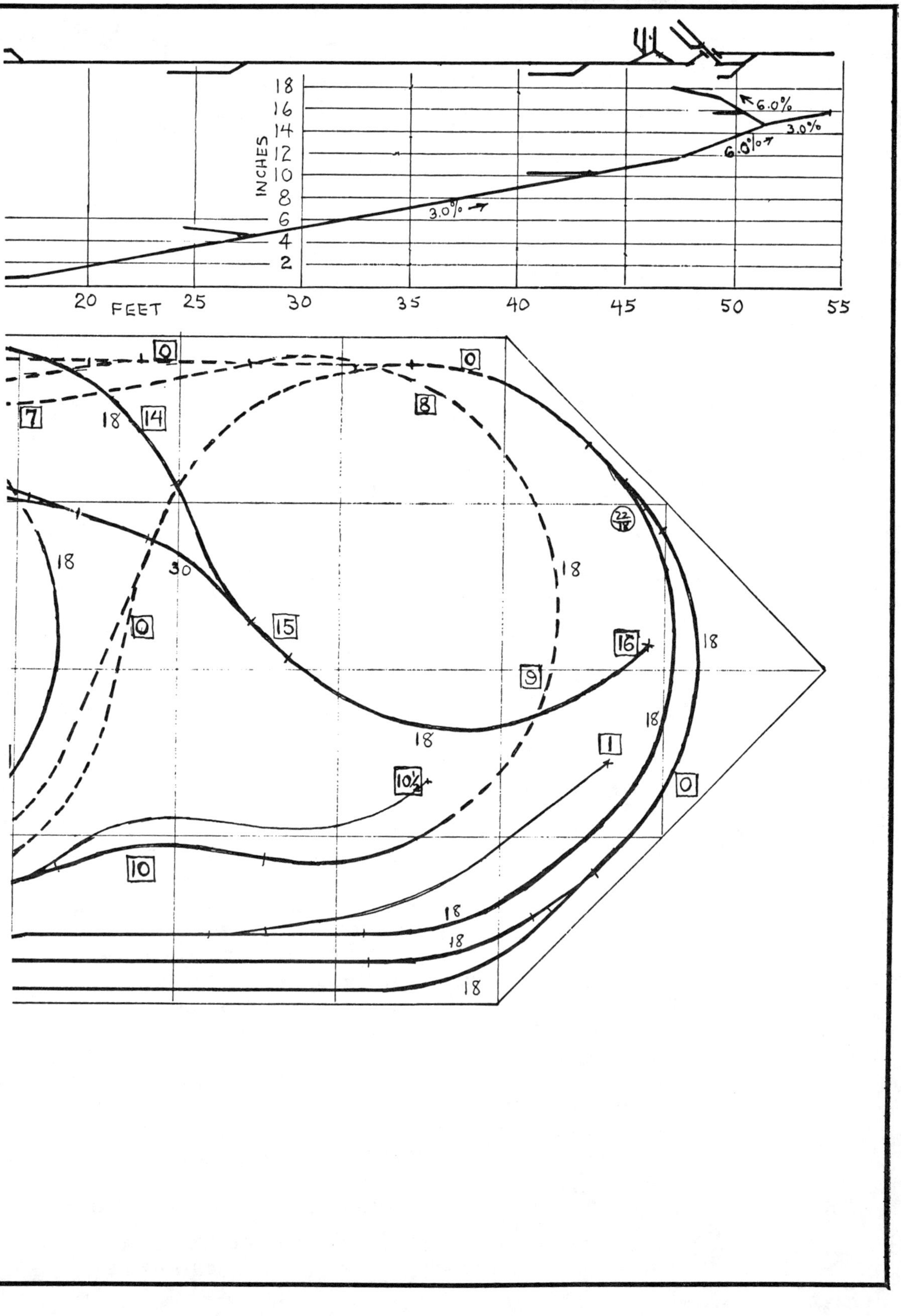

INCHES
18
16
14
12
10
8
6
4
2
FEET
20
25
30
35
40
45
50
55
6.0%
3.0%
6.0%
3.0%
0
0
7
18
14
8
22/18
18
18
30
18
0
15
16
18
9
18
18
1
10½
0
10
18
18
18

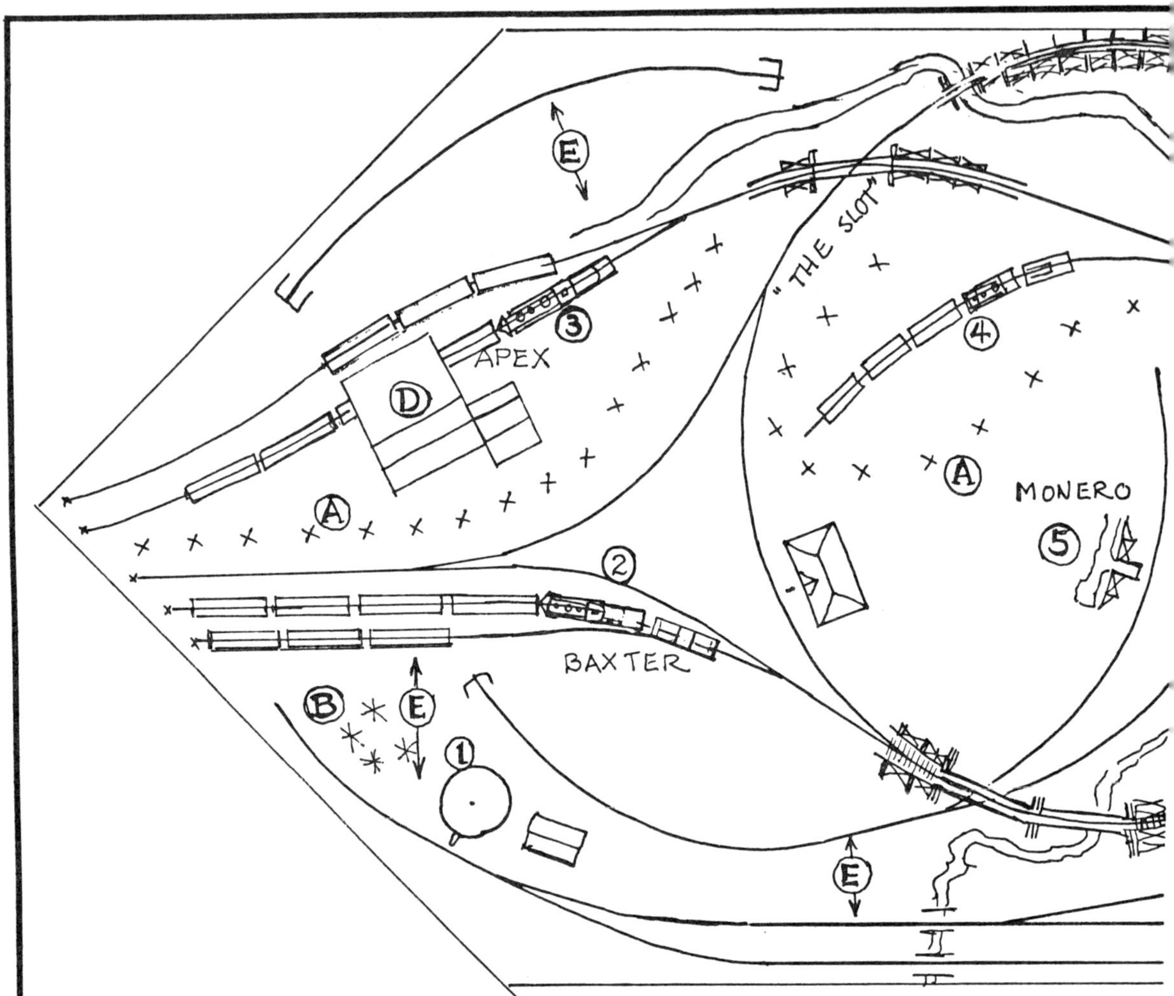

OPERATIONAL NOTES:

(1) LONG, DOUBLE-HEADED TRAIN ARRIVES AT LOBATO FROM HIDDEN, LOWEST-LEVEL LOOP. CARS SET OUT TO REDUCE TONNAGE FOR 3% GRADE. HELPER ENGINE MOVED TO REAR END; COAL & WATER TAKEN.

(2) TRAIN SPLIT AT BAXTER – ROAD ENGINE TURNS ON WYE, PULLS FIRST CUT OF CARS BACKWARD UP 6% TO SWITCHBACK AT REVUELTA. PUSHER SETS OUT REAR CUTS IN BAXTER SPUR, TURNS ON WYE FOR RETURN TRIP.

(3) ROAD ENGINE SETS EMPTIES INTO APEX CONCENTRATOR LOADING TRACK; LOADS ALLOWED TO ROLL PAST ENGINE TOWARD REVUELTA, WHERE UPGRADE STOPS THEM ON TAIL TRACK. ENGINE PRECEDES CARS ON 6% DESCENT TO BAXTER, WHERE DOWNHILL TRAIN IS MADE UP FROM ACCUMULATED LOADS.

(4) MINING CO. SWITCHER SHUTTLES CARS OF WASTE TO DUMP.

(5) OTHER MOVEMENTS: COAL FROM MONERO TO LOBATO COAL DOCK, LIVESTOCK FROM MORO LOADING PENS.

Fig. 3-23. Top-level view only.

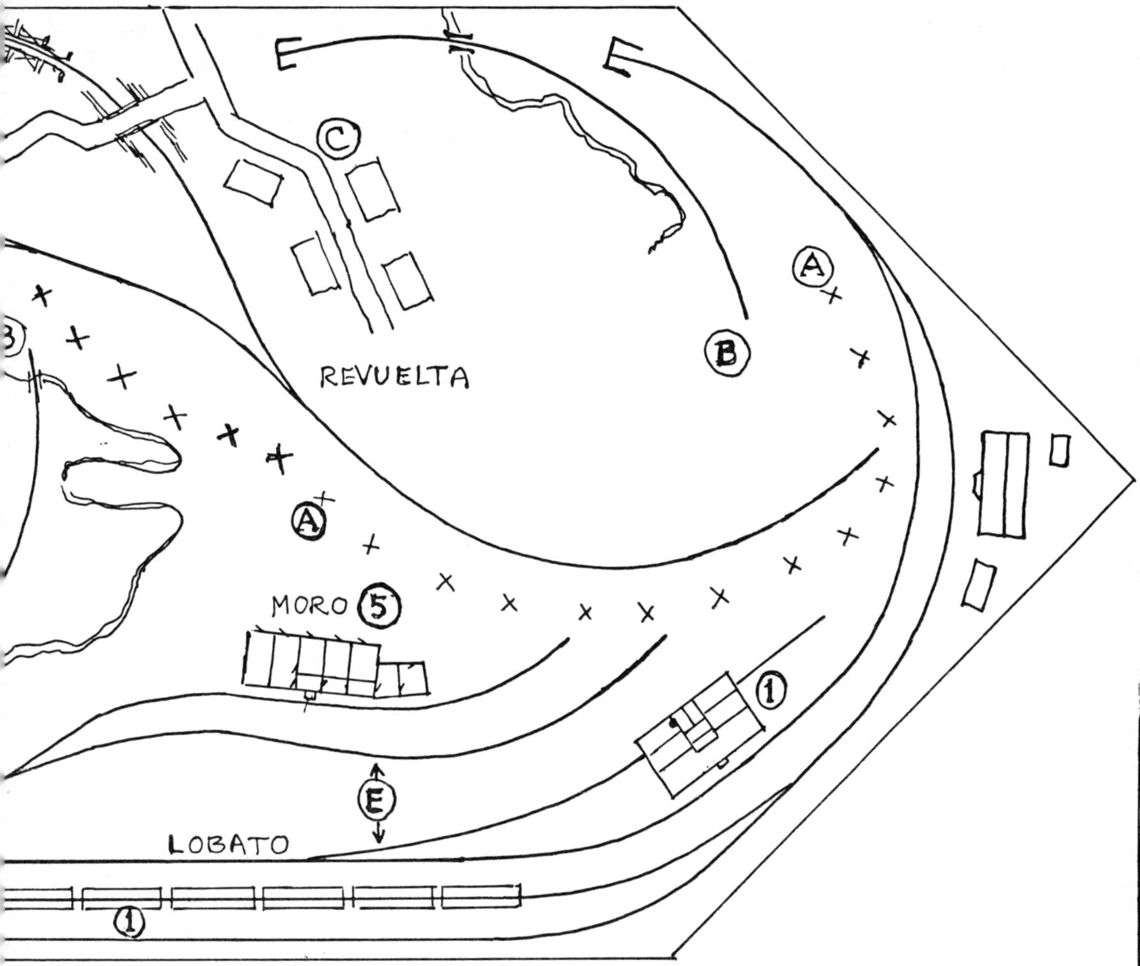

Scenic-Treatment Notes:

Ⓐ "CONTINENTAL DIVIDE" — MOUNTAIN RIDGE SCENICLY SEPARATES TWO SIDES OF LAYOUT: LOBATO-BAXTER ON ONE SIDE, REVUELTA-APEX AT HIGHER LEVEL ON OTHER, CONNECTED ONLY BY RAILROAD LINE THROUGH "THE SLOT."

Ⓑ WHEREVER PRACTICAL, TRACK DISAPPEARS AROUND CLIFF OR BEHIND TREES RATHER THAN INTO TUNNEL PORTAL.

Ⓒ MINING TOWN — GHOST OR VIOLENTLY ALIVE, AS APPPROPRIATE FOR TIME & PLACE.

Ⓓ LARGE SIDE-HILL ORE CONCENTIZATOR AND AUXILIARY BUILDINGS

Ⓔ SCENIC SEPARATION BETWEEN ADJACENT AREAS ACHIEVED BY VIOLENT DIFFERENCES IN ELEVATION RESULTING FROM STEEP GRADES ON RAILROAD, HIGHLY APPROPRIATE FOR NARROW GAUGE LINE.

Schematic: point-to-loop, with switchback
Recommended construction: open grid; extreme differences in elevation (up to 18 in. above datum) provide access from side or below to lower-level track and turnouts

Trackwork options: standard turnouts; curvable track recommended; priority addition if modest additional space available: turntable at Lobato for pusher locomotives, saving trip around hidden loop

4

Medium Size Track Plans

The average pike appears, from various polls, to occupy an area in the vicinity of 60 square feet, which is perhaps some justification for calling a model railroad in the 45 to 150 square foot (5 × 9 up to 10 × 15 ft. equivalent) range *medium size*. Possibilities really proliferate, with choices to be made between investing the extra space in more liberal curvature standards, less cramped scenery and more versatile operations—more trains, or longer ones.

Five by nine becomes a most popular size, partly because plywood for table-tennis tops is fairly widely available in 4½ × 5 ft. segments and more properly because that's about the largest *island* pike with a reasonably accessible center. The spare room railroad, in the most luxurious space of all especially if any interfering windows can be blanked out, is likely to provide about 100 square feet of which somewhat over 60 percent is useable without getting into "my arm's too short" trouble. Down in the basement, in the smallest gauges the cost is likely to be the factor keeping things down to such proportions. Per square foot, an N gauge railroad is a lot more expensive than HO, of course, and a modest but complete pike may well be more fun than an overextended empire.

Here are some of those medium-sized track plans that have proven most enjoyable over the years. Some grow into their full flowering from smaller beginnings, others can expand later into basement-fillers with a minimum of lost motion.

THE MEDIUM BIG TIME

This plan (Fig. 4-1) incorporates the same main-line philosophy as Fig. 3-4, but the increase in size allows the use of a radius accommodating all classes of rolling stock, larger engine terminal, passenger station, and optional (single direction) reversing connection. Trains can originate or terminate in a modest yard.

This is primarily an easily-constructed starter railroad, with trackage components readily useable on a later larger pike. There's room for considerable modification to the character of the railroad by expansion or reduction of engine servicing, passenger station, yard or industrial trackage and facilities.

Size: 5 × 10 ft. island or peninsula
Gauge: HO
Curvature standards: conventional
Schematic: multiple-track oval; single reversing connection optional
Recommended construction: flat top
Trackwork options: standard trackwork items; curvable track recommended for laying exactly parallel two- and three-track curves with easements

THE PRETZEL

This is the layout (Fig. 4-2) for the man who is satisified with running fairly short trains but wants the fun of running many of them. There's infinite variety in their many meeting and passing man-

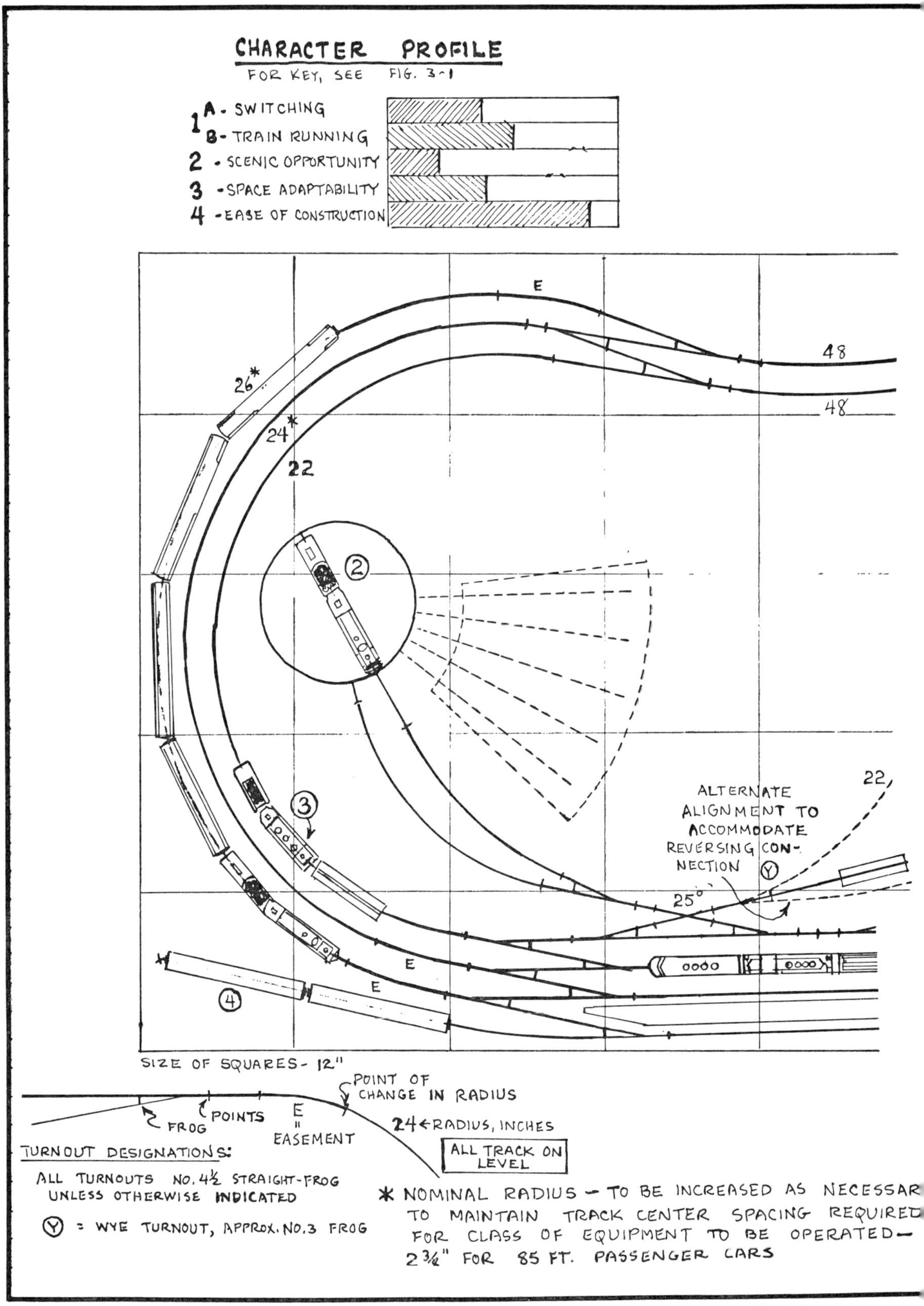

Fig. 4-1. The Medium Big Time track plan for HO gauge. For scenic treatment notes on this plan see Fig. 3-4.

OPERATIONAL NOTES

(1) DOUBLE-TRACK, RIGHT-HAND OPERATION ON MAIN LINE. CONVENTIONAL-RADIUS CURVES WITH SHORT EASEMENTS ALLOW OPERATION OF 85 FT. PASSENGER CARS AND APPROPRIATE LOCOMOTIVES WITH REASONABLY GOOD APPEARANCE.

(2) ROOM FOR UP TO 100 FT. TURNTABLE (87 FT. SHOWN) AND LONG-STALL ROUNDHOUSE — ALTERNATIVE: DIESEL SERVICING TRACKS

(3) SEE OPERATIONAL NOTE (3) ON FIG. 5-4 THIRD TRACK (SLIGHTLY SUB-STANDARD RADIUS) SERVES AS SWITCHING LEAD.

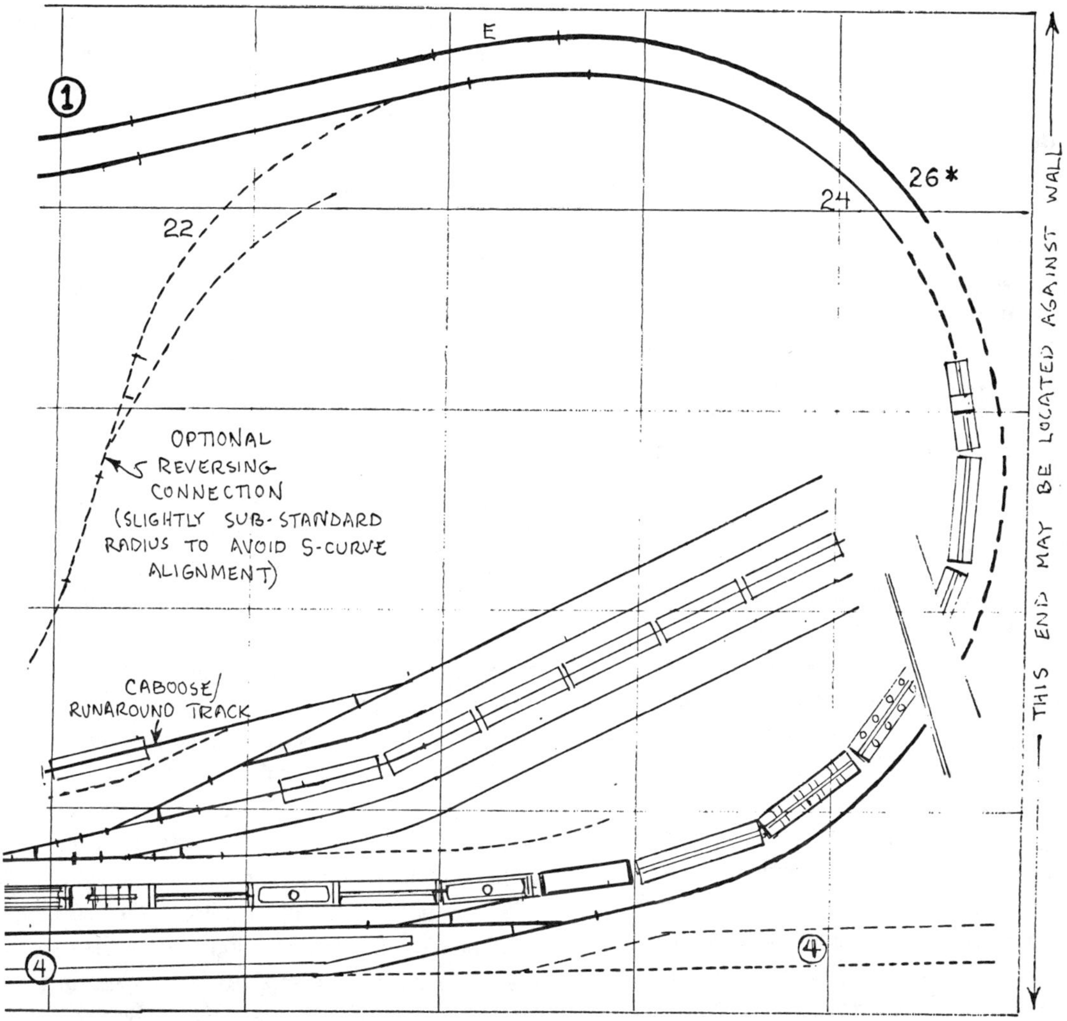

(4) PASSENGER PLATFORM, PASSENGER CAR SET-OUT SPUR AND EVEN ROOM FOR AN (OPTIONAL) TWO-TRACK "COACH YARD" FOR THOSE INTERESTED IN MORE REPRESENTATIVE VARNISH OPERATION.

euvers, not to mention the conflicting movements that all those crossings introduce!

For further development the large area can absorb almost limitless attention to detail in building and installing structures in matching scenic settings. Since a flat top railroad such as this can be dismantled and its components reused in a more complex layout with very little loss or wastage, that's usually the best route to follow should this pike ever be fully "completed."

Size: 8 × 12 L (two 4 × 8 rectangles) island or in corner
Gauge: HO
Curvature standards: sharp; extra sharp on some spur tracks
Schematic: twisted oval with crossings at grade; single track
Recommended construction: flat top
Trackwork options: all trackwork components standard; curvable track recommended for parallel tracks on curves and sweeping curves where they can improve appearance without wasting space

A PROGRESSIVE PIKE TRILOGY

The next three plans illustrate the development of a layout designed to be built and operated in stages. The first-stage pike (Fig. 4-3) is a middle-of-the-roader, with a small yard, out-and-back train-running possibilities, and a single-track main line that can keep two short trains moving. For its 4½ × 10 ft. size, it provides as much HO operating variety as you can expect on a flat-top railroad. From the beginning, or later on if you choose, its scenic possibilities can be enhanced by making it into a cookie-cutter job, with differences in track elevation and moderate grades for the trains to climb. Should expansion be indefinitely postponed, the *Happy Acorn* will continue to provide railroading fun.

The two follow-on plan examples (Fig. 4-4, 4-6) illustrate expansion in two radically different directions. The *Long, Long Trail* goes after a lot of single-track running, with trains of about the same length as those suitable for its predecessor, while its double-track alternative accommodates long trains by eliminating the necessity for fitting consists into passing tracks. There's an angle, though. Interlacing trackage at three levels to allow for long terminal tracks provides an excuse for a 4 percent grade on the branch leading to the main line. It'll take a pusher to get the heavy ones out of the yard, so that crossover designed to let engines escape from incoming trains is also useful in getting the helper engine behind the caboose when leaving town.

Pikes which grow to 16 to 18 ft. lengths usually encounter obstacles, so these plans illustrate the possibilities that come from bending a plan into an L—either the *concave* variety that fits into a corner, or the less-often-encountered *convex* configuration that wraps *around* a corner to make good use of otherwise-wasted areas fairly typical of finished basements. Either plan can be bent out straight if a longer, and generally more desirable from an access standpoint, space is available.

THE LIMITS OF SHARP CURVES

Track plans that can be built in stages are highly desirable. A close look at these plans will show that most of the first-stage trackage remains in place, so a minimum of the labor it represents is lost. Progressively-built pikes that start out within an area limiting their main-line trackage to sharp-radius curves do pose a problem, though. No matter how big the railroad ultimately becomes, its rolling stock will have to be able to get around those same curves unless the original part is completely rebuilt. These plans provide easements for all important main-line curves, so their expanded versions represent the best in model railroading operation and appearance that can be achieved within the sharp-curve format.

For dieselized, primarily-freight railroading this limitation may not be serious. Nevertheless, if there are good prospects for developing into a large pike, such as half-garage size or bigger, conventional or broad curvature is usually a better choice for the first stage, and the plans in Fig. 4-4 and 4-6 are about as large as they come in sharp-curve railroading. Without the easements, these plans would represent severely restricted use of the space, time and money.

THE HAPPY ACORN

Yard capacity at this stage (Fig. 4-3) is sacrificed in favor of capability for running and ter-

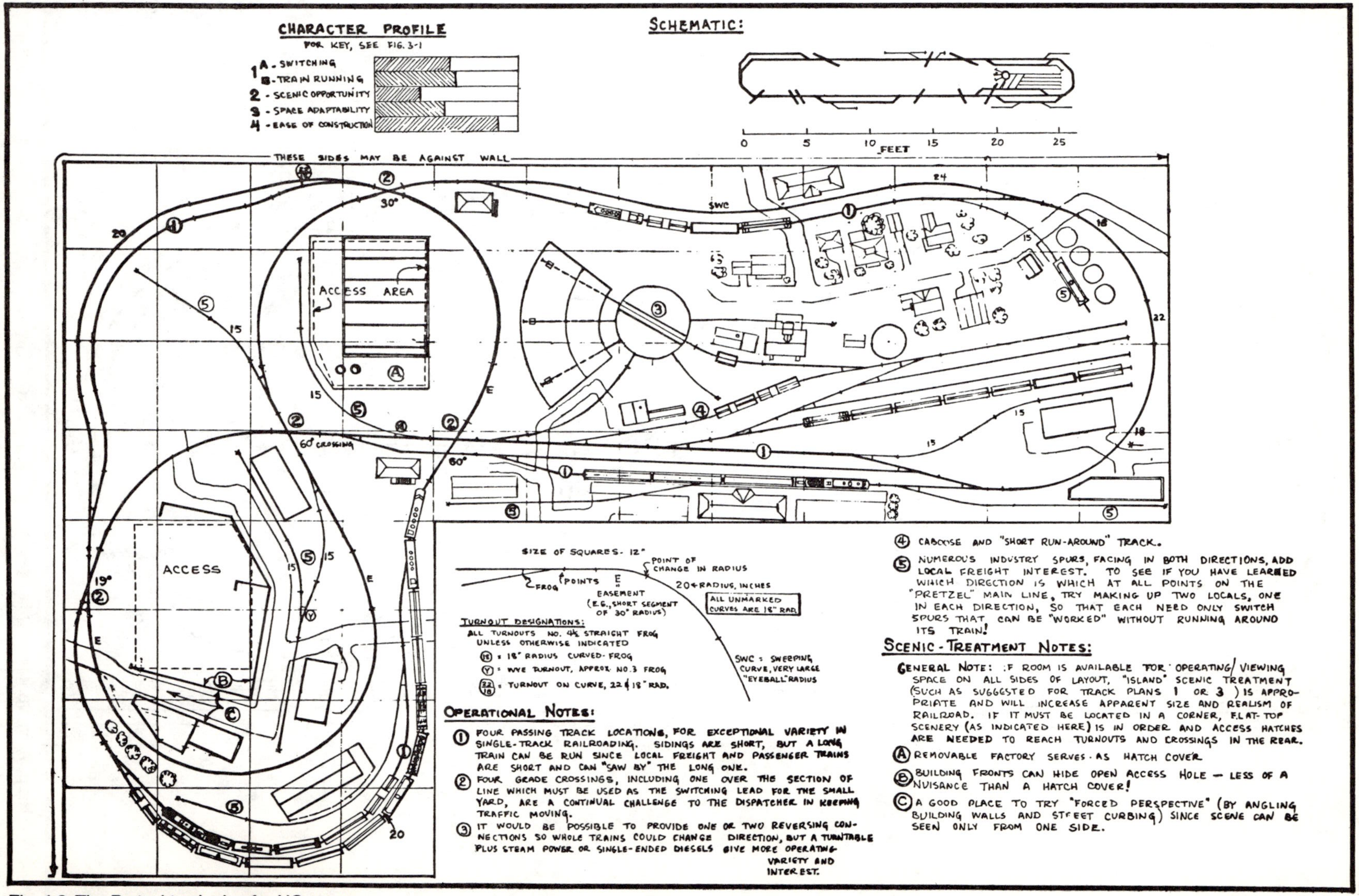

Fig. 4-2. The Pretzel track plan for HO gauge.

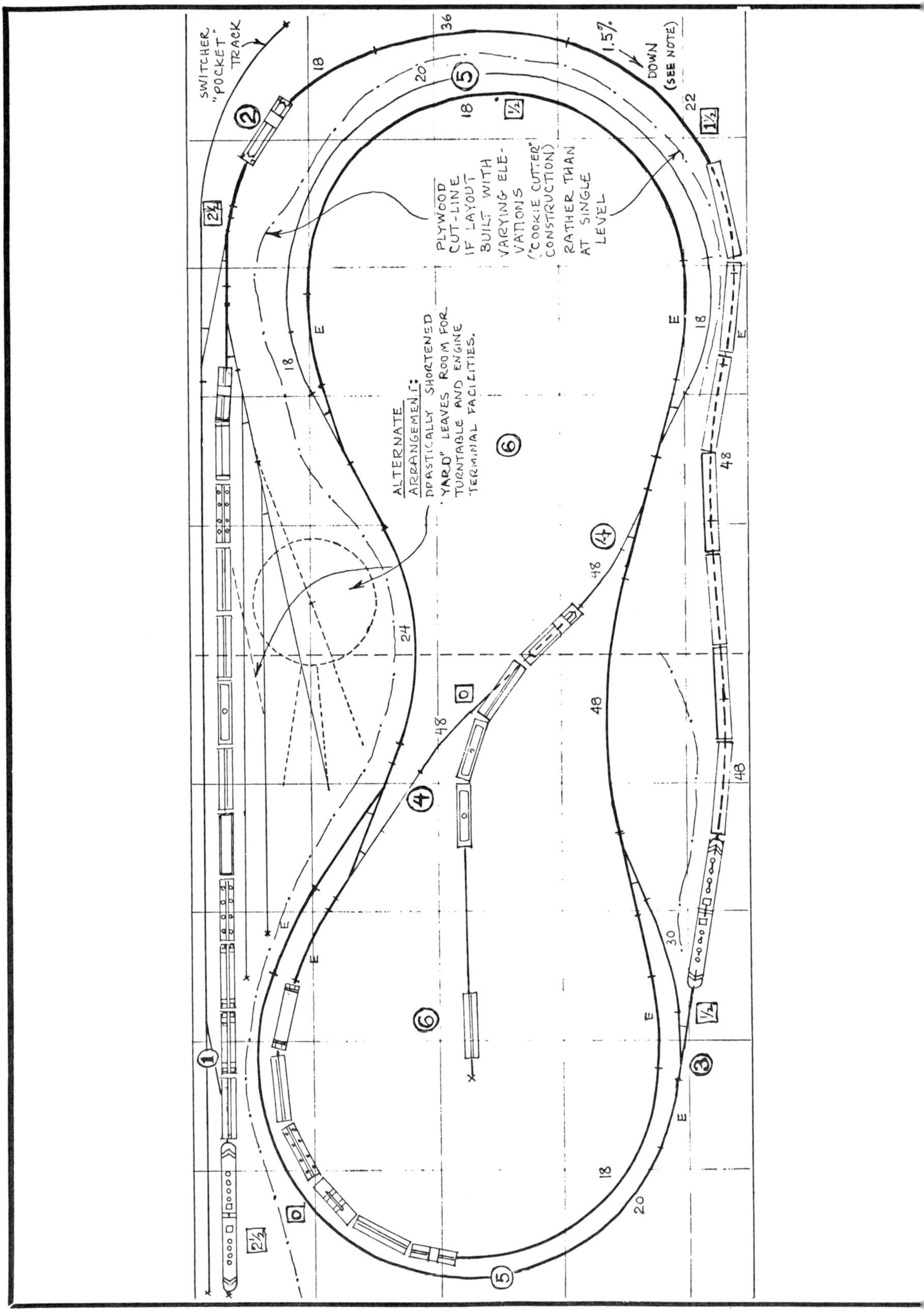

Fig. 4-3. The Happy Acorn track plan for HO gauge.

CHARACTER PROFILE

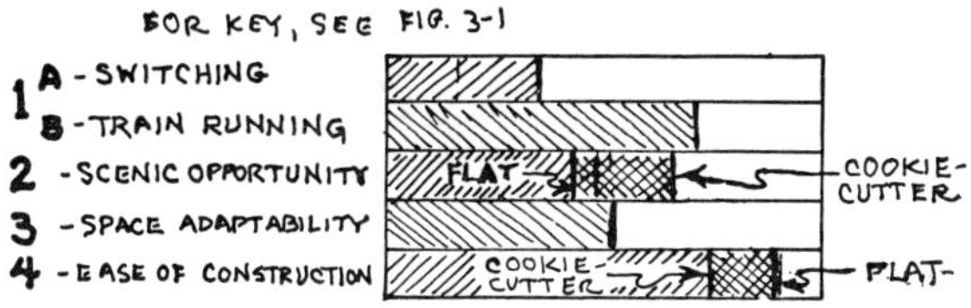

SCHEMATIC:

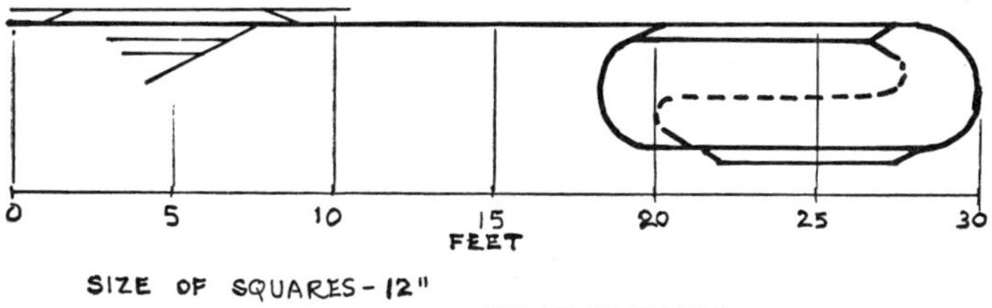

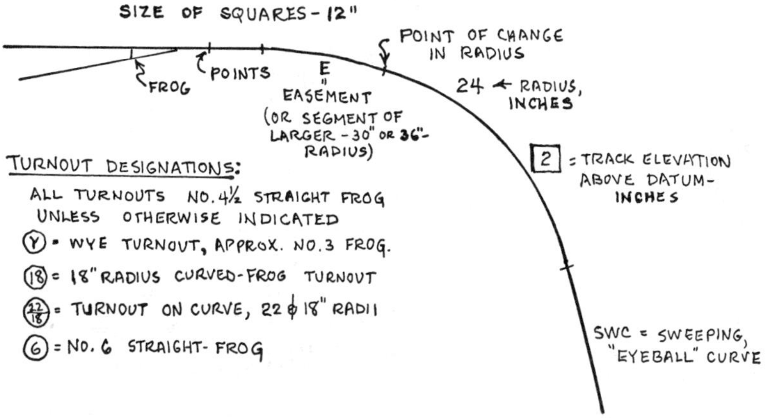

OPERATIONAL NOTES:

① RUN-AROUND CROSSOVER ONE ENGINE-LENGTH FROM BUMPERS LETS TRAINS UP TO ABOUT NINE CARS RELEASE LOCOMOTIVE IN A SINGLE MOVE. AFTER ARRIVING AT TERMINAL.

② SWITCH EMERGES FROM "POCKET" TO SWITCH LONGER ARRIVING CONSISTS. "YARD" CAPACITY EXTREMELY LIMITED.

③ JUNCTION WITH MAIN LINE OVAL — A FAIRLY LONG RUN FROM TERMINAL, AND SO CONNECTED THAT TRAIN OFF BRANCH CANNOT DIRECTLY ENTER THE...

④ SINGLE REVERSING CONNECTION. IN DIRECTION TO ALLOW OUT-AND-BACK OPERATION FROM TERMINAL.

⑤ PASSING TRACKS APPROXIMATELY AS LONG AS TERMINAL RUN-AROUND, BUT ENOUGH DIFFERENT IN CAPACITY TO MAKE THE DISPATCHER KEEP TRAIN LENGTHS IN MIND IN PLANNING MEETS.

⑥ AMPLE ROOM FOR INDUSTRY-TRACK DEVELMENT — IF RAILROAD ACCESSIBLE FROM ONLY ONE SIDE, ACCESS HATCHES ARE NEEDED IN THESE AREAS.

SCENIC-TREATMENT NOTES:

BEST SCENIC TREATMENT DEPENDS ON WHETHER LAYOUT IS AGAINST WALL OR IS A FREE-STANDING "ISLAND." IN FIRST CASE, ACCESS HATCHES OR OPENINGS (HIDDEN BY SCENERY OR STRUCTURES) ARE NEEDED AND ALL TERRAIN SHOULD BE PLANNED FOR VIEWING FROM OPEN (YARD) SIDE. FOR ISLAND PIKE, CENTRAL VIEW-BLOCK APPROACH (SEE FIG. 3-2 j)

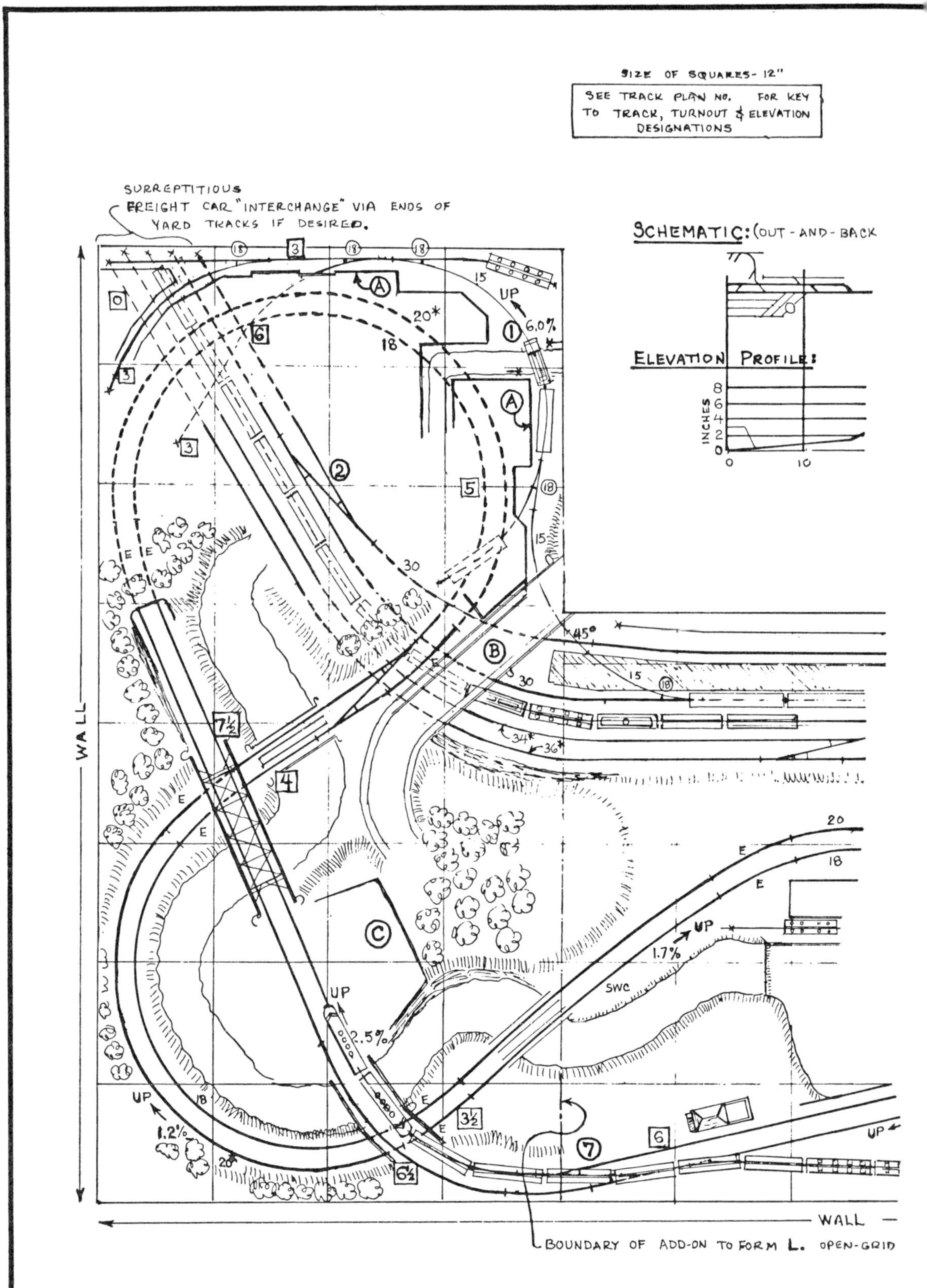

Fig. 4-4. Long Trains with a Push track plan for HO gauge. For operational notes, see Fig. 4-5.

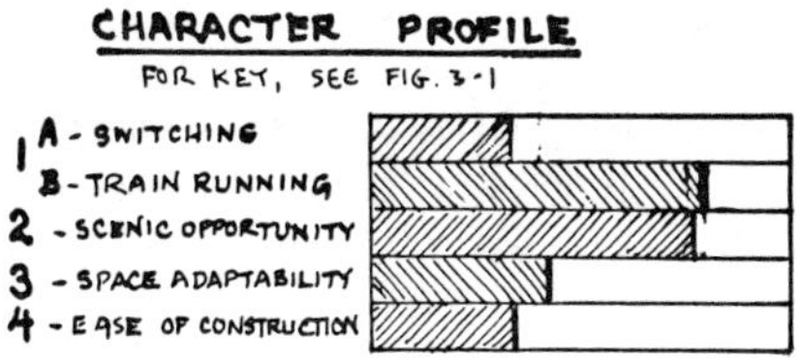

TRIP ILLUSTRATED)

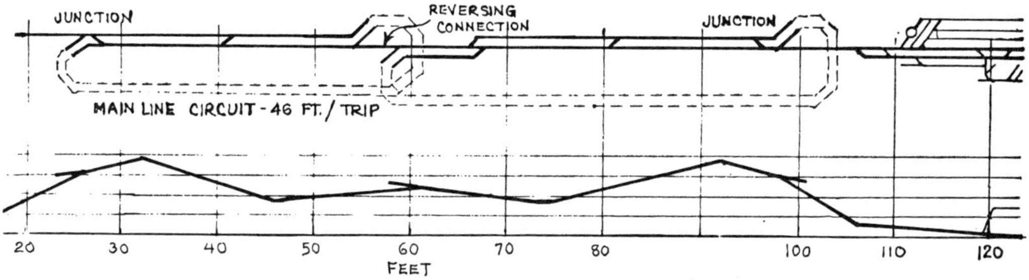

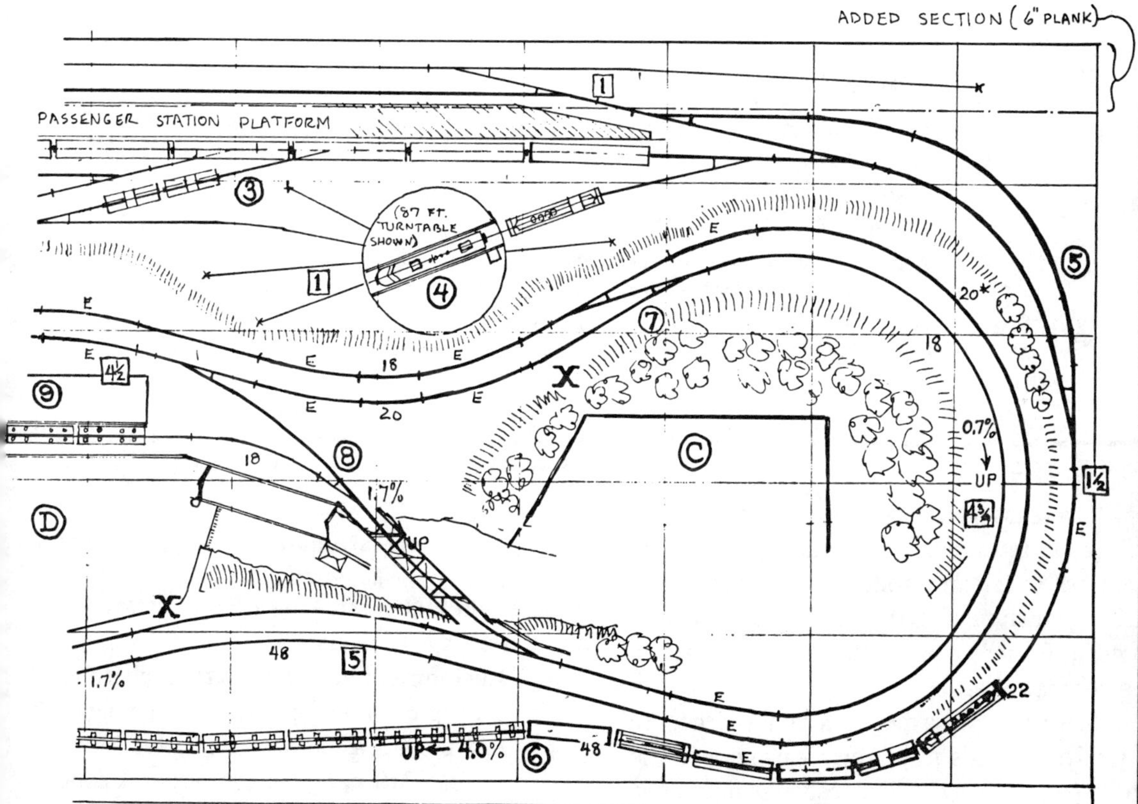

CONSTRUCTION RECOMMENDED FOR ADD-ON SECTION.

OPERATIONAL NOTES:

1. STEEP BRANCH SERVING INDUSTRIES WITH SPURS EXTENDING INTO AND BETWEEN BUILDINGS. SHORT-WHEELBASE SWITCHER REQUIRED.
2. ENGINE-ESCAPE CROSSOVER. CONCEALED BY BUILDINGS BUT ACCESSIBLE FROM ABOVE WHEN NEED BE.
3. CABOOSE AND RUN-AROUND TRACK ADJACENT TO YARD LADDER TRACK. NO. 4½ TURNOUTS LESS RESTRICTIVE THAN SHARP MAIN-LINE CURVES.
4. ENGINE FUEL & SERVICE FACILITY — CHOICE OF TURNTABLE OR STRAIGHT-THROUGH TRACKS DICTATED BY MOTIVE POWER IN USE.
5. SECOND YARD TRACK EXTENDED AND CONNECTED TO MAIN TRACK TO ALLOW QUICK HANDLING OF LONG CONSISTS ARRIVING & DEPARTING
6. "HELPER-ENGINE DISTRICT" EXTENDS UP SEVERE GRADE TO JUNCTION. MAIN-LINE GRADES MUCH LESS SEVERE.
7. CROSSOVERS TO ALLOW PROMPT RETURN TO RIGHT-HAND TRACK FOR NORMAL-DIRECTION-OF-TRAFFIC RUNNING AFTER COMING OFF BRANCH OR USING REVERSING CONNECTION.
8. REVERSING CONNECTION FOR OUT-AND-BACK OPERATION. SECOND REVERSING CONNECTION X-X OPTIONAL — SEE TEXT.
9. MAJOR INDUSTRY, SUCH AS BARGE-LOADING TERMINAL INDICATED

SCENIC-TREATMENT NOTES:

A. BUILDINGS CONCEAL TRACKAGE FROM DIRECT VIEW, JUSTIFY INDUSTRIAL BRANCH.
B. HIGHWAY BRIDGE TO LET YARD TRACKS DISAPPEAR QUIETLY, IN AN APPROPRIATELY URBAN SETTING
C. MAJOR MOUNTAINS WITH OPENINGS ON BACK SIDE, TO CONCEAL ACCESS OPENINGS WITHOUT NUISANCE OF HATCH-COVERS.
D. RIVER TERMINAL BASIN, DAMS AND LOCK JUSTIFY DROP-DOWN WATER SURFACE AS ACCESS HATCH COVER IN THIS AREA — NO CRACKS TO HIDE!

Fig. 4-5. Operational and scenic treatment notes for Long Trains with a Push track plan. See Fig. 4-4 for track plan.

minating reasonably long trains. Out-and-back connection to continuous oval provides any desired mix of terminal switching and single-track main-line train running. You have here a fine opportunity for finding out which aspects of operation are your favorites.

This track plan is the acorn from which more extensive railroads may grow, leaving open the option of developing in the direction of more train running or more fancy dispatching, with terminal facility development to suit.

Size: 4½ × 10 ft. island or peninsula with access openings
Gauge: HO
Curvature standards: sharp, with easements on all curves
Schematic: stub terminal/oval; single reversing connection
Recommended construction: single-level flat top or two-level cookie-cutter optional; may be built as flat top, converted later
Trackwork options: all trackwork components standard; curvable track recommended

LONG TRAINS WITH A PUSH

The double-track main line (Fig. 4-4) lets you run long trains, and yard trackage is extended to match. Extra-steep grade out of yard provides bigger differences in elevation between various tracks, greatly enhancing scenic opportunities (Fig. 4-5) as well as providing an interesting helper-engine operation. A train loaded to capacity for the main-line climbs won't be able to reach the junction without assistance.

A slight shortening of the main-line oval in the added section leaves room for an industrial branch; its extra-sharp curves may restrict this trackage to a smaller class of switch engine.

The railroad can be built in a rectangular space 5 × 18 to 20 ft. by rotating add-on section 90 degrees. Industrial spurs on the main line can be added and expanded considerably, but reasonable access requires that they be located primarily toward the front edges of the railroad.

A second reversing connection can be extended between points marked "X" on the plan, crossing the existing track at grade and requiring relocation of the industry spur. The added flexibility in switching from following train to opposing train running on the main line which the second connection provides is interesting, but not as important as it would be on a pike without the train-turning capabilities of the terminal yard.

Size: 8 × 14 ft. L; in a corner, if necessary
Gauge: HO
Curvature standards: sharp, with easements on all main-track curves
Schematic: stub terminal/oval (multi-track) with single reversing connection
Recommended construction: cookie-cutter original section; open grid add-on section
Trackwork options: all trackwork components standard; curvable track recommended

THE LONG, LONG TRAIL

This plan (Fig. 4-6) favors extensive single-track running for moderate-length trains supplied from a small but very flexible terminal on long branch, with three main-line passing tracks plus one on branch. An out-and-back trip with single circuit of main line amounts to 2.3 scale miles. The yard at the terminal encourages use of switcher to rearrange arriving consists for departure; other switching capabilities are severely limited in favor of main-line length.

If the add-on section is built open grid, which is preferable to cookie-cutter from the standpoint of access to lower-level trackage, 4 × 8 ft. dimensions can easily be modified to accommodate a passenger station of less limited facilities. Spread out concentric loops to improve scenic possibilities and otherwise let the tightly confined railroad breathe a little more comfortably.

Because of the tight main-line trackage with its sharp, but eased, curves winding around in search of length of run, there are few places where industry spur tracks can be attached comfortably. Points of departure for such embellishments are indicated, but the local freight will never be the main operating interest on this railroad.

If a long, straight area is available, rather than an L, the add-on section can rather readily be "bent" 90 degrees, retaining the same schematic in a total space of about 4½ × 18 to 20 ft.

Size: 8 × 14 ft. L; island, or as few as two exposed sides
Gauge: HO
Curvature standards: sharp with easements on all main-track curves
Schematic: stub terminal/oval; multi-lap with single reversing connection
Recommended construction: cookie-cutter or open grid of add-on section
Trackwork options: all trackwork components standard; curvable track recommended

THE SUPER SWITCHING RAILROAD

Use of the company intra-plant railroad theme (Fig. 4-7) allows a large variety of point-to-point car movements within the confines of a medium-size pike, along with extensive interchange with a main-line railroad. A steel mill is illustrated, but any industry such as quarrying or heavy manufacturing where loads are large and diverse enough to require rail transportation can also serve as a prototype. By omitting or simplifying some steps in the process, for example no stockpiling of raw materials is portrayed here, the system is made to fit the space available (Fig. 4-8).

Use of hand-laid trackwork of more flexible geometry will allow numerous additional spur tracks at various points. If some additional width is

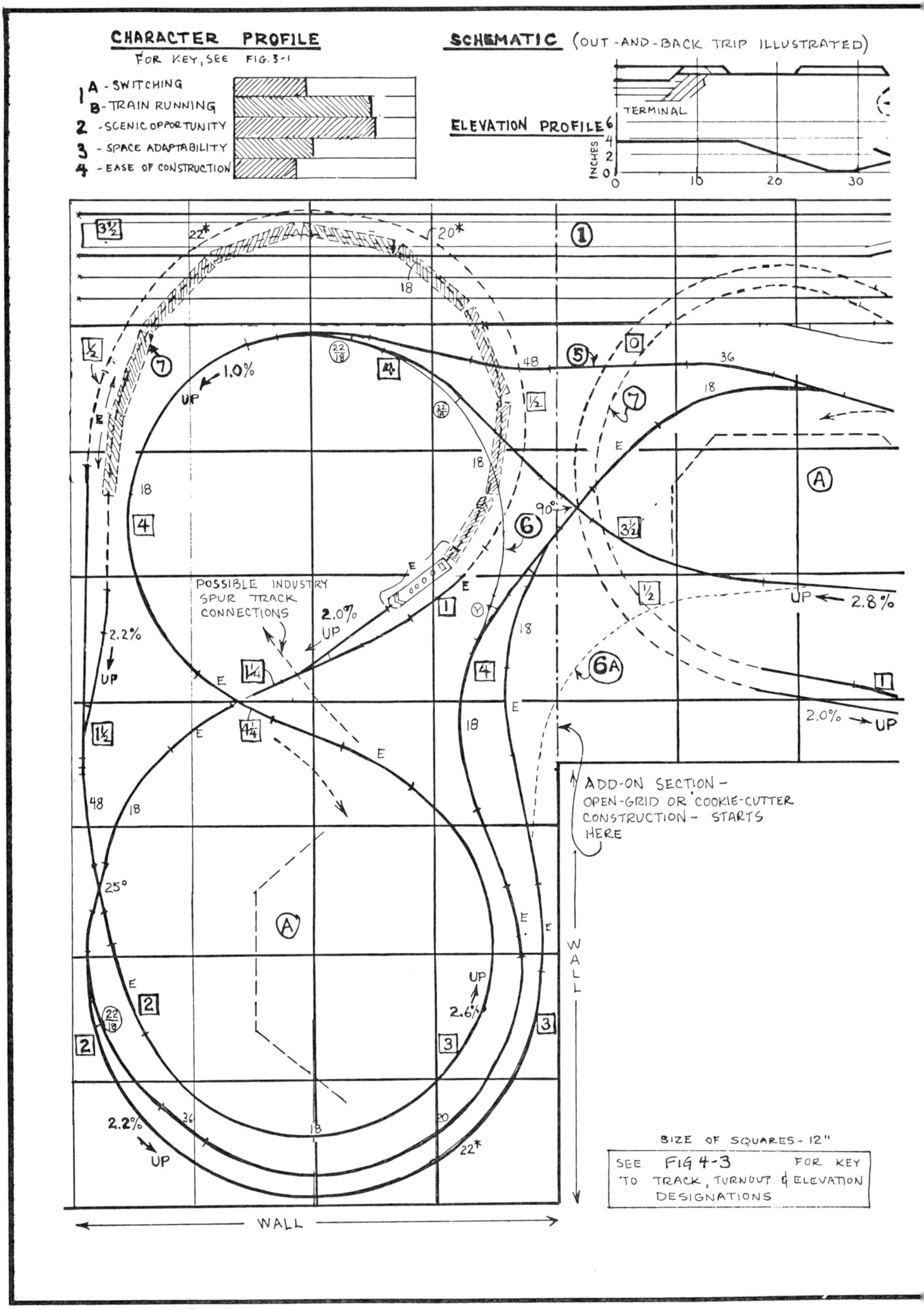

Fig. 4-6. The Long, Long Trail track plan for HO gauge.

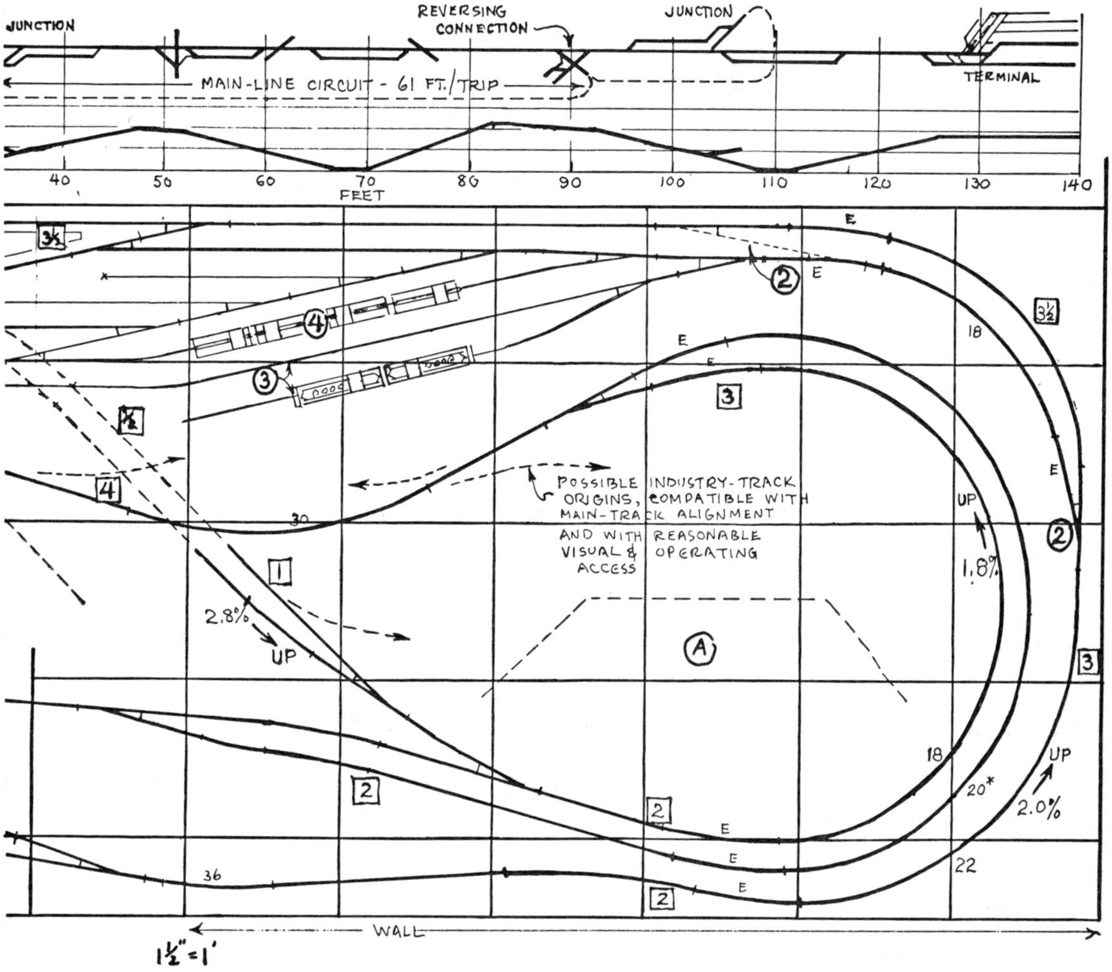

OPERATIONAL NOTES:

① PASSENGER-STATION PLATFORM. ADDITIONAL YARD TRACK AND ENGINE-ESCAPE CROSSOVER MAY BE SUBSTITUTED IN THE SAME SPACE.

② SECOND TRACK INTO TERMINAL RECONNECTED "AROUND THE CORNER" TO GIVE SWITCHER MORE WORKING ROOM AND ALLOW LONGER TRAINS TO BE HANDLED QUICKLY ON ARRIVAL. EXISTING CROSSOVER MAY BE RETAINED FOR FURTHER FLEXIBILITY.

③ DIESEL SERVICING & FUEL TRACKS — ALTERNATIVE: ENGINE TERMINAL WITH TURNTABLE AS ON FIG 4-4, OR SINGLE-ENDED DIESEL TRACKS (MORE USABLE YARD-TRACK SPACE).

④ CABOOSE AND RUN-AROUND TRACK.

⑤ REVERSING CONNECTION FOR OUT-AND-BACK OPERATION — ARRANGED TO LOOK LIKE INTERCHANGE CONNECTION BETWEEN TWO RAIL LINES AT THEIR CROSSING.

⑥ OPTIONAL CONNECTING TRACK — COMPLETES WYE AT CROSSING SO TRAINS OR ENGINES MAY BE TURNED (AS IF TERMINATING LOCAL RUNS AT THIS POINT) OR CARS CAN BE "INTERCHANGED" BETWEEN TWO LINES. OPTIONAL CONNECTION (6A) WOULD ALLOW "RE-REVERSING" TRAINS HEADED BACK TOWARD TERMINAL BUT IS MUCH LESS TYPICAL OF A REAL RAILROAD JUNCTION.

⑦ LOWER-LEVEL PASSING-TRACK SEGMENTS MAY BE USED TO HIDE TRAINS FOR LAYOVER PURPOSES, INCREASING APPARENT SIZE OF RAILROAD. ("SHORTY" (65 FT.) PASSENGER CARS ILLUSTRATED).

SCENIC-TREATMENT NOTES

Ⓐ SEE NOTES FOR FIG 4-3 REGARDING GENERAL APPROACH AS AFFECTED BY LOCATION OF LAYOUT IN ROOM. IF LAYOUT IS AGAINST WALLS AS INDICATED (THE MOST RESTRICTIVE YOU'RE LIKELY TO ENCOUNTER), ACCESS AREAS ARE NEEDED AT POINTS INDICATED — EITHER HATCHES OR OPEN AREAS SHIELDED FROM VIEW BY STRUCTURES OR TERRAIN BETWEEN VIEWERS AND HOLES.

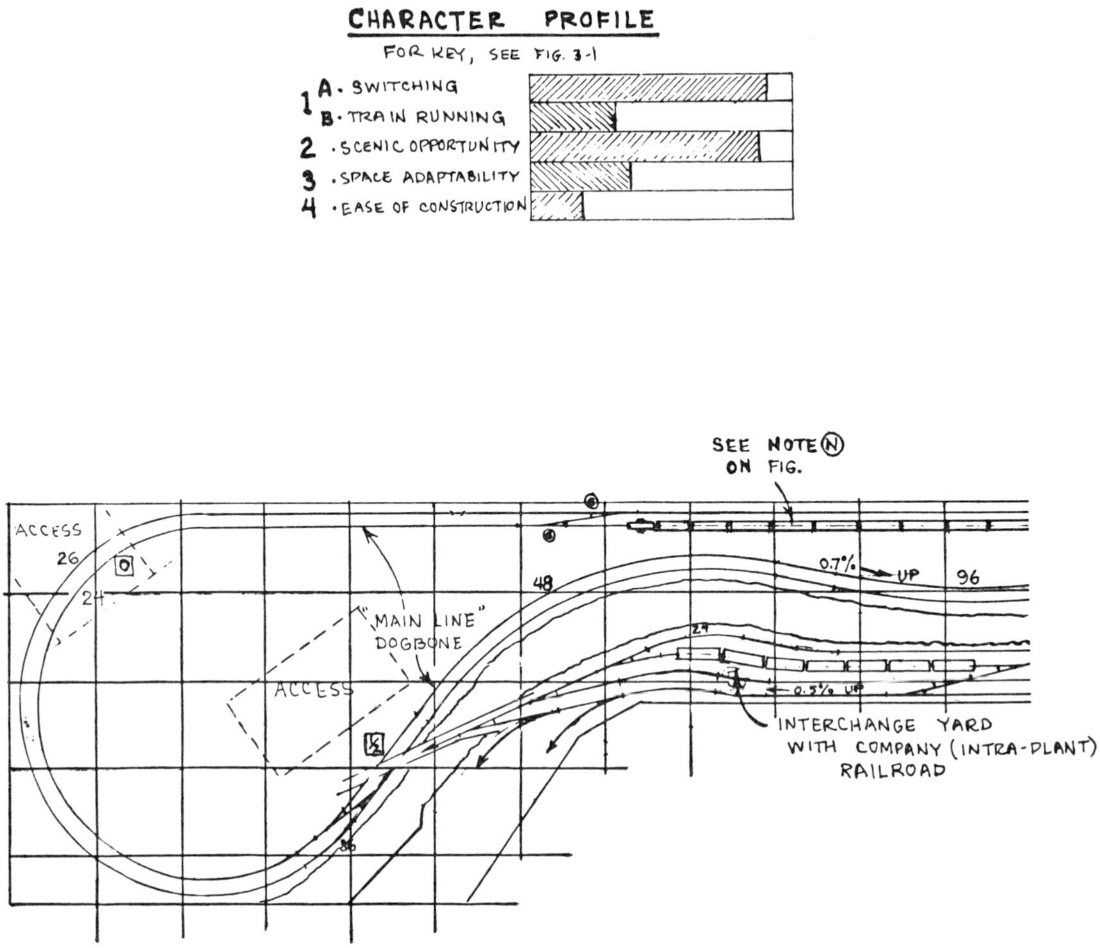

Fig. 4-7. The Super Switching Railroad track plan for HO gauge.

available, a priority modification would be more hidden layover tracks alongside the main line to accommodate more trains.

The flexible nature of intra-plant trackage with its sharp curves makes it relatively simple to adapt a plan of this type to radically different-shaped areas—bend it into an L, or even a U!

With the intricacy of such industrial elements as blast furnaces, with their accompanying hot-air stoves, skip hoists and gas piping, the opportunities for super detailing with this railroad are limitless.

Size: 4½ × 24 ft. with short *panhandle*, 27 in. wide *waist*

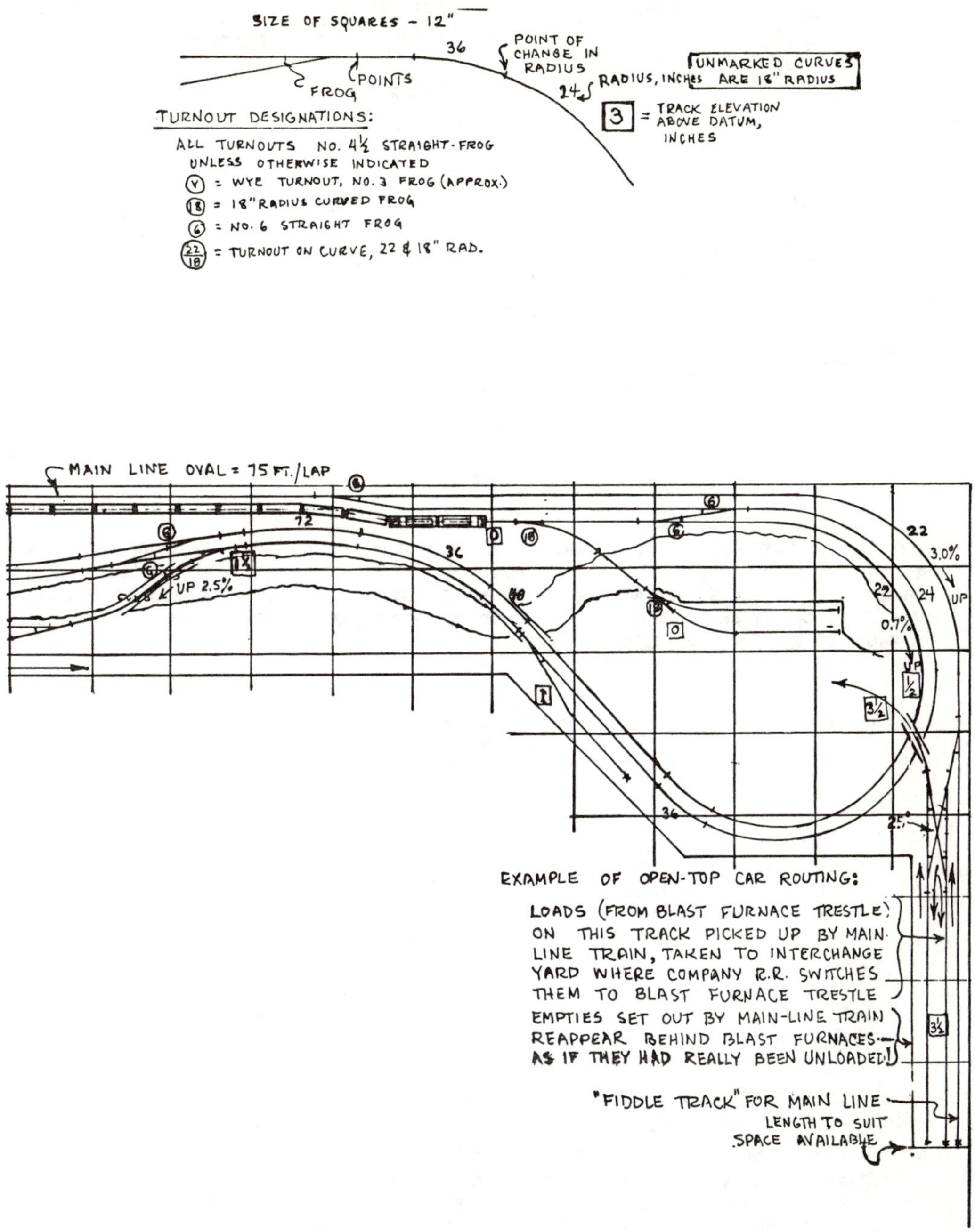

Gauge: HO

Curvature standards: conventional (main line); sharp (company switching railroad through tracks); extra sharp (individual spur tracks)

Schematic: double-track dogbone main line; point-to-point switching trackage connected via double-ended interchange yard and hidden switchback connection

Trackwork options: all trackwork elements standard; main-line curves beyond range of sectional-track radii, curvable track recommended

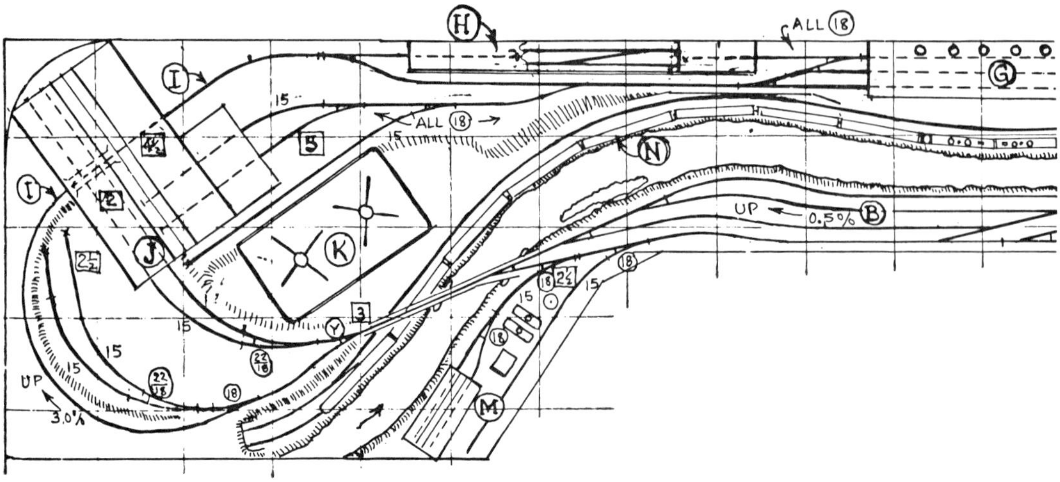

OPERATIONAL & SCENIC-TREATMENT NOTES

WITH RAILROAD OPERATIONS CENTERED ABOUT INTRA-PLANT MOVEMENTS IN THE MULTI-STEP PROCESSING THAT CONVERTS RAW MATERIALS INTO FINISHED PRODUCTS, THE PLANT BUILDINGS & FACILITIES THAT ARE MAJOR ELEMENTS OF THE "SCENERY" ALSO DETERMINE THE PATTERN OF SWITCHING AND TRANSFER RUNS THAT KEEP THE COMPANY'S LOCOMOTIVES AND THEIR CREWS BUSY.

(A) SOME RAW MATERIALS ARRIVE BY BARGE AT THE DOCK JUST BELOW THE FIRST RAPIDS THAT MARK THE UPPER LIMIT OF NAVIGATION. LOADED CARS TO PLANT R.R. VIA MAIN-LINE R.R.

(B) INTERCHANGE YARD CONNECTING PLANT R.R. WITH THE OUTSIDE WORLD. NEVER QUITE BIG ENOUGH FOR THE JOB!

(C) UNLOADING TRESTLE SERVING BLAST FURNACES FOR SMELTING ORE — COAL, LIMESTONE & IRON ORE IN, IF THIS IS A STEEL MILL. "LOADS OUT/ EMPTIES BACK" ARRANGMENT FOR OPEN-TOP CARS VIA HIDDEN TRACKS CONNECTING TO MAIN LINE ON LOWER LEVEL. PHONEY "UNLOADING" HIDDEN BEHIND BLAST FURNACES.

(D) MOLTEN PIG IRON IN "HOT METAL" CARS PULLED OUT VIA TRACK PASSING THROUGH FOUNDRY. SOME GOES TO FOUNDRY (E), MOST TO OPEN HEARTH (G) FOR DIRECT CONVERSION TO STEEL.

(E) FOUNDRY — MOLTEN IRON, SCRAP IN; PIG IRON AND CASTINGS OUT, MOSTLY IN GONDOLAS TO MAIN-LINE INTERCHANGE.

(F) SCRAP HANDLING YARD — GONDOLAS IN & OUT.

(G) OPEN-HEARTH FURNACES — MOLTEN IRON, IRON ORE, SCRAP IN; HOT INGOTS OUT, MOSTLY TO SLABBING MILL ADJACENT.

(H) SLABBING MILL, WHERE INGOTS START THE ROLLING PROCESSES EVENTUALLY MAKING THEM INTO BARS, RAILS, PLATE, SHEET, WIRE OR WHATEVER. ROOF OF MILL LIFTS UP FOR ACCESS TO MAIN-LINE CROSSOVER BELOW. HOT SLABS OF STEEL ON SPECIAL FLAT CARS TO ROLLING MILL (J)

(I) "MAIN LINE" OF PLANT RAILROAD PASSES THROUGH UPPER LEVEL OF ROLLING MILL BUILDING — LOCATION OF MILL IN NARROW RIVER VALLEY HAS RESULTED IN MUCH BACK-AND-FORTH MOVEMENT WITHIN PLANT, WHICH IS WHY IT MAKES SUCH A GOOD MODEL RAILROAD!

Fig. 4-8. A top-level only view of the Super Switching Railroad track plan.

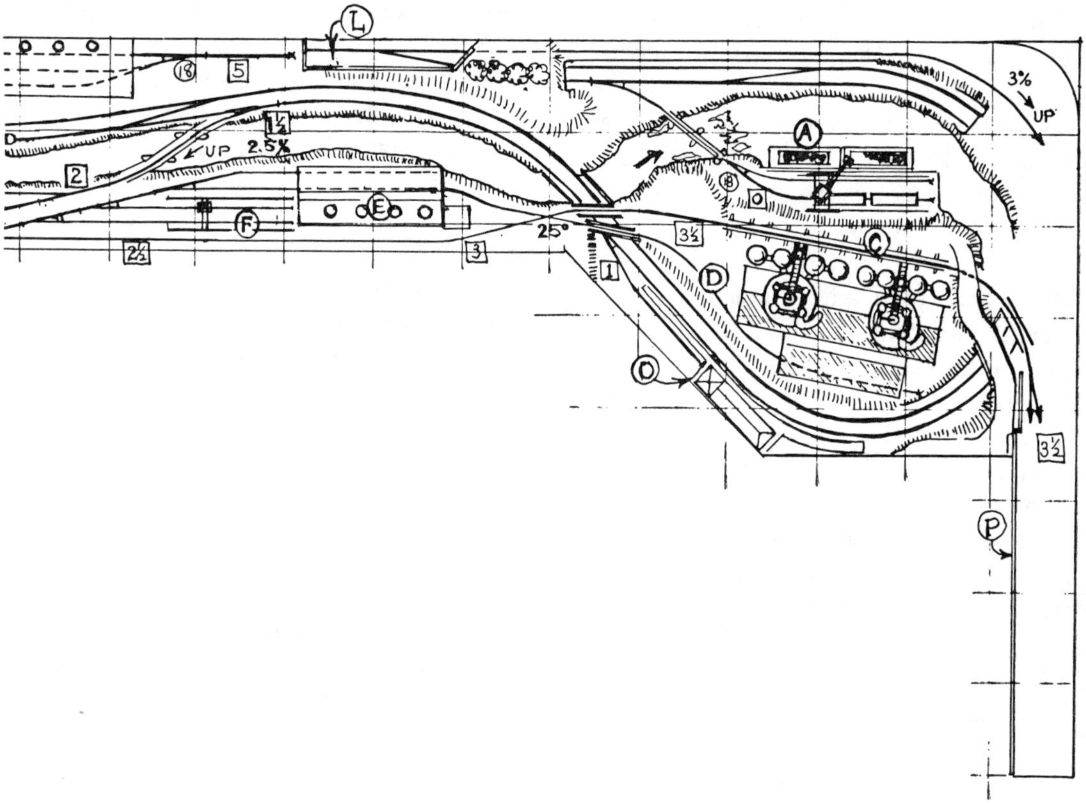

Ⓙ ROLLING MILL — HOT SLABS IN, FINISHED STEEL OUT IN MILL GONDOLAS, COIL STEEL CARS, ETC. VIA INTERCHANGE YARD. ALL PROCESSING BUILDINGS ALSO GENERATE SCRAP STEEL, TO BE RECYCLED WITHIN PLANT.

Ⓚ WATER SETTLING POND SERVES AS LID TO HATCH PROVIDING ACCESS TO MAIN-LINE TRACKAGE IN CORNER— ROOF OF ROLLING MILL REMOVABLE.

Ⓛ ROOFLESS PLANT ADMINISTRATION BUILDING — NO RAIL TRAFFIC, BUT IT DOES PROVIDE ACCESS TO TURNOUT ON LOWER LEVEL.

Ⓜ COMPANY-RAILROAD ENGINE SERVICING FACILITIES — STEAM OR DIESEL AS APPROPRIATE FOR THE ERA. OUT IN FRONT, OF COURSE.

Ⓝ SWEEPING CURVES ALONG RIVER MAKE FOR BEAUTIFUL APPEARANCE OF TRAINS OF FULL-LENGTH PASSENGER CARS. HIDDEN LAYOVER TRACKAGE AT REAR, LOWER LEVEL, FOR MAIN-LINE CONSISTS, BUT NO LEGITIMATE SWITCHING FACILITIES FOR THEM.

Ⓞ JUST ENOUGH ROOM FOR AN INTERESTING PASSENGER STATION ON THE MAIN LINE.

Ⓟ BUILDING FALSE-FRONTS HIDE "FIDDLE YARD" WHERE DIRTY WORK OF EXCHANGING LOADS FOR EMPTIES, MESSING WITH MAIN-LINE CONSISTS, INTRODUCING NEW ROLLING STOCK CAN TAKE PLACE.

AROUND-THE-WALL PLANS

Once a room is big enough to take a horseshoe-shaped layout with suitably gentle return bends, you can have an ideal situation—a walk-in arrangement that lets you reach most of the track comfortably and watch the trains run from close-up vantage points. Closet doors and windows which must still be reachable after the railroad is built can throw a monkey wrench into the proceedings, but it's often practical to fit a most satisfactory track plan into such an area.

By definition, only one side of the around-the-wall sections can be out front, and getting a reasonably long main-line run usually means more than one *lap* of track. This in turn favors multi-level trackage, perhaps including sections where two separate levels are treated as two separate scenes, one above the other. At the very least, this makes the track plan hard to draw! It also can be hard to judge whether or not it's going to be possible to get to hidden trackage well enough to build, maintain and run trains over it satisfactorily.

The apparent mess of overlapping lines on the diagram may give too pessimistic an impression, so several of the track plans of this type are accompanied by cross-sections at key points. In combination with the schematics and top-level supplementary plans they should let you assess the practicability of the design for your purposes.

A multi-level pike *has* to be buildable in stages. Start from the bottom level and work up and it's a pleasure; laying track underneath an upper level is something else! It's extremely helpful for the reliability of the completed railroad to have the lower-level trackage form some sort of continuous circuit so it can be operated extensively while its trackage is still easy to get at and adjust. Running trains is the best, and most enjoyable, way to find and eliminate any problems.

THE COLLECTOR'S FRIEND

In this plan (Fig. 4-9) you have unrestricted main-line running of long trains in both first and second-stage versions. Out-and-back operation from branch terminal suitable for turning long consists is greatly expanded in second stage (Fig. 4-10). Major complete-train layover and storage capacity on hidden tracks is parallel to main line. There are very limited local freight opportunities. Additional crossovers in second stage allow varied "wrong track" running opportunities in leaving and entering branch and passing slower trains.

As a layout emphasizing spacious scenery and the display of long trains running freely, room for industrial development is limited, but with some ingenuity enough spur trackage can be worked in along the branch around the terminal yard and on the inside of the main line, adjacent to the operating area, to make for an interesting local-freight traffic.

Size: 7 × 11 ft., somewhat adjustable to match room size
Gauge: N
Curvature standards: conventional and broad
Schematic: double-track twisted dogbone with branch, single reversing connection for out-and-back operation
Recommended construction: first stage: flat top with river sawed out and dropped below rest of platform; second stage: partial cookie-cutter
Trackwork options: all trackwork items standard, with most curves to available sectional-track radii, curvable recommended for sweeping curves

A TWO-LAYER ROOMFUL

Hidden layover trackage on simple main-line oval (Fig. 4-11) favors running a variety of trains of moderate length, with timetable scheduling through the yard at branchline connection if desired. There are ample engine-servicing facilities at the yard, with long branch of more restrictive curvature capable of handling two trains at once. There's room for several fair-sized industries, some with their own switchers. Substantial but not extreme grades are used on both main and branch lines. Upper level trackage is shown in Fig. 4-12.

As a single-track line, the entire plan may be reversed to fit a different door location, with no effect on operation. A second passing track on the branch may be added or the existing siding lengthened. The grade from the junction to the passing track may be made much steeper, with a corresponding flattening on the upper end of the branch to avoid getting too close to the ceiling, justifying the use of pusher engines or requiring the crew to *double the hill* and take their train to the passing track in two pieces.

With minor modifications, perhaps reducing the minimum radius to 22 in. in places, the main line may be made double track, favoring the running of longer and more frequent trains.

The branch, as a self-contained point-to-point operation, can be built to narrow gauge, with enough dual-gauge trackage to let the slim-track locos reach the engine terminal and some easily-made yard modifications to simulate trans-loading freight between the different-gauge cars. For operating notes and suggestions for scenic treatment see Fig. 4-13.

Size: 10 × 14 ft., somewhat adjustable
Gauge: HO
Curvature standards: main line, conventional; branch line, sharp with easements
Schematic: main line, folded oval with single reversing connection; branch, stub terminal with wye, switchback continuation
Trackwork options: all trackwork components may be standard; curvable track recommended

SPAGHETTI ON THE ROLLING PIN

This layout (Fig. 4-14) is a *real* railroad, effectively simulating a busy line climbing over a mountain range to connect two terminals. Somewhat cramped stub terminals will test your yardmasters in finding ways to make up the long (18-car) freights which can be accommodated by the three main-line passing tracks. But continuous-running connection allows trains to increase length of run before entering far terminal and requiring turning. For operational notes see Fig. 4-15.

Lineside industrial development needs further development, and some spaces are available. Layout is deficient in track space for holding rolling stock; lengthening one or both terminal yards in the future would remedy this quickly. Optional subterranean *interchange yard* indicated would provide both storage capacity and interesting switching problems, with some advanced special trackwork required as a good project to make use of the experience acquired in building the basic railroad.

Size: 10 × 11 ft. L; diagonal central section 4 ft. wide, length of legs somewhat adjustable
Gauge: N
Curvature standards: conventional
Schematic: point-to-point with continuous-running connection completing three-lap oval; optional reversing connection for out-and-back operation from one terminal
Recommended construction: open grid, access from below simplifies and improves scenic treatment
Trackwork options: all trackwork items standard, with sectional track useable for easemented curves in most cases, if curvable track, preferred, is not used

NOTCHING THE L

The *L-shaped pike* is a favorite of long standing, but in medium-size format has serious access problems. With a walk-in *notch* at the root of its two arms, however, it can expand to a point where the larger gauges (S and O) can be accommodated and still let you reach all operating points with ease and comfort. Figures 4-16, 4-18, 4-19 show how varied the railroads can be that fit into the same size and shape area, an L with 13 and 16-ft. arms.

If you have one large corner of a basement available, don't overlook the possibilities of building a railroad in a large scale, with the benefits of detail you can *see*, much heavier rolling stock that tracks well, and minimized electrical contact and dirt problems.

THE EXHIBITIONIST

This plan (Fig. 4-16) is primarily a railroad for displaying long trains and big locomotives in main-line action, with a big enough passenger station to represent a city where trains might terminate their runs. Consists not in action at the moment can thus logically remain visible, parked at the platforms between trips.

Freight traffic can include some switching, with the limitation that facing-point spurs would be a real problem to handle, but operation of heavy, through trains is primary. See Fig. 4-17 for suggestions on scenery development.

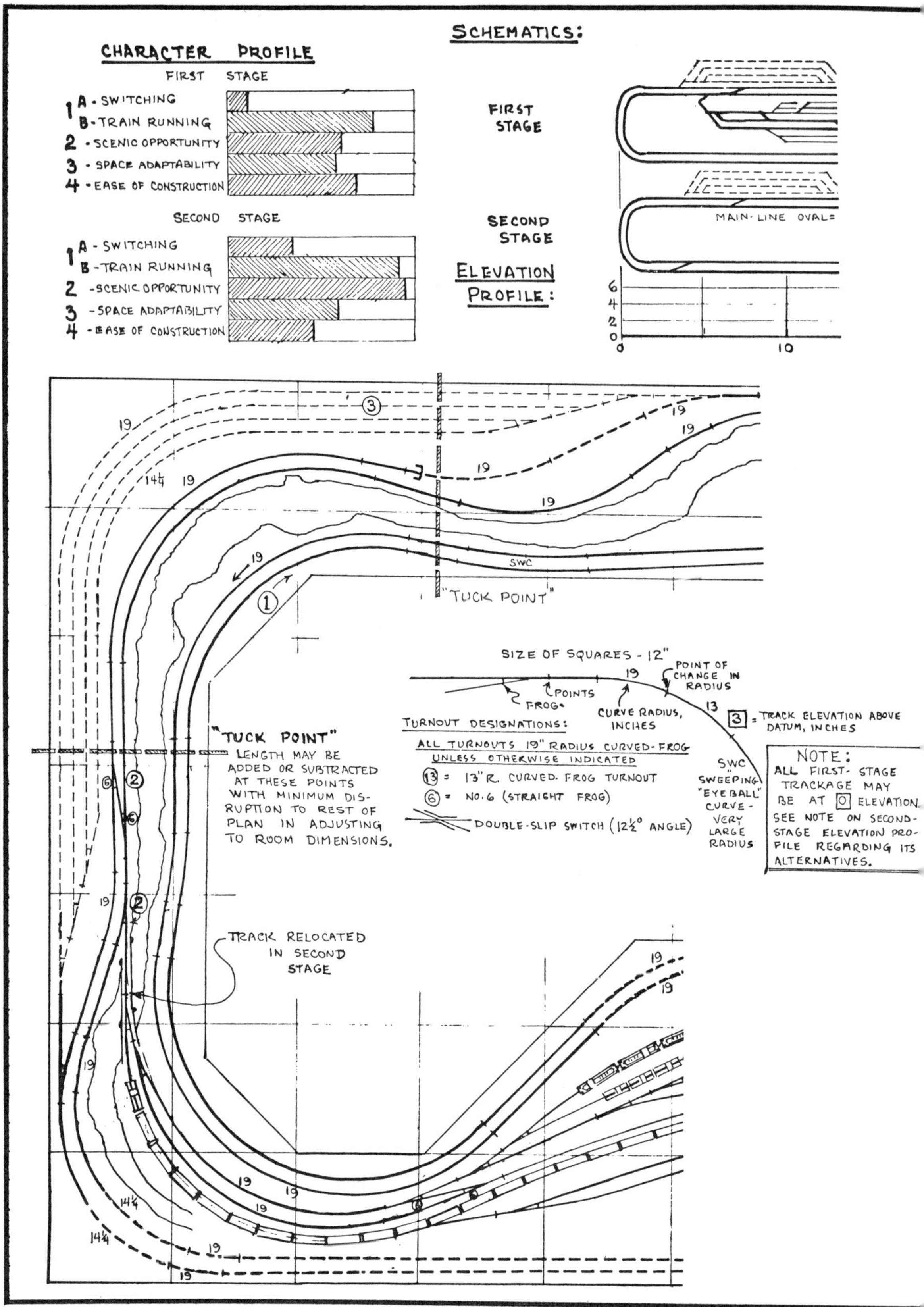

Fig. 4-9. The Collector's Friend track plan for N gauge.

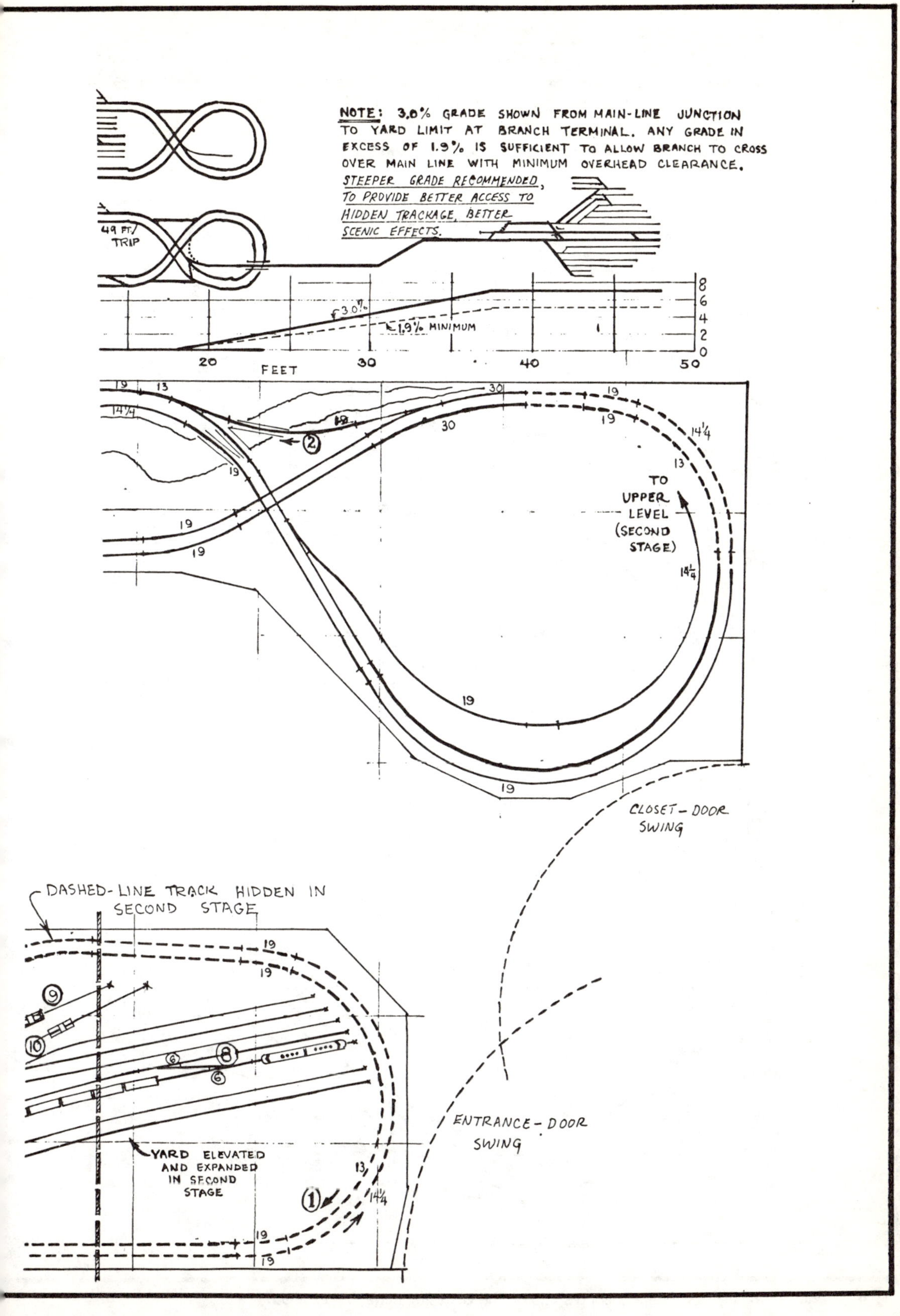

NOTE: 3.0% GRADE SHOWN FROM MAIN-LINE JUNCTION TO YARD LIMIT AT BRANCH TERMINAL. ANY GRADE IN EXCESS OF 1.9% IS SUFFICIENT TO ALLOW BRANCH TO CROSS OVER MAIN LINE WITH MINIMUM OVERHEAD CLEARANCE.
STEEPER GRADE RECOMMENDED, TO PROVIDE BETTER ACCESS TO HIDDEN TRACKAGE, BETTER SCENIC EFFECTS.
49 FT./TRIP
3.0%
1.9% MINIMUM
FEET
TO UPPER LEVEL (SECOND STAGE)
CLOSET-DOOR SWING
DASHED-LINE TRACK HIDDEN IN SECOND STAGE
YARD ELEVATED AND EXPANDED IN SECOND STAGE
ENTRANCE-DOOR SWING

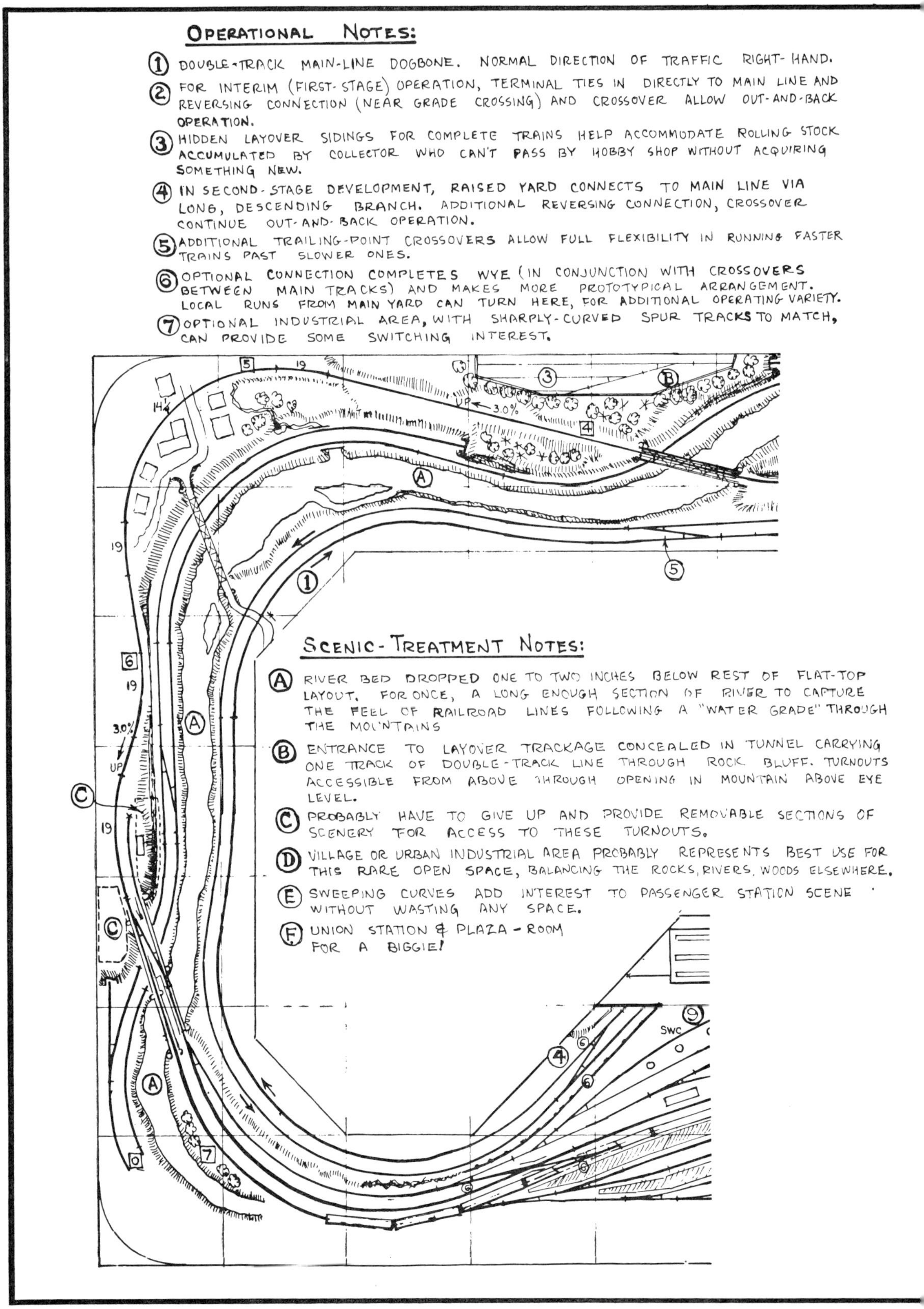

Fig. 4-10. A top-level only view of the second stage of The Collector's Friend track plan.

(8) ENGINE-ESCAPE CROSSOVER. SWITCHER WORKS INCOMING TRAINS FROM REAR END.

(9) DIESEL FUEL/SAND/SERVICE TRACK. CORRESPONDING STEAM FACILITIES OPTIONAL.

(10) CABOOSE TRACK. ALSO SERVES AS RUN-AROUND IN SECOND STAGE WHEN ROOM IS AVAILABLE.

(11) DIESEL SHOP.

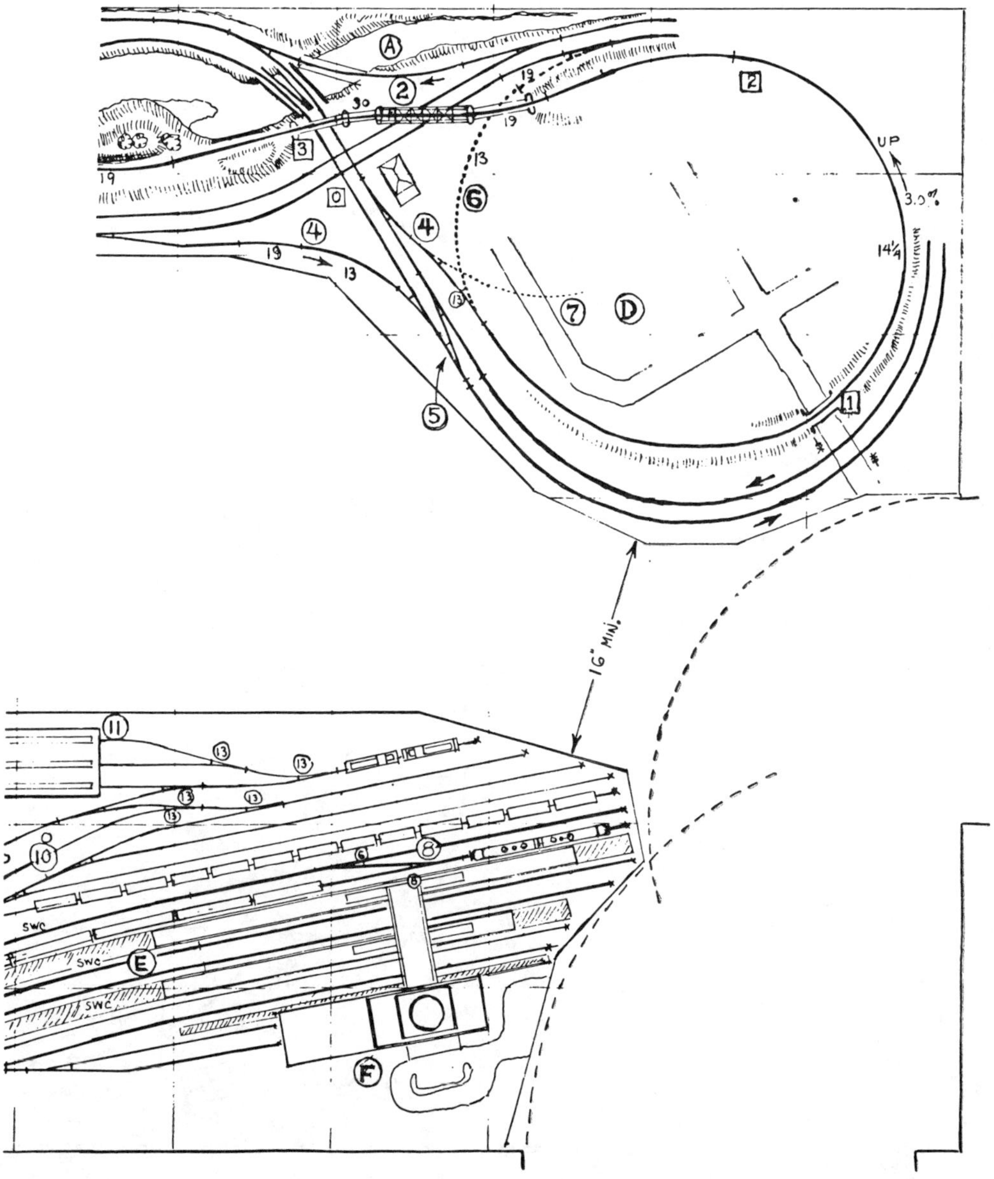

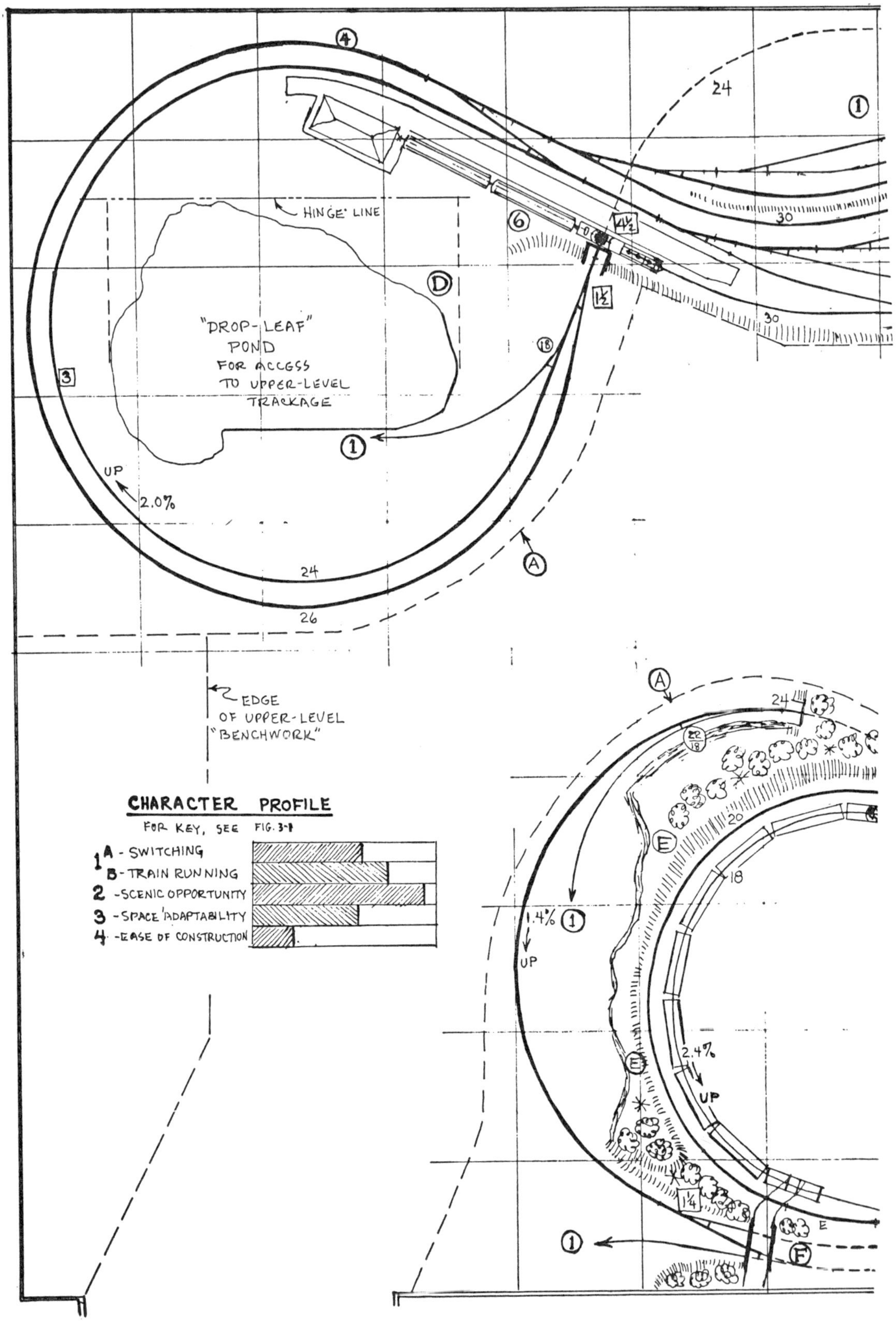

Fig. 4-11. A Two-Layer Roomful track plan for HO gauge.

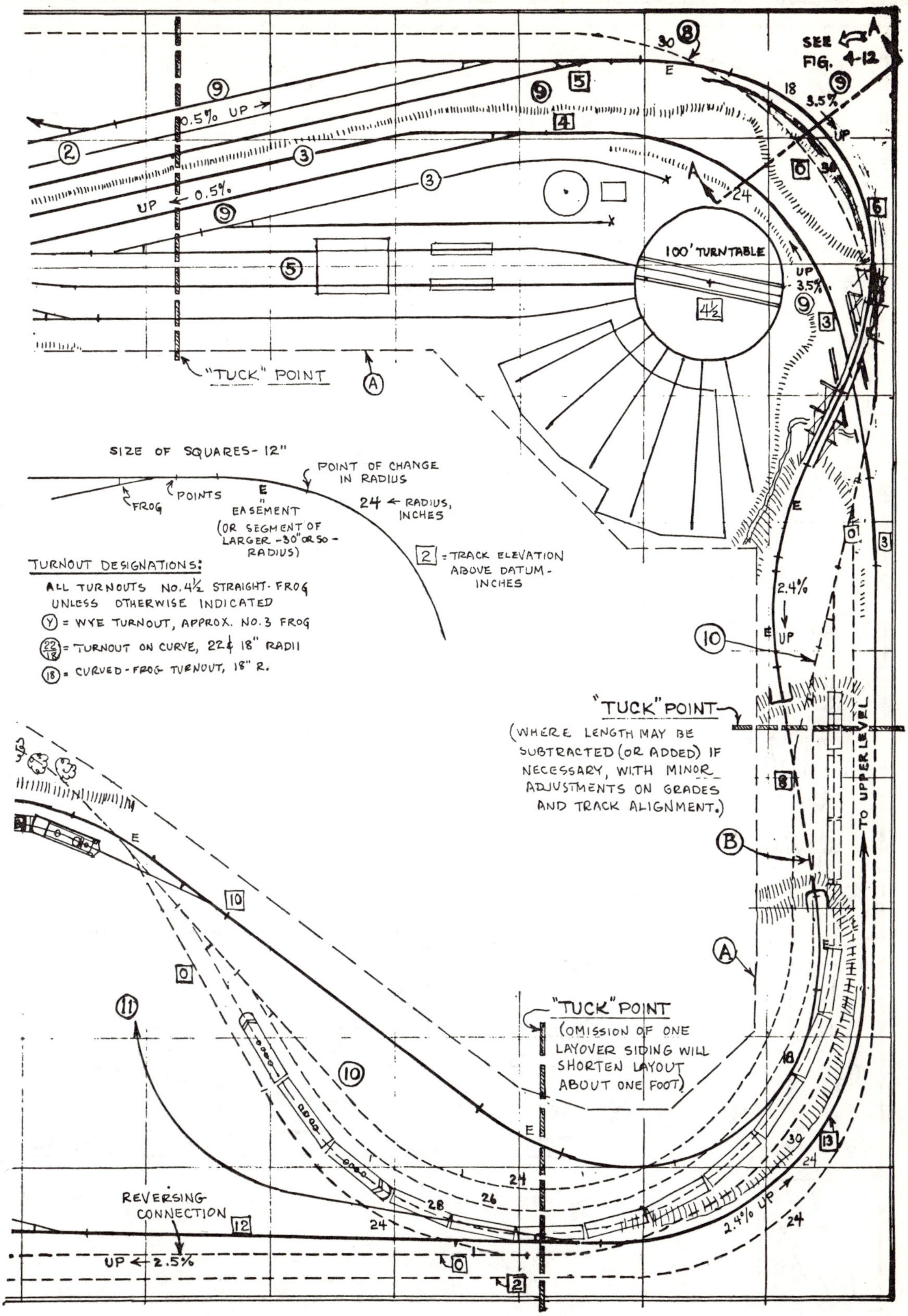
SEE FIG. 4-12
100' TURNTABLE
0.5% UP
UP 0.5%
UP 3.5%
3.5% UP
"TUCK" POINT
SIZE OF SQUARES- 12"
POINT OF CHANGE IN RADIUS
FROG
POINTS
EASEMENT (OR SEGMENT OF LARGER -30" OR SO- RADIUS)
24 ← RADIUS, INCHES
2 = TRACK ELEVATION ABOVE DATUM-INCHES
TURNOUT DESIGNATIONS:
ALL TURNOUTS NO. 4½ STRAIGHT-FROG UNLESS OTHERWISE INDICATED
Y = WYE TURNOUT, APPROX. NO. 3 FROG
22/18 = TURNOUT ON CURVE, 22 & 18" RADII
18 = CURVED-FROG TURNOUT, 18" R.
2.4% UP
"TUCK" POINT (WHERE LENGTH MAY BE SUBTRACTED (OR ADDED) IF NECESSARY, WITH MINOR ADJUSTMENTS ON GRADES AND TRACK ALIGNMENT.)
TO UPPER LEVEL
"TUCK" POINT (OMISSION OF ONE LAYOVER SIDING WILL SHORTEN LAYOUT ABOUT ONE FOOT)
REVERSING CONNECTION
UP ← 2.5%
2.4% UP

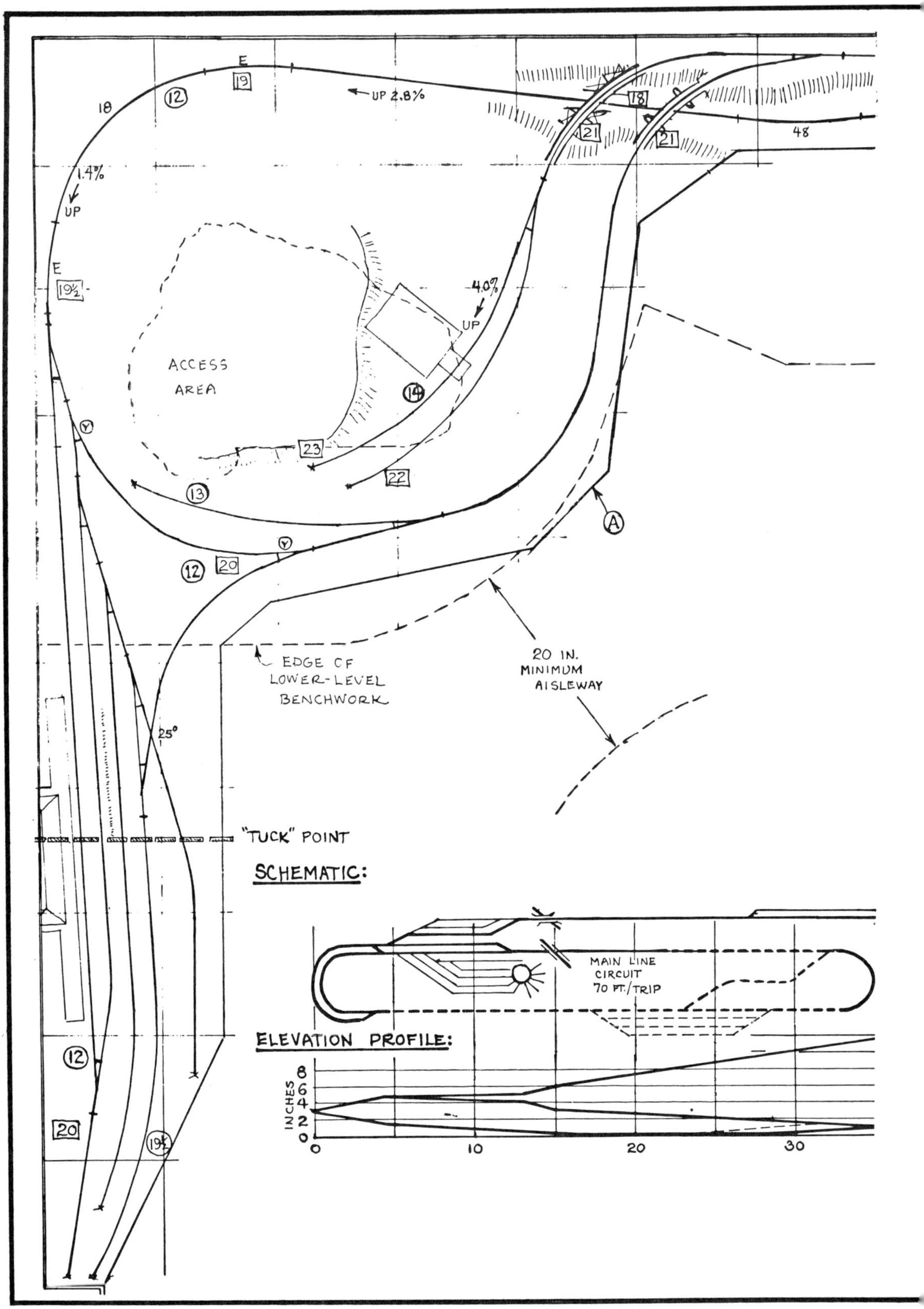

Fig. 4-12. A top-level view of A Two-Layer Roomful track plan. For operational and scenic treatment notes see Fig. 4-13.

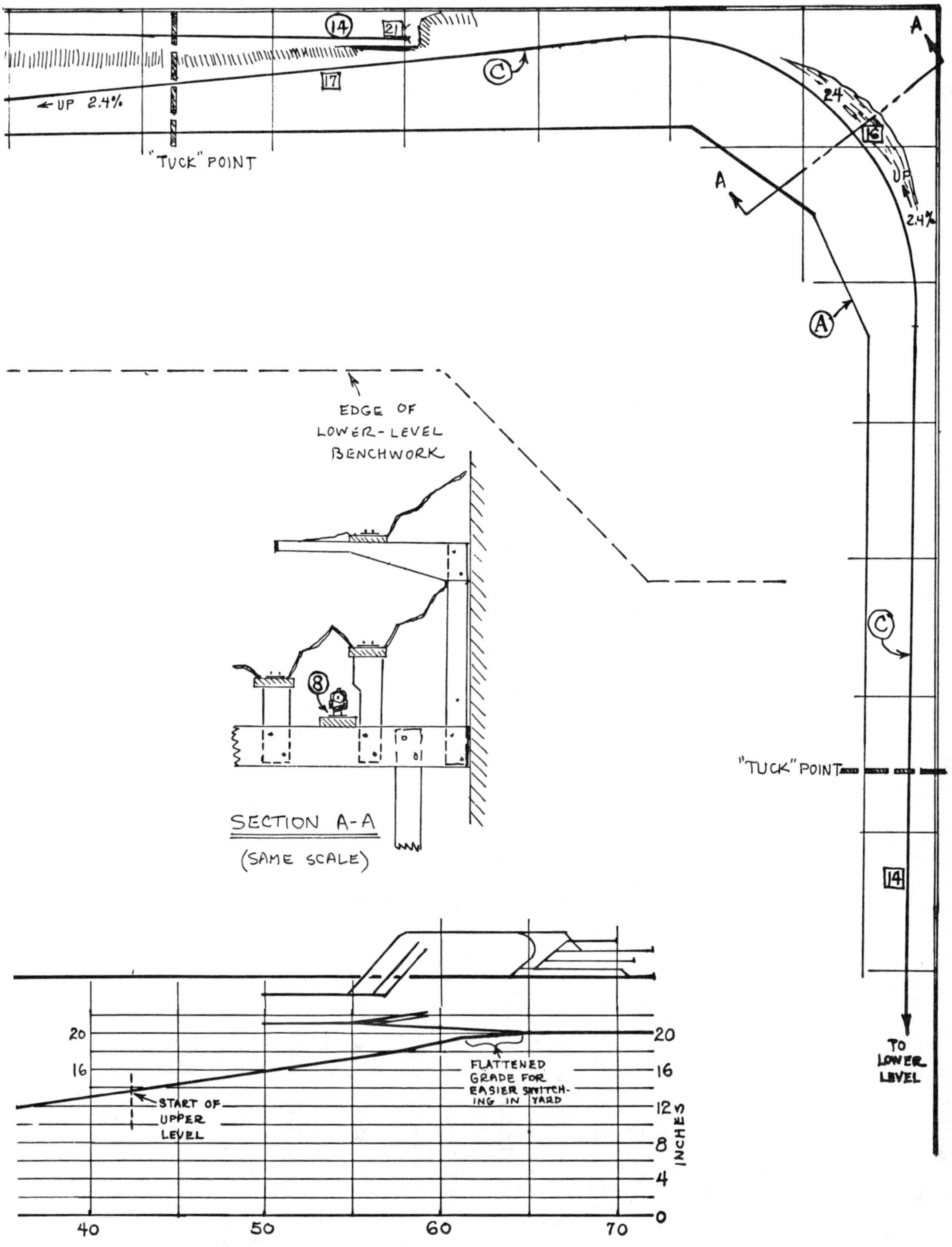
14
21
17
C
UP 2.4%
"TUCK" POINT
A
A
24
16
UP
2.4%
A
EDGE OF
LOWER-LEVEL
BENCHWORK
8
SECTION A-A
(SAME SCALE)
C
"TUCK" POINT
14
TO
LOWER
LEVEL
20
16
FLATTENED
GRADE FOR
EASIER SWITCHING IN YARD
START OF
UPPER
LEVEL
20
16
12
8
4
0
INCHES
40
50
60
70

OPERATIONAL NOTES

1. ROOM FOR MAJOR INDUSTRIES (SMELTER, LUMBER MILL OR WHATEVER) PROCESSING MATERIALS ORIGINATING ON BRANCH.
2. RECEIVING/MAKE-UP YARD FOR BRANCHLINE FREIGHTS; ALSO SERVES INDUSTRIES IN VICINITY
3. "INTERCHANGE" TRACKS BETWEEN MAINLINE AND BRANCH FOR FREIGHT TRAFFIC, WHEN NOT REQUIRED FOR OTHER PURPOSES (EXTENSION OF PASSING TRACK, ENGINE STORAGE, ETC.)
4. COMBINATION MAIN-LINE PASSING TRACK AND SWITCHING LEAD FOR YARDS AT JUNCTION.
5. LARGE ENGINE TERMINAL (TURNTABLE CAN BE LENGTHENED IF NECESSARY FOR EXTRA-BIG POWER) WITH APPROPRIATE FUEL, SAND, WATER, ASH FACILITIES. SOME MAINLINE ENGINE RUNS TERMINATE HERE.
6. BRANCHLINE LOCAL PASSENGER TRAIN MAKES SWITCH-BACK MOVEMENT (USING TURNTABLE LEAD AS A THOROUGHFARE TRACK) TO LEAVE FROM AND RETURN TO MAIN-LINE PASSENGER STATION PLATFORM, LIE OVER BETWEEN TRIPS.
7. IT'S A LONG REACH TO THIS TRACK, WITH NO GOOD PLACE FOR ACCESS FROM BELOW — WHICH MAKES IT IMPORTANT THAT THERE ARE NO TURNOUTS OR OTHER COMPLICATIONS LIKELY TO REQUIRE "WRECKER SERVICE" MORE THAN RARELY.
8. REASONABLY EASY ACCESS TO HIDDEN TRACK FROM BELOW, WITH 6" CLEARANCE BETWEEN LEVELS. EXTRA-BROAD RADIUS INSURES AGAINST FREQUENT TROUBLE.
9. GRADE IN YARDS HELD TO 0.5% FOR EASIER SWITCHING, WITH STEEPER (BUT SHORT) GRADES TO GET BRANCH OVER MAIN LINE LATER ON.
10. HIDDEN LAYOVER TRACKS FOR MAIN-LINE TRAINS — TURNOUTS READILY ACCESSIBLE FROM SIDE.

(11) ROOM FOR TIMBER-PRODUCING OR OTHER INDUSTRIAL AREA TO FEED BRANCH. CONNECTING SPUR TO UPPER LINE GIVES LONGER RUN TO THE JUNCTION FOR CARS PICKED UP OR SET OUT.

(12) BRANCHLINE TERMINAL YARD — SMALL BUT ADEQUATE, WITH RUN-AROUND TRACK AND WYE. MINIMUM-RADIUS APPROACH CURVE, ALSO USED AS SWITCHING LEAD, HAS EASEMENTS TO INSURE RELIABLE OPERATION OF ANY EQUIPMENT SUITABLE FOR THE BRANCH.

(13) MINIMAL ENGINE-SERVICE FACILITIES — MOST SERVICING DONE AT JUNCTION END OF BRANCH.

(14) MINE OR OTHER INDUSTRY SERVED BY SWITCHBACK EXTENSION OF BRANCH — CURVES AND GRADES COULD BE EVEN WORSE (REQUIRING USE OF GEARED OR OTHER SMALL LOCOMOTIVES) IF DESIRED.

SCENIC-TREATMENT NOTES

(A) APPROXIMATE CONTOUR OF EDGE OF BENCHWORK — SHOWN AS STRAIGHT-LINE SEGMENTS TO DISTINGUISH IT FROM TRACKAGE ON THE DRAWINGS, BUT USUALLY BUILT WITH CURVES TO MATCH THE TERRAIN AND TRACK WHEN USING "OPEN GRID" CONSTRUCTION.

(B) LOWER LEVEL OF BRANCH LINE DUCKS INTO SHORT TUNNEL TO LET SCENERY SWITCH INCONSPICUOUSLY FROM SINGLE-LEVEL TO TWO-LEVEL.

(C) TRACK SHOULD INCORPORATE GENTLE CURVES FOR SCENIC INTEREST — EXACT CONFIGURATION YOUR CHOICE!

(D) FAIRLY LOW-PROFILE SCENE IN THIS AREA — APPROXIMATELY 16" CLEARANCE BELOW UPPER DECK.

(E) SCENIC SEPARATION BETWEEN MAIN LINE & BRANCH — CUTS, CLIFFS, QUARRIES, TREES.

(F) THE OLD "TRACK DISAPPEARS UNDERNEATH OVERPASS" TRICK AT THIS END OF HIDDEN SECTION OF MAINLINE TRACKAGE.

Fig. 4-13. Operational and scenic treatment notes for A Two-Layer Roomful track plan. For track plan see Fig. 4-12.

OPERATIONAL NOTES:

① YARD CAPACITY LIMITED BY AVAILABLE LENGTH – TO BE INCREASED BY SIMPLY LENGTHENING BODY TRACKS IF MORE SPACE AVAILABLE.

② SUBTERRANEAN "INTERCHANGE YARD", BETWEEN MAIN-LINE TRACK LEVELS & CONNECTED VIA SPECIAL TRACKWORK (HAND-BUILT CROSSINGS OR HIGHLY MODIFIED COMMERCIAL ITEMS), CAN PROVIDE MAJOR CAR-STORAGE CAPACITY PLUS INTRICATE SWITCHING.

③ OPTIONAL REVERSING CONNECTION (HUMP-BACKED TO MATCH ELEVATION OF TRACK IT MUST CROSS AT GRADE) ALLOWS OUT-AND-BACK OPERATION (101 FT. ROUND TRIP) FROM MAJOR YARD. HIDDEN LOCATION MEANS THAT TRACK SHOULD BE INSTALLED DURING LAYOUT CONSTRUCTION IF IT IS EVER GOING TO BE WANTED. –

④ A GOOD PLACE FOR ADDING A PUSHER FOR THE LONG CLIMB TO THE SUMMIT.

⑤ PASSENGER TRAINS ARE LIKELY TO BE SHORT ON THIS RAILROAD, SO FREIGHTS EVEN LONGER THAN THE LIBERAL PASSING TRACKS CAN BE RUN BY "SAWING BY" AT THE MEETING POINTS.

⑥ WHEN RAILROAD IS BEING RUN FROM THE "FRONT" (LEFT) SIDE, TRAINS ON THESE SIDINGS ARE OUT OF SIGHT AND A "CENTER LAY-OVER" OPERATING SCHEME IS POSSIBLE, SIMULATING VERY LONG TRIPS FROM ONE TERMINAL TO THE OTHER.

⑦ PRACTICAL LOCATIONS FOR INDUSTRY SPUR CONNECTIONS.

⑧ ENGINE-TURNAROUND FACILITIES OF SPACE-SAVING CONFIGURATION. MAY BE OMITTED (IN FAVOR OF INDUSTRY TRACKAGE) IF NOT NEEDED.

SCENIC-TREATMENT NOTES:

Ⓐ CENTRAL RIDGE, EXTENDING ABOVE EYE LEVEL, SEPARATES TWO SIDES OF LAYOUT AND PRESERVES THE EFFECT OF TRAINS GOING IN THE SAME DIRECTION AS THEY PROCEED FROM ONE TERMINAL TO THE OTHER. LAYOUT SHOULD BE BUILT HIGH, TO ALLOW EASY DUCK-UNDER TO REAR-SIDE OPERATING/VIEWING AREA (A-1), WHICH IS ALSO FULLY SCENICKED AS A SEPARATE SERIES OF SCENES.

Ⓑ IF HOLLOW MOUNTAIN IS BUILT HIGH ENOUGH ABOVE TRACKS, THERE WILL BE ADEQUATE ACCESS FROM BELOW TO THE HIDDEN TRACKWORK AND NO AWKWARD HATCHES WILL BE NEEDED.

Ⓒ BUILDING "FLATS" HIDE TRACKAGE BUT ALLOW EMERGENCY ACCESS FROM ABOVE

Ⓓ "ZERO SPACE" PASSENGER STATIONS ("FLATS" AGAINST WALL) CONNECTED TO PLATFORMS VIA OVERPASS, CROSS-TRACK WALKWAYS OR UNDERPASS, AS DESIRED.

Ⓔ THIS SECTION OF TRACK, WHICH SERVES AS SWITCHING LEAD FOR YARD, IS LEFT EXPOSED FOR CONVENIENCE, VISIBLE FROM FRONT SIDE OF LAYOUT.

Fig. 4-15. Operational and scenic treatment notes for Spaghetti on the Rolling Pin track plan.

Major rail-served industries and additional passenger-station trackage can be added, as indicated, in the rather large areas currently undeveloped.

Despite appearances of two-way traffic, the direction of travel of a train *on any one particular track* cannot be reversed, and maneuvers such as having one train pass another by using the left-hand track are not possible. Adding two or three crossovers between the main line, and accepting

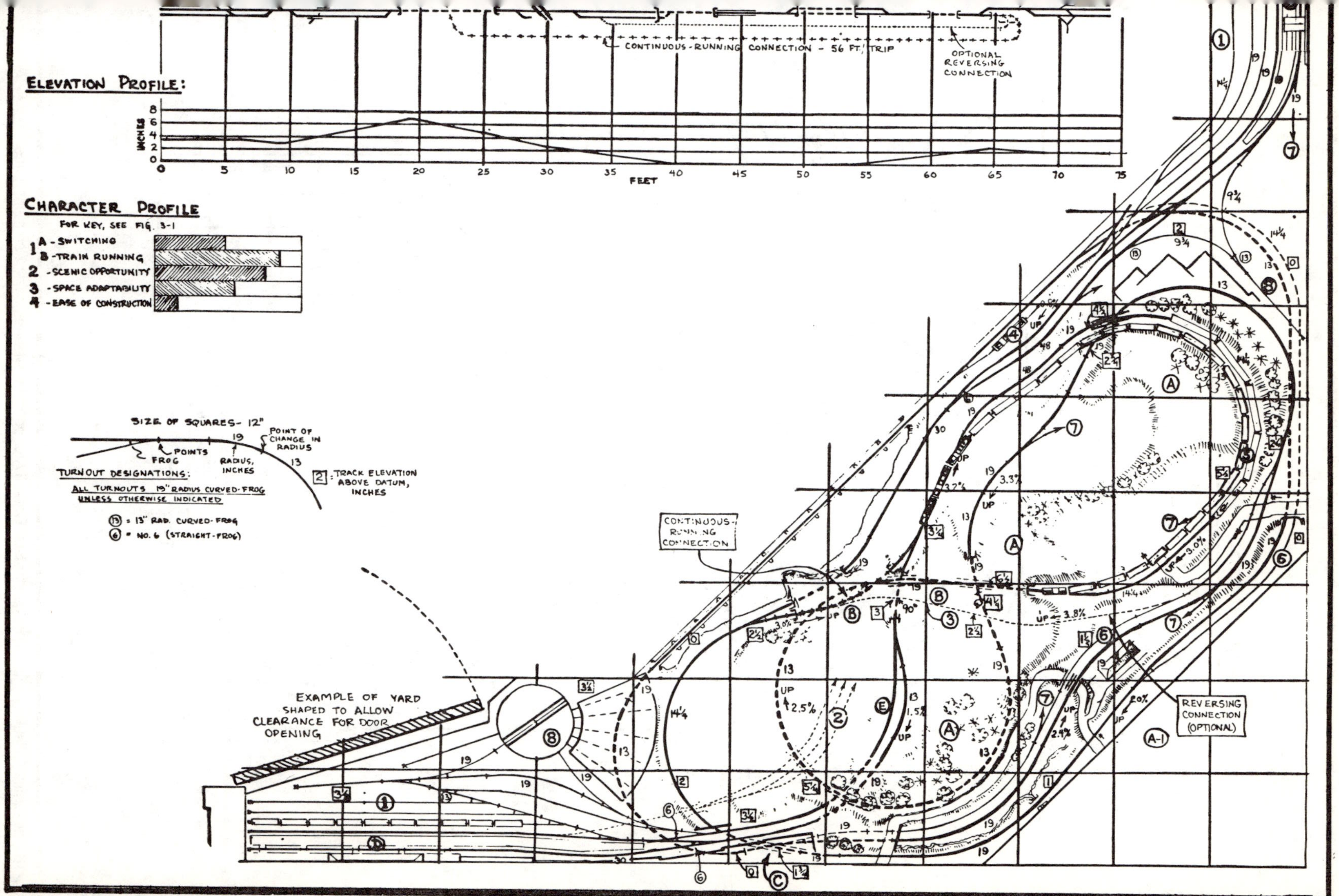

Fig. 4-14. Spaghetti on the Rolling Pin track plan for N gauge.

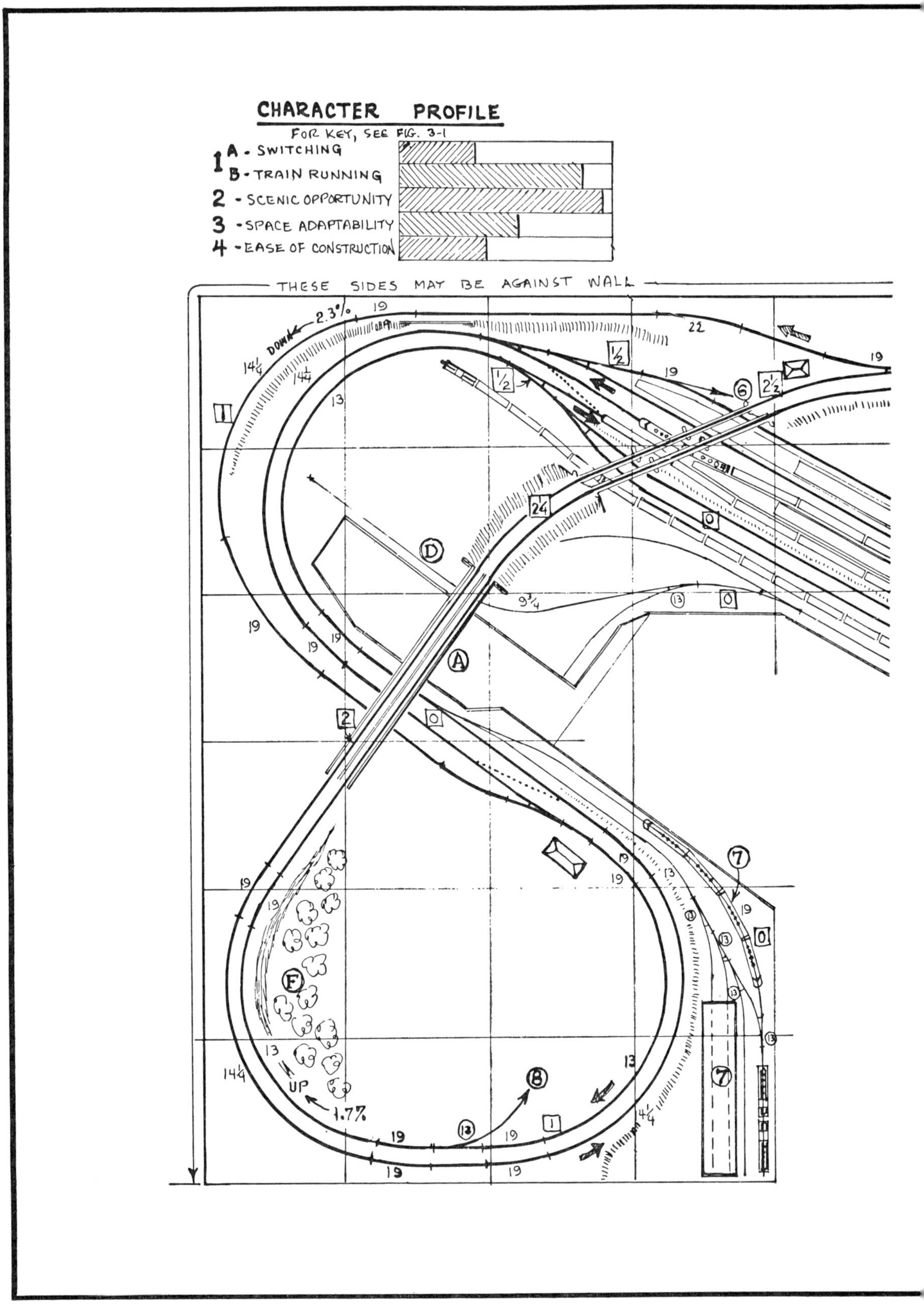

Fig. 4-16. The Exhibitionist track plan for N gauge. See Fig. 4-17 for operational and scenic treatment notes.

SCHEMATIC:

ELEVATION PROFILE:

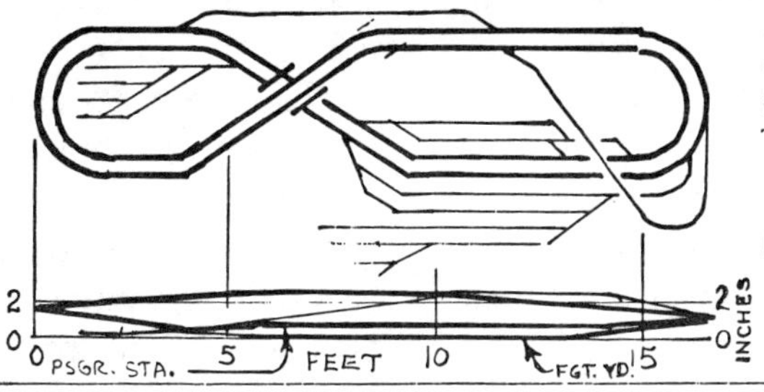

NOTE THAT THERE ARE NO ELECTRICAL REVERSING CONNECTIONS IN THIS TRACK PLAN, ALTHOUGH TRAINS MAY TRAVERSE THE DOUBLE-TRACK MAIN LINE IN EITHER DIRECTION. ADDING A CROSSOVER BETWEEN MAIN LINES WOULD CREATE A REVERSING CONNECTION SITUATION.

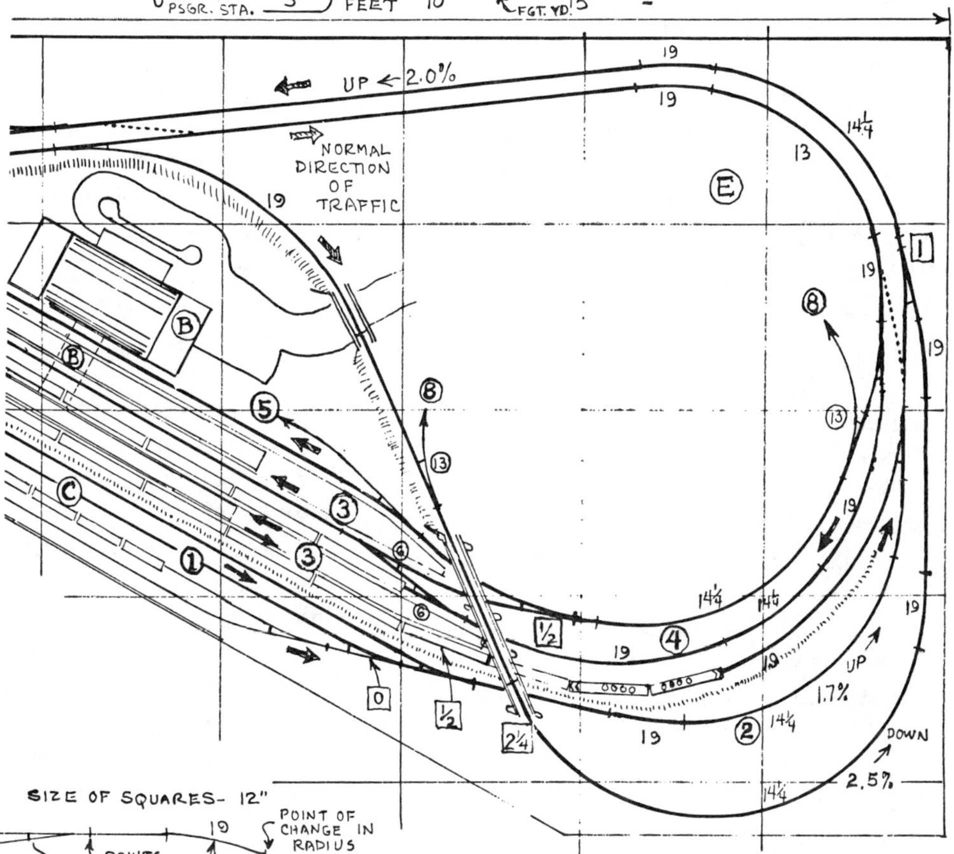

SIZE OF SQUARES- 12"

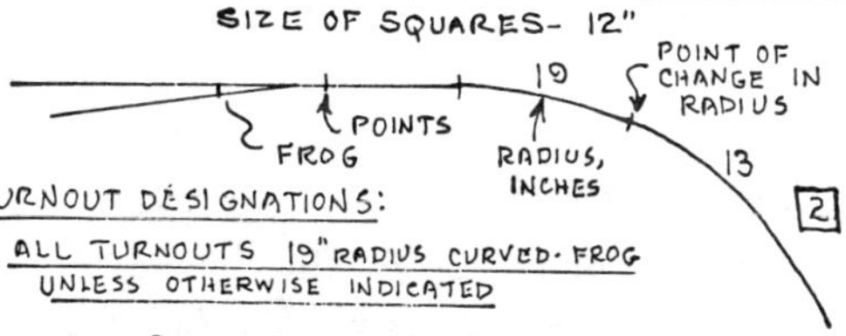

[2] = TRACK ELEVATION ABOVE DATUM, INCHES

TURNOUT DESIGNATIONS:

ALL TURNOUTS 19" RADIUS CURVED-FROG UNLESS OTHERWISE INDICATED

(13) = 13" RAD. CURVED-FROG

(6) = NO. 6 (STRAIGHT-FROG)

LOCATIONS SUITABLE FOR MAIN-LINE CROSSOVERS (OPTIONAL, SEE NOTES) the mild complication of adding wiring to handle the electrical reversing-connection situation that results, is a logical development, particularly if local freight operations are expanded.

Size: 6 × 10 ft., with walk-in notch
Gauge: N
Curvature standards: conventional
Schematic: double-track oval with two-way direction-of-travel capapability; no *electrical* reversing connections
Recommended construction: cookie-cutter, with commercial bridges/piers at crossing points
Trackwork options: all trackwork items standard, with sectional track usable for easemented curves if curvable track, preferred, not used

ANOTHER MEDIUM BIG TIME RAILROAD

With its conventional curvature standards, this railroad (Fig. 4-18) can expect to handle full-length rolling stock in fairly long trains. The main line is double track with enough crossovers for considerable flexibility in routing trains to and from the moderate-size yard. Optional reversing connection allows out-and-back operation from the yard. A third track serves as switching lead without interfering with main-line traffic.

More industry tracks can be added, but turnouts on curves will be required, which is no problem if you're building your own!

Size: 13 × 16 ft. L, with walk-in notch
Gauge: S
Curvature standards: conventional
Schematic: one and a half times around overlapped dogbone; double track, with optional single reversing connection
Recommended construction: open grid; cookie-cutter only in yard area
Trackwork options: all turnouts standard, primarily No. 5 straight-frog hand-built or otherwise; curvable or hand-laid track

BOTH SIDES OF THE MOUNTAIN

This railroad (Fig. 4-19) is primarily a main line log carrier whose basic job is to haul trainloads of logs from a loading site over a mountain and down to a mill where they can be converted to lumber. In-the-woods logging operations can be added. In this medium-sized pike the main line is long enough to represent, with the aid of 4 percent grades, both sides of the mountain and still attain moderately dizzying altitudes with tall trestles. See Fig. 4-20 for operational notes.

The ease with which prefabricated loads of logs can be put on and taken off skeleton flatcars makes it practical to run loads to the mill and empties back, with correspondingly different hauling capabilities for the same locomotives. Relatively large (2-8-2, 2-6-6-2) narrow-gauge locomotives will be at home on such a line.

Additional dual-gauge trackage can be added in the mill area and the logging operations with geared locomotives further developed.

This plan can be built as a standard-gauge railroad in S scale with only minor revisions. The track center spacing of three inches is about right and overhead clearances adequate at points where tracks cross. In this gauge it could represent a more general-purpose line, a mineral-hauler, with suitably different processing facilities at the ends of the line, or keep the timber-country approach.

Size: 13 × 16 ft. L, with walk-in notch
Gauge: On3
Curvature standards: conventional (for narrow gauge)
Schematic: point-to-loop with single switchback
Recommended construction: open grid
Trackwork options: all turnouts standard, primarily No. 5 straight-frog, hand-built or otherwise; curvable or hand-laid track

ALL THE ESSENTIALS

In a moderate space, with stand-up access to virtually all important areas, this plan (Fig. 4-21) provides the essentials for varied single-track operation. These include three meeting points, a yard for make-up and break-up of trains, engine servicing and turning facilities, and enough industry spurs to support local freight operations.

You could further develop the plan primarily in the direction of squeezing in a few more industry tracks by using more imaginative turnouts, such as curved-frogs on curves, and the additional structures and scenic detailing that go with them.

OPERATIONAL NOTES:

1. FREIGHT YARD & LAYOVER/MAKE-UP TRACK FOR THROUGH & LOCAL TRAINS.
2. SWITCHING LEAD TRACK, CLEAR OF MAIN LINE FOR MOVES OF UP TO 8 CARS.
3. MAIN-LINE PASSENGER PLATFORMS FOR 8-10 CAR TRAINS.
4. PASSENGER (REAR-END) SWITCHING LEADS CLEAR OF MAIN LINE FOR MOVES OF UP TO 4 CARS.
5. SLEEPING CAR SET-OUT TRACK (OPTIONAL)
6. HEAD-END (MAIL/EXPRESS) CAR SET-OUT TRACK (OPTIONAL - REQUIRES ADDITIONAL BRIDGES).
7. DIESEL SHOP AND LOCOMOTIVE FUEL/SAND SERVICING FACILITIES. (LOCATED SOME DISTANCE FROM STATION/YARD TO SPREAD OUT POINTS OF MAJOR INTEREST, PROVIDE BETTER VIEW OF MOTIVE POWER BETWEEN RUNS)
8. CONNECTION POINTS FOR SPUR TRACKS SERVING MAJOR INDUSTRIES.

SCENIC-TREATMENT NOTES:

- (A) HARBOR, SPANNED BY STONE-ARCH BRIDGES. — SHINY ENOUGH "WATER" FOR INTERESTING REFLECTIONS.
- (B) "UNION STATION" — A BIG ONE, WITH UNDERPASS TO PLATFORMS (RATHER THAN OVERPASS) SUGGESTED TO LEAVE TRAINS MORE VISIBLE FOR CLOSE INSPECTION.
- (C) FREIGHT TRACKS IN FOREGROUND AT SLIGHTLY LOWER LEVEL THAN STATION TRACKS — FOR A BETTER LOOK AT THE TRAINS, AGAIN!
- (D) HARBORSIDE STRUCTURES/INDUSTRIES, TO SUIT.
- (E) URBAN SCENE — COMPATIBLE WITH STATION, AND HIGH ENOUGH TO INTERRUPT VIEW OF PASSING TRAINS, BREAK UP ROUND-AND-ROUND EFFECT.
- (F) MORE RUSTIC AREA, SEPARATED LOGICALLY FROM CITY BY WATERWAY, WITH CUT & TREES HIGH ENOUGH TO HIDE SOME PART OF TRAINS' SERPENTINE COURSE, MAKE RAILROAD SEEM A BIT LARGER.

Fig. 4-17. Operational and scenic treatment notes for The Exhibitionist track plan. See Fig. 4-16 for track plan.

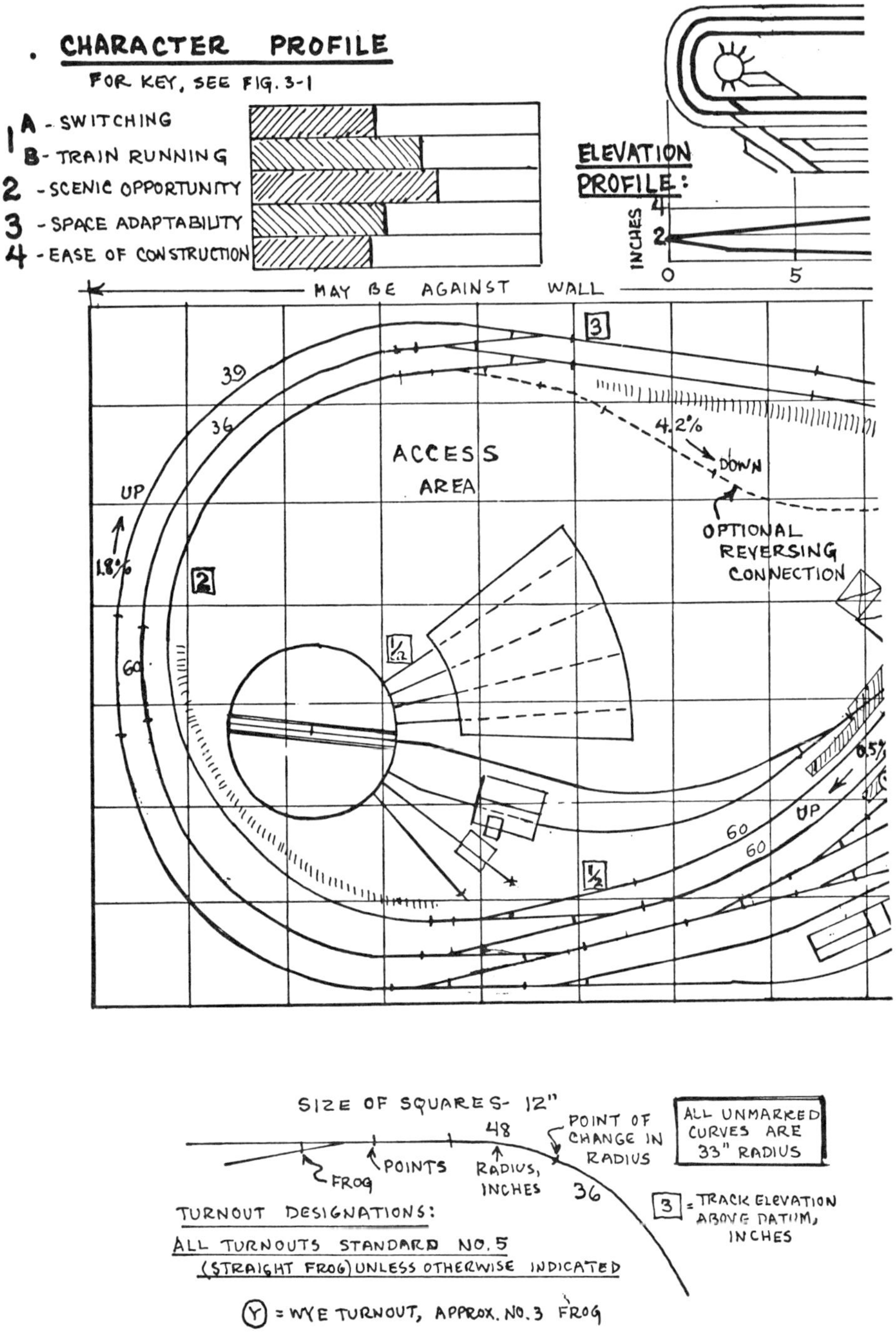

FOR OPERATIONAL NOTES APPLYING TO THIS PLAN, SEE FIGS. 3-4 AND 4-1.

FOR SCENIC-TREATMENT SUGGESTIONS, SEE NOTES FOR FIGS. 4-20 AND 4-21.

Fig. 4-18. Another Medium Big Time Railroad track plan for S gauge.

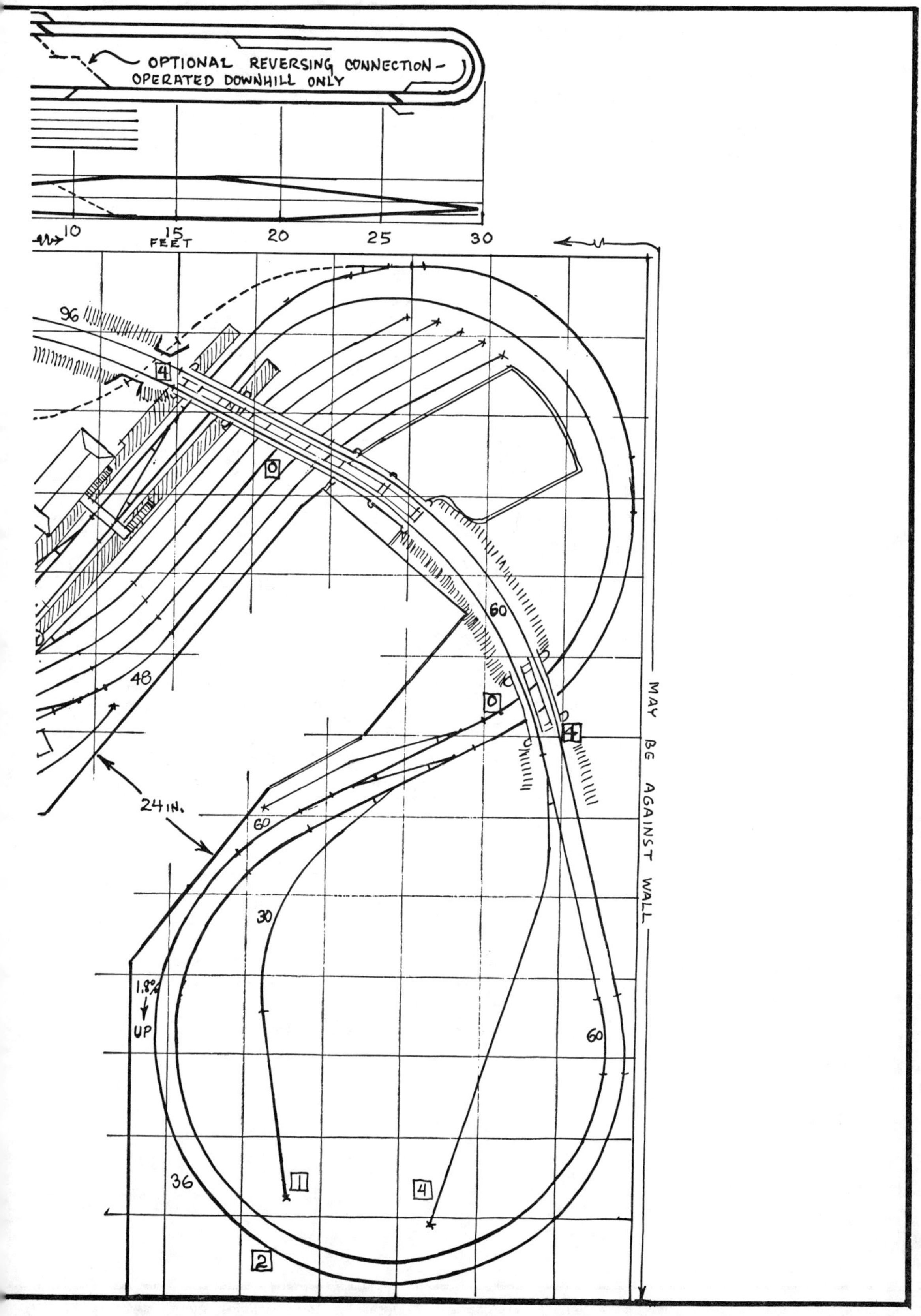

OPTIONAL REVERSING CONNECTION - OPERATED DOWNHILL ONLY
10
15
FEET
20
25
30
96
4
0
60
48
0
4
24 IN.
60
30
1.8%
UP
60
36
1
4
2
MAY BE AGAINST WALL

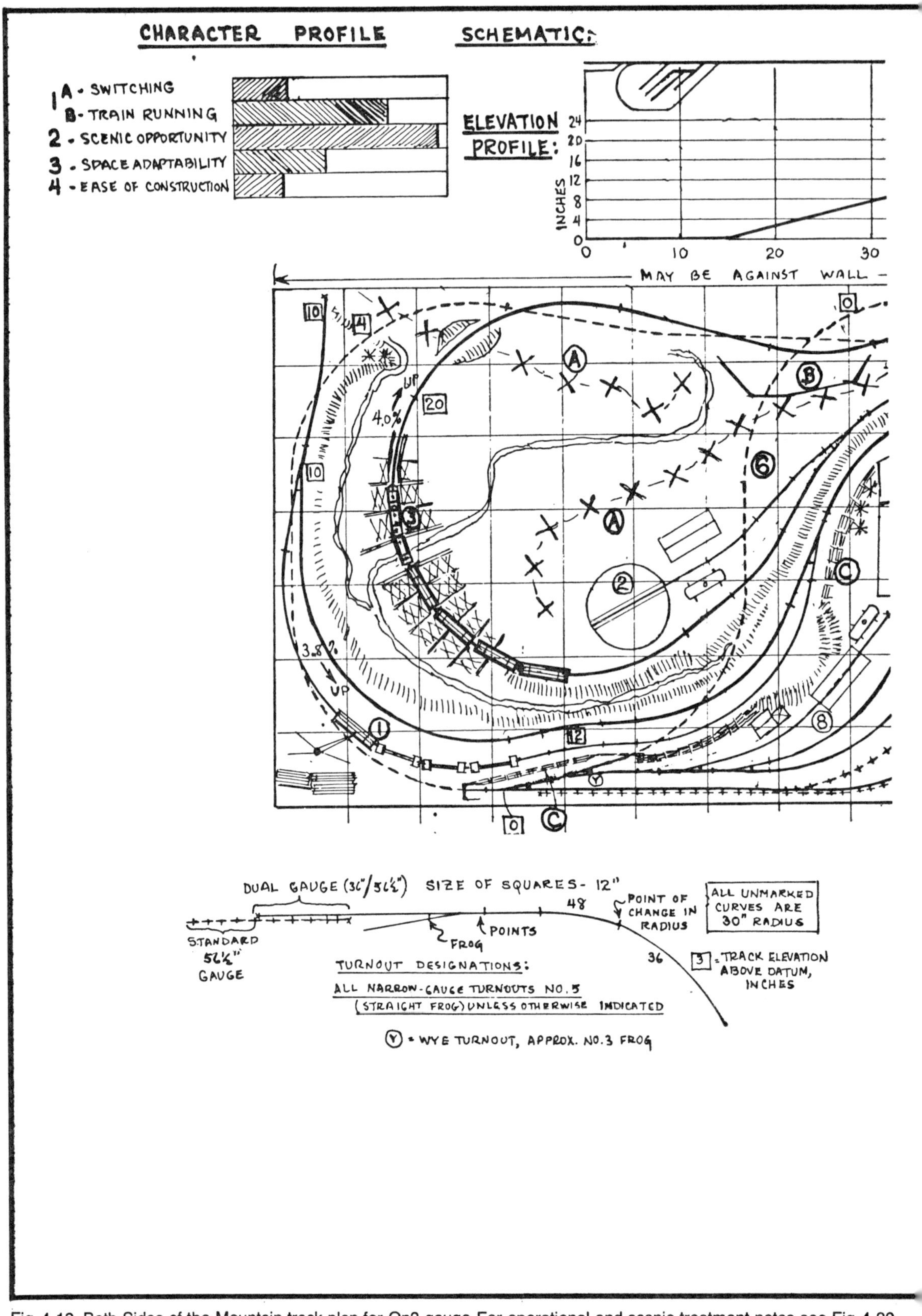

Fig. 4-19. Both Sides of the Mountain track plan for On3 gauge. For operational and scenic treatment notes see Fig. 4-20.

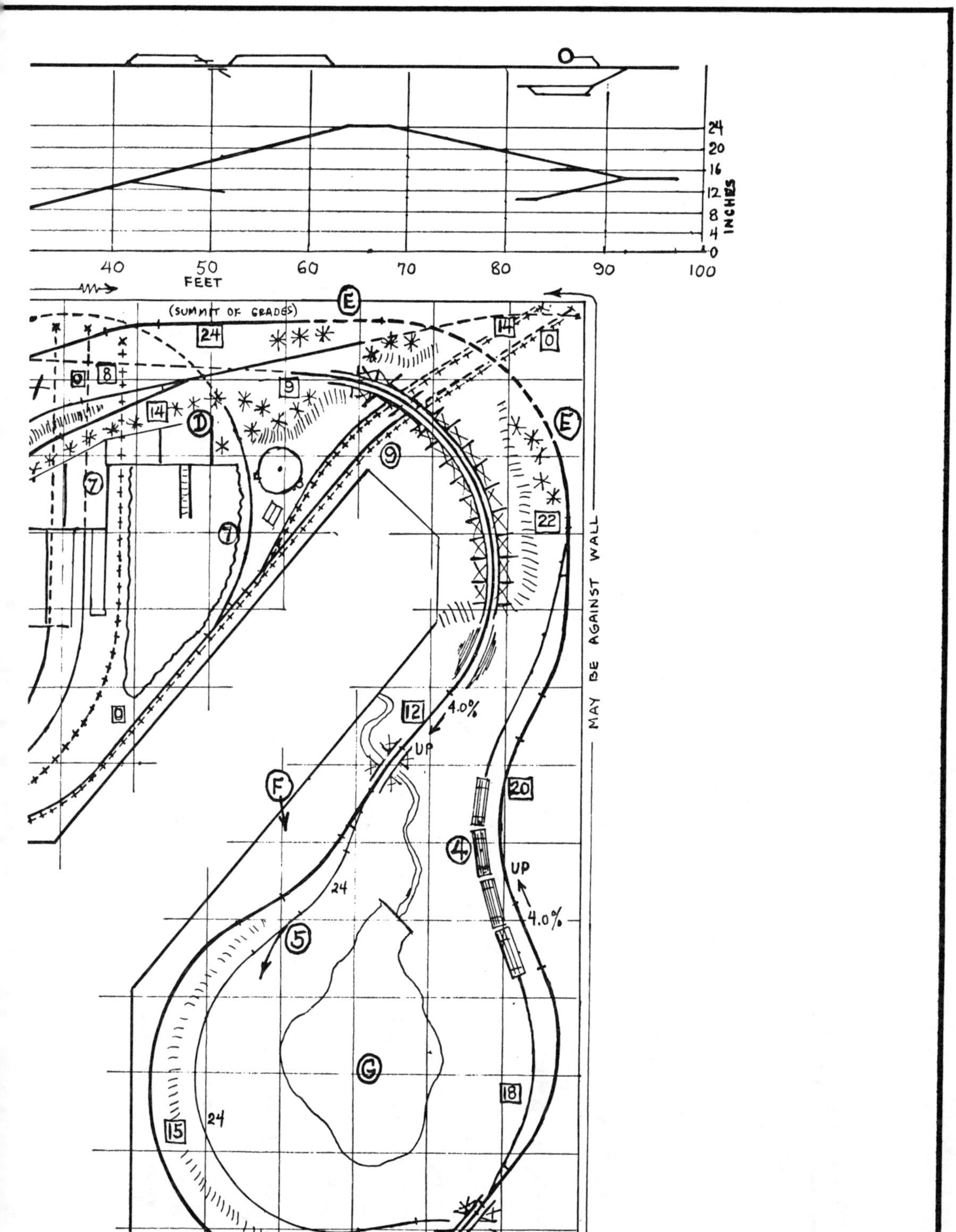
24
20
16
12
8
4
0
INCHES
40
50
60
70
80
90
100
FEET
(SUMMIT OF GRADES)
E
24
14
0
8
9
14
D
7
9
E
22
7
0
12
4.0%
UP
F
20
4
UP
4.0%
24
5
G
18
15
24
9
30
ELEV.
× 25
MAY BE AGAINST WALL

OPERATIONAL NOTES:

1. "LANDING" AREA — LOGS LOADED ON SKELETON FLAT CARS; EMPTIES DROPPED INTO LOADING POSITION BY GRAVITY.
2. THEIR BEING NO SUITABLE PIECE OF LEVEL GROUND BIG ENOUGH FOR A TURNTABLE NEARER THAN THIS TO THE END OF THE "MAIN LINE", LOCOMOTIVES RUN BACKWARD THE REST OF THE WAY — EXCEPT THAT SWITCHBACK PUTS THEM IN FORWARD MOTION AGAIN ON THE FINAL SECTION TO THE LANDING.
3. LOADED CARS TAKE OVER SUMMIT IN 4-CAR CUTS (TONNAGE LIMIT ON 4% GRADE).
4. SIDING FOR REASSEMBLING TRAIN FOR DOWNHILL TRIP TO THE MILL. AS THE ONLY PASSING TRACK ON MAIN LINE, MUST ALSO BE MEETING POINT WITH UPHILL TRAIN OF EMPTIES.
5. CLOSER-IN LOGGING OPERATION WITH GEARED LOKEYS, ADDITIONAL TRACKAGE OF EXTRA-SHARP CURVATURE ADDED IN FUTURE DEVELOPMENT.
6. BALLOON TRACK TAKES CARE OF TURNING TRAINS AT THE MILL END OF THE MAIN LINE.
7. LOG UNLOADING TRACK AT MILL POND. SOME LOGS ALSO PUT DIRECTLY INTO MILL.
8. LOCO SERVICING TRACKS — FUEL, SAND AND MINIMAL RUNNING REPAIRS. FOR NARROW-GAUGE ENGINES, OPEN SHED SUFFICIENT — RAILROAD SHUTS DOWN IN WINTER WHEN LOGGING STOPS.

(9) STANDARD-GAUGE CONNECTION FOR OUTBOUND LUMBER, INBOUND SUPPLIES — DUAL-GAUGE TRACKAGE FOR SWITCHING THE MILL

SCENIC-TREATMENT NOTES:

(A) ABOVE-EYELEVEL VIEW-BLOCKS (MOUNTAIN RIDGES AND TREES) SEPARATE SCENES IN TWO STREAM VALLEYS, HIDE ORIGIN AND DESTINATIONS OF CREEKS AND TRACKS, GIVE REASON FOR THE SWITCHBACK TO REACH LOG LOADING AREA.

(B) OPEN-REAR MOUNTAIN PROVIDES EMERGENCY ACCESS TO TOP-LEVEL TRACK. (LOWER LEVELS EASILY REACHED FROM BELOW).

(C) EXTENSIVE CRIBWORK (TIMBER, OF COURSE) SUPPORTS UPPER-LEVEL TRACKAGE.

(D) TREES SOFTEN & HIDE THE QUICK SWITCH FROM LOWER-LEVEL MILL BUILDINGS TO UPPER-LEVEL TRACKAGE ON THE MOUNTAINSIDE.

(E) TRACKAGE OVER SUMMIT IN OPEN BUT HIDDEN BEHIND TREES — TUNNELS INAPPROPRIATE FOR LOGGING RAILROAD IF IN ANY WAY AVOIDABLE.

(F) VIEW UP VALLEY TOWARD HORSESHOE CURVE. SURROUNDED BY HILLS.

(G) DROP-DOWN POND FOR ACCESS IN CONSTRUCTING LOGGING TRACKAGE

Fig. 4-20. Operational and scenic treatment notes for Both Sides of the Mountain track plan. For track plan see Fig. 4-19.

CHARACTER PROFILE

FOR KEY, SEE FIG. 3-1

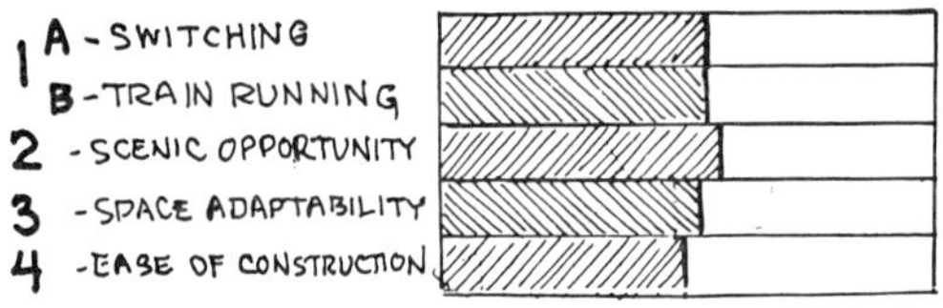

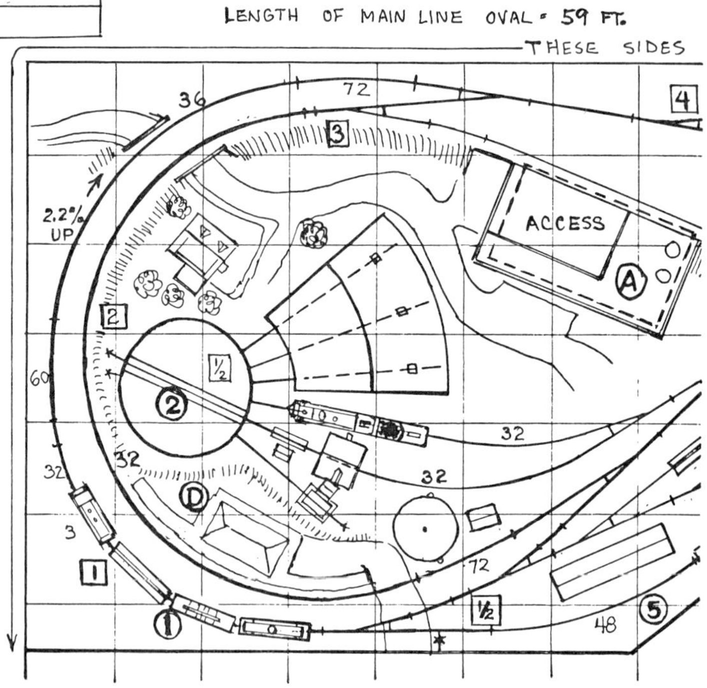

OPERATIONAL NOTES:

(1) ONE OF THE THREE PASSING SIDINGS DOUBLES AS THE SWITCHING LEAD FOR THE YARD. GRADE IN YARD HELD TO 0.5% MAXIMUM FOR EASY SWITCHING.

(2) 72 FT. TURNTABLE SHOWN, ADEQUATE FOR TURNING SINGLE-ENDED DIESELS OR ANY STEAM LOCOS APPROPRIATE FOR SHARP CURVATURE OF MAIN LINE. ROUNDHOUSE STALL-LENGTHS TO MATCH.

(3) FOUR-INCH TRACK-CENTER SPACING SHOWN. IF RESTRAINT IS USED ON MAXIMUM-CAR AND LOCOMOTIVE LENGTHS ON RAILROAD (SEE CHAPTER 2), SPACING CAN BE REDUCED TO 3½ IN., INCREASING RADIUS OF INSIDE TRACKS.

(4) BARE-MINIMUM (20 FT.) RAILHEAD-TO-RAILHEAD CLEARANCE SHOWN IMPLIES THIN BRIDGE FLOORS. CLEARANCE CAN BE RAISED BY INCREASING GRADES TO 2.8%, NO GREAT OBSTACLE FOR RELATIVELY SHORT TRAINS LIKELY TO BE OPERATED.

(5) CABOOSE/RUNAROUND/SWITCHER "POCKET" TRACK. MAKE EVERY TURNOUT WORK HARD FOR ITS KEEP!

SCENIC-TREATMENT NOTES:

(A) FACTORY IN O SCALE CAN EASILY BE LARGE ENOUGH TO SERVE AS COVER FOR GENEROUS-SIZED ACCESS HATCH NEAR SEVERAL KEY TURNOUTS.

(B) OPEN-REAR HILL HIDES THIS HOLE; PROVIDING EMERGENCY ACCESS TO TURNOUTS JUST A BIT TOO FAR FROM THE NOTCH THAT MAKES THE REST OF THE IMPORTANT TRACKAGE EASILY REACHABLE.

(C) A VIEW-BLOCK IS HIGHLY DESIRABLE, SEPARATING INDUSTRIES AND BREAKING UP ROUND-AND-ROUND EFFECT.

(D) A NOD TO PASSENGER SERVICE — HAVE TO SETTLE FOR CURVED PLATFORMS.

(E) NO EXTRA SPACE REQUIRED FOR A LARGE-RADIUS CURVE HERE, AND IT DOES MAKE THE TRAINS LOOK NICE!

Fig. 4-21. All the Essentials track plan for 0 gauge.

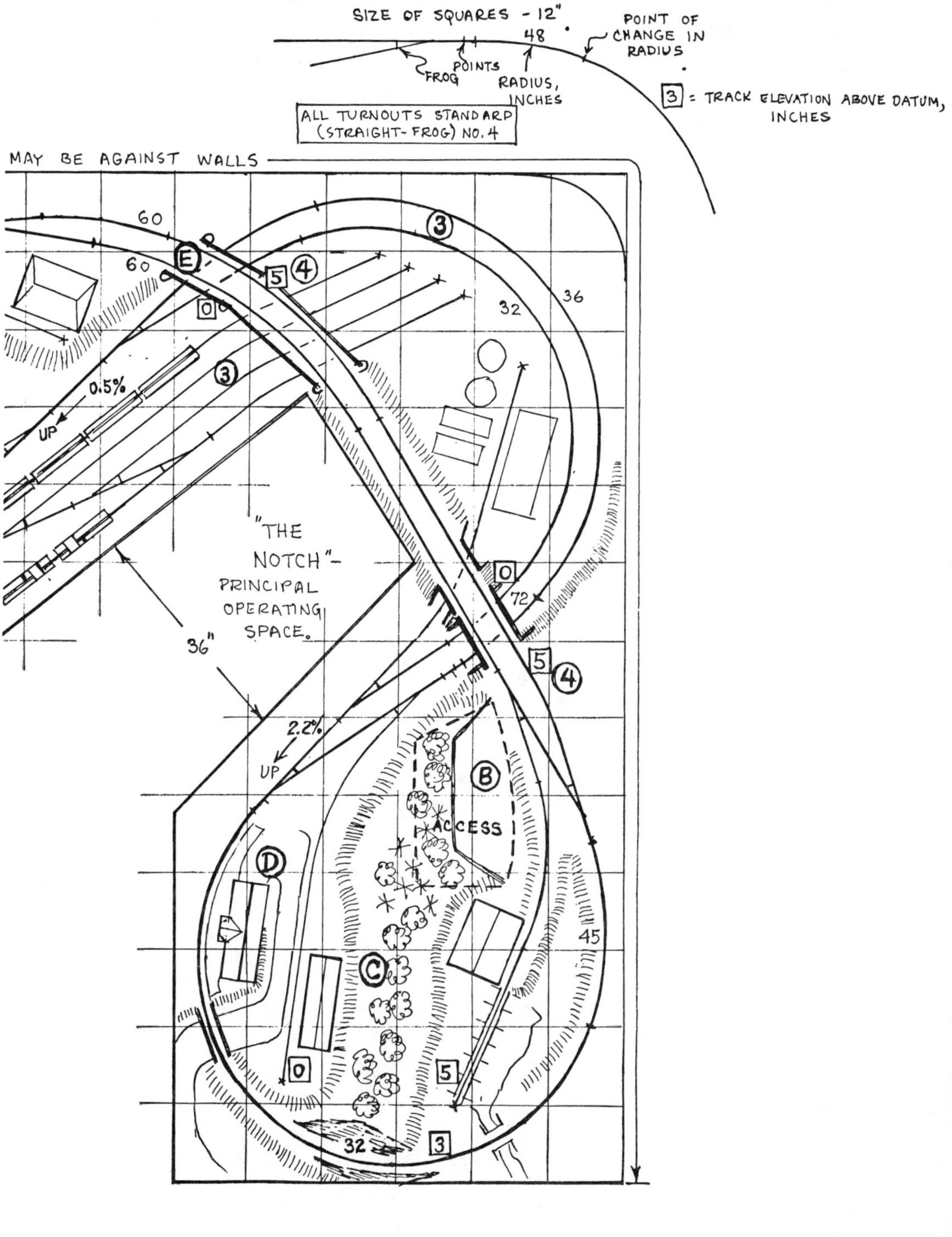

SIZE OF SQUARES - 12"
POINT OF CHANGE IN RADIUS
48
FROG
POINTS
RADIUS, INCHES
3 = TRACK ELEVATION ABOVE DATUM, INCHES
ALL TURNOUTS STANDARD (STRAIGHT-FROG) NO. 4
MAY BE AGAINST WALLS
60
60
E
5
4
3
0
32
36
3
0.5%
UP
"THE NOTCH" - PRINCIPAL OPERATING SPACE.
36"
0
72
5
4
2.2%
UP
B
ACCESS
D
45
C
0
5
32
3

Size: 13 × 16 ft. L, with walk-in notch
Gauge: 0
Curvature standards: sharp, with easement curves approaching most main-line curves
Schematic: one and a half times around overlapped dogbone, single track
Recommended construction: open grid; cookie-cutter only in yard area
Trackwork options: all turnouts standard No. 4, hand-built or otherwise; curvable or hand-laid track

5

Larger Track Plans

When all is said and done, a good big pike beats a good little pike, once it's completed to the point that the trains are running smoothly and the scenic aspects have progressed far enough to provide a suitable background for the railroad operations. The larger layouts, using about 200 square feet as our lower limit in separating them from the medium-size category, can afford to use broader curves for better appearance and operation, need not be so severe in reducing the number of tracks to a bare minimum, and can include a greater variety of passing-points, industries and other points of interest.

The larger pike, of course, is a bigger project. It takes longer to build and often involves more time and effort in preparing the space to receive it. A softening-up campaign on other members of the family may be required to obtain a franchise for additional occupancy rights, or an unfinished space may need paneling, heating, air conditioning or whatever. Larger areas are more likely to have peculiarities such as odd shapes, protruding pipes and supporting columns, or requirements for access to doors or windows. These conditions may greatly affect the track plan that will be practical.

The track plans in this chapter, therefore, are those which are relatively flexible in matching up to typical spaces. Some, despite their size, may adapt to your space with only minor adjustments; others are more likley to serve as springboards which are not directly useable but will point the direction and provide segments for working out your own plan.

It's always easier and safer to expand a smaller plan to fill a larger space than vice versa; therefore, the six plans in this chapter are planned to fit garages, basements or other areas that are of smaller-than-average dimensions. You'll have no problem adding a few inches or feet here and there to adjust them to take advantage of more liberal situations.

Modular model railroading is an idea that has only recently become a major aspect of the hobby. With its opportunities for the apartment dweller or other space-limited modeler to take active part in the operation of very large layouts, it has much to recommend it.

If you're able to consider building a *very* extensive railroad—one that will take you a matter of years to bring to full operation, or one where space limitations are really of secondary importance—you will do best to design it from scratch.

GARAGE RAILROADS

A typical single *stall,* in either a one-car or multi-car attached or detached garage, is a prime site for an extensive model railroad. The area of about 11 × 21 ft. or more is the ideal oblong shape and big enough for heavy-duty train running.

An often-used configuration is the *doughnut* with a large central operating area reached by ducking under the railroad or opening a drawbridge

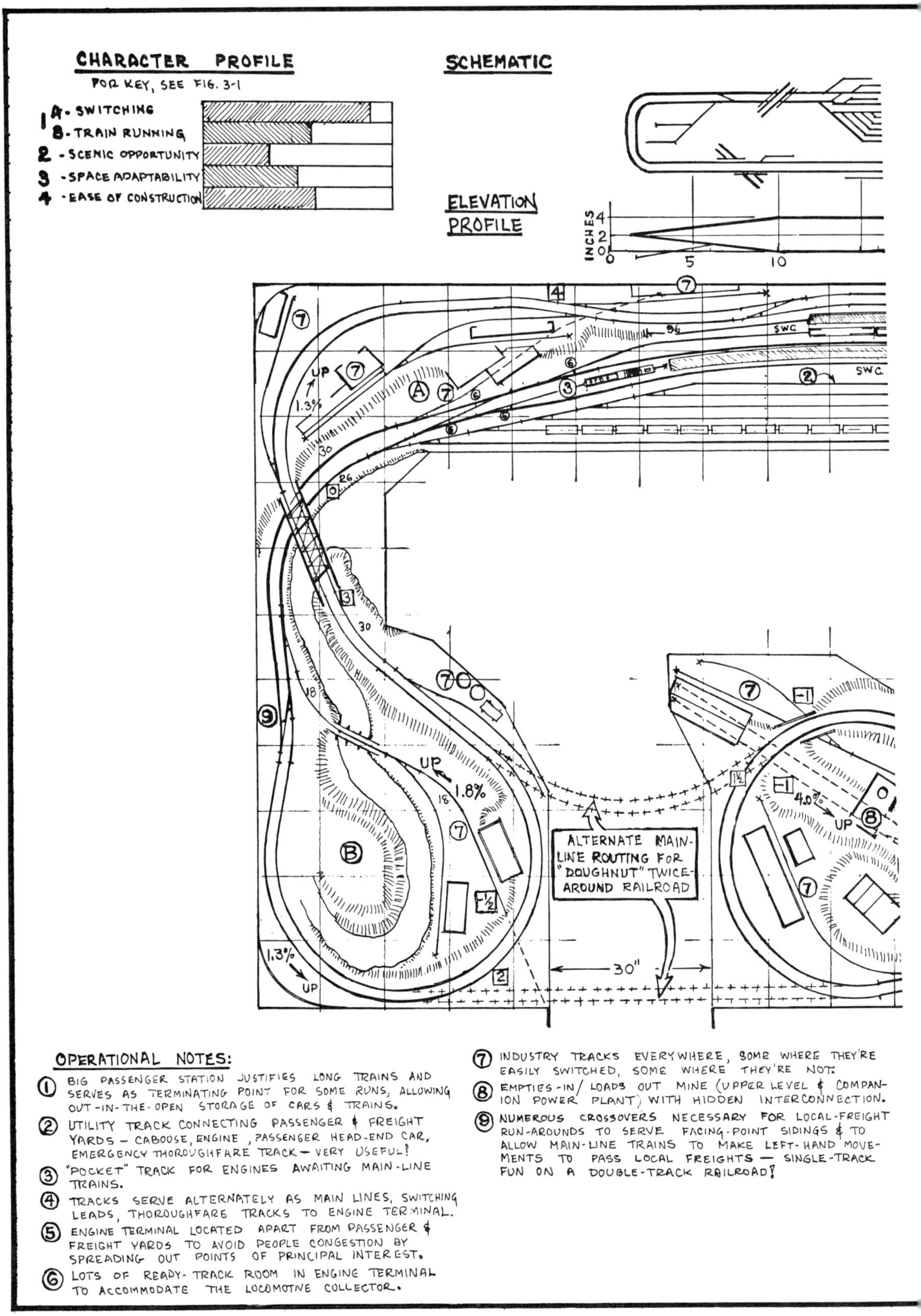

Fig. 5-1. A Garage Full of Way Freight Fun track plan for HO gauge.

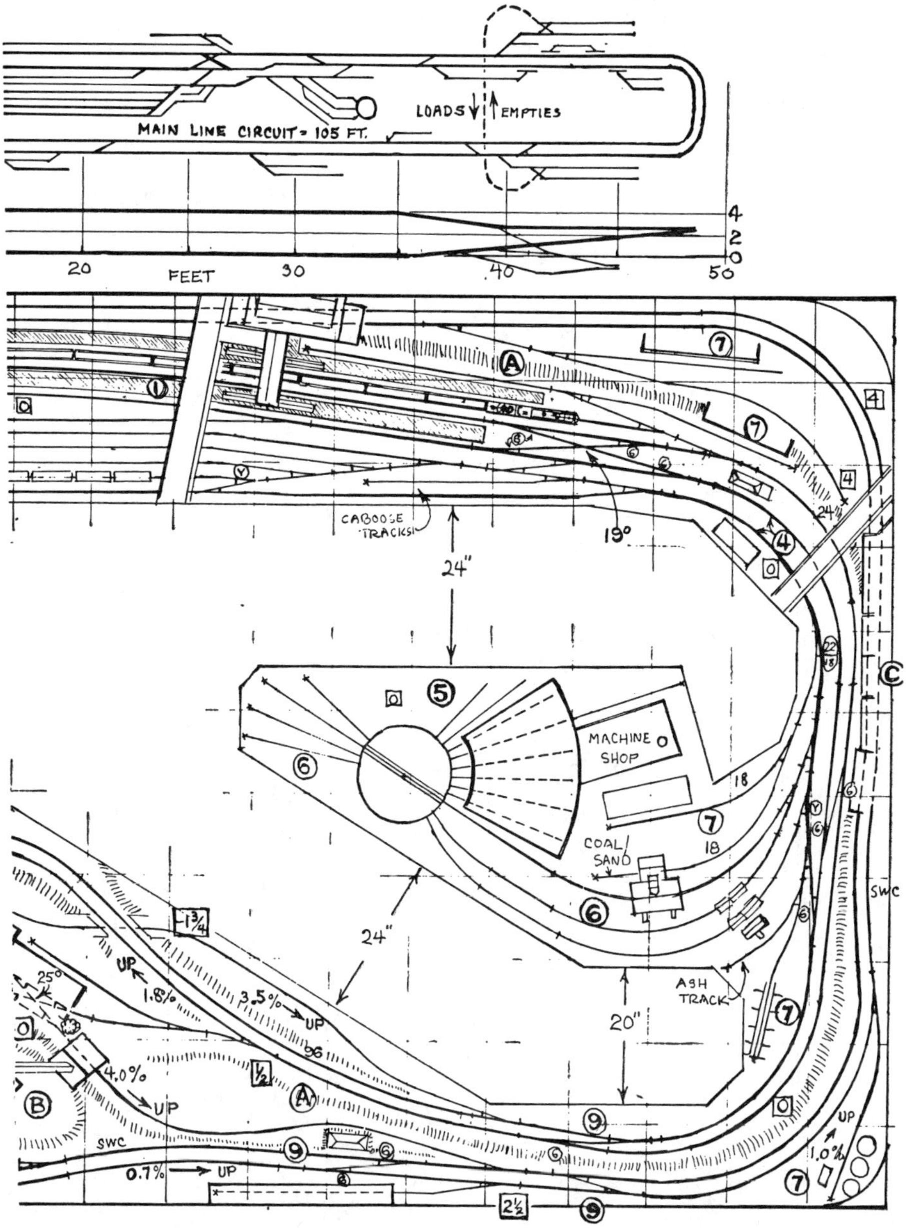

SIZE OF SQUARES = 12"

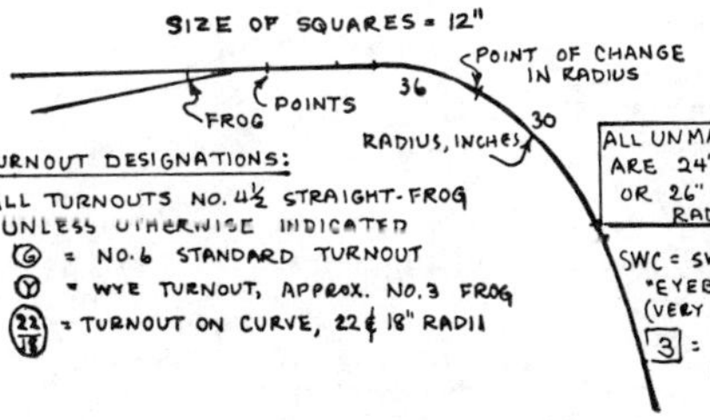

TURNOUT DESIGNATIONS:

ALL TURNOUTS NO. 4½ STRAIGHT-FROG UNLESS OTHERWISE INDICATED

- Ⓖ = NO. 6 STANDARD TURNOUT
- Ⓨ = WYE TURNOUT, APPROX. NO. 3 FROG
- 22/18 = TURNOUT ON CURVE, 22 & 18" RADII

ALL UNMARKED CURVES ARE 24" (INSIDE TRACK) OR 26" (OUTSIDE TRACK) RADIUS

SWC = SWEEPING "EYEBALL" CURVE (VERY LARGE RADIUS)

3 = ELEVATION ABOVE DATUM, INCHES

SCENIC-TREATMENT NOTES:

Ⓐ DIFFERENCE IN ELEVATION WITH EMBANKMENTS & RETAINING WALLS USED TO SEPARATE PARALLEL MAIN LINES AT MOST POINTS.

Ⓑ SCENERY HIGH ENOUGH TO HIDE TRAINS TRAVERSING THE TURN-BACK CURVES, BREAK UP THE CONTINUOUS ROUND & ROUND PATTERN SOMEWHAT

Ⓒ URBAN BUILDING FLATS HIDE REAR TRACK, SEPARATE MAIN LINES AT THIS PARTICULARLY TIGHT POINT.

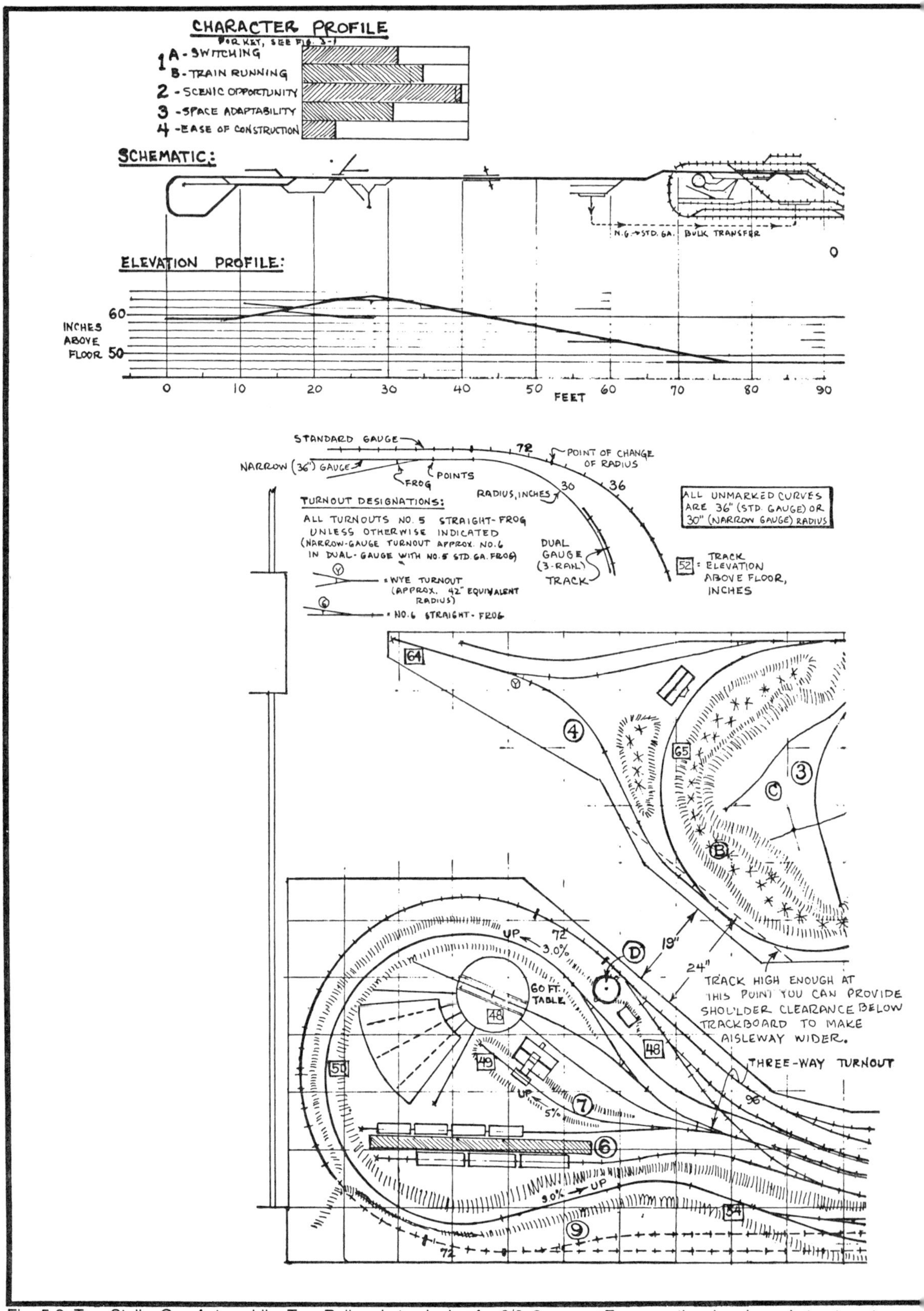

Fig. 5-2. Two Stalls, One Automobile, Two Railroads track plan for 0/0n3 gauge. For operational and scenic treatment notes see Fig. 5-3.

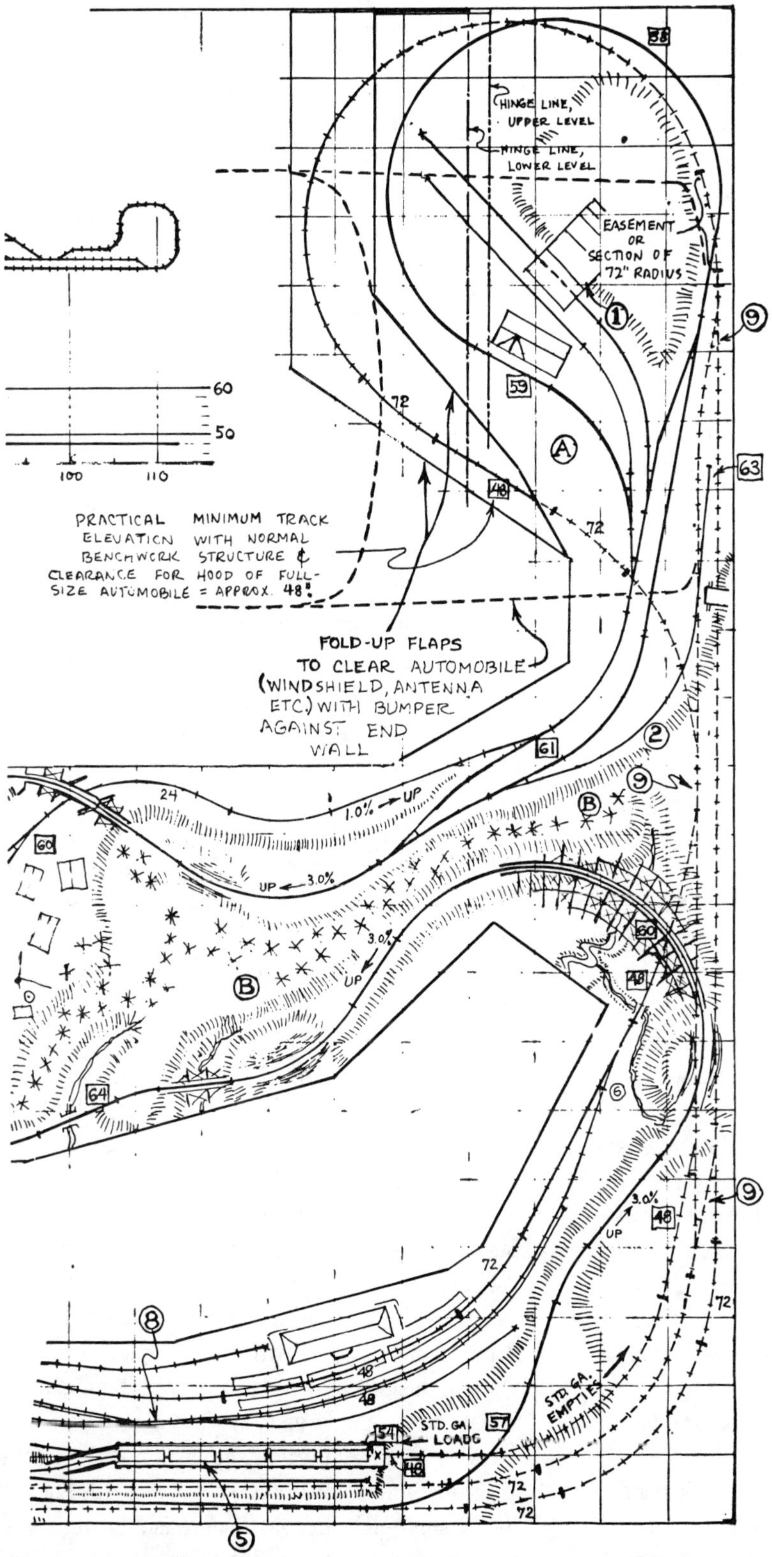
HINGE LINE, UPPER LEVEL
HINGE LINE, LOWER LEVEL
EASEMENT OR SECTION OF 72" RADIUS
PRACTICAL MINIMUM TRACK ELEVATION WITH NORMAL BENCHWORK STRUCTURE & CLEARANCE FOR HOOD OF FULL-SIZE AUTOMOBILE = APPROX. 48"
FOLD-UP FLAPS TO CLEAR AUTOMOBILE (WINDSHIELD, ANTENNA ETC.) WITH BUMPER AGAINST END WALL
1.0% UP
UP 3.0%
3.0% UP
STD. GA. EMPTIES
STD. GA. LOADS
60
50
100
110

arrangement. Figure 5-1 illustrates what can be done in a walk-in arrangement where no-stoop access to the operating area is via either a side pedestrian door or from the other stall area in a two-car garage. The track plan is such that the exact position of the walk-in can be varied considerably to match the actual door locaion without greatly disturbing the operating scheme. Rearrangement into a *U* to accommodate an end door is also feasible.

Adding the railroad usually means demoting one of the automobiles to outdoor storage, but many successful pikes have been built as *lift-ups*, with counterweighted suspensions allowing the whole platform to be raised high enough between operating sessions to readmit the car to its habitat. The doughnut configuration is ideal for such a layout.

With overhead heating, and even air-conditioning, and insulation as the climate may require, the garage represents territory not to be overlooked!

A GARAGE FULL OF WAY FREIGHT FUN

This track plan (Fig. 5-1) simulates the operations of a railroad carrying general freight and passenger traffic through a highly industrialized area. The 16 or so spurs along the main line serving carload freight customers represent a principal facet of the business, with way freights busy switching them while ducking out of the way of through traffic. The engine terminal, passenger and through freight facilities also are well developed. Realistic through-freight operation in open-top cars is easy because the continuous-oval format lets loaded cars travel in one direction, empties in the other. In addition, there are provisions for empties-in/loads-out mineral traffic originating and terminating at points on the layout.

The ample walk-in operating area provides elbow room for the several operators who can be kept busy running the way freights, dispatching the through trains and hustling engines to and from the big engine-servicing area.

The relatively simple main-line track configuration means that broad-radius curves can be substituted if the area is about a foot larger in each dimension.

Additional industry tracks may be worked in at various points, particularly if special turnouts are used. As shown, grades are moderate and not a real factor in train operation, except on some of the spur tracks. But a steep main-line grade, perhaps requiring helper engines, can be created if desired by simply increasing some elevation figures rather drastically.

Size: 11 × 12 ft. walk-in around-the-wall
Gauge: HO
Curvature standards: conventional
Schematic: double-track oval folded into dogbone
Recommended construction: open grid; flat top in yard areas
Trackwork options: all trackwork components standard; curvable or hand-laid track

TWO STALLS, ONE AUTOMOBILE, TWO RAILROADS

The standard-gauge railroad (Fig. 5-2) is limited to an oval, much of it hidden, providing connecting trackage for the narrow gauge. For operating variety in its limited area, full train-reversing flexibility and an empties-in/loads-out car-exchange are provided.

The narrow gauge, which may be expected to have a more limited supply of rolling stock, keeps all of it in the open, generating tonnage at three major points to be hauled and pushed over the mountain to the two points of interchange with the standard gauge.

Standard and narrow gauges will have fun operating in the cramped yard while staying out of each other's way. The amount and complexity of dual-gauge trackage has been minimized in the interest of simplicity of construction.

As it stands, the yard must be worked jointly but separately by engines of the two different gauges, each moving its own cars. A logical extension is to provide much more dual-gauge trackage. A switcher equipped with dual couplers can then work both sides of the problem creating additional variety in the same space.

The 3 percent grade shown is actually on the low side for many prototype narrow-gauge lines. If the ceiling height permits, increasing it to 4 percent would be a good idea. For operational and scenic treatment notes see Fig. 5-3.

Size: 11 × 21 plus 11 × 4 ft. (half of two-car garage)

Gauge: 0/0n3

Curvature standards: standard gauge: sharp, with easements; narrow gauge: conventional equivalent

Schematic: standard gauge: oval with two reversing connections; narrow gauge: point to-loop

Recommended construction: open grid; flat top for lower end loop areas, with large openings for access

Trackwork options: most trackwork components to standard geometry; limited dual-gauge trackage; curvable or hand-laid track

THE BIG Z

This plan (Fig. 5-4) features the realism of a long main line so arranged that the engineer can

OPERATIONAL NOTES

1. ORE CONCENTRATOR OR OTHER BULK PRODUCT PLANT SHIPPING VIA NARROW GAUGE
2. SMALL COAL MINE, PRODUCING ENOUGH FOR THE NARROW GAUGE & LOCAL INDUSTRIES.
3. ALTITUDE HIGH ENOUGH FOR TREES — SO WE HAVE A LUMBERING OPERATION ON THIS SHORT BRANCH.
4. WYE FOR HELPER ENGINES WORKING UP BOTH SIDES TOWARD THE SUMMIT.
5. TWO-LEVEL BULK TRANSFER FACILITY — NARROW-GAUGE ON TOP, DUMPING INTO STD. GAUGE CARS BENEATH. SECOND SPUR ALONGSIDE IS NEEDED SO ROAD ENGINE HAS A PLACE TO STASH EMPTIES BEFORE SPOTTING LOADS — UPGRADE TOO STEEP TO PARK THEM ON MAIN LINE. "EMPTIES-IN/LOADS-OUT" ON THE STD. GAUGE.
6. BOXCAR TRANSFER PLATFORM BETWEEN NARROW & STD. GAUGES. (STD. GAUGE LOCATED TO REAR SO YOU CAN SEE THE LITTLE N.G. CARS).
7. IF THERE'S NO COAL ON THE BRANCH, SPUR WILL HAVE TO BE CONNECTED TO STANDARD-GAUGE TRACKAGE INSTEAD!
8. JUST ENOUGH DUAL-GAUGE SO THE NARROW GAUGE HAS A RUN-AROUND TRACK & CAN REACH THE PASSENGER STATION.
9. DIFFERENCE IN ELEVATION BETWEEN "LEVELS" IS ENOUGH TO PROVIDE ADEQUATE ACCESS TO TURNOUTS, WITH SOME CARE IN LOCATING SUPPORTS FOR UPPER-LEVEL TRACKAGE.

SCENIC-TREATMENT NOTES:

A. DESERT COUNTRY COMES IN HANDY FOR SIMPLIFYING SCENERY ON SECTIONS WHICH MUST FOLD UP TO CLEAR AUTOMOBILE.
B. UNLESS YOU'RE 6'5", IT'S EASY TO EXTEND TERRAIN (WITH SOME HELP FROM EVERGREENS) HIGH ENOUGH FOR VIEW-BLOCK WITHOUT RESORTING TO BACKDROP.
C. A SECLUDED VALLEY FOR LOGGING OPERATIONS.
D. A DUAL-GAUGE WATER TANK.

Fig. 5-3. Operational and scenic treatment notes for Two Stalls, One Automobile, Two Railroads track plan. For track plan see Fig. 5-2.

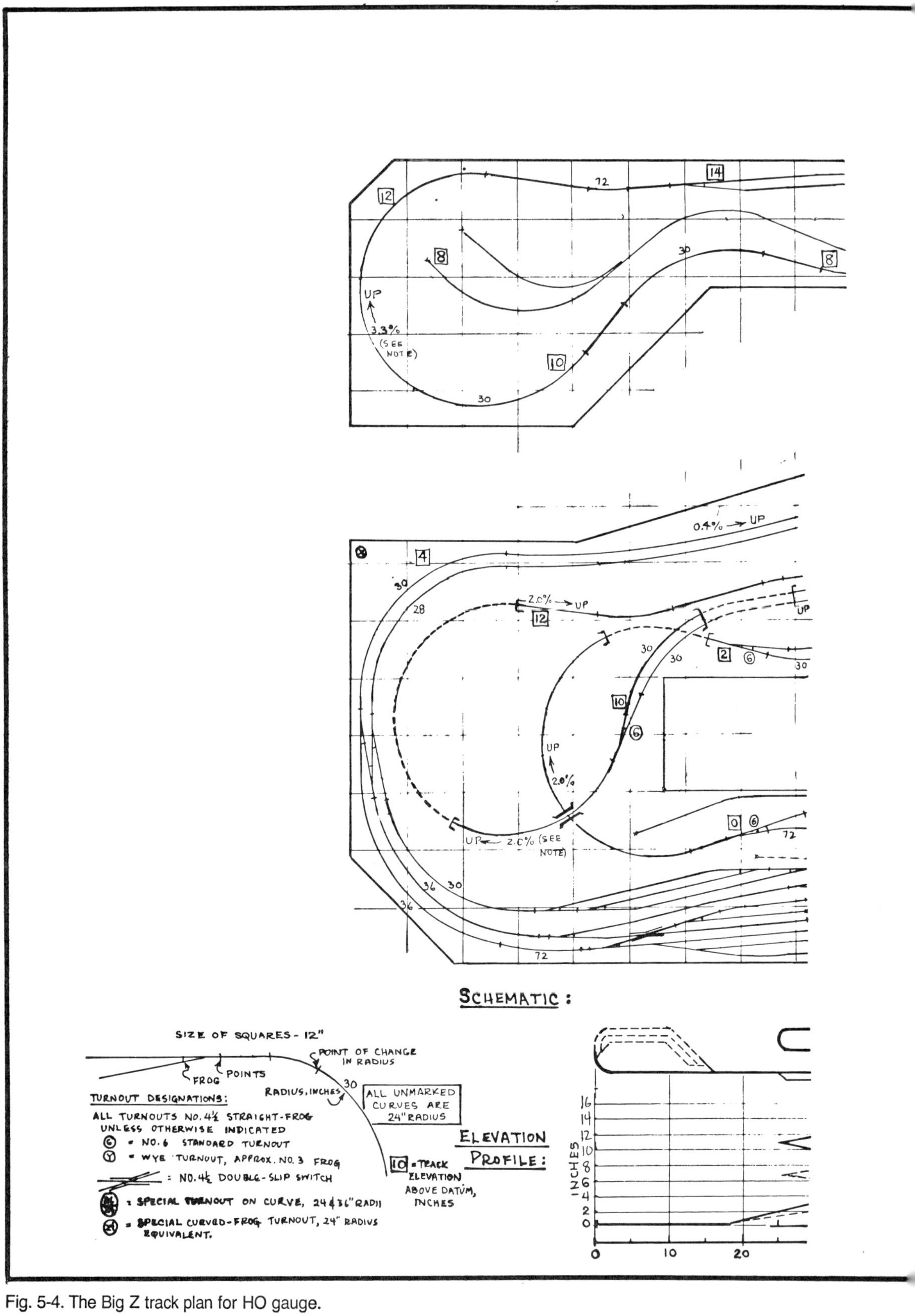

Fig. 5-4. The Big Z track plan for HO gauge.

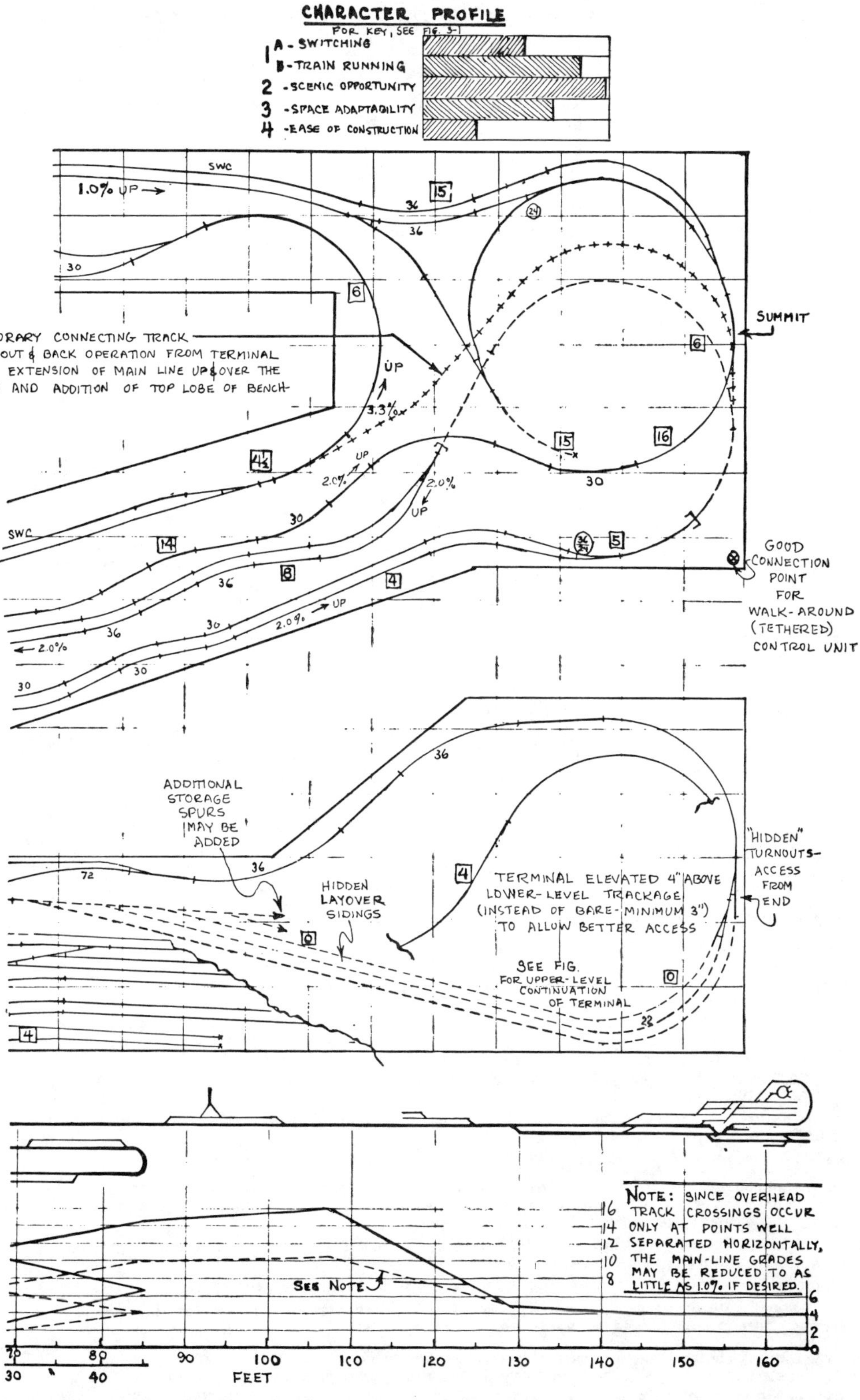
CHARACTER PROFILE
FOR KEY, SEE FIG. 3-1
1 A - SWITCHING
B - TRAIN RUNNING
2 - SCENIC OPPORTUNITY
3 - SPACE ADAPTABILITY
4 - EASE OF CONSTRUCTION
TEMPORARY CONNECTING TRACK ALLOWS OUT & BACK OPERATION FROM TERMINAL PENDING EXTENSION OF MAIN LINE UP & OVER THE MOUNTAIN AND ADDITION OF TOP LOBE OF BENCH-WORK.
SUMMIT
GOOD CONNECTION POINT FOR WALK-AROUND (TETHERED) CONTROL UNIT
1.0% UP
SWC
ADDITIONAL STORAGE SPURS MAY BE ADDED
HIDDEN LAYOVER SIDINGS
TERMINAL ELEVATED 4" ABOVE LOWER-LEVEL TRACKAGE (INSTEAD OF BARE-MINIMUM 3") TO ALLOW BETTER ACCESS
SEE FIG. FOR UPPER-LEVEL CONTINUATION OF TERMINAL
"HIDDEN" TURNOUTS-ACCESS FROM END
NOTE: SINCE OVERHEAD TRACK CROSSINGS OCCUR ONLY AT POINTS WELL SEPARATED HORIZONTALLY, THE MAIN-LINE GRADES MAY BE REDUCED TO AS LITTLE AS 1.0% IF DESIRED.
SEE NOTE
FEET

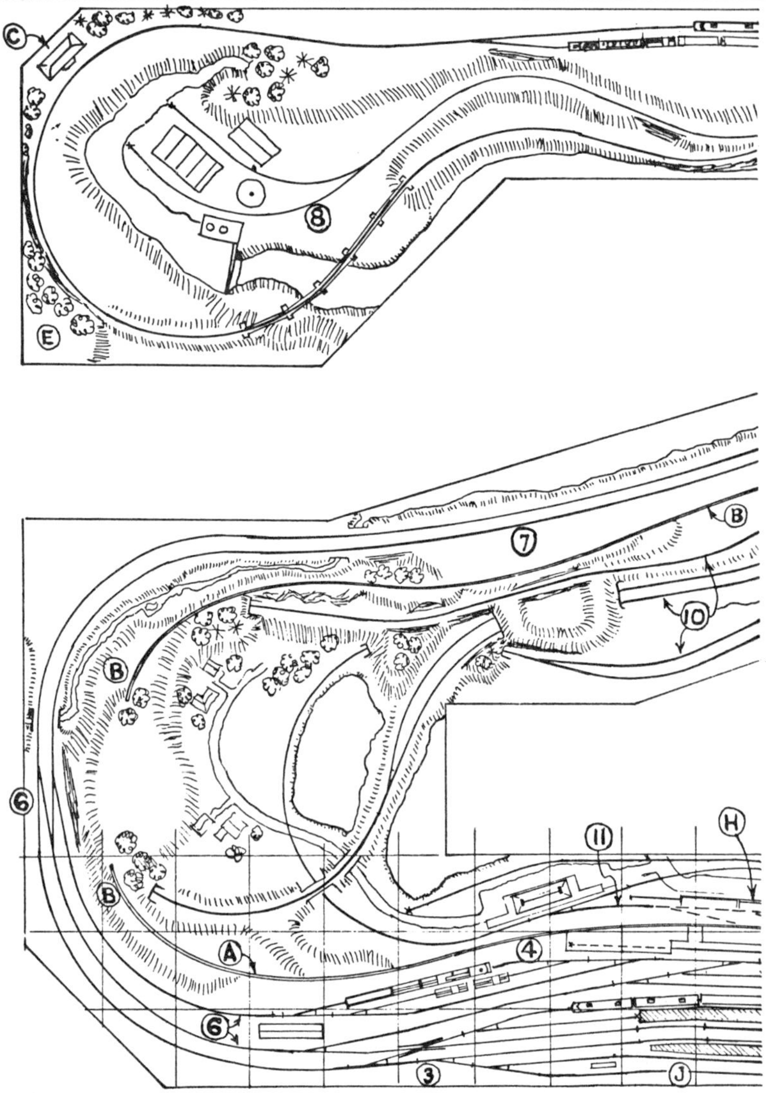

Operational Notes:

1. ENORMOUS BULK-LOADING FACILITY ON BALLOON TRACK SERVES UNIT TRAINS ORIGINATING AT THE TERMINAL END OF LINE.—SOLID TRAINS OF COVERED GRAIN HOPPERS, FOR EXAMPLE. BALLOON TRACK ALSO SERVES FOR TURNING LOCOMOTIVES, OBSERVATION CARS, ETC. IF DIESEL-TYPE ENGINE TERMINAL IS SELECTED.
2. DIESEL FUEL, SAND AND SERVICE TRACKS AND SHOP SHOWN. ROOM IS AMPLE FOR STEAM FACILITY WITH 100 FT. OR LONGER TURNTABLE IF DESIRED.
3. ENGINE-ESCAPE CROSSOVER.. FOR PASSENGER TERMINAL TRACKS. DOUBLE-SLIP SWITCH AT STATION THROAT GIVES IMPRESSION OF BIGGER TERMINAL; TWO REGULAR TURNOUTS MAY BE SUBSTITUTED WITHIN SPACE AVAILABLE.
4. CABOOSE TRACKS, WRECK-TRAIN READY TRACK, SHORT-RUNAROUND TRACK PROVIDED BY THIS SMALL, DOUBLE-ENDED SUB-YARD. VERY HANDY!
5. INDUSTRIAL DISTRICT — TRACKAGE CAN BE AS COMPLEX & SHARPLY-CURVED AS DESIRED.
6. THROAT ARRANGED SO THAT TWO SWITCHERS CAN WORK PASSENGER & FREIGHT TRACKS AT THE SAME TIME WITHOUT INTERFERING WITH EACH OTHER, WHILE LEAVING ONE LEAD TRACK CLEAR FOR TRAINS ENTERING OR LEAVING TERMINAL.
7. DOUBLE TRACK LEAVING TERMINAL AND APPROACHING THE STEEP SIDE OF THE MAIN LINE MOUNTAIN CROSSING. HELPERS ADDED AS NECESSARY.
8. MAJOR INDUSTRY ON SHORT BRANCH — TRACKAGE TO BE ARRANGED TO SUIT.
9. WYE NEAR SUMMIT FOR TURNING HELPER ENGINES FOR RETURN TO FOOT OF HILL IN EITHER DIRECTION. ACCESS TO REAR TURNOUT FROM BENEATH SCENERY VIA INCONSPICUOUS OPENING.
10. "THREE-RUNG LADDER" OF MAIN TRACKS DESCENDING MOUNTAIN — LOOP-BACK HORSESHOES IN TUNNELS. SEE NOTE ON ELEVATION PROFILE DIAGRAM REGARDING CHOICE OF GRADE.
11. TRAINS SNEAK INTO OR OUT OF LAYOVER TRACKS ON LOOP AT END OF MAIN LINE.

Fig. 5-5. Upper level trackage view for the Big Z track plan.

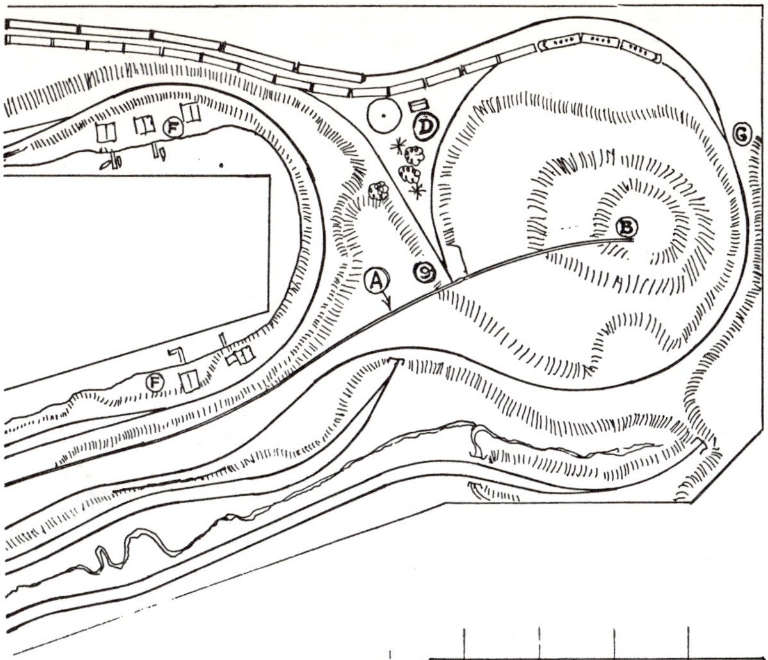

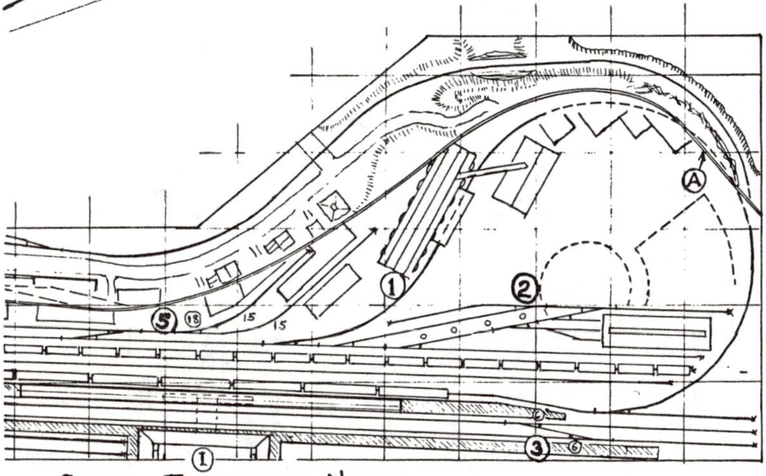

SCENIC-TREATMENT NOTES:

Ⓐ DOUBLE-FACED, FREE-STANDING (1/8" TEMPERED HARDBOARD) BACKDROP. EXTENDS WELL ABOVE EYE LEVEL, SEPARATING RAILROAD LINES ON OPPOSITE SIDES OF NARROW SECTIONS OF LAYOUT. NOTE THAT THIS TRACK PLAN APPROACHES THE "WALK-IN" IDEAL, IN WHICH ONLY A SINGLE SECTION OF MAIN LINE IS VISIBLE FROM ANY ONE POINT — JUST AS WOULD BE THE CASE IN REAL LIFE.

Ⓑ ENDS OF BACKDROP DISAPPEAR INTO MOUNTAIN, AT POINTS WHERE CREST IS ABOVE EYE LEVEL.

Ⓒ LEAVE THE REAR SIDE OF THE STATION OPEN FOR AN IMPRESSIVE VIEW (THROUGH THE STATION WINDOWS) OF TRAINS STRUGGLING UPHILL AROUND THE HORSESHOE CURVES.

Ⓓ TREES AND THINGS TO KEEP DISAPPEARANCE OF WYE TAIL TRACK OUT OF SIGHT.

Ⓔ TREES ON BLUFF TO KEEP YOU FROM SEEING FARTHER BEYOND THE BEND OF THE RIVER THAN YOU'RE SUPPOSED TO.

Ⓕ SQUATTER'S SUMMER SHACKS ALONG THE RIVER'S EDGE (ONLY REACHED BY TRESPASSING ON R.R. PROPERTY.

Ⓖ FOR ONCE, THERE'S NO NEED FOR A TUNNEL AT THE SUMMIT OF THE MOUNTAIN CROSSING!

Ⓗ SMALL-TOWN BUILDING FRONTS DO FINE JOB OF HIDING SNEAK-OFF TRACKAGE WITHOUT IMPAIRING ACCESS TO ITS TURNOUTS.

Ⓘ PASSENGER STATION AT SIDE OF TERMINAL TRACKS HELPS GIVE IMPRESSION THAT RAILROAD CONTINUES ON ACROSS THE CONTINENT, EVEN THOUGH ALL TRAINS END THEIR RUNS HERE. ABSENCE OF UMBRELLA SHED ON FIRST PLATFORM LEAVES TRAINS MORE VISIBLE.

Ⓙ COACH YARD - SMALL, BUT WHERE THE CARS CAN BE PROPERLY ADMIRED.

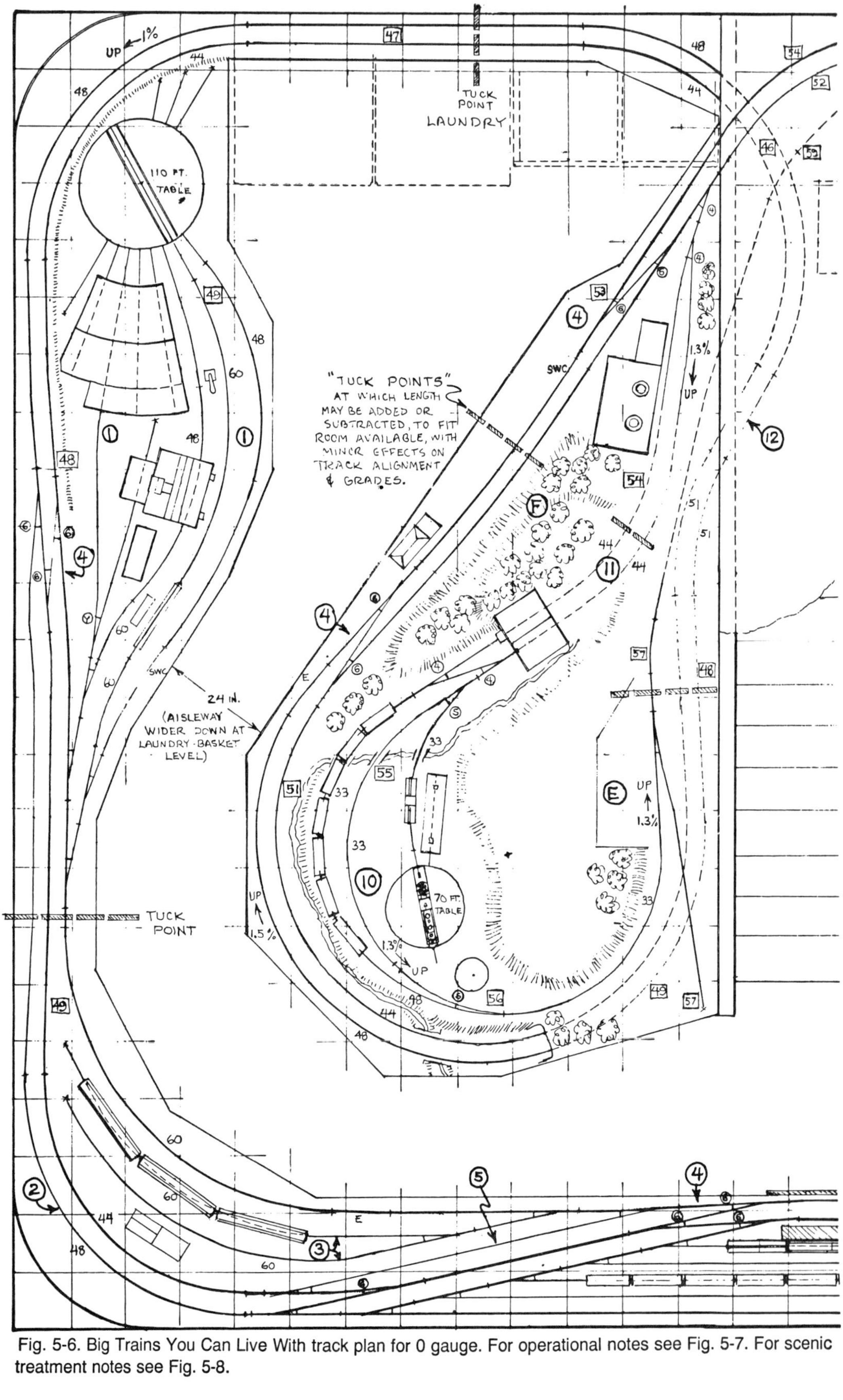

Fig. 5-6. Big Trains You Can Live With track plan for 0 gauge. For operational notes see Fig. 5-7. For scenic treatment notes see Fig. 5-8.

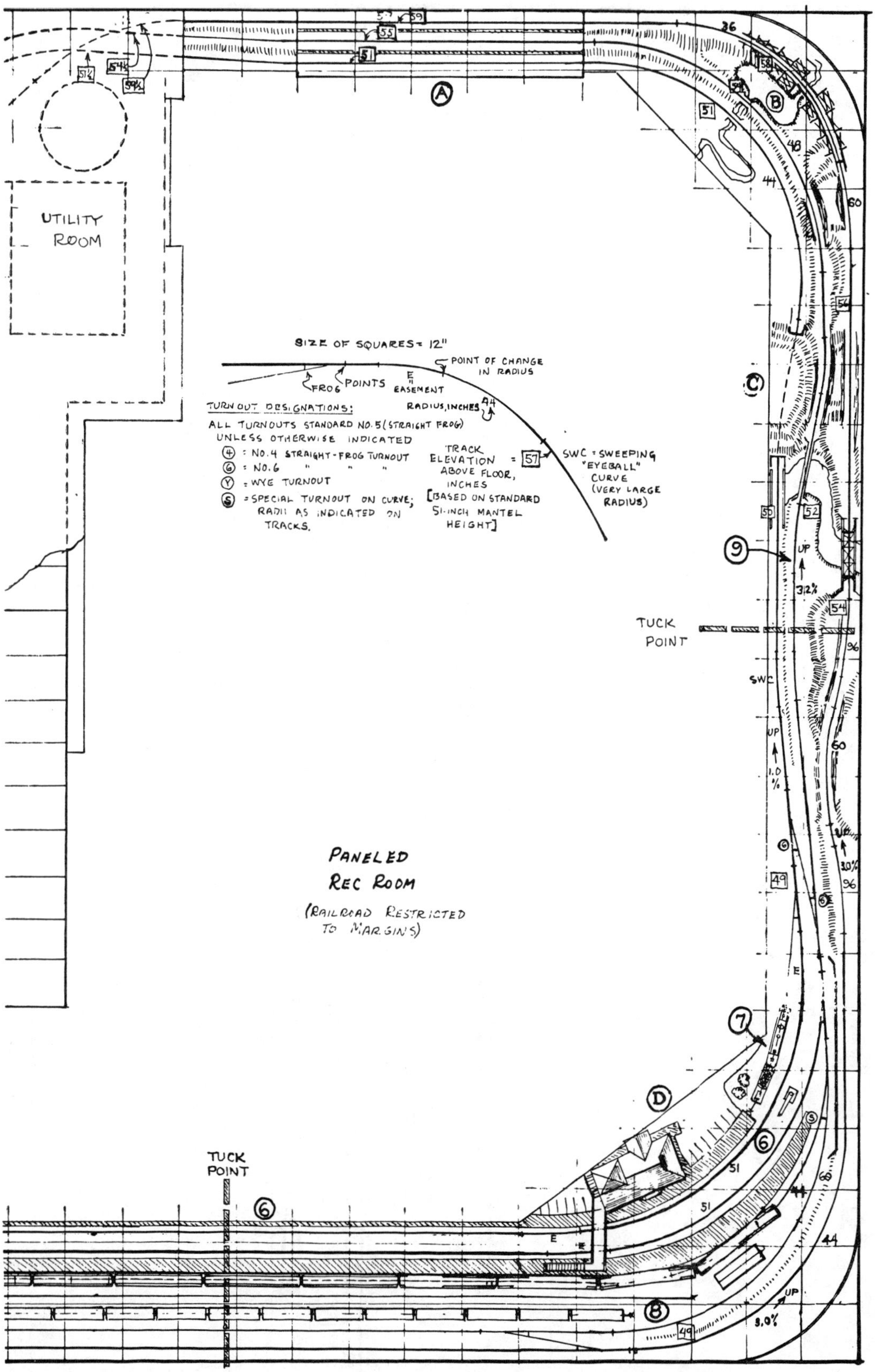

UTILITY ROOM
SIZE OF SQUARES = 12"
POINT OF CHANGE IN RADIUS
FROG
POINTS
E EASEMENT
RADIUS, INCHES
44
TURNOUT DESIGNATIONS:
ALL TURNOUTS STANDARD NO. 5 (STRAIGHT FROG) UNLESS OTHERWISE INDICATED
④ = NO. 4 STRAIGHT-FROG TURNOUT
⑥ = NO. 6 " " "
Ⓨ = WYE TURNOUT
Ⓢ = SPECIAL TURNOUT ON CURVE; RADII AS INDICATED ON TRACKS.
TRACK ELEVATION ABOVE FLOOR, INCHES = 57
[BASED ON STANDARD 51-INCH MANTEL HEIGHT]
SWC = SWEEPING "EYEBALL" CURVE (VERY LARGE RADIUS)
PANELED REC ROOM
(RAILROAD RESTRICTED TO MARGINS)
TUCK POINT
TUCK POINT
UP 3.2%
UP 1.0 %
UP 3.0%
SWC

CHARACTER PROFILE

FOR KEY, SEE FIG. 3-1

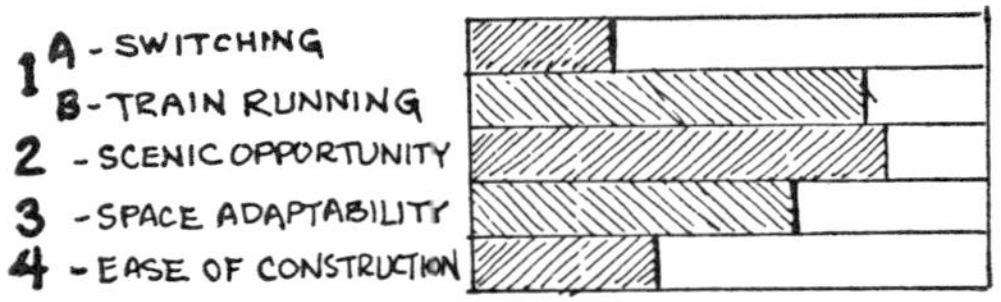

SCHEMATIC

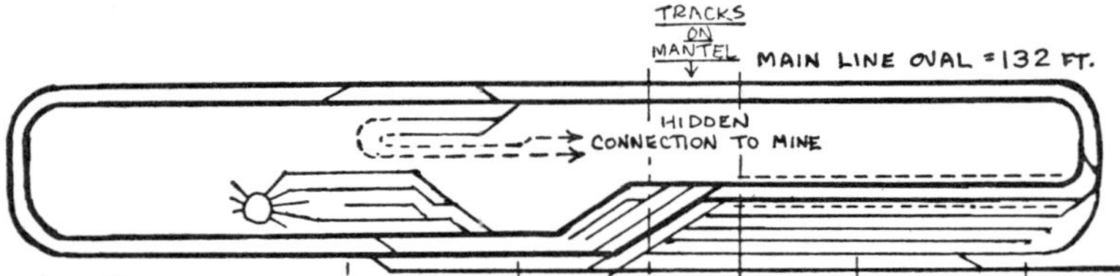

ELEVATION PROFILE

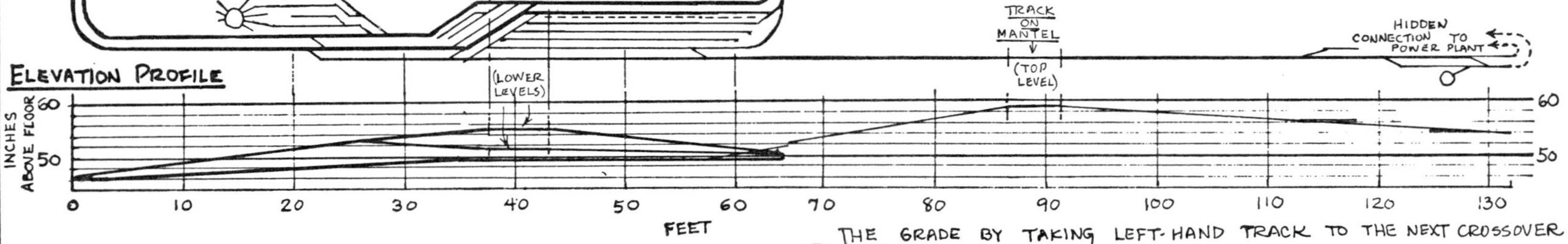

OPERATIONAL NOTES:

1. LONG ENGINE SERVICING TRACKS IN APPROACH TO TURNTABLE MAKE UP FOR DEFICIENCY IN ROUNDHOUSE STALLS. FOURTH TRACK TO TABLE (THROUGH ENGINE HOUSE STALL) IS A GOOD WRECK CRANE TRACK – BIG HOOK CAN BE SENT OUT, HEADED EITHER WAY, IN A HURRY.
2. OUTSIDE TRACK SERVES AS FREIGHT YARD: SWITCHING LEAD OR AS A THIRD MAIN TRACK IN GETTING TRAINS THROUGH YARD.
3. COACH YARD (PASSENGER-TRAIN SERVICING) - MODERATE CURVATURE FOR BETTER APPEARANCE.
4. LONGER CROSSOVER TURNOUTS USED WHEREVER THEY WILL IMPROVE PASSENGER TRAIN APPEARANCE WITHOUT WASTING SPACE.
5. CABOOSE TRACK – ALSO SERVES AS SHORT RUN-AROUND TRACK. NOTE THAT FREIGHT & PASSENGER SWITCHING CAN GO ON AT SAME TIME WHILE STILL LEAVING ONE CLEAR TRACK THROUGH YARD.
6. RELATIVELY LONG PASSENGER PLATFORMS, OUT FRONT WHERE YOU CAN SEE THE CAR DETAIL, WITH BROADER-RADIUS CURVES. THIRD TRACK SERVES ALTERNATELY AS PART OF FGT. YARD OR PASSENGER STATION.
7. ENGINE POCKET OR BUSINESS-CAR SET-OUT TRACK. DISTANCE TO ENGINE TERMINAL MAKES THIS USEFUL IN ENGINE-CHANGE OPERATIONS.
8. SINGLE-ENDED FGT. YARD TRACKS AVOID SOME TURNOUT-ON-CURVE PROBLEMS WITH MINOR EFFECT ON OPERATIONAL FLEXIBILITY.
9. A STIFF GRADE FOR COUNTER-CLOCKWISE TRAFFIC, BUT THE YARD IS HANDY TO PROVIDE A PUSHER. NOTE THAT TRAINS CAN AVOID THE GRADE BY TAKING LEFT-HAND TRACK TO THE NEXT CROSSOVER
10. MINIMAL BRANCHLINE TERMINAL – RUNAROUND TRACK, SHORT TURN-TABLE IF STEAM OR SINGLE-ENDED POWER USED ON THIS LINE.
11. THE OLD EMPTIES-IN/LOADS OUT HIDDEN CONNECTION. MAY NEED TO SET HANDBRAKE ON [STICK A CHOCK IN FRONT OF] FREE-ROLLING CARS.
12. THIS TRACK MAY BE USED AS A HIDDEN LAYOVER BY RUNNING ALL TRAFFIC ON OTHER TRACK. LEAVE CROSSOVERS REVERSED AS REMINDER!

Fig. 5-7. Schematic, profile and operational notes for Big Trains You Can Live With track plan. For track plan see Fig. 5-6. For scenic treatment notes see Fig. 5-8.

follow his train from one end to the other without back-tracking or ducking under. The alternative of a balloon track at stub terminal makes operation of heavy main-line traffic with minimal switching available when desired. Optional steep grades will require helper engines or heavy motive power on the moderately long trains accommodated by the passing tracks. Figure 5-5 shows upper level trackage.

Overall design is such that a single, moderately-graded cut-off track will allow full operation to begin when only two-thirds of the benchwork and half the main-line trackage is in place.

Considering the sparsely-populated territory usually associated with a major mountain crossing such as represented here, the limited industry trackage along the main line is appropriate. However, many additional shippers and their spur tracks can be added should the other types of operation over this extensive single-track railroad ever begin to become too routine.

If an exceptionally large quantity of rolling stock is to be accommodated, several extra storage spurs can be added beneath the terminal. This is of course best done at the start rather than as an afterthought!

Size: 14 × 20 ft., walk-in island
Gauge: HO
Curvature standards: conventional
Schematic: point-to-loop/loop-to-loop, stub terminal with balloon track; single track
Recommended construction: open grid
Trackwork options: 95 percent of trackwork components standard; a few special turnouts where space saving is particularly useful; curvable or hand-laid track

BIG TRAINS YOU CAN LIVE WITH

This plan (Fig. 5-6) has a large yard with emphasis on passenger-station scenes and operations and, for once, extensive locomotive servicing and ready-track facilities keeping a lot of motive power on display. The double-track main line emphasizes train running with minimum complications but enough crossovers for interesting passing maneuvers. A mineral-hauling branch with

SCENIC TREATMENT NOTES:

(A) A THREE-LEVEL MANTELPIECE DISPLAY OF ROLLING STOCK AT EYE LEVEL — CHANGES ITEMS EVERY TIME YOU RUN THE RAILROAD.

(B) NOT MUCH OF A POND — BUT IT'S RIGHT WHERE IT CAN REFLECT TRAINS PASSING BY ON THE BRANCHLINE TRESTLE.

(C) MOUNTAIN RIDGE DIVIDES RAILROAD SCENE INTO VIGNETTES & BREAKS UP ROUND 'N' ROUND EFFECT. DIFFERENCES IN TRACK ELEVATION MAKE TUNNEL/CUT COMBINATION LOGICAL.

(D) PASSENGER STATION — MOST TRAINS PASS THROUGH (AFTER A STOP & MAYBE SOME SWITCHING) BUT STATION IS BIG ENOUGH TO EXPLAIN WHY SOME TRAINS END THEIR RUNS HERE AND ARE REARRANGED FOR THE RETURN TRIP.

(E) OPEN-REAR MOUNTAIN FOR ACCESS TO SPUR TURNOUT.

(F) RIDGE & TREES COMBINE WITH CURVATURE IN HIDDEN CONNECTING TRACKAGE TO MAKE MINE & POWER PLANT APPEAR MILES APART, COMPLETELY UNRELATED EXCEPT FOR THE LONG TRIP BY BRANCH & MAIN LINE

Fig. 5-8. Scenic treatment notes for Big Trains You Can Live With track plan. For track plan see Fig. 5-6. For operational notes see Fig. 5-7.

empties-in/loads-out connection exercises the smaller motive power realistically. See Fig. 5-7 for schematic.

Overall, the plan permits other family uses of the rec room area with a minimum of lost space. A three-level rolling-stock display on the fireplace mantel can be arranged without lifting anything off the track and even provides an excuse for a short helper grade on the main line. See Fig. 5-8 for scenic treatment notes.

A branch line can logically be added after the main line and its supporting facilities are in place and operating.

As indicated by the *tuck points*, the basic plan can be adjusted to fit different room sizes and shapes, with minor effect on operating and scenic possibilities.

A main deficiency in the plan as shown is the lack of local freight switching apart from the big mine/power plant shuttle. Adding numerous industry tracks, a logical improvement, can be done by expanding the railroad width a bit at various points or, if more challenging main line running is also a goal, reducing much of the line to single track and using the space for a variety of spur tracks.

Size: 23 × 30 ft., adjustable; around-the-wall with large open center
Gauge: 0
Curvature standards: conventional (main line); sharp (branch)
Schematic: figure-8 oval, double track
Recommended construction: open grid; flat top/cookie-cutter for yard and engine terminal areas
Trackwork options: 90 percent of trackwork components standard; a few special turnouts where space saving is particularly useful; curvable or hand-laid track

6

Modifying and Combining Track Plans

Versatile as most of the plans in this book have tried to be, there are bound to be many situations in which major modifications are the key to making them do the job. The operating pattern may be what you want but the curves too sharp for the equipment you'd like to run, or the engine terminal with its diesel orientation may spoil things for your Gay Nineties desires. There are some changes that can be considered.

CHANGING SCALE OR GAUGE

The most fundamental modification is to build a railroad to a different scale or to change from standard to narrow gauge or vice versa. As discussed in the introduction, this may lead to some problems in aisle widths, access to turnouts, and finger space. When it comes to gauge and scale, though, most of us are far more willing to fight than switch, so Table 6-1 provides equivalent space requirements for the track plans in the previous chapters if built in any of the common gauges other than the one in which they were designed.

In the case of solid rectangular or L-shaped pikes the new size is simply the original multiplied by the *scale factor*. A layout four feet wide in HO becomes 87.1/160th as wide in N, or 2 ft. 2 in. The character of the railroad may become entirely different, though. While it is often necessary to put a 4 × 8 pike against a wall, it's highly unlikely that one only half that width need be so located, and the scenic treatment should be changed to recognize this. Table 6-1 indicates the probable wall-bound sides of the layouts accordingly. When an N or HO plan is expanded to one of the larger scales, the usual problem is the length of arm needed to reach the middle of the resulting expanse of tablework. This is noted in appropriate places. It's not necessarily a fatal defect, since you can *see* the larger-scale models at the greater distance, but it does mean making provisions, such as access hatches, open-rear mountains, openings from below, to make building, maintaining and operating the railroad comfortable and practical.

Walk-in railroads, such as Fig. 5-4, however, must change shape so that aisleways will remain about the same size as the people who use them. As a result, an O-scale version may be only about 2½ times as wide as its N-scale counterpart, rather than the 3 1/3 ratio of the scales themselves. The figures have been adjusted to reflect these effects. The results are approximate, of course. The exact size of a large layout is more likely to be determined by the room available, but the figures will tell you whether a plan is likely to be useable or not. Figure 6-1 illustrates the process of using the square grid of the track plan to modify and adapt it to the change of scale.

The elevation figures also change, of course. Figure 6-2 is a nomogram that will let you convert figures from the original scale to any other, with emphasis on the HO or N scale used for the majority of the plans in this book. If the plan is modified to keep the aisleways the same width, the grades will also change a little, becoming more gentle if

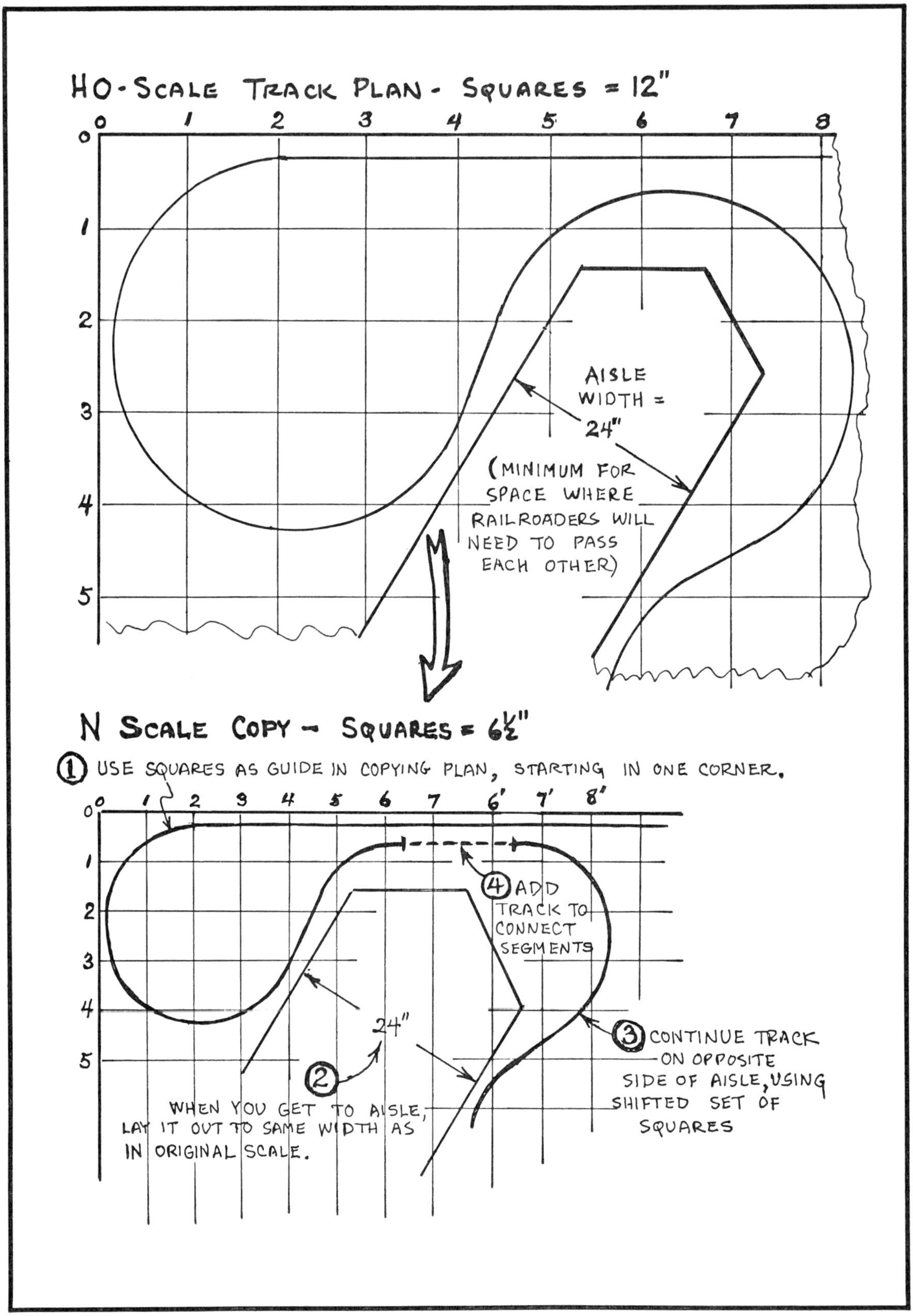

Fig. 6-1. New scale, same aisle conversions.

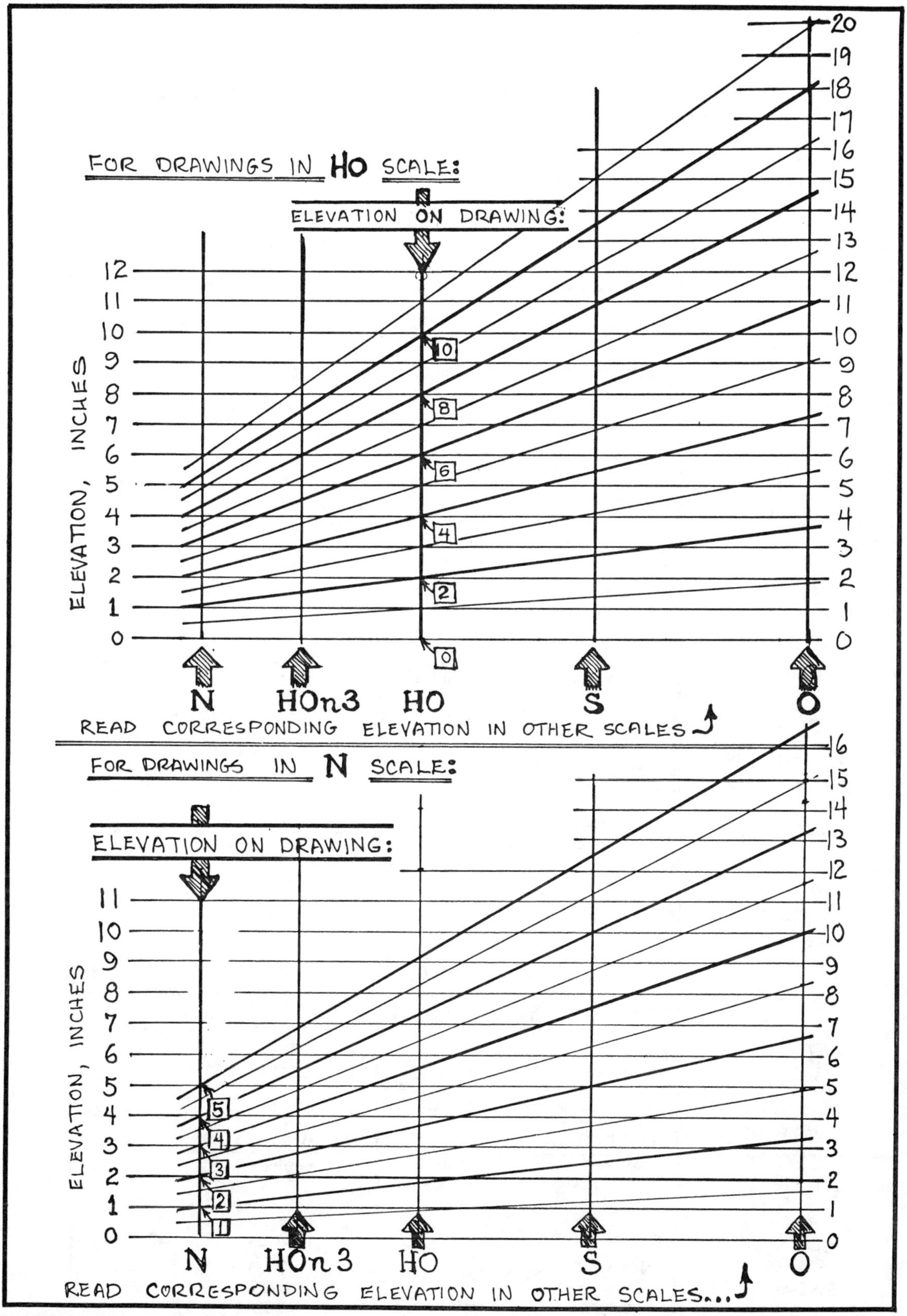

Fig. 6-2. Elevation conversion nomogram.

Table 6-1. Scale-Gauge Conversion Possibilities. (continues through page 201)

FIGURE NUMBER	N	HOn3*
Fig. 3-2 "LET'S GET STARTED"	2'2" × 3'3" 9¾" MIN. R. 6½"	3' × 4'6" 13½" MIN. R. 9" — OR — 4' × 6' (IF 18" R. KEPT) 12"
Fig. 3-3 "THE IMPROVED OVAL"	3'6" × 7' 13" R. CURVES 12"	4'10" × 9'8" 18" MIN. R. MULTI-TRACK PLAN NOT APPROPRIATE FOR N.G. IN U.S. 17"
Fig. 3-4 "THE LITTLE BIG TIME"	2'2" × 4'4" 9¾" MIN. R. 6½"	3' × 6' 13½" MIN. R. MULTI-TRACK PLAN NOT APPROPRIATE FOR N.G. IN U.S. 9"
Fig. 3-5 "THE PRAIRIE DIVISION POINT"	3' × 6'8" 9¾" CURVES 12"	4'2" × 9'2" 13½" MIN. R. 17"
Fig. 3-6 "CONSTRICTED CONNECTING R.R."	1' × 10' 9¾" R. CURVES 12"	1'3" × 13'9" 13½" MIN. R. SUITABLE FOR NARROW GAUGE INTRA-PLANT RAILROAD 17"
Fig. 3-7 "HAMMERLOCK INDUSTRIAL DISTRICT"	2'2" × 5'5" × 10' 7⅝" MIN. R. 6½" GRADES SHOULD BE INCREASED FOR CLEARANCE ON LOWER LEVEL	3' × 7'5" × 12' 11" MIN. R. 9" SUITABLE FOR NARROW-GAUGE INTRA-PLANT RAILROAD
Fig. 3-8 "BIG SCALE IN A SMALL PACKAGE"	1'10" × 4'3" × 6½" 7" MIN. R. (FGT.) N GAUGE TRACTION, ANYBODY? 3½"	10" MIN. R. (FGT.) 6" MIN. R. (TRACTION) INTRA-PLANT N.G. + STREET RY. 5"

HO	S/On3	O
4'×6' 18" R. CURVES 12"	5'5"×8'2" 24" MIN. R. 16"	7'3"×10'11" 33" MIN. R. VERY LONG REACH TO CENTER 22"
6'6"×13' 24" MIN. R. LONG REACH TO CENTER 22"	8'9"×17'6" 33" MIN. R. VERY LONG REACH TO CENTER 30"	11'8"×23'4" 44" MIN. R. IMPOSSIBLY LONG REACH TO CENTER 40"
4'×8' 18" R. CURVES 12"	5'5"×10'10" 24" MIN. R. 16"	7'3"×14'6" 33" MIN. R. VERY LONG REACH TO CENTER 22"
5'6"×12'3" 18" MIN. R. 22"	7'6"×16'8" 24" MIN. R. VERY LONG REACH TO CENTER 30"	10'×22'3" 33" MIN. R. VERY LONG REACH TO CENTER 40"
1'10"×18'4" 18" MIN. R. 22"	2'6"×25' 24" MIN. R. 30"	3'4"×33'4" 33" MIN. R. WIDTH APPROACHING THE LIMIT FOR COMFORTABLE OPERATION 40"
4'×10'×1'6" 15" R. CURVES 12"	5'5"×13'7"×2'0" 20" MIN. R. 16"	7'3"×18'2"×2'9" 27" MIN. R. GRADES CAN BE REDUCED IF DESIRED 22"
13" MIN. R. (FGT.) 11" MIN. R. (TRACTION) 6½"	4'6"×10'6"×16" 18" MIN. R. (FGT.) 11" MIN. R. (TRACTION) 9"	6'×14'×1'9" 24" CURVES (FREIGHT) 15" CURVES (TRACTION) 12"

Table 6-1. Scale-Gauge Conversions Possibilities (continued).

FIGURE NUMBER	N	HOn3
Fig. 3-10 "TWICE-AROUND," VIA CROSSING	2'2" × 4'4" 9¾" MIN. R. 6½"	3' × 6' 13½" MIN. R. VERY UNLIKELY TERRAIN FOR NARROW GAUGE! 9"
Fig. 3-10 "TWICE AROUND," VIA BRIDGE	2'2" × 4'4" 9¾" MIN. R. 6½"	3' × 6' 13½" MIN. R. 9"
Fig. 3-11 "THE IRON RANGER"	2'2" × 4'4" 9¾" MIN. R. (7" IN MINE) STEEPER GRADES NEEDED FOR LOWER-LEVEL ACCESS 6½"	3' × 6' 13½" MIN. R. (10" R. IN MINE) 9"
Fig. 3-13 "THE ACCESSIBLE WATERWINGS"	2' 4' × 8' 19" R. CURVES (13" ON BRANCH) 12"	5'6" × 11' DOUBLE TRACK PLAN NOT APPROPRIATE FOR NARROW GAUGE IN U.S. 17"
Fig. 3-14 "UNDERBED SPECIAL"	4' × 5'8" 13" R. CURVES (9¾" R. ON BRANCH) 6"	5'6" × 7'10" 18" MIN. R. (13½" ON BRANCH) 8¼"
Fig. 3-16 "THE TRADITIONAL COFFEE-TABLE R.R"	2' × 4' —OR— 2'6" × 5' 7⅝" R. CURVES (2'×4') —OR— 9¾" R. (2½'×5') 6" OR 7½"	2'9" × 5'6" 18" MIN. R. 8¼"
Fig. 3-17 "LONG TRAINS FOR THE COFFEE TABLE"	2'6" × 6'6" 9¾" R. CURVES (MAIN TRACKS) 12"	3'5" × 9' 18" MIN. R. (MAIN TRACKS) HEAVY-DUTY TRAFFIC NOT TYPICAL OF NARROW GA. IN U.S. 17"

* ARBITRARILY ASSUMED (PRIMARILY ON BASIS OF LENGTHS OF TYPICAL ROLLING STOCK) THAT EQUIVALENT DIMENSIONS AND RADII FOR HOn3 = 75% OF CORRESPONDING HO FIGURES.

HO	S/On3	O
4' x 8' 18" R. CURVES 12"	5'5" x 10'10" 24" MIN. R. 16"	7'3" x 14'6" 33" MIN. R. 22"
4' x 8' 18" R. CURVES 12"	5'5' x 10'10" 24" MIN. R. 16"	7'3" x 14'6" 33" MIN. R. 22"
4' x 8' 18" R. CURVES (13" R. IN MINE) 12"	5'5" x 10'10" 24" MIN. R. (18" IN MINE) 16"	7'3" x 14'6" 33" MIN. R. (24" IN MINE) 22"
3'8" 7'4" x 14'8" 35" MIN. R. (24" ON BRANCH) 22"	5' 10' x 20' 48" MIN. R. (33" ON BRANCH) ACCESS O.K. IF AN ISLAND LAYOUT 30"	6'8" 13'4" x 26'8" 63" MIN. R. (43" ON BRANCH) MAKE IT AN ISLAND, BUT "NOTCH" DEEPER FOR ACCESS 40"
7'4" x 10'5" 24" MIN. R. (18" ON BRANCH) 11"	10' x 14'2" 33" MIN. R.; 24" ON BRANCH VERY LONG REACH TO CENTER 15"	13'4" x 18'11" 45" MIN. R.; 33" ON BRANCH IMPOSSIBLY LONG REACH TO CENTER 20"
3'8" x 7'4" 24" MIN. R. 11"	5' x 10' 33" MIN. R. 15"	6'8" x 13'4" 44" MIN. R. LONG REACH TO CENTER, BUT SIDES CAN BE SLIMMED 20"
4'7" x 12' 24" MIN. R. (MAIN TRACKS) 22"	6'3" x 16'3" 33" MIN. R. (MAIN TRACKS) LONG REACH TO CENTRAL AREAS 30"	8'4" x 21'8" 44" MIN. R. (MAIN TRACKS) CENTRAL ACCESS HATCHES NEEDED 40"

* ARBITRARILY ASSUMED (PRIMARILY ON BASIC OF LENGTHS OF TYPICAL ROLLING STOCK) THAT EQUIVALENT DIMENSIONS AND RADII FOR HOn3 = 75% OF CORRESPONDING HO FIGURES.

Table 6-1. Scale-Gauge Conversion Possibilities (continued).

FIGURE NUMBER	N	HOn3
Fig. 3-19 "THE COFFEE TABLE UPPER LIMIT"	2'2" x 5'1" 9" MIN. R. 9"	3' x 7' 12" R. CURVES 12"
Fig. 3-20 "GRAND CENTRAL, JUNIOR"	4' x 10' 16" R. CURVES 12"	5'6" x 13'9" 22" MIN. R. HEAVY PASSENGER TRAFFIC NOT APPROPRIATE FOR NARROW GAUGE IN U.S. 17"
Fig. 3-22 "CENTENNIAL PEAK BRANCH"	2'10" x 7'3" 13" MIN. R. 9"	4' x 10' 18" R. CURVES 12"
Fig. 4-1 THE "MEDIUM BIG-TIME"	2'9" x 5'5" 13" MIN. R. 6½"	3'9" x 7'6" 18" MIN. R. MULTI-TRACK MAIN LINE NOT APPROPRIATE FOR N.G. IN U.S. 9"
Fig. 4-2 "THE PRETZEL"	4'4" x 6'6" x 2'2" 9¾" MIN. R. 6½"	6' x 9' x 3' 13½" MIN. R. VERY UNLIKELY TERRAIN FOR NARROW GAUGE! 9"
Fig. 4-3 "THE HAPPY ACORN"	2'6" x 5'5" 9¾" MIN. R. 6½"	3'5" x 7'6" 13½" MIN. R. 9"
Fig. 4-4 "LONG TRAINS-WITH A PUSH"	4'4" x 7'7" x 2'9" 9¾" MIN. R. 6½"	6' x 10'6" x 3'9" 13½" MIN. R. DOUBLE-TRACK MAIN NOT APPROPRIATE FOR N.G. IN U.S. 9"

HO	S/On3	O
4' x 9'4" 16" MIN. R. 16"	5'5" x 12'9" 22" MIN. R. 22"	7'3" x 17' 30" MIN. R. A LONG REACH TO CENTER FOR CONSTRUCTION BUT ACCESS O.K. FOR OPERATION 30"
7'4" x 18'4" 30" MIN. R. 22"	10' x 25' 40" MIN. R. CENTRAL ACCESS AREAS NEEDED 30"	13'4" x 33'4" 54" MIN. R. CENTRAL OPERATING AREAS NEEDED 40"
5'4" x 13'4" 24" MIN. R. 16"	7'3" x 18'2" 33" MIN. R. A LONG REACH TO CENTER FOR CONSTRUCTION BUT ACCESS O.K. FOR OPERATION 22"	9'8" x 24'2" 45" MIN. R. CENTRAL ACCESS AREAS NEEDED 30"
5' x 10' 24" R. CURVES 12"	6'10" x 13'7" 33" MIN. R. 16"	9'1" x 18'2" 45" MIN. R. A LONG REACH TO CENTER FOR CONSTRUCTION BUT ACCESS O.K. FOR OPERATION 22"
8' x 12' x 4' 18" R. CURVES 12"	10'10' x 16'3" x 5'5" 24" MIN. R. MUST BE ISLAND FOR ADEQUATE ACCESS 16"	14'6" x 21'9" x 7'3" 33" MIN. R. MUST BE ISLAND—ACCESS HOLES NEEDED 22"
4'6" x 10' 18" R. CURVES 12"	6'2" x 13'7" 24" MIN. R. 16"	8'2" x 18'2" 33" MIN. R. VERY LONG REACH TO CENTER—NEEDS ACCESS 22"
8' x 14' x 5' 18" R. CURVES 12"	10'10" x 19' x 6'8" 24" MIN. R. ACCESS O.K. IF PENINSULA WITH SOME HATCHES 16"	14'6" x 25'5" x 9' 33" MIN. R. MUST BE ISLAND, WITH SOME ACCESS HATCHES 22"

Table 6-1. Scale-Gauge Conversion Possibilities (continued).

FIGURE NUMBER	N	HOn3
Fig. 4-6 "THE LONG, LONG TRAIL"	4'4"x7'7" x 2'6" 6½"	6'x10'6" x 3'4" 9"
Fig. 4-7 "THE SUPER SWITCHING R.R."	2'6" x 13' WIDTH KEPT AT 2'-EXTRA ROOM! 13" & 9¾" MIN. RADII END-CURVE GRADES SHOULD BE INCREASED FOR BETTER CLEARANCE BETWEEN LEVELS 6½"	3'6" x 18' TO 20' MAIN LINE SHOULD REMAIN STD. GAUGE (18" MIN. R.); PLANT R.R. → NARROW GAUGE, 13½" R. 9"
Fig. 4-9 "THE COLLECTOR'S FRIEND"	7'x11' 16" 13" R. CURVES 12"	18" MIN. R. DOUBLE-TRACK MAIN NOT APPROPRIATE FOR NARROW GAUGE IN U.S. 17"
Fig. 4-11 "THE TWO-LAYER ROOMFUL"	7'x10' 30" 20" 16"/13" MIN. R. INSUFFICIENT CLEARANCE BETWEEN DECKS IN SMALLER RM. 6½"	8'x11'6" 30" 20" 18"/13½" MIN. R. 9"
Fig. 4-14 "SPAGHETTI ON THE ROLLING PIN"	4' 10'x11' 13" R. CURVES 12"	5'6" 13'9" x 15'2" 18" MIN. R. 17"
Fig. 4-16 "THE EXHIBITIONIST"	6'x10' 13" R. CURVES 12"	8'3" x 13'9" 18" MIN. R. DOUBLE TRACK NOT APPROPRIATE FOR N.G. IN U.S. 17"
Fig. 4-18 "ANOTHER MEDIUM-BIG-TIME RAILROAD"	24" 6'x7'2"x2'10" 13" MIN. R. 4¾"	24" 8'x9'4"x4'5" 18" MIN. R. DOUBLE TRACK NOT APPROPRIATE FOR N.G. IN U.S. 6½"
Fig. 4-19 "BOTH SIDES OF THE MOUNTAIN"	24" 6'x7'2"x2'10" 12" MIN. R. 4¾"	24" 8'x9'4 x 4'5" 16" MIN. R. 6½"

HO	S/On3	O
 8'×14'×4'6" 18" R. CURVES 12"	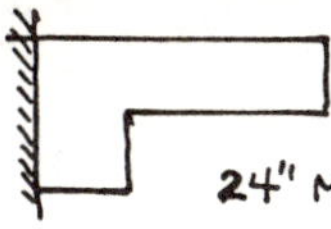 10'10"×19'×6'1" 24" MIN. R. ACCESS O.K. IF PENINSULA OR ISLAND, WITH HATCHES 16"	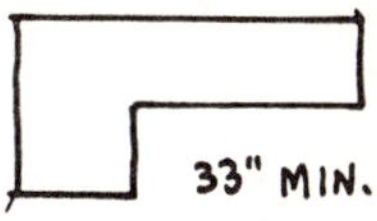 14'6"×25'5"×8'2" 33" MIN. R. MUST BE ISLAND, WITH SOME ACCESS HATCHES 22"
 2'3" 4'6"×24' + PANHANDLE 24" CURVES (MAIN LINE) 18" R. CURVES (SWITCHING R.R.) 12"	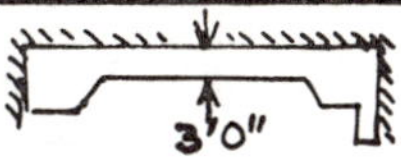 3'0" 6'1"×32'8" 33" & 24" MIN. RADII PROBABLY BENT AROUND A CORNER—NO PROBLEM! 16"	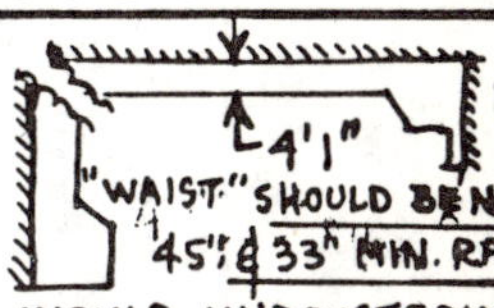 4'1" 8'2"×43'6" "WAIST" SHOULD BE NARROWED 45" & 33" MIN. RADII WOULD UNDOUBTEDLY BE BENT AROUND A CORNER—OR TWO 22"
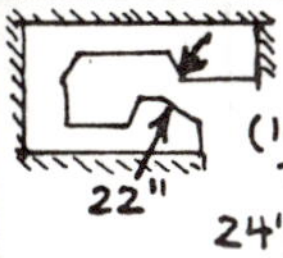 12'6"×20' (INCREASE AISLE TO 22" MIN. WIDTH) 22" 24" MIN. R. 22"	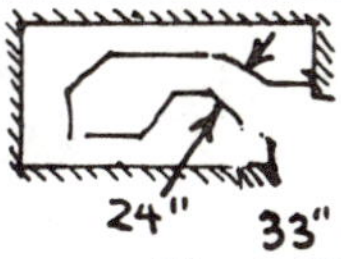 16'×24' 24" 33" MIN. R. NEEDS LESS AISLE, DOORWAY CLEARANCE SPACE (IN PROPORTION) 30"	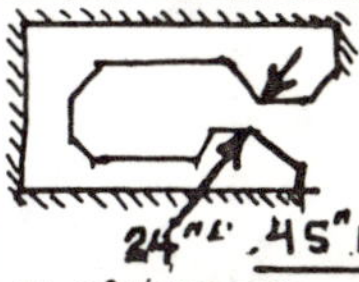 21'×33' 24" 45" MIN. R. ADJUSTED TO RETAIN 24" AISLE, SAME DOORWAY SPACE 40"
 10'×14' 30" 20" 24"/18" CURVES, MAIN/BRANCH LINE 12"	 24" 30" 12'9"×18' 33"/24" MIN. RADII 16"	 30" 24" 17'×23'6" 45"/33" MIN. RADII REDUCE GRADE TO KEEP FROM HITTING CEILING! 22"
 7'4" 18'4"×20'2" 24" MIN. R. ACCESS FROM BENEATH TO HIDDEN TRACKAGE 22"	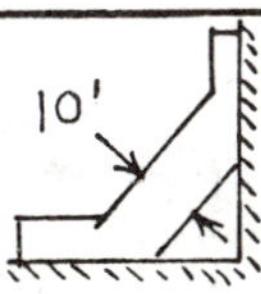 10' 25'×27'6" 33" MIN. R. ACCESS FROM BENEATH TO HIDDEN TRACKAGE 30"	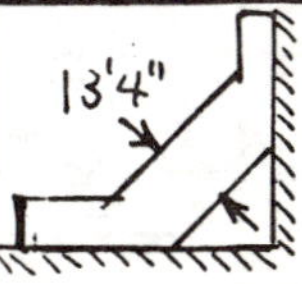 13'4" 33'4"×35'8" 45" MIN. R. ACCESS FROM BENEATH TO HIDDEN TRACKAGE 40"
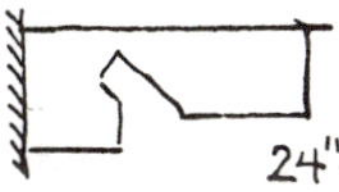 11'×18'4" 24" MIN. R. BETTER AS PENINSULA (FOR ACCESS) 22"	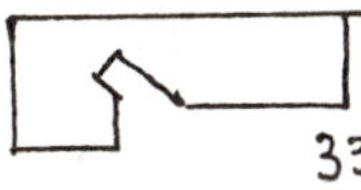 14'6"×24' 33" MIN. R. MUST BE ISLAND ACCESS HOLES NEEDED 30"	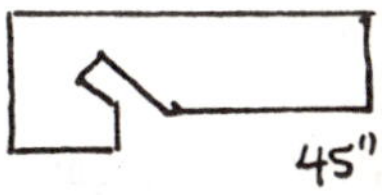 18'6"×31' 45" MIN. R. MUST BE ISLAND—ACCESS HOLES NEEDED 40"
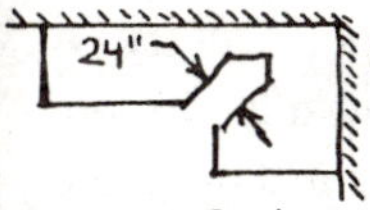 24" 10'×12'4"×5'8" 24" MIN. R. 8¾"	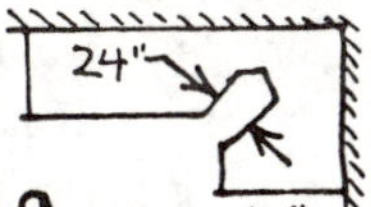 24" 13'×16'×7' S GAUGE ONLY—NOT APPROPRIATE FOR NARROW GA. 33" R. CURVES 12"	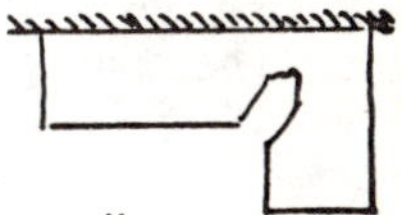 17'×20'9"×8'10" 44" MIN. R. 16"
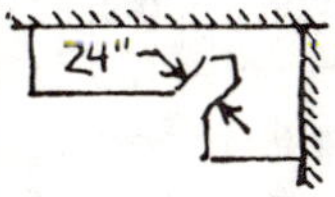 24" 10'×12'4"×5'8" 22" MIN. R. 8¾"	 24" 13'×16'×7' 30" R. CURVES On3 OR S GAUGE O.K. 12"	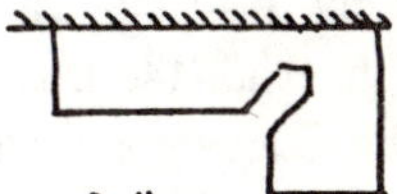 17'×20'9"×8'10" 40" MIN. R. 16"

Table 6-1. Scale-Gauge Conversion Possibilites (continued).

FIGURE NUMBER	N	HOn3
Fig. 4-21 "ALL THE ESSENTIALS"	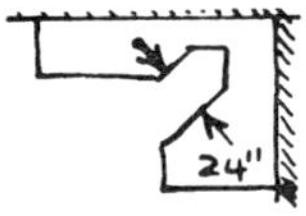 5' x 6' x 2' 24" 9¾" MIN. R. 3½"	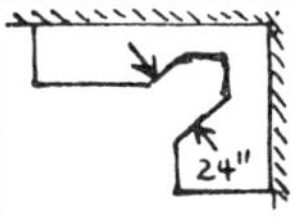 5'8" x 6'9" x 2'9" 24" 13½" MIN. R. 5"
Fig. 5-1 "A GARAGE FULL OF WAY-FREIGHT FUN"	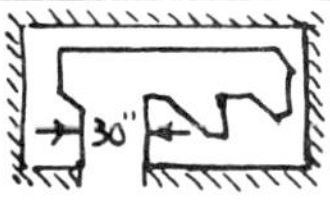 30" 8' x 13'6" 13" MIN. R. 6½"	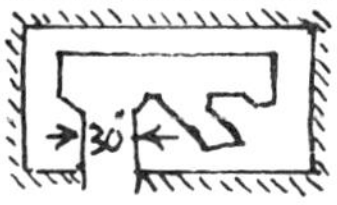 30" 9'8" x 18' 18" MIN. R. 9"
Fig. 5-2 "TWO STALLS, ONE AUTOMOBILE, TWO RAILROADS"	11" MIN. R. (N), 7½" MIN. R. (Z) 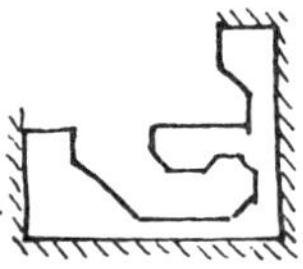 8' x 8' x 5' N = STD. GAUGE Z ≈ Nn3½ 3½"	HOn3 INCLUDED IN HO RAILROAD
Fig. 5-4 "THE BIG Z"	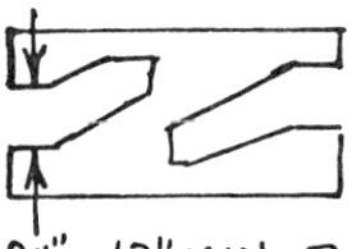 8'8" x 11'6" 24" 13" MIN. R. 6½"	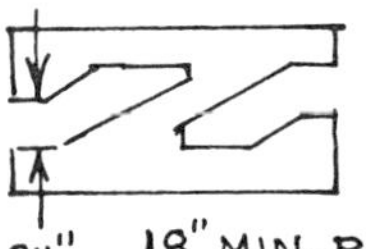 11' x 15'9" 24" 18" MIN. R. 9"
Fig. 5-6 "BIG TRAINS YOU CAN LIVE WITH"	 24" 9' x 12'6" 13"/9¾" MIN. RADII 3½"	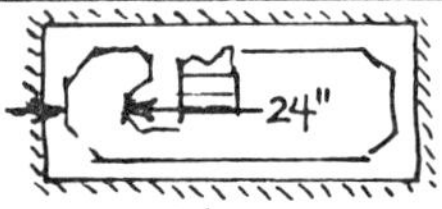 24" 14' x 19' 24"/15" MIN. RADII BRANCH LINE ONLY CONVERTED TO NARROW GAUGE 5"

the pike is spread out to maintain walk-in access in a smaller scale. It's usually desirable to keep the grade at the original slope in such a case, though. Increasing the elevations helps fight the tendency for finger room to become tight as the scale gets tinier.

INAPPROPRIATE CHANGES

Not all the possible transformations make sense, though. Since the narrow-gauge railroads in the United States were all relatively lightly-trafficked lines, usually far from cities of any size, a slimmed-down version of a double-track trunk line serving a big passenger terminal isn't a logical model railroad. Narrow gauge was most often used in the mountains where its ability to wind around sharp curves while ascending at a rate of three or four percent made it the practical choice for penetrating the mining or timber country. A flat-land HOn3 empire is also unlikely, except perhaps as a starter railroad. Such inappropriate combinations have been noted on Table 6-1, but the figures are still provided. In South Africa, Japan and some other exotic places you'll find very heavy-duty railroading on 3½ ft. or meter (39 ⅜ inches) gauge, and we're seeing the import of more and more foreign-prototype rolling stock of attractive quality and, sometimes, price. It just might grab your interest!

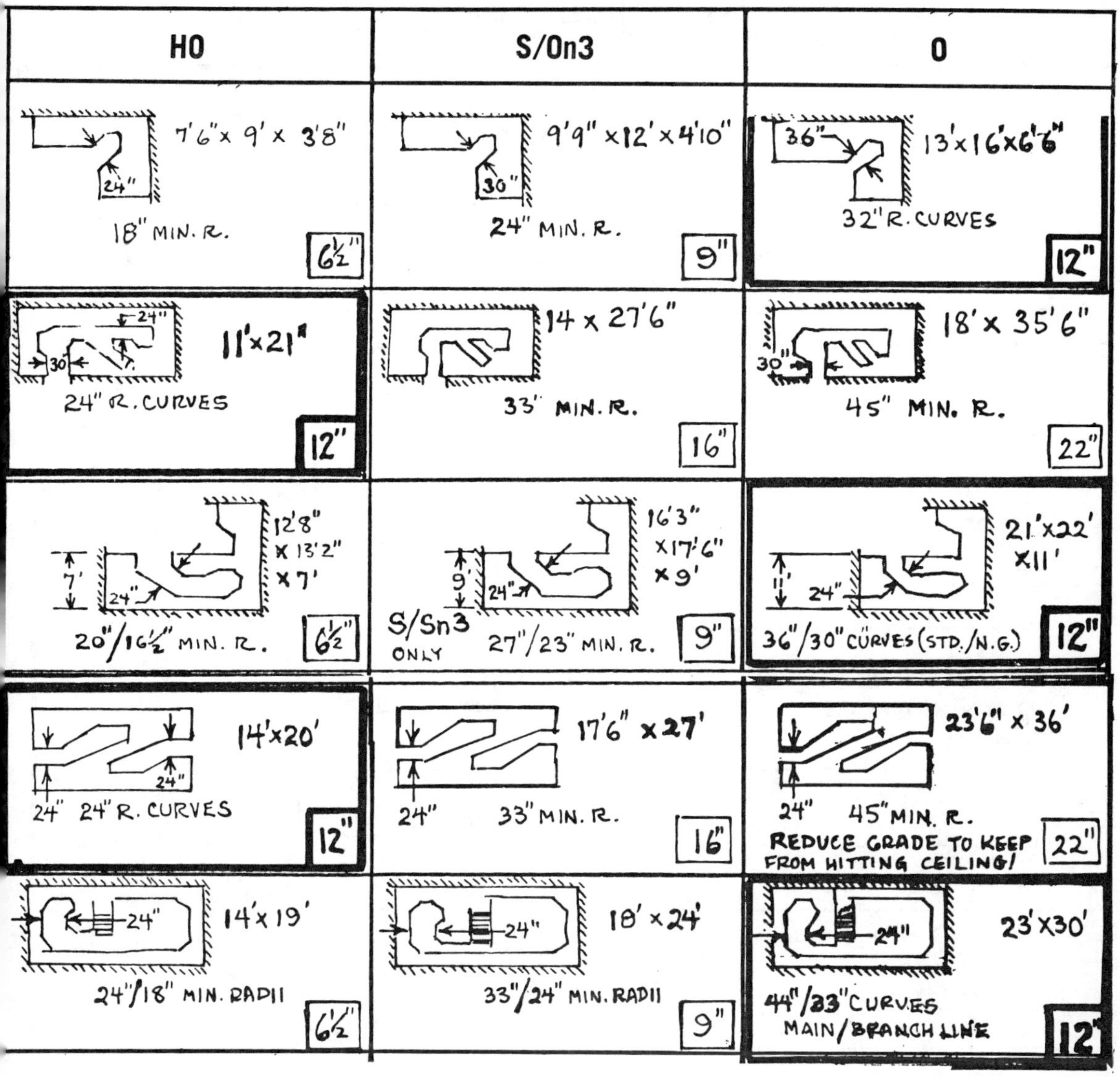

CHANGING CURVATURE STANDARDS

The most important single characteristic of a track plan in determining the size of equipment that can run on it reliably and attractively is its curvature. If the track plan you like is based on sharp standards and you're a passenger train nut, something has to give. Converting the plan, in the same gauge, to conventional or broad standards may be quite feasible. Conversely, if you don't have quite enough room for your favorite plan but can do without its liberal radii in accommodating the modest length of your rolling stock, the reverse process may be the answer. Table 6-2 tabulates the effect of such modifications on the overall size of the track plans in Chapters 3, 4, and 5.

Modifying the plans in this way is rather straightforward. You simply substitute the corresponding size square (from Table 6-2) in redrawing the plan with different-radius curves. The *straight-away* sections of the plan, if there are any, need not be affected, so the *minimum* effect on the size of the layout depends greatly on whether it's a bowl of spaghetti or a string bean. On a highly convoluted plan like Fig. 3-16 or Fig. 4-14, an increase of 25 percent in minimum radius increases its length and width by almost the same proportion. On an around-the-wall pike or one of those skinny switching railroads you can change the radius by 50 percent and scarcely change the length.

Table 6-2. What Changing the Minimum Radius Does to Layout Size. (continues through page 209

FIGURE NUMBER	GAUGE/SHAPE	SHARP
Fig. 3-2 "LET'S GET STARTED"	HO 	4' × 6' [12"]
Fig. 3-3 "THE IMPROVED OVAL"	N 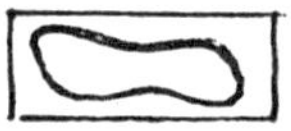	2' 8" × 5' 3" SEE NOTE BELOW [9"]
Fig. 3-4 "THE LITTLE BIG-TIME"	HO 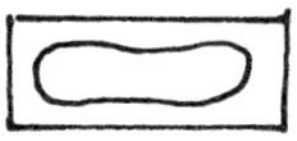	4' × 8' [12"]
Fig. 3-5 "THE PRAIRIE DIVISION POINT"	N 	3' × 6' 8" [12"]
Fig. 3-6 "CONSTRICTED CONNECTING R.R"	N 	1' × 10' [12"]
Fig. 3-7 "HAMMERLOCK INDUSTRIAL DISTRICT"	HO  (EXTRA-SHARP CURVES)	2' 7" × 6' 6" × 12" [15"]
Fig. 3-8 "BIG SCALE IN A SMALL PACKAGE"	O 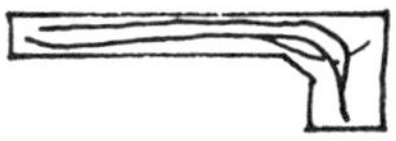 (EXTRA-SHARP CURVES)	7' 2" × 16' 10" × 2' 1" [15"]
Fig. 3-10 "TWICE AROUND VIA CROSSING"	HO 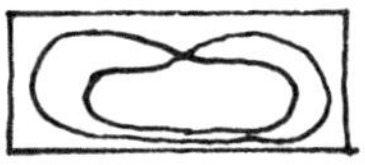	4' × 8' [12"]
Fig. 3-10 "TWICE AROUND VIA BRIDGE"	HO 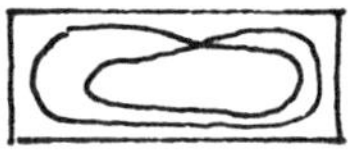	4' × 8' [12"]
Fig. 3-11 "THE IRON RANGER"	HO 	4' × 8' [12"]

STANDARD MAIN-LINE CURVATURE*

CONVENTIONAL	**BROAD**	**SUPER BROAD**
5'4" x 7'4" MIN. 5'4" x 8' [16"]	6'8" x 8'8" MIN. 6'8" x 10' [20"]	8' x 10' (MIN.) 8' x 12' [24"]
3'6" x 7' [12"]	4'5" x 7'11" MIN. 4'5" x 8'9" [15"]	5'10" x 9'4" 5'10" x 11'8" [20"]
5'4" x 9'4" MIN. 5'4" x 10'8" [16"]	6'8" x 10'8" MIN. 6'8" x 13'4" [20"]	8' x 12' MIN. 8' x 16' [24"]
4' x 8'3" MIN. 4' x 8'10" [16"]	5' x 10' MIN. 5' x 11'1" [20"]	6' x 11'6" 6' x 13'4" [24"]
1'4" x 11' MIN 1'4" x 13'4" [16"]	1'8" x 12' MIN. 1'8" x 16'8" [20"]	2' x 13' MIN. 2' x 20' [24"]
3'2" x 7'2" x 15" MIN. 3'4" x 8'3" x 15" [19"]	3'8" x 7'8" x 18" MIN. 4'2" x 10'4" x 19" [24"]	4'4" x 8'4" x 21" MIN. 5'2" x 13' x 24" [30"]
8' x 18' x 2'3" MIN. 9'1" x 21'4" x 2'8" [19"]	9'6" x 19' x 2'4" MIN. 11'6" x 27' x 3'3" [24"]	11' x 20' x 2'6" MIN. 14'4" x 33'8" x 4'2" [30"]
5'4" x 10'6" MIN. 5'4" x 10'8" [16"]	6'8" x 13' MIN. 6'8" x 13'4" [20"]	8' x 15'6" MIN. 8' x 16' [24"]
5'4" x 10'6" MIN. 5'4" x 10'8" [16"]	6'8" x 13' MIN. 6'8" x 13'4" [20"]	8' x 15'6" MIN. 8' x 16' [24"]
5'4" x 10'8" MIN. 5'4" x 10'8" [16"]	6'8" x 13'4" MIN 6'8" x 13'4" [20"]	8' x 16' MIN. 8' x 16' [24"]

Table 6-2. What Changing the Minimum Radius Does to Layout Size (continued).

FIGURE NUMBER	GAUGE/SHAPE		SHARP
Fig. 3-13 "THE ACCESSIBLE WATERWINGS"	N		2'7" × 5'2" SEE NOTE BELOW 7"
Fig. 3-14 "UNDERBED SPECIAL"	N	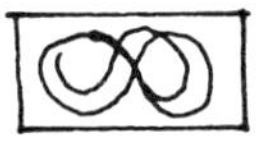	3'2" × 4'6" SEE NOTE BELOW 9"
Fig. 3-16 "THE TRADITIONAL COFFEE-TABLE R.R."	N (EXTRA-SHARP CURVES)	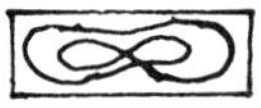	2'6" × 5' (ALTERNATE VERSION ON TRACK PLAN) 7½"
Fig. 3-17 "LONG TRAINS FOR THE COFFEE TABLE"	N	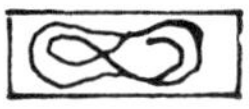	2'6" × 5' 12"
Fig. 3-19 "THE COFFEE TABLE UPPER LIMIT"	HOn3	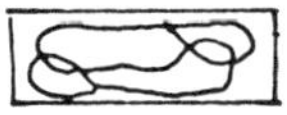	3' × 7' 12"
Fig. 3-20 "GRAND CENTRAL, JUNIOR"	N	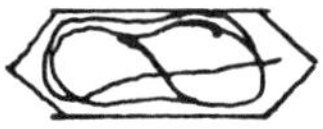	2'9" × 6'3" SEE NOTE BELOW 7"
Fig. 3-22 "CENTENNIAL PEAK BRANCH"	HOn3	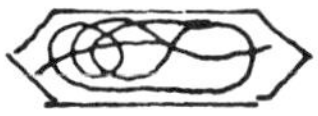	3'3" × 7'8" SEE NOTE BELOW 9"
Fig. 4-1 "THE MEDIUM BIG-TIME"	HO	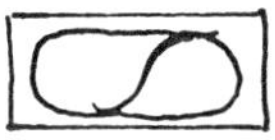	3'11" × 7'8" SEE NOTE BELOW 9"
Fig. 4-2 "THE PRETZEL"	HO	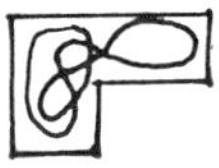	8' × 12' × 4' 12"
Fig. 4-3 "THE HAPPY ACORN"	HO	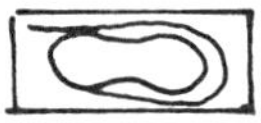	4'6" × 10' 12"

* SEE FIG. 1-1 FOR RADIUS EQUIVALENTS IN THE VARIOUS SCALES.
NOTE: LAYOUT SIZE DOESN'T SHRINK IN PROPORTION TO MINIMUM RADIUS BECAUSE TRACK CENTER SPACING MUST BE MAINTAINED.

STANDARD MAIN-LINE CURVATURE		
CONVENTIONAL	**BROAD**	**SUPER BROAD**
3'2" × 6'4" SEE NOTE BELOW [9"]	4' × 8' [12"]	5' × 10' MIN. 5' × 10' [15"]
4' × 5'8" [12"]	4'10" × 7' MIN. 5' × 7'1" [15"]	6'5" × 9'4" MIN. 6'8" × 9'5" [20"]
3'3" × 6'5" MIN. 3'3" × 6'6" [10"]	4' × 7'10" MIN. 4' × 8' [12"]	5' × 9'9" MIN. 5' × 10' [15"]
3'3" × 6'4" MIN. 3'3" × 6'6" [16"]	4' × 7'9" MIN. 4' × 8' [20"]	5' × 9'8" MIN. 5' × 10' [24"]
3'8" × 8' MIN. 4' × 9'4" [16"]	4'6" × 10'2" MIN. 5' × 11'8" [20"]	5'4" × 12' MIN. 6' × 14' [24"]
3'4" × 7'10" SEE NOTE BELOW [9"]	4' × 10' [12"]	5' × 11'3" MIN. 5' × 12'6" [15"]
4' × 10' [12"]	4'10" × 12'3" MIN. 5' × 12'5" [15"]	6'5" × 16'5" MIN. 6'8" × 16'8" [20"]
5' × 10' [12"]	6'2" × 12'5" MIN. 6'3" × 12'6" [15"]	8'2" × 16'6" MIN. 8'4" × 16'8" [20"]
10'8" × 14'4" × 5'4" MIN. 10'8" × 16' × 5'4" [16"]	13'4" × 16'8" × 5' MIN. 13'4" × 20' × 6'8" [20"]	16' × 19' × 8' MIN. 16' × 24' × 8' [24"]
5'10" × 12' MIN. 6' × 13'4" [16"]	7'4" × 15' MIN. 7'6" × 16'8" [20"]	8'9" × 17' MIN. 9' × 20' [24"]

Table 6-2. What Changing the Minimum Radius Does to Layout Size (continued).

FIGURE NUMBER	GAUGE/SHAPE	SHARP
Fig. 4-4 "LONG TRAINS, WITH A PUSH"	HO 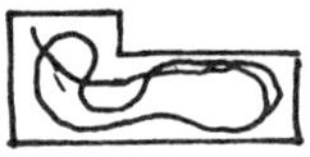	8'×14'×5' 12"
Fig. 4-6 "THE LONG, LONG TRAIL"	HO 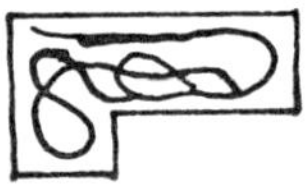	8'×14'×4'6" 12"
Fig. 4-7 "THE SUPER SWITCHING R.R."	HO 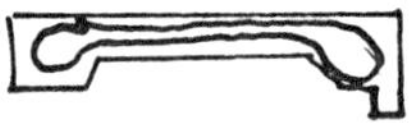	3'7" × 18'6" SEE NOTE BELOW 9"
Fig. 4-9 "THE COLLECTOR'S FRIEND"	N 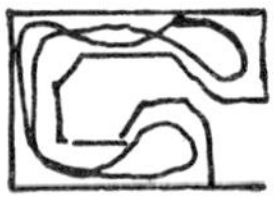	5'6" × 8'6" SEE NOTE BELOW 9"
Fig. 4-11 "THE TWO-LAYER ROOMFUL"	HO 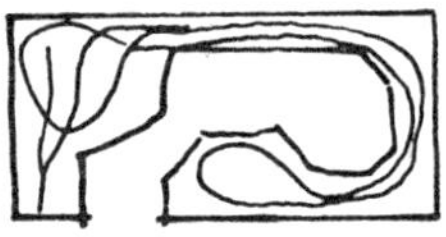	8'3" × 11'6" SEE NOTE BELOW 9"
Fig. 4-14 "SPAGHETTI ON THE ROLLING PIN"	N 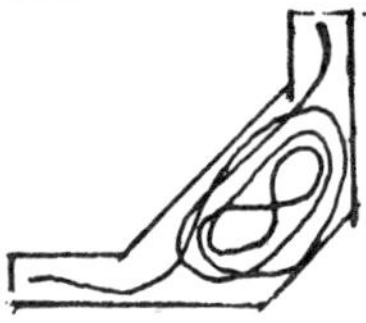	8' × 8'9" SEE NOTE BELOW 9"
Fig. 4-16 "THE EXHIBITIONIST"	N 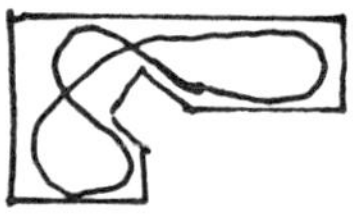	4'10" × 7'10" × 3'6" SEE NOTE BELOW 9"
Fig. 4-18 "ANOTHER MEDIUM-BIG-TIME RAILROAD"	S 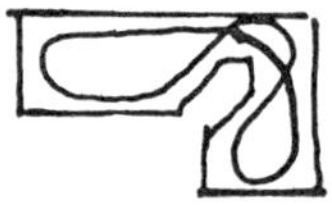	10'6" × 12'9" × 5'8" SEE NOTE BELOW 9"
Fig. 4-19 "BOTH SIDES OF THE MOUNTAIN"	S/On3 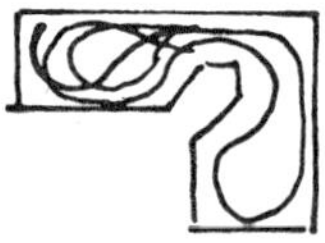	13'×16'×7' 12"

STANDARD MAIN-LINE CURVATURE		
CONVENTIONAL	**BROAD**	**SUPER BROAD**
10'7" x 17'4" x 6'6" MIN. 10'8" x 18'8" x 6'8" [16"]	13'2" x 20'8" x 8' MIN. 13'4" x 23'4" x 8'4" [20"]	15'9" x 24' x 9'6" MIN. 16' x 28' x 10' [24"]
10'7" x 17'4" x 5'10" MIN. 10'8" x 18'8" x 6' [16"]	13'2" x 20'8" x 7' MIN. 13'4" x 23'4" x 7'5" [20"]	15'9" x 24' x 8'6" MIN. 16' x 28' x 9' [24"]
4'6" x 24' (+ PANHANDLE) [12"]	5'6" x 27' MIN. 5'8" x 30' [15"]	7'2" x 32' MIN. 7'6" x 40' [20"]
7' x 11' [12"]	8'2" x 12'8" MIN. 8'9" x 13'9" [15"]	10'2" x 15'6" MIN. 11'8" x 18'4" [20"]
10' x 14' [12"]	11'2" x 16'2" MIN. 12'6" x 17'6" [15"]	14' x 20'4" MIN. 16'8" x 23'4" [20"]
10' x 11' (4' WIDE) [12"]	12'3" x 13'3" MIN (4'10" WIDE) 12'6" x 13'9" [15"]	16' x 17'6" MIN. (6'6" WIDE) 16'8" x 18'4" [20"]
6' x 10' x 4'3" [12"]	7'4" x 12'4" x 5' MIN. 7'6" x 12'6" x 5'4" [15"]	9'6" x 16'4" x 6'6" MIN. 10' x 16'8" x 7'1" [20"]
13' x 16' x 7' [12"]	15'8" x 19' x 8'6" MIN. 16'3" x 20' x 8'9" [15"]	20'6" x 24'6" x 11' MIN. 21'8" x 26'8" x 11'8" [20"]
16'9" x 20'8" x 9' MIN. 17'4" x 21'3" x 9'3" [16"]	20'4" x 25'4" x 11'5" MIN. 21'8" x 26'8" x 11'8" [20"]	24' x 30' x 13'8" MIN. 26' x 32' x 14' [24"]

Table 6-2. What Changing the Minimum Radius Does to Layout Size (continued).

FIGURE NUMBER	GAUGE/SHAPE		
			SHARP
Fig. 4-21 " ALL THE ESSENTIALS"	O	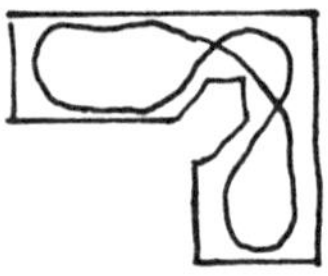	13' x 16' x 6'6" 12"
Fig. 5-1 "A GARAGE FULL OF WAY-FREIGHT FUN"	HO	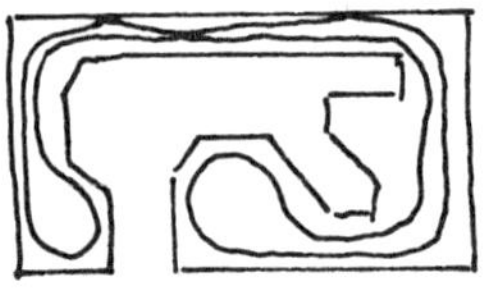	9' x 16'9" SEE NOTE BELOW 9"
Fig. 5-2 "TWO STALLS, ONE AUTOMOBILE, TWO RAILROADS"	O/On3	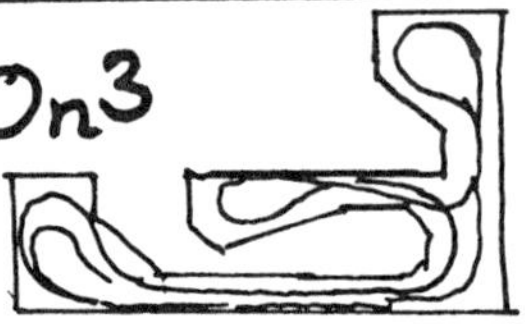	21' x 22' x 11' 12"
Fig. 5-4 "THE BIG Z"	HO	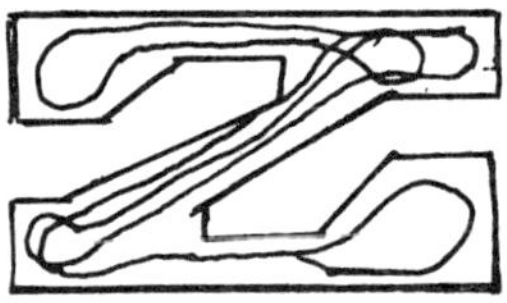	11'10" x 15'8" SEE NOTE BELOW 9"
Fig. 5-7 "BIG TRAINS YOU CAN LIVE WITH"	O	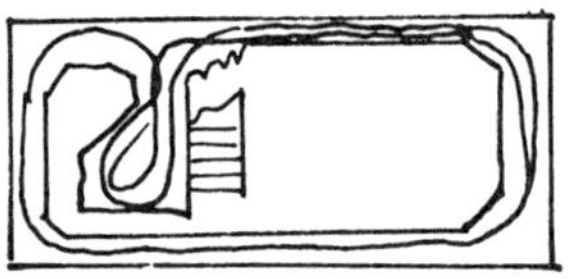	18'6" x 23'9" SEE NOTE BELOW 9"

NOTE: LAYOUT SIZE DOESN'T SHRINK IN PROPORTION TO MINIMUM RADIUS BECAUSE TRACK CENTER SPACING AND AISLE WIDTHS MUST BE MAINTAINED.

The simplest way of reworking a plan to different curve standards is to expand or contract the whole thing uniformly. If this makes it too big, *only the sections whose size is controlled by the curves they contain need be expanded*; straightaways and aisleways are kept the same length. Wherever a plan is being expanded to allow gentler curves, Table 6-2 gives it both ways; the minimum dimensions represent the case where the selective process has been followed.

EFFECT ON GRADES

Since the vertical clearance required to let one track cross over another isn't directly affected by the minimum radius, expanding the plan to accommodate bigger curves will cause the grades to become somewhat gentler. Using tighter curves will have the opposite effect. Figure 1-6 gives the good, or bad news.

Theoretically there are some 780 possible revisions when you consider changing both the gauge and the curvature standards independently. Many of these, of course, don't make sense. If you converted Fig. 3-2 to 0 scale with super-broad curves it would be 15 ft. across and cover this vast expanse with so little track as to be clearly a misuse of the space. Nevertheless, many combinations are thoroughly practical. The transcription can be made in one step. You take the size of square corresponding to the desired *scale* and then multiply this by the *ratio* of the square size for the desired curvature (Table 6-2) to the 12 in. square

STANDARD MAIN-LINE CURVATURE		
CONVENTIONAL	BROAD	SUPER BROAD
16'9"×20'8"×8'6" MIN. 17'4"×21'3"×8'8" [16"]	20'4"×25'4"×10'7" MIN. 21'8"×26'8"×10'10" [20"]	24'×30'×12'8" MIN. 26'×32'×13' [24']
11'×21' [12"]	13'2"×25' MIN. 13'9"×26'3" [15"]	17'3"×33' MIN. 18'4"×35' [20"]
27'4"×28'8"×14' MIN. 28'×29'4"×14'8" [16"]	34'9"×35'4"×17' MIN. 35'×36'8"×18'4" [20"]	40'×42'×20' MIN. 42'×44'×22' [24"]
14'×20' [12"]	17'×23' MIN. 17'6"×25' [15"]	22'3"×28' MIN. 23'4"×33'4" [20"]
23'×30' [12"]	27'×33'6" MIN. 28'9"×37'6" [15"]	35'×42' MIN. 38'4"×50' [20"]

size that corresponds to the original plan's scale.

Here's an example. Fig. 4-6 (HO scale, sharp curvature) is to be converted to N scale with broad curvature.

1. From Table 6-1: for N scale, use 6½ in. for each 12 in. square on the original drawing.
2. From Table 6-2: for broad curvature, use 20 in. squares to correspond to the 12 in. squares of the drawing.
3. Multiply 6½ × 20/12 = 10⅞ in., or 11 in. is certainly close enough.

Redrawing the plan with each square equal to 11 inches vs. the 12 inches of the original plan will result in a layout of the desired broad-curve, N-gauge proportions. It will then be necessary to adjust the track centers (as determined from Table 1-4) to make it into a truly N gauge plan, but you can be confident that things *will* fit. In this case, since the overall size will change only slightly, you also know in advance that the access arrangement suitable for the original HO railroad will probably be suitable for its small-scale cousin.

IT'S ALL APPROXIMATE

In general, all the dimensions generated by the above processes are only approximate. They're on the conservative side, calling for a little more space than will actually be needed in the interest of avoiding severe cases of frustration.

They do assume that tracks will run near the edge, just as they do in the basic planes in many cases. One of the best things you can do when you find that there *is* a little extra is to keep the same track plan but put it on a somewhat more liberally proportioned bench or work table. In addition to providing some protection against that one-way trip to the floor, space between the track and the edge of the layout vastly improves the scene. The sharp edge of the railroad is something that doesn't exist in the prototype.

Track plans in this book generally show the layout edge as a series of straight lines, often at nice standard angles such as 30 or 45 degrees with each other. This is primarily to be sure that a track isn't easily confused with the outline of the benchwork. In actually building your railroad, a free-form curve is preferred from an artistic sense. It is almost as easily achieved with any of the benchwork-building methods that are more sophisticated than the standard tabletop, and often (in a plan such as Fig. 4-9 or 5-4) lets you make better use of the aisle space. So, don't take those sharp corners as a *recommended* part of the design!

Available turnout sizes don't change in exact proportion as you vary the minimum curve radius, either. As a result, there will be some track plan adjustments, in addition to those mentioned above, to center the distance spacing between parallel tracks into line. With the figures given, these also should be in the safe rather than the sorry direction.

CHANGING CHARACTER

Other less drastic changes can do much to change the character of the railroad to suit your desires. If you crave the more demanding dispatching that goes with single-track railroading, a double-track main line can be reduced to single track by eliminating the second set of rails at various points. In many cases the location of crossovers on the basic plan will provide ready-made alignments for the trackage at the end of what will become passing sidings. When you go from double track to single, there's no doubt that there will be adequate room. The caution pointed out in Fig. 2-14 does apply. In going from single track to double, of course, you may expect to have space problems. It's usually necessary to increase the overall size of the plan by about the equivalent of that required to raise the curvature standard by one notch (Table 6-2).

DIESELIZING OR STEAMIZING?

The track plans in this book deliberately show a variety of steam-only,diesel-only andcombination engine-service facilities. Putting the right locomotive terminal on your plan may mean swapping the one shown for one on some other plan that suits the type of motive power you are determined to use. If it's shown in another scale you can use the relationships above and count squares to see what will and won't fit. Fortunately, the number, length and arrangement of such tracks is rather flexible.

Similar considerations apply in tailoring the yard capacity and characteristics to suit. Omitting platforms and substituting tracks can convert a passenger-oriented terminal to one suitable for a freight-only line. The reverse is usually harder to make fit, which is why so many of the plans lean toward providing accommodations for the varnished trains that are at least as extensive as you are likely to desire on a plan of its size.

MORE FREIGHT CAR CAPACITY

Yards never are big enough, of course, and Fig. 1-18 shows how various ladder-track arrangements other than the simple ladder of Fig. 1-17 can add track space in the same area. Most of the yards in our track plans are shown with simple ladders, nevertheless, because they typically provide a fair balance between freight car space in the yard and caboose-track and engine-terminal capacity when the total space is limited. You may well find it fits your desires better to substitute one of the more unusual arrangements from Chapter 1 in personalizing your yard.

Industry sidings represent another opportunity for using your ingenuity in boosting the fun you'll get out of your railroad. While tinkering with the main line alignment at one point may lead to troubles elsewhere in some of these close-packed plans, spurs can be worked in at many ponts without hazard. The way they look *on the railroad,* as opposed to on the plan, is the best guide. Often the availability of a particularly attractive building or structure can be the inspiration for departing from the plan and making something really worthwhile out of some otherwise less used corner of the scene.

LET YOURSELF GO!

Don't be afraid of using up a few sheets of paper, and maybe some lengths of track, in experimenting, mentally or physically, with various combinations. You'll probably find that all the pieces you need for your own dream pike plan can be found somewhere among the 30-odd specific plans, the trackwork examples of Chapter 1, and the schematics of Chapter 2. Go to it, and good luck!

Glossary of Railroad Terms

Many of the terms used by trainmen on the prototypes are slang to which they have become accustomed, rather than a purely technical application of the words used in the rule book. Others, while they might often appear to be slang in ordinary usage, are likely to be extracted from the technical jargon which necessarily develops in any specialized field. To *set out* a car is technically accurate for switching a car from a train to a side track. To *set out* people means, to the railroader, to verbally put them in their place.

In the list below, notations in italics indicate whether a word is railroad slang (*S*) or is restricted to model railroading (*M*). Where no letter appears a term is either one of general use or is used on prototye and model railroads to mean the same thing.

Abutment: A mass or structure which supports the end of a bridge, frequently with retaining walls to support the bridge approaches.

Agent: Employee in charge of tracks, turnouts, waiting rooms, ticket office, fixed signals, and employees at stations where there is no yardmaster or trainmaster.

Air *S*: The air brake system. A trainman who cannot attract the attention of the engineer on a moving train to signal for an emergency stop can "pull the air" to set the brakes by operating a lever or pulling a cord in the caboose or passenger car.

Alternating current: The flow of electricity which reverses direction at regular intervals as it travels through two wires to an operational device.

Approach: A section of track leading to a bridge, structure, or track device.

Automatic car identification: A system which employs an electro-optical trackside scanner and reflective car markings to trace car movements. The scanner reports location of a car at a given point and time to a central computer, and the information is used to calculate freight charges and record the car's journey for the owning company.

Automatic speed regulation *M:* An electrical or electronic arrangement in the throttle circuit which senses changes in power requirements to a locomotive's motor and automatically adjusts power pack output to maintain constant speed.

Automatic train control: A centralized system for starting and stopping trains and operating turnouts and other track devices to insure safe movement of trains with a minimum of manual operations.

Auxiliary reversing switch *M*: A double-pole, double-throw electrical switch wired to a power pack so as to be independent from the main reversing switch for the control of special track sections such as turning loops.

Backdrop *M*: A painted cloth, paper, or panel mounted at the back of a layout to continue the effect of landscaping beyond the limits of the layout.

Bad order: Any defective railroad equipment whose malfunction is serious enough to prevent its normal use.

Ballast: Crushed rock, stone, slag, cinders, or other coarse material placed between and around ties to provide support, stability, and drainage to the track.

Base level *M:* The level of the main yard or main operating area on a layout. *See also* **datum level.**

Big hole: Emergency stop.

Big hook *S*: Railroad crane used to hoist locomotives and cars back onto rails or salvage cars at the scene of a wreck or serious derailment.

Black diamonds *S:* Coal.

Blinds *S:* Space between tender and first car of passenger train. Used by hoboes since it is "blind" to the train crew viewing the train from the locomotive or passenger boarding steps. A hazardous place to ride.

Block: A length of track with definite limits, the use of which by trains is controlled by fixed signals.

Block control: The use of blocks to maintain safe distances between trains on the same main track. In model railroading control is by switches at the control panel.

Body track: A storage track for cars in a yard or industrial area.

Bolster: Cross member on a car's body or truck through which the weight of the body is transferred to the truck.

Boomer *S:* A railroader who changes jobs frequently, traveling from one railroad to another.

Brains *S*: Conductor of a train.

Brakeman: Trainman whose duties, under the supervision of the conductor, is to insure safe handling of trains by aligning turnouts, watching for equipment failures, and protecting the train from collision when it is stopped on a track where another train may be expected.

Bull *S:* Special agent or railroad detective.

Bum *S:* Hobo.

Butcher *S:* Concessionaire who sells magazines, newspapers, sandwiches, snacks, and sundries to passengers on board a train.

Cab: The part of a locomotive occupied by the engineer and fireman and housing the controls for normal operation. *M:* The electrical control unit for adjusting speed and changing direction.

Cab control *M:* A method of operating a single locomotive from one throttle unit independent of other locomotives running at the same time on different blocks of a layout.

Caboose: A special car to carry part of a freight train's crew (conductor and brakeman) assigned to ride at the rear of a train. The caboose probably has more slang names than any other railroad component, operating or otherwise. A few are: **crummy, hack, palace, brain bin, carriage, cage,** and **bobber.**

Caboose bounce *S (also* **Caboose hop):** A train consisting of a locomotive and caboose, used to transfer a crew to pick up a train at another station where there is no eligible crew available.

Call boy: An employee whose duty was to notify train crew members of the time to report for duty. Today this job is included in that of another yard office employee.

Car: Any flanged-wheel vehicle used on a railroad to transport passengers, livestock, merchandise, raw materials, railroad equipment, and crews. Locomotives, tenders, and some other special or self-propelled vehicles are called by their appropriate names instead of *cars.*

Car knocker *S:* Car inspector or repairman (often use interchangeably with **car toad**).

Car toad *S:* Car inspector who frequently "frog walks" between the rails underneath standing cars to examine and make minor repairs on brake and other gear.

Cascade *M*: Sequential operation of several electrical devices from a single control, as an arrangement of switch machines for rapid route selection in a yard ladder.

Catwalk: A wooden or metal walkway on a car or locomotive to permit trainmen to reach hand brakes on a moving train.

Centerpin: A thick vertical rod which passes through car and truck bolsters to secure their position and allow the truck to pivot on curves.

Chain gang *S*: A method of scheduling freight train crews for duty from the home terminal on a first-in, first-out basis for moving all trains, schedule and extra.

Classification signals: Lamps and flags displayed on the front of a locomotive to indicate class, section, or other designation as required by the rules.

Common rail *M*: A rail whose electrical continuity is maintained from block to block to provide a single return for the entire series of blocks so wired.

Common return *M:* Any single electrical conducting wire or element used to complete one leg of two or more circuits.

Conductor *1:* A trainman vested with the general direction and government of a train. 2: Wire or other material capable of transmitting an electrical current.

Consist: The cars and their contents which make up a train, excluding the locomotive and caboose.

Contacts: Points or surfaces of two or more conductors arranged to connect or disconnect electrical circuits by mechanical means.

Control Rail *M:* Gapped rail which is used to control an individual block when used in conjunction with a common rail return.

Cornfield meet *S*: Head-on collision.

Coupler: Mechanical device for linking one car to another.

Cowcatcher: Pointed, plow-shaped project on the front of a locomotive between coupler and rails, intended to clear the track of livestock and other movable obstructions.

Crossing: Intersection of two railroad tracks or a railroad track and a street or highway.

Crossover: A track arrangement consisting of two turnouts, one on each of two adjacent tracks, so connected as to allow trains running in either direction to be routed to either track.

Cupola: Part of a caboose raised above roof level to increase trainmen's visibility in maintaining surveillance over the cars in a moving train.

Cushions *S:* Passenger train.

Cut *1:* Removal of part of a hill to allow construction of a roadbed with a suitable gradient. *2:* Separation of one or more cars from a train or yard string.

Datum level *M:* Reference point for elevation measurements on a layout.

Deadheading: Free transportation (with or without mileage pay) for a trainman relieved from duty or moving to a new assignment. Deadheading is related to duty but is used in a slang sense for vacationing employees riding on a pass.

Derail *1:* To cause a locomotive or car to leave the track. *2:* A removable track device intended to derail free-rolling cars before they travel far enough to block another track.

Design *M:* Usually intended to mean the configuration of a layout's two main features: the track plan (dogbone, point-to-point, etc.) and spatial arrangement (shelf, table, etc.).

Detail scenery *M:* Any scenery added after the final terrain coat and base color have been applied to a layout.

Detection circuit *M:* An arrangement of electronic circuitry used to detect and signal the presence of a train in a track segment.

Diorama *M:* Progressive reduction of the scale of scenic elements beyond the most distant track to give the effect of greater distance.

Direct current: Unidirectional flow of electrical current through one conductor to the point of use and back to the power source through a second conductor.

Dispatcher: Employee responsible for safe movement of trains according to timetable schedule and for issuing train orders to authorize movements not provided by timetables.

Division: One of the major sections of a railroad governed by a superintendent and subdivided into districts.

Doubleheading: The use of two locomotives at the head of a train to pull more tonnage than a single locomotive could handle.

Doubling: Train movements which require the train to be cut into two segments. For example, a train too long for a single siding must be doubled over by setting part of it on another auxiliary track to clear the main for a meet or pass. Also a heavy train may require doubling a hill.

Draft gear: The assembly of coupler, springs, and other parts contained in a coupler pocket which transfers the pulling force from one car to the next.

Drag *S:* A slow freight.

Drop: *See* **running switch.**

Dry texturing *M:* Adding dry powder or other materials to a wet scenery surface for detail effects of texture and color.

Elevation *M:* Distance above or below the datum level, shown in scale feet with a plus or minus sign to indicate height and depth.

Extra board: A list of trainmen, according to seniority, who has not been assigned to a regular crew. A regular brakemen who has passed the examination for conductor can be placed on the extra conductor board to be called for that job when it opens without losing his regular job as brakeman.

Fill: Part of a low area of the terrain which has been filled with earth and rubble to support a roadbed at a suitable level.

Fireman: Employee responsible for keeping a steam locomotive supplied with steam. On a diesel he assists engineer in operation of the locomotive.

Fishplate: A flat steel plate used to stabilize the position of a rail on a tie. Spike holes in it near the rails allow spiking it and the rail to the tie.

Flagman: An employee (usually a brakeman) assigned to protect a train.

Flange: The vertical extension of a wheel beyond the tire designed to keep the wheel on the rail.

Flangeway: The space between a guard rail, wing rail, or other track accessory part through which a flange passes as it travels over turnouts, crossings, bridges, and other track assemblies.

Flimsy *S:* Train order.

Frog: That part of a turnout or railroad crossing designed to allow wheels to pass over one rail while traveling to another.

Fusee: A chemical flare used by flagmen to protect a train.

Gandy dancer *S*: Section hand or track worker.

Gage: Distance between the two rails of a track.

Goat *S:* Engine, especially a yard engine used for switching.

Grab iron: Steel hand holds on rolling stock.

Grade *1:* The level of land at any given point. *2:* Slope of a trackbed (more properly this should be called *gradient*).

Helper: A locomotive used to add tractive force to a train over short distances on steep grades. It is usually coupled on the rear or near the middle of a train as opposed to doubleheading.

Hobo: An unauthorized passenger on a freight train or on the blinds of a passenger train.

Hog *S:* A road engine.

Hogger *S:* Engineer.

Hole *S:* Siding (take the hole). *Also see* **big hole.**

Home guard *S:* A steady employee as opposed to a boomer.

Hoop: A bamboo or wooden loop used to pass train orders from the ground to a passing trainman.

Hostler: Engine handler assigned to moving locomotives around the shops and ready tracks and, on some railroads, to and from trains in the yard.

Hotbox: An overheated bearing indicated by a smoking or flaming journal.

House track: A siding or spur which serves a railroad freight house.

Hump: The hill at the end of a classification yard. A string of cars pulled to the top can be cut as required and allowed to roll into the yard below slowed, as needed, by speed arresters attached to the tracks.

Independent block system *M:* The arrangement of a series of blocks in which the ends of both rails in each block are gapped.

Intiial station: The station at which a train enters a district or originates therefrom. A train must not leave its initial station without a clearance card.

Interchange: A track or tracks on which cars are routed to another railroad.

Interlocking: An arrangement of switch, lock, and signal appliances so interconnected that their movement must succeed each other in a predetermined order. Often remote-controlled interlockings are used to protect the trains of one railroad from those of another at a heavily used crossing.

Interurban: A self-propélled passenger car for use between nearby cities.

Jungle *S:* Camp near a railroad where hoboes gather.

Kick: A switching movement in which a car is pushed, uncoupled from the locomotive, and allowed to roll by itself to a designated track.

Kit-bashing *M:* Construction method in which parts from two or more kits are combined to form a hybrid structure.

Ladder track: A yard track which serves several storage tracks through a series of turnouts.

Local: A train which makes frequent stops at stations between major terminals to serve the needs of small communities.

Main reversing switch *M:* Locomotive direction-reversing switch used in switching and other moves in the regular blocks or tracks of a layout.

Markers: Train signals (lamps and flags) attached to the rear of the last car in a train to indicate conditions of movement.

Meet: Arrival at a station and passing of two trains traveling in opposite directions.

Motor *1:* Device for transforming electrical energy into rotational mechanical energy. *2:* An electric-powered locomotive.

No bill *S:* Derogatory term for nonunion railroad employee, from troublesome movements of cars which have no waybills to give clear instructions on handling and contents.

Normal *M:* A turnout alignment to the track most frequently used (as the main line) and signals displayed to indicate normal position.

Old man *S:* The superintendent or trainmaster.

On the advertised *S:* Arrival on time according to the timetable.

On the ground *S:* Derailed.

Open circuit: Any part connection which prevents electric current from flowing when a circuit is turned on.

Pass *1:* To overtake and run ahead of another train traveling in the same direction. *2:* Authorization for employees and members of their families to ride a passenger train free or at reduced fare. *3:* The surface route between mountain peaks.

Peddler *S:* Local train or switch train.

Pull the pin: Uncouple a car.

Pulse power: Direct current taken unmodified from a half-wave rectifier and applied to an electrical motor. Used to make slow starts with model locomotives, but should not be used for continuous running.

Rail *S:* Railroader on prototye or model pike.

Ramp: A short incline for vehicle and pedestrian traffic as at a depot. *M* A track device for uncoupling cars.

Rattler *S:* A freight train comprised of empty cars, especially boxcars.

Reefer *S:* Refrigerator car.

Relay: An electromagnetic device for completing or interrupting the flow of electricity in a circuit.

Reversing section *M:* A track arrangement or device for turning locomotives or trains to face the opposite direction. A loop, wye, or turntable.

Rheostat: A voltage-control resistive device for electric circuits.

Right-of-way: Railroad property on which tracks are laid, especially taken to mean the tracks and adjacent land along the road.

Rolling stock: All vehicles fitted with flanged wheels and intended for rail service.

Roundhouse: A locomotive repair shop built as part of a circle segment with rails leading from a turntable to stalls in the building.

Runaround track: Any track or siding with both ends joined to another track to permit a locomotive to handle cars from either end of a train or string of stored cars.

Running switch: A switching move in which a locomotive facing a switch moves toward it with a car or cars trailing, slows to allow the cars to be uncoupled, then speeds up through the switch so that it can be thrown to send the cars down the auxiliary or second branch of the turnout (Rule 104e).

Scenery *M:* The complete details of the upper surface of a layout excluding tracks, track control devices, and rolling stock.

Scissors crossover: Two crossovers combined with a crossing between two adjacent tracks used to conserve space while improving route selection.

Scratch building *M:* Construction method in which a model structure is built from raw stock. Rolling-stock models may have some parts ready-made and still qualify as scratch built.

Shack *S:* Caboose or rear brakeman.

Siding: A track joined at both ends of a main line, used by one train to allow another to pass in either direction.

Slack: Sufficient relief of tractive effort to separate the mating surfaces of the knuckles of two couplers joined together.

Spot: To locate a car at a loading or unloading site.

Spur: A track which has access through a turnout at one end only.

Switch machine *M:* Any device, mechanical or electrical, used to move the points of a turnout to change routes through it.

Signals: Any of the visible or audible communications or appliances used to indicate track conditions affecting the movement of trains.

Tender: Car used to supply fuel and water to a locomotive.

Terrain: The geological features of a scene including the bulk shapes, soil, and types of rock formations.

Texture paint *M:* A powdery plaster material which forms a paint-like mixture when added to water and hardens on drying to form a shell almost as hard as plaster.

Throttle: A device for controlling locomotive speed. *M:* A rheostat, potentiometer, or variable transformer for the same purpose.

Tower: A structure situated at a junction, interlocking, or other track control point for the purpose of operating turnouts, derailers, and signal appliances governing the use of tracks. A towerman frequently has the additional duties of passing train orders to trainmen.

Trainmaster: An employee who supervises train crews in the performance of their duties. The trainmaster's authority extends to all employees in train or engine service, both on the road and in yards where no trainmaster is employed.

Train order: An order delivered to the conductor and engineer of a train with instructions for movements to be made under the authority of the chief train dispatcher. A train order confers rights over trains of any class at the dispatcher's discretion.

Traveling engineer: An engineer who is especially competent to handle and understand the principles of each type of locomotive used by a railroad. He is employed in the education of other engineers and firemen in the proper use of locomotives and accessory equipment.

Trolley: An overhead electric power line used to supply energy to locomotives, interurbans, and streetcars.

Uncoupling ramp *M:* A device installed between the rails at selected locations to uncouple cars.

Variable transformer: A transformer whose output voltage can be varied by sliding a contact along the secondary coil, the best of ordinary start-and-stop controllers for model railroading.

Water plug: Penstock, pipe, or sluice used to convey water to a tender for boiler feed.

Wing rail: The flared ends of the closure rails attached to the flangeways of a frog to help guide wheels through a turnout.

Wye: An arrangement of three turnouts joined together to form a triangle upon which locomotives and cars can be turned to head in the opposite direction.

Zip texturing *M:* Rapid finishing of terrain using such techniques as coloring large areas with dye either mixed in a plaster coat or added to the surface after the coat has been applied; adding dry material to wet plaster or painted surfaces to produce a particular soil or vegetation effect; or cutting or brushing cracks, striations, and grain features into simulated rocks while they are still wet.

Appendix A
Freight Car Insignias of Major Railroads

Appendix B
Rules and Regulations

RULES AND REGULATIONS

Any train must be under some controlling precept or special instruction wherever it travels on the layout, whether the rule is intended to avoid collision, derailment, or passenger complaints.

Rules for Movement of Trains

86. An inferior train must clear the time of a superior train, in the same direction not less than 5 minutes, but must be clear at the time a first-class train in the same direction is due to leave the next station in the rear where time is shown.

87. An inferior train must keep out of the way of opposing superior trains and, failing to clear the main track by the time required by rule, must be protected as prescribed by Rule 99.

88. At meeting points between trains of the same class, the inferior train must clear the main track before the leaving time of the superior train.

90. Trains must stop at scheduled meeting stations, if the train to be met is of the same class, unless the switch is right and the track clear. Superior trains must approach all sidings prepared to stop until all overdue inferior trains of the same class have been met.

91. Unless some form of block signal is used, trains in the same direction must keep at least 5 minutes apart, except in closing up at stations.

92. A train must not arrive at a station in advance of its scheduled arriving time. A train must not leave a station in advance of its scheduled leaving time.

97. Extra trains must not be run without orders from the chief train dispatcher.

98. Trains must approach the end of double track, junctions, railroad grade crossings at grade, and drawbridges prepared to stop unless the switches and signals are right and the track is clear. Where required by law, trains must stop.

99. When a train stops or is delayed under circumstances in which it may be overtaken by another train, the flagman must go back immediately with stop signals a sufficient distance to insure full protection. One-fourth mile from the rear of the train he will place one torpedo on the rail; continuing back one-half mile from the rear of his train, he will place two torpedoes on the rail, two rail lengths apart. He may then return to the single torpedo, where he must remain until he is relieved by another flagman or is recalled by the whistle of his locomotive. When recalled, if he does not see or hear an approaching train, the single torpedo will be removed. If conditions warrant, a red fusee (standing flare) will be displayed to protect his train while returning.

Should a train be seen or heard approaching before flagman has reached the required distance, he must, by night or during foggy or stormy weather, display a red fusee, continuing in the direction of the approaching train. Under no circumstances may a flagman allow a train which he must stop, to pass him, without having placed one torpedo on the rail.

The front of the train must be protected in the same manner when necessary. Conductors are responsible for the full protection of their trains in both directions and under all conditions.

In block signal districts where the automatic home block signal governing the track in use can be plainly seen at the rear of the train to be at *stop*, its location being not less than one-half mile from the train to be protected, it will be unnecessary for the flagman to go back.

104. Switches must be left in proper position after having been used. A switch must not be left open for a following train unless in the charge of a trainman of such train.

All main-line switches and those required by rule and special instructions to be locked must be left in that condition.

Trainmen and other employees must not unlock main-track switches nor stand within 20 ft of such switches until trains to be met or passed or all of the trains for which switch was opened have cleared the entire switch. If practicable they will take position on the opposite side of the track from the switch stand while trains are passing. Neither switch to a crossover must be unlocked during the passage of a train on either track.

Running switches will be made only when absolutely necessary, in which case the train must be brought to a stop before movement is commenced.

Main-track switches will show green when the switch is set for the main track, red when set for sidings, crossings, or junction tracks.

161. Where reduced speed is required the entire train must pass over the designated territory at the reduced speed.

These are samples of prototype rules which can be applied or adapted to model railroading. The list is far from complete but is sufficient to indicate how a model pike must be governed. Obviously there will be less than the full crew operating a model train. Usually there are no more than two, and most of the time, only the man at the throttle who must maintain surveillance over the whole train. He is responsible for the protection of his own train.

Conduct of Employees and Train Movement Control

700. Civil, gentlemanly deportment is required of all employees in their relations with the public, their subordinates, and each other. Boisterous, profane, or vulgar language is forbidden. Courtesy and attention to patrons is demanded.

702. All employees must devote themselves exclusively to the company's service, attending to their duties during prescribed hours and obeying instructions promptly.

703. Employees who are careless of the safety of themselves and others will not be continued in service.

706. No appointment or promotion to the position of conductor or engineman will be made until after the applicant has been examined as to knowledge and understanding of all rules which relate to his duties.

719. In case of damage to trains or structures, wherein the security of freight or company property is involved, it is the duty of all concerned to see that watchmen are immediately stationed and that arrangements are promptly made for the protection of such property.

720. Minors will not be employed in yard, train, or engine service; when employed in other service it must be with the written consent of parent or guardian.

723. Employees whose duties connect with the movement of trains must not be absent themselves from, exchange duties with, nor substitute others in their place, without proper authority.

755. Before starting on any district upon which they have not been running or when absent for 6 days or over, train and enginemen must inquire for and know that they have the current timetable and supplements.

757. Trains must not be permitted to stand across another railroad at grade.

758. Trains must be opened to clear all public crossings while standing at stations, and in no case block a crossing longer than 5 minutes.

759. Cars must not be backed nor cut loose and allowed to run over a street, highway, or private crossing without a flagman on the front of, or preceding, the leading car.

800. At stations where a yard force is employed, trains or engines without trains will be under control of the yardmaster, and all employees in train or engine service will be subject to his direction. Road crews of trains entering such stations will be responsible for their respective trains and engines until the same are taken charge of by the yardmaster or his representative.

801. Yardmasters will be responsible for the proper position and security of all yard switches. Main-line switches in yards, except when in use, must invariably be clocked for the main track.

802. Yardmasters will keep advised of important trains such as stock fruit, and manifest, and make every effort to get them through the yard with the least possible delay. They must see that cars loaded with explosives and flammable material are placed in the train the prescribed distance from the engine and caboose.

813. The general direction and government of a train is vested in the conductor, and all persons employed on the train will obey his instructions.

820. Conductors must inspect the running gear and brake and draft rigging of trains as often and as closely as practicable while on the road, require their men to assist in such inspection, remedy as far as possible any defects discovered, and remove from the train cars which are unsafe to run.

821. In leaving cars on sidetracks, conductors must see that they are left clear of other tracks and also of any street. Conductors must not leave cars on sidings when there is room for them on other tracks. If so left, immediately notify train dispatcher.

863. Conductors must see that the words *bad order* are written with chalk on both sides of bad-order cars left at stations, and defective parts marked with a cross. They must also attach damaged-car card.

865. Conductors must not take freight, either in carload or less-than-carload lots, from a station where there is an agent, without the regular waybills or cardbills.

882. While switching, the engineman and fireman must remain on the engine. Exercise great care in handling engine while yardmen or others are making couplings and give close attention to signals.

887. If a train makes an improper station stop, it must not be moved until the conductor gives the proper signal to do so. If, after making a stop at a water station, it should be necessary to move the engine to take water, it must not be done while passengers are leaving or entering the train.

889. Keep a constant and vigilant lookout. Carefully note all signals. See whether other trains are displaying signals; observe the position of switches while running; and frequently look back, especially when rounding curves, to see whether the train is intact. After having seen a fixed signal affecting movement of his train, the engineman must call its indication to fireman and require fireman to do likewise.

897. Report to master mechanic any defect or improper condition of engine, and at the end of each trip enter on the workbook the repairs required.

899. Engines must not be left without a man in charge, except at designated places, and must not be left standing in such position as to block movements on adjoining tracks. Never allow engine to stand on main track unless properly protected under the rules.

900. Engines must not be permitted to stand nearer than 100 ft to a street or highway crossing; under any bridge, when it can be avoided; in the vicinity of waiting rooms, telegraph, or telephone offices; nor near cars occupied by passengers where the noise or smoke will disturb the occupants.

901. Exercise caution and good judgment in starting or stopping trains to avoid violent or sudden movements which migh cause discomfort or injury to passengers, or damage to property.

Definitions for Rules

Engine: A locomotive propelled by any form of energy.

Train: An engine, or more than one engine, coupled, with or without cars, and displaying markers.

Regular train: A train authorized by a timetable schedule.

Section: One of two or more trains running on the same schedule displaying signals or for which signals are displayed.

Extra train: A train not authorized by a timetable schedule (either any extra train or specifically a *work extra*).

Train of superior right: A train given precedence by train order.

Train of superior class: A train given precedence by timetable.

Train of superior direction: A train given precedence in the direction specified in the timetable as between trains of the same class.

Timetable: The authority for the movement of regular trains subject to the rules. It contains the classified schedules of trains with special instructions relating thereto.

Main track: A track extending through yards and between stations, upon which trains are operated by timetable and train order, or the use of which is controlled by block signals.

Single track: A main track upon which trains are operated in both directions.

Double track: Two main tracks upon one of which the current of traffic is in a specified direction, and upon the other in the opposite direction.

Three (or more) tracks: Three (or more) main tracks, upon any of which the current of traffic may be in either specified direction.

Station: A place designated on the timetable by name, at which a train may stop for traffic, or to enter or leave the main track, or from which fixed signals are operated.

Siding: A track auxiliary to the main track for meeting or passing trains.

Fixed signal: A signal or fixed location indicating a condition affecting the movement of a train. (Covers such signals as slow boards, stop boards, yard limits, switch, train order, block, interlocking, semaphore, disc, ball, or other means indicating "stop," "caution," or "proceed."

Yard: A system of tracks within defined limits provided for the making up of trains, storing of cars, and other purposes, over which movements not authorized by timetable or train order may be made, subject to prescribed signals and regulations.

Under control: To be able to stop within the distance track is seen to be clear.

Appendix C
Connecting Power to the Rails

CONNECTING POWER TO THE RAILS

Even the simplest toy train, chasing its caboose around a circle of track, must be connected to a transformer if it is to move. The most complex model railroad imaginable is faced with the same problem—the only differences are that it is repeated much more, and in the complicated model the operator must be able to change the power connections at will to meet operation requirements.

The problem of furnishing electrical power to the rails can be solved in any of several ways. We will examine the usual techniques, comparing their advantages and disadvantages, and offering recommendations. No one technique outshines any of the others, so the final choice must be determined by your own desires.

Using Terminal Tracks

The conventional toy train of bygone years used special terminal track sections to make a connection from the transformer to the rails. These sections were prewired from rails to electrical connectors, and all you had to do was run a wire from the connector to the terminal on the transformer.

Railroaders who work in either HO- or N-scales can use similar terminal track sections. Both these scales are featured in today's train set trade, and every such train set contains a terminal track section.

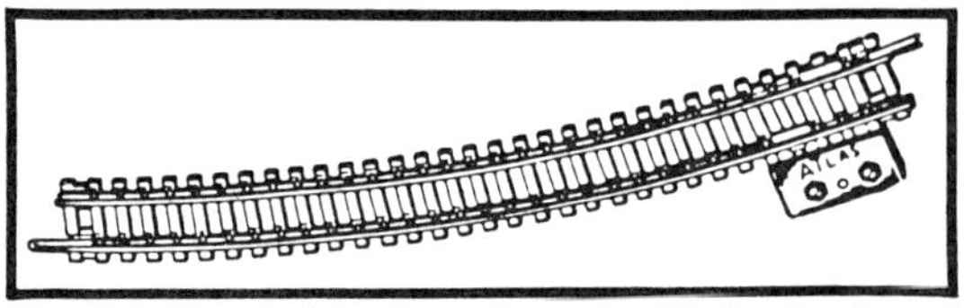

Fig. C-1. Terminal track sections simplify the feeding of power to the rails, but the terminal block is hard to disguise.

Using a terminal track section to make your electrical connections to the rails offers advantages. The first is that you need make no electrical connections direct to the rails; the connections are already made for you by the manufacturer. Secondly, since you do not have to deal with the rails themselves, you cannot cause damage to the track while attempting to make the connections, and there is little chance of altering the track dimensions and causing future derailment of trains.

Balanced against these advantages are two major disadvantages: The terminal track section has a rather unrealistic appearance, unless you go to considerable extra trouble to disguise it, and if you have many different control blocks, each requiring its own terminal track, it can get expensive.

When we balance the advantages and the disadvantages against each other, we reach this conclusion: Terminal tracks are fine for beginners who are building uncomplicated layouts. They are not recommended for the long haul.

A close relative of the terminal track idea, which combines all the advantages of terminal

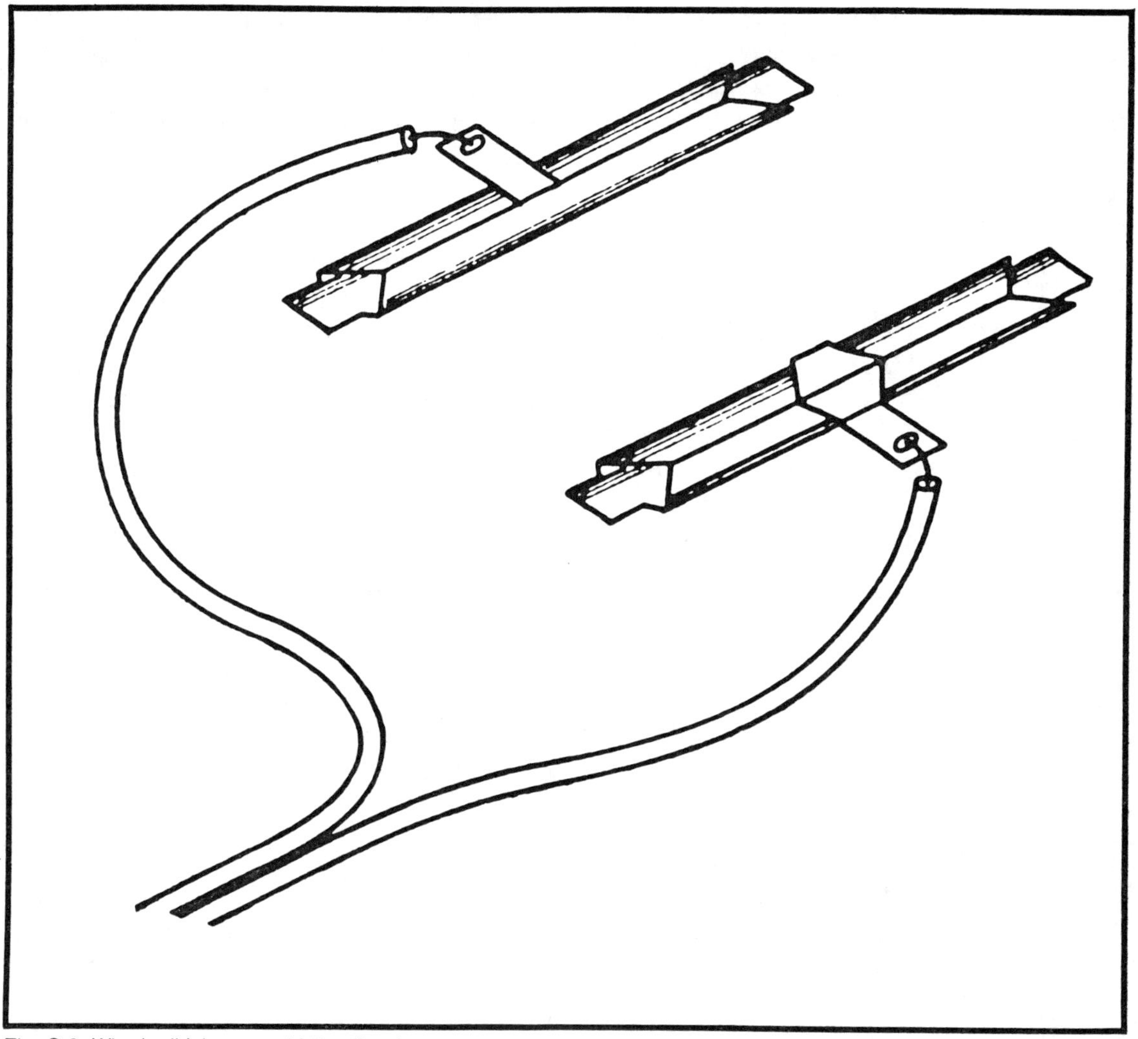

Fig. C-2. Wired rail joiners avoid the disguise problem.

track while escaping its disadvantages, is the device known as a wired rail joiner.

Prefabricated track in both HO- and N-scales is made in sections. To assemble a track plan, these sections must be joined by brass rail joiners. The wired joiner consists of a length of wire permanently fastened to two rail joiners; by using them instead of the ordinary brass joiner, you make an electrical connection from the wire to the rails.

The connections are no more difficult than any joining of sectional track. No damage can result, and there is no more chance of a derailment than there is at any other track joint. The wire is easily camouflaged when you ballast the track, eliminating the terminal track disadvantage of unrealistic appearance, and while the wired rail joiner is more costly then the plain rail joiner, it is far less expensive than the terminal track sections.

The primary problem with wired rail joiners is the fact that they can be placed only between rail sections. If you are using prefabricated sections, this is no problem at all, because you will have a rail joint every 5 to 10 inches. If, however, you are using the popular *flex* track, or hand-laying track using separate rails and ties, you can install wired rail joiners only between the longer lengths of track. These probably will not match the desired control blocks.

An alternative is to cut the track into smaller sections, wherever you want to connect the electrical power, and this defeats the major reason for using flex track in the first place—which is its freedom from frequent rail joints.

If you are modeling in TT-, S-, or O-scales, you need not worry about the advantages or disadvantages of terminal track or wired rail joiners. As far as we know, they are not available in those scales. This leaves you no alternative but soldering your connections directly to the rails.

Soldering to the Rails

For large or complicated track plans, the most popular method for making electrical connections to the rails is soldering. In this technique, a short length of small, relatively flexible wire is soldered to the outside of each rail and run through a hole drilled between the ties. This wire connects to a terminal beneath the layout, and the main power connection is then made to the terminal. The small flexible wire removes physical strain from the rails, while the fact that it is short in length makes it capable of carrying more current than a locomotive ever needs.

The advantages of the solder connection technique are that connections can be installed anywhere on the layout, and the cost is minimal. The disadvantages of this technique are several: Soldering skill is necessary to do it properly. If you overheat the rails, you may damage or destroy the plastic tie strips. (This is the most frequent problem beginners encounter in their first attempts to solder connections to rails; the only preventative for it is experience. Practice first on some scrap rail before trying on your beautifully detailed oper-

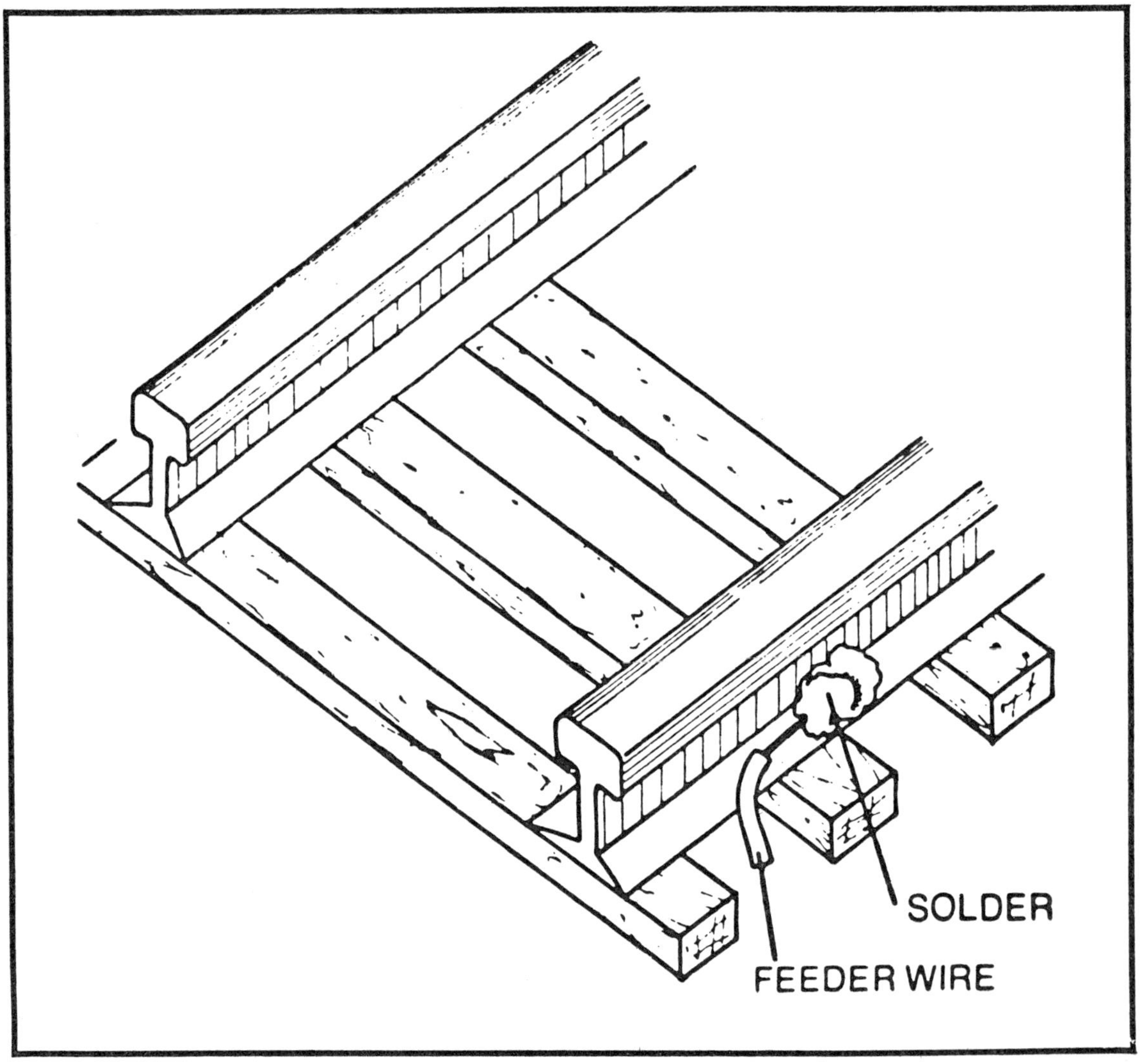

Fig. C-3. The most versatile method of feeding power to the rails is by individually soldered connections.

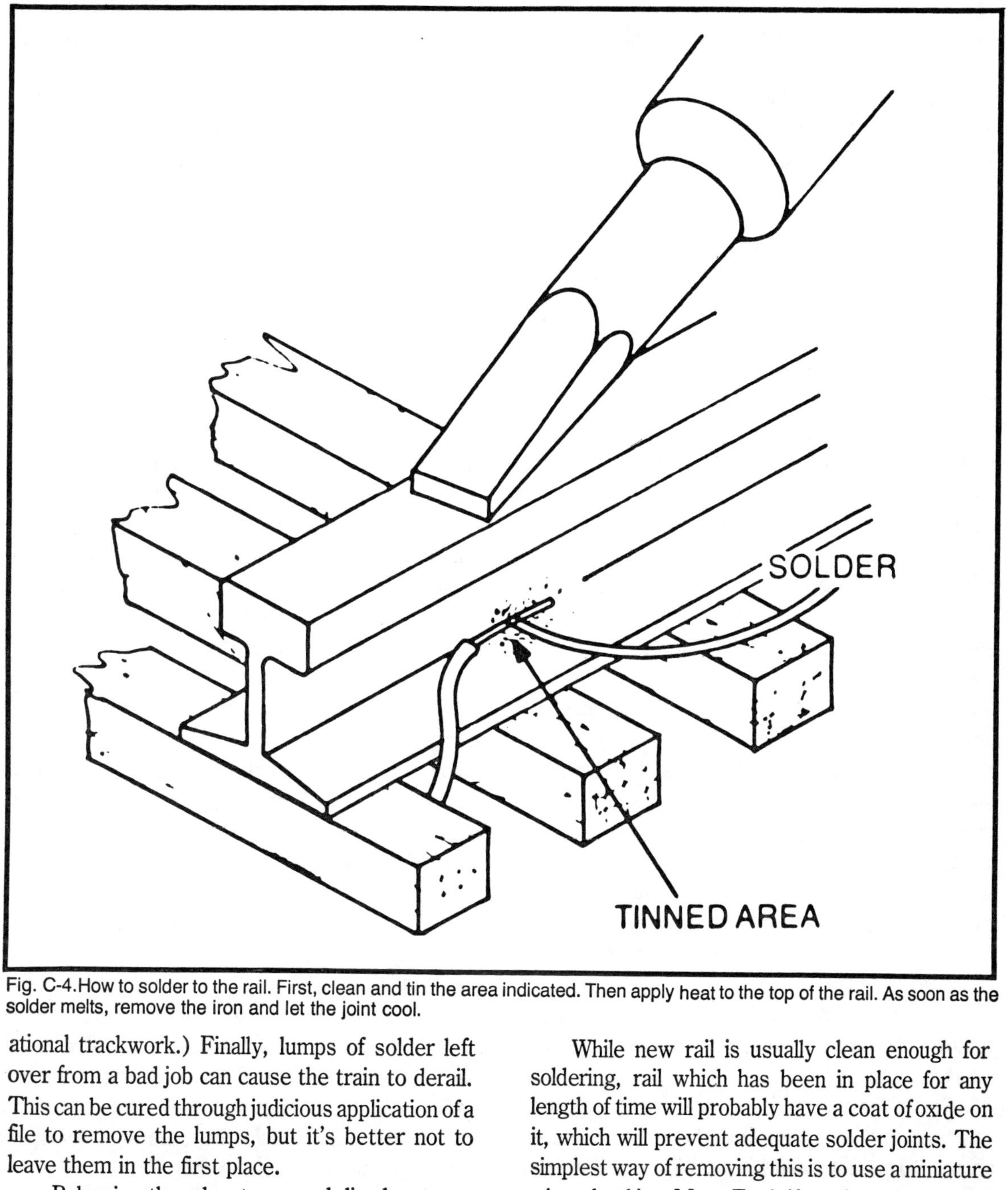

Fig. C-4. How to solder to the rail. First, clean and tin the area indicated. Then apply heat to the top of the rail. As soon as the solder melts, remove the iron and let the joint cool.

ational trackwork.) Finally, lumps of solder left over from a bad job can cause the train to derail. This can be cured through judicious application of a file to remove the lumps, but it's better not to leave them in the first place.

Balancing the advantages and disadvantages of the soldering technique, we reach the conclusion that it is best for complicated layouts and not bad for even the simplest. It is highly recommended.

Since rail is not made to be soldered to, but rather is intended to be a resonable replica of the real thing and to guide the wheels of the train, you must take special precautions to get a good connection.

While new rail is usually clean enough for soldering, rail which has been in place for any length of time will probably have a coat of oxide on it, which will prevent adequate solder joints. The simplest way of removing this is to use a miniature wire wheel in a Moto-Tool, if you have one available. If not, you can scrape the rail bright and clean with a pocket knife, a screwdriver tip, or fine sandpaper. In any event, the metal should be shiny before you attempt to solder to it.

Once you have brightened the metal, it should be tinned, using rosin core solder, before attempting to make the joint itself. If you use steel rail (not common in smaller scales, but popular in the larger gauges) you may have to use acid flux rather than rosin core. If so, you must clean off all traces of acid after the tinning job is done.

The next step in making the connections is to drill the hole for the feeder wire. A 1/16-inch drill will make a large enough hole for any feeder wire. The first preference is telephone switchboard wire, which is approximately wire gauge number 24 in size. The bare tinned wire sold by radio parts houses under the name "bus bar conductor," in 24 or smaller gauge, will also serve adequately. Do not attempt to use larger wire—its stiffness introduces stress, which will subsequently give you nothing but problems.

With the hole drilled to the tinned spot on each rail, on the outside of the rail rather than between the rails, thread the wire up from the bottom and bend its tip. The wire tip should, of course, be clean of insulation and tinned just as the rail was before doing this.

Now clamp the wire tightly against the tinned spot on the rail (using a pair of long-nosed pliers), and apply heat from the soldering iron directly to the rail above the point where the connection is to be made. Be sure the iron is hot when you do this; the major cause of damage to plastic ties is applying a cool iron for too long a time. Strangely enough, an extremely hot iron causes less damage to adjacent plastic than a cool one.

While the iron is in contact with the top of the rail, watch the tinned areas closely. When they change from a dull surface to a shiny, wet-looking appearance, remove the iron and quickly wipe over the top of the rail with a piece of cloth to remove any remaining lump of solder which might interfere with the wheels.

Do not permit the joint itself to move during this process—you must hold the pliers in place another 10 to 15 seconds after the iron is removed. You can tell when the joint sets, because it will lose its wet look and go back to a satin-finish appearance. When this happens, you can remove the pliers. The connection is complete.

Assuring Track Continuity

Every modeler who has built a layout with sectional track has had the experience—everything works nicely at first, but as time passes the trains apparently get tired. Instead of smooth roars of power through the model countryside, the locomotives stagger and lurch, surging ahead at one place, almost halting elsewhere. You did nothing to change it; it changed itself from a "working" to a "non-working" layout.

The culprit is oxidation. Sectional track depends upon brass rail joiners between the rail sections to establish electrical continuity from one length of rail to the next. When everything is shiny new, this works well. As time passes, and the air oxidizes the brass to a dark—and insulating—finish, problems appear.

When this happens, you have basically two choices. One is to tear everything up, polish away the oxide, and then put the track back down. Operation will be fine again—until the process repeats itself. (If you are trying one track plan after another, while attempting to determine how you want to put things down permanently, this is the best way to deal with oxidation.)

However, if you are constructing your permanent layout, and intend to apply ballast and other scenic effects, you will not be able to tear things up and clean periodically. Then you must follow the other alternative—soldering electrical feeders around the offending joiners to provide a solid metallic connection wherever you want the electricity to go.

Most textbooks on wiring model railroads advise you to bond all rail joints with small lengths of flexible wire soldered at each end of each piece of rail, bridging around the joints, or joiner. For large scales this is undoubtedly the best way. For N-scale operation, however, there is no need to use the separate wire. The joiner itself can be soldered to the ends of both rails.

In large scales, soldering rails together may lead to problems when the metallic rails expand and contract with temperature changes.

On the prototype, welded rail is laid down in lengths of hundreds of feet and causes no problems in thermal expansion and contraction. Some modelers have applied this lesson to their small scale layouts—brazing the ends of rail lengths together to provide the equivalent of extra long prototype welded rails.

This is practical only if you intend to hand-lay rail, since the brazing process raises the rail's

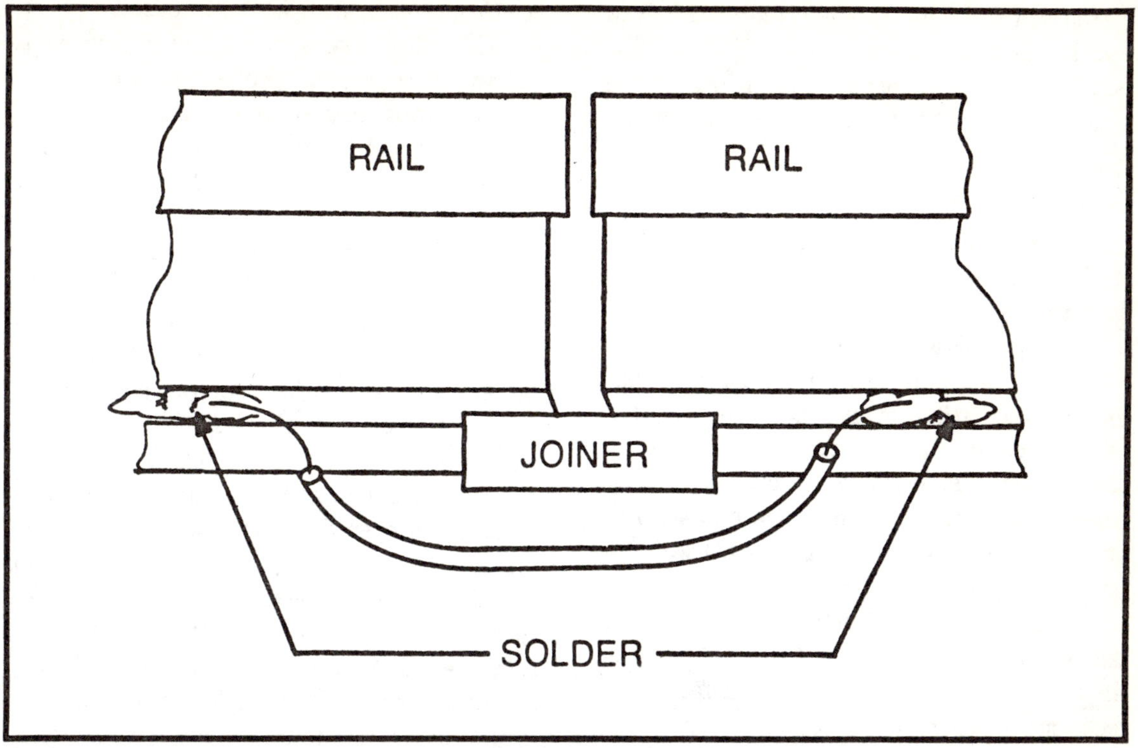

Fig. C-5. Most authorities recommend bonding the electrical path around each rail joiner, like this.

temperature too much for plastic tie strips to survive. The technique involves clamping two lengths of rail together, end to end, in a special fixture made of sheet aluminum, then using a propane gas or acetylene torch to braze the rail ends together. However the joint is made, it is filed to the same cross-section as the rest of the rail. Lengths of up to 50 feet have been handled on some club layouts by this technique.

Another approach for insuring electrical continuity completely ignores bonding of the joints and, instead, runs a separate feeder wire to every separate piece of track. When this is done, it doesn't matter if the physical joint between the rail

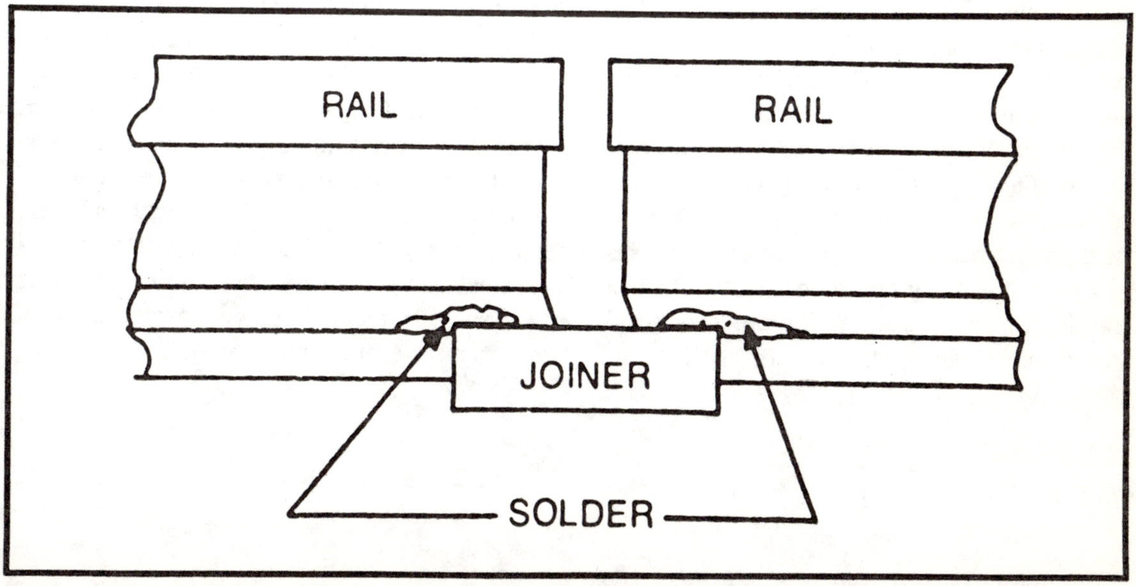

Fig. C-6.. There are not many problems bonding N-scale rails this way. It might not work with larger track, however.

corrodes. The electrical power is fed separately to each length of track from cabling beneath the layout. This is the technique used on one of the largest model railroads ever built—that of the Model Railroad Club, in New Jersey.

Common-Rail Track Circuits

Up to this point, all our discussion of connecting feeder wires, installing gaps, and so forth, has assumed that connections would have to be made to both rails. This is not necessary in many cases.

While it hurts nothing to provide individual feeders to both rails in every control block, it is not really necessary to do so except in the case of turning sections. All other trackwork can be supplied by what is known as the *common-rail* system. In this system, one rail has electrical continuity throughout all sections. Gaps do not appear in this rail—they are only in the supply rails. This rail, which is common to all sections, is known as the common rail; that is where the name of the technique comes from. The common rail provides the electrical return path for all control blocks and should, for safety, be grounded to a water pipe.

Common rail has a number of advantages when compared to the independent power system. The most obvious of these advantages is that common rail requires fewer insulated rail gaps, and only half as much wiring to provide the same control capabilities. By requiring less wiring, it makes the track circuits that much simpler. By grounding the common rails, a safety feature is added. Because the common rail has the same voltage potential everywhere, troubleshooting is easier when something goes wrong.

In fact, the only severe disadvantage to common rail (in comparison to an independent supply of power) is that more than one power supply must be used to provide more than one throttle—this can mean that every throttle must have its own transformer and rectifier. With independent control, a single oversize transformer and rectifier combination can supply all the throttles.

If the dual-power supply system is employed, only two power supplies are necessary no matter how many cabs are used with common rail. In this case, the junction of the two power supplies goes to the common rail, and the other pole of each power supply goes to all the throttles.

Nothing, of course, keeps you from applying the common rail idea and still cutting both gaps at every gap point. All that is necessary to make this work is to connect all the south rail feeders together, for instance, while supplying power to the north rail feeders through block control techniques.

Operationally, it is exactly the same as common-rail operation. Mechanically, however, the presence of the gaps makes it possible to provide independent control for specific blocks such as turning sections, or to remove power completely from certain sections by simply disconnecting the common-rail feeder for that section, to help eliminate certain areas while troubleshooting.

Independent Power Control

For reversing loops, common rail cannot be used. The reason is simple—either the north or the south rail must be made common to employ common-rail techniques. In a reversing section, neither rail is exclusively north or south. The roles of the rails reverse when the reversing loop does. Therefore, independent control of a reversing section is the only way to achieve operation.

It will hurt nothing to provide the power independently to all other control blocks as well, but will require twice as much feeder wire. There is no need to do so, unless you have some compelling reason to operate multiple cabs with only one power supply. To do this, you must provide independent control to every block, as the two blocks will short out the common power supply if common-rail operation is attempted.

Appendix D
Preventive Maintenance for Locomotives

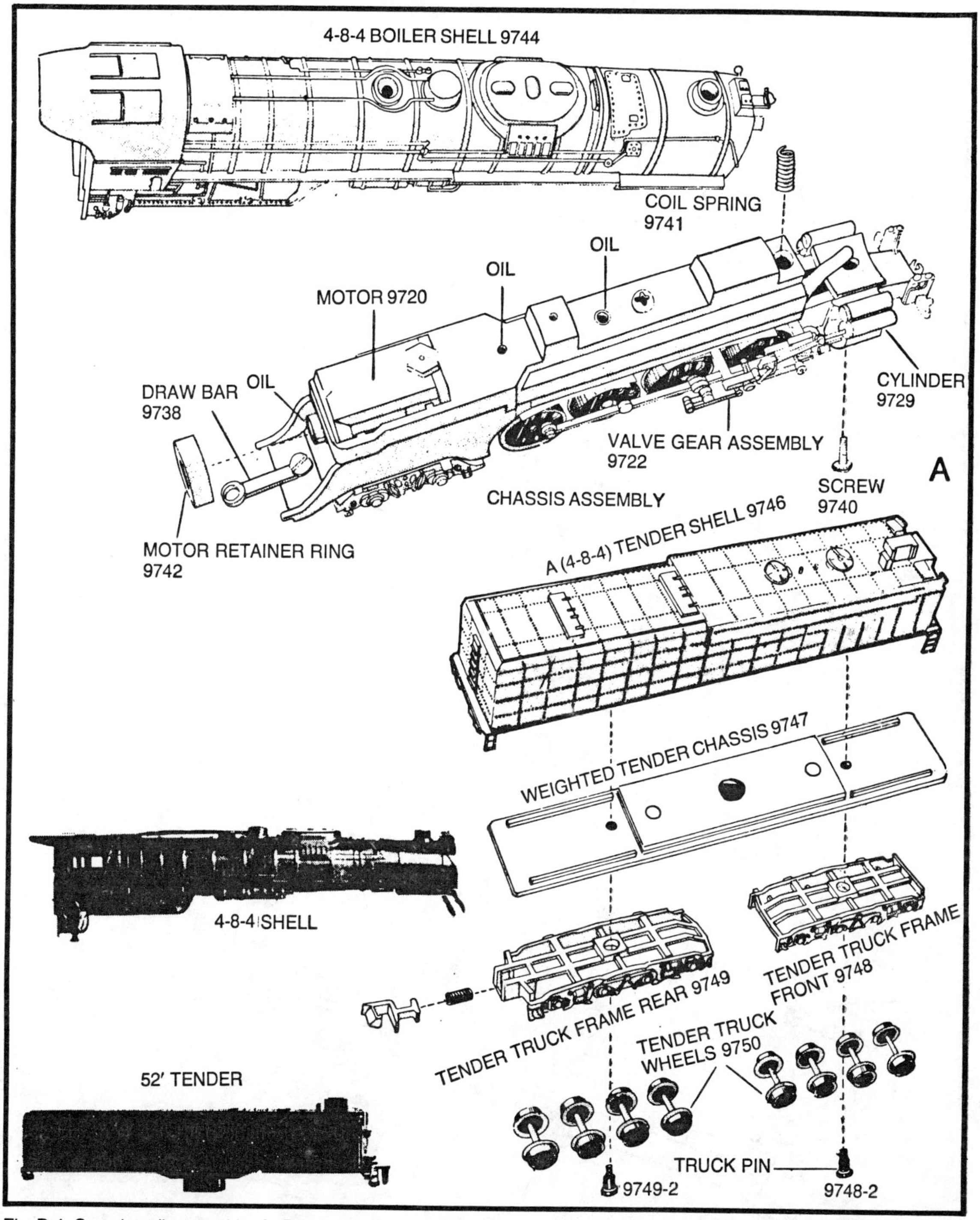

Fig. D-1. Complete disassembly of a Bachmann N-scale 4-8-4 begins with lifting the shell after removing the single screw in the frame below the smokestack. Die cast top frame supplies the wright needed to keep the tiny locomotive pulling heavy loads. After it has been removed, the motor can be slipped out for inspection. Clean all electrical contacts from pickup shoes to brushes. Unless necessary don't take snap-pin parts apart, since they wear with frequency removal. (Continued on pages 232 through 236).

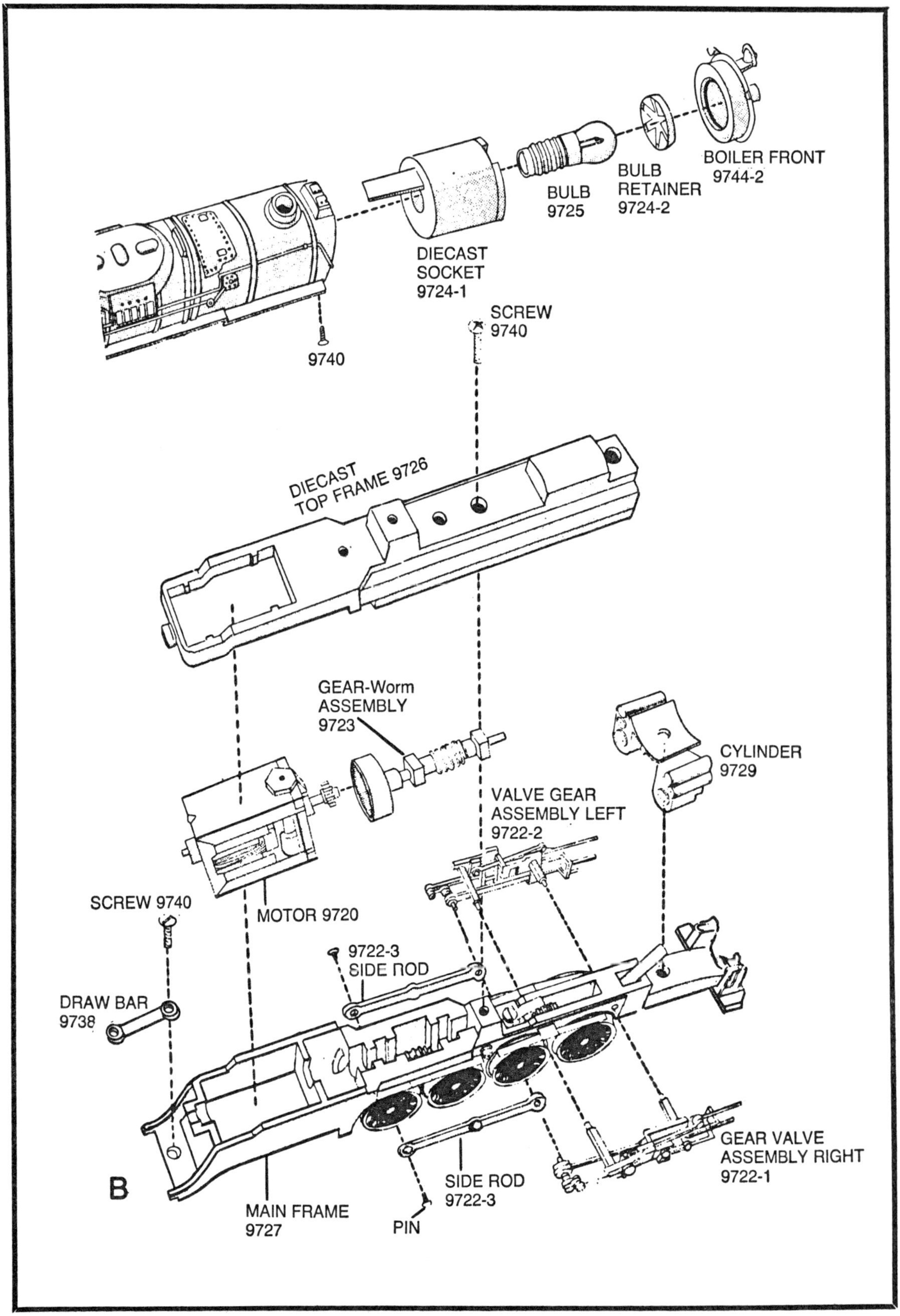
BOILER FRONT
9744-2
BULB
RETAINER
9724-2
BULB
9725
DIECAST
SOCKET
9724-1
9740
SCREW
9740
DIECAST
TOP FRAME 9726
GEAR-Worm
ASSEMBLY
9723
CYLINDER
9729
VALVE GEAR
ASSEMBLY LEFT
9722-2
SCREW 9740
MOTOR 9720
9722-3
SIDE ROD
DRAW BAR
9738
GEAR VALVE
ASSEMBLY RIGHT
9722-1
B
SIDE ROD
9722-3
MAIN FRAME
9727
PIN

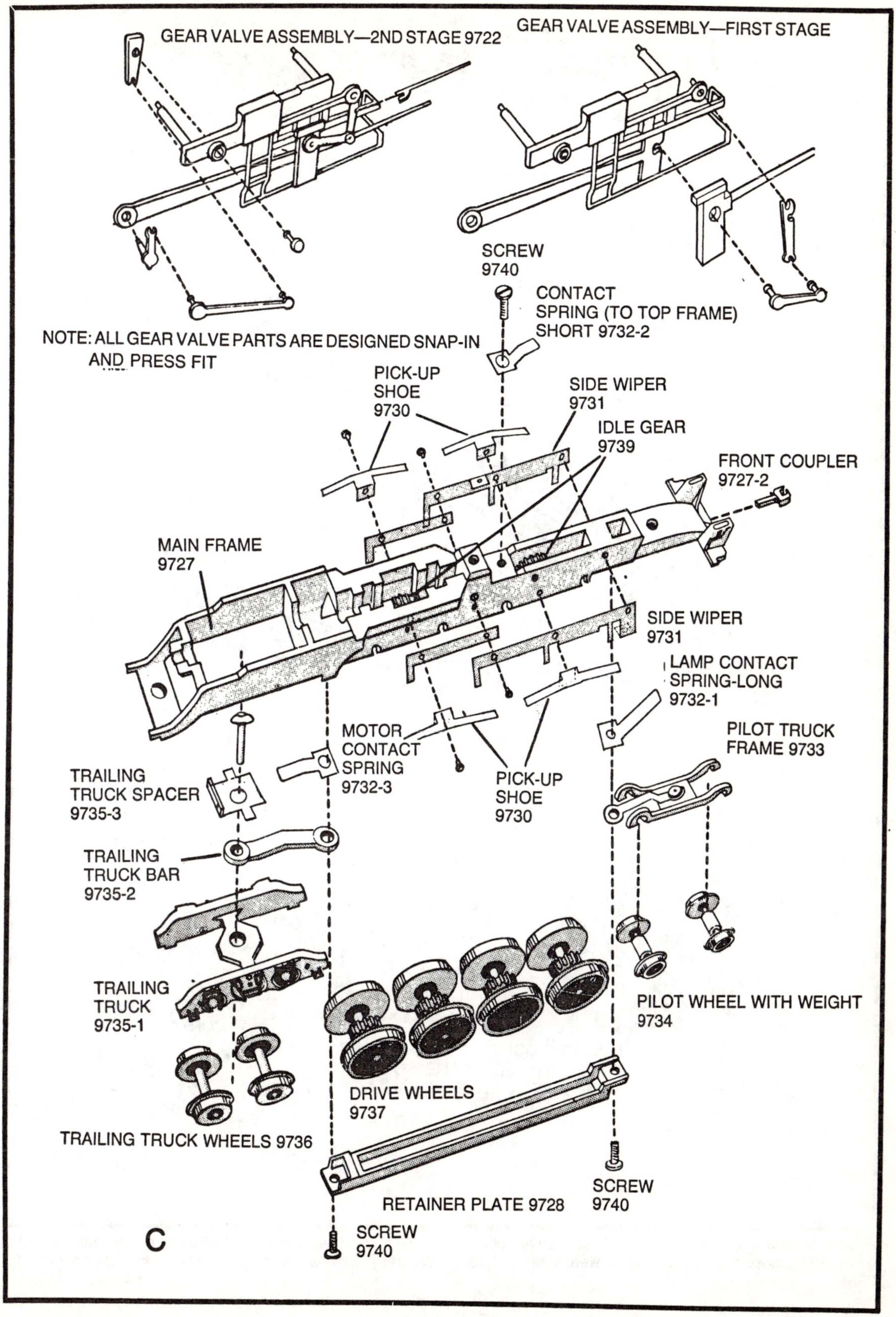
GEAR VALVE ASSEMBLY—2ND STAGE 9722
GEAR VALVE ASSEMBLY—FIRST STAGE
SCREW 9740
CONTACT SPRING (TO TOP FRAME) SHORT 9732-2
NOTE: ALL GEAR VALVE PARTS ARE DESIGNED SNAP-IN AND PRESS FIT
PICK-UP SHOE 9730
SIDE WIPER 9731
IDLE GEAR 9739
FRONT COUPLER 9727-2
MAIN FRAME 9727
SIDE WIPER 9731
LAMP CONTACT SPRING-LONG 9732-1
MOTOR CONTACT SPRING 9732-3
PILOT TRUCK FRAME 9733
TRAILING TRUCK SPACER 9735-3
PICK-UP SHOE 9730
TRAILING TRUCK BAR 9735-2
TRAILING TRUCK 9735-1
PILOT WHEEL WITH WEIGHT 9734
DRIVE WHEELS 9737
TRAILING TRUCK WHEELS 9736
SCREW 9740
RETAINER PLATE 9728
C
SCREW 9740

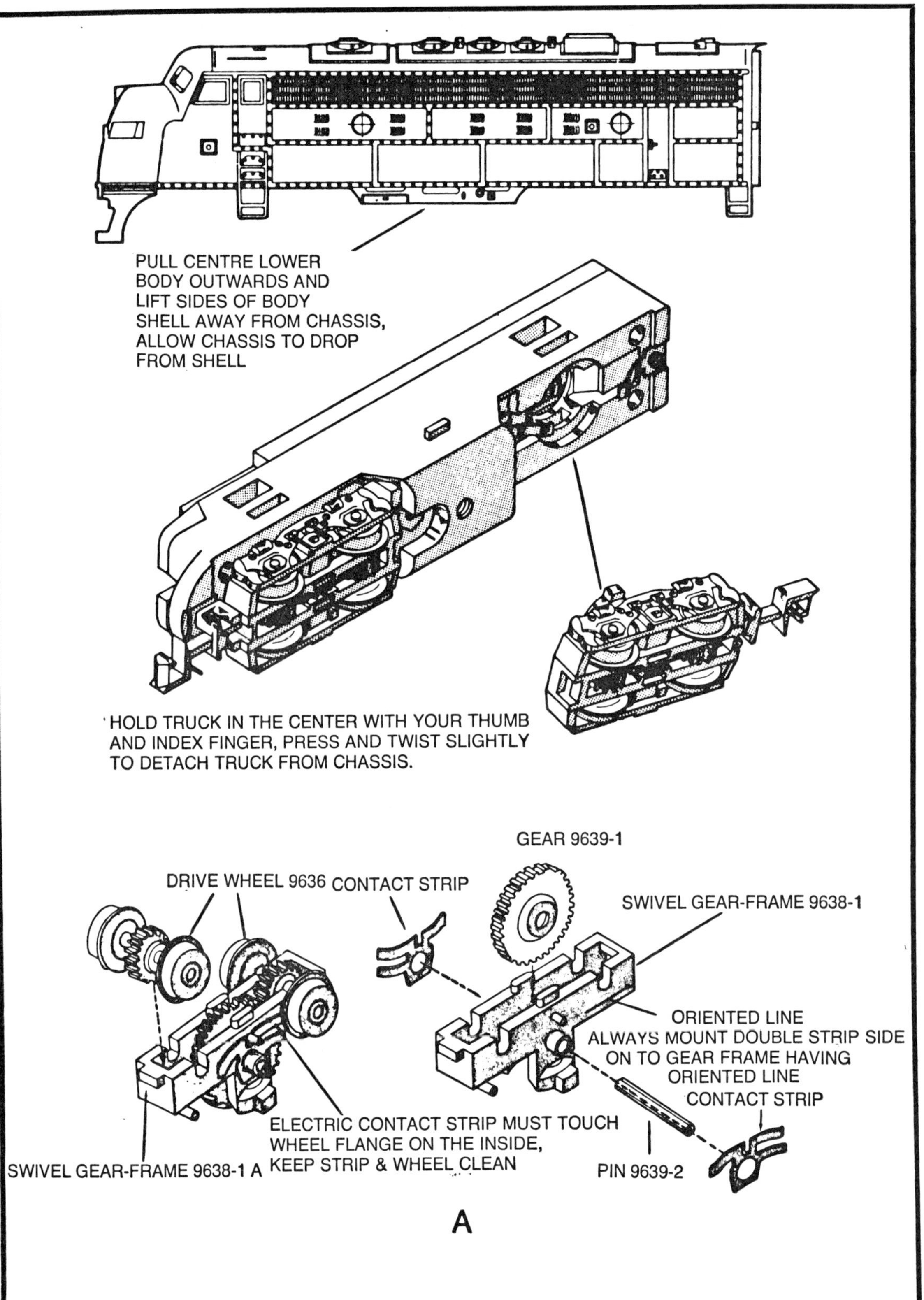

App. D-2. Diesels are as different inside as they are outside. Swivel trucks carry the power to the wheels through a chain of gears. These need regular cleaning but wear suprisingly long. (Courtesy Bachmann Brothers, Inc.) (Continued on pages 235, 236)

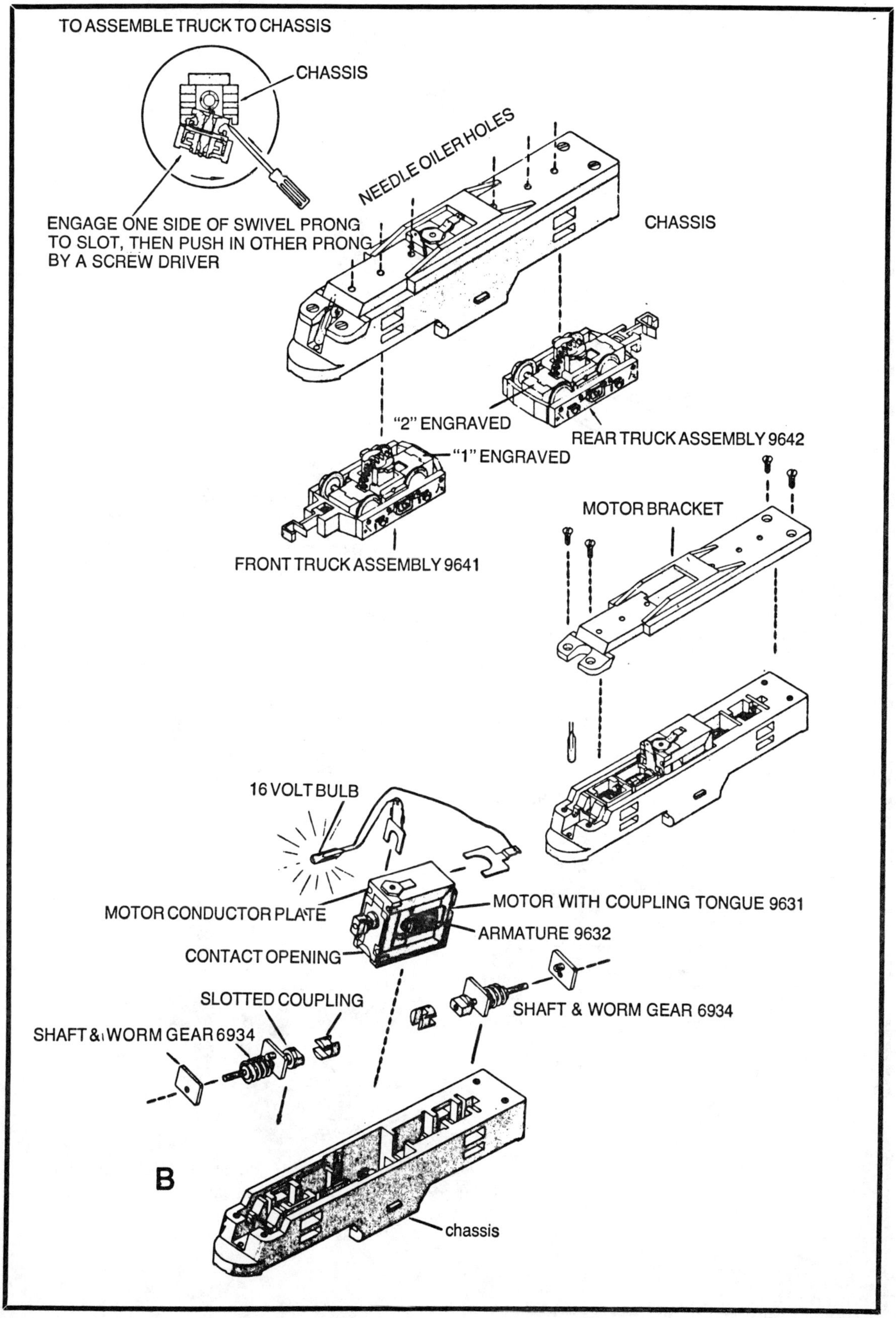
TO ASSEMBLE TRUCK TO CHASSIS
CHASSIS
NEEDLE OILER HOLES
ENGAGE ONE SIDE OF SWIVEL PRONG TO SLOT, THEN PUSH IN OTHER PRONG BY A SCREW DRIVER
CHASSIS
"2" ENGRAVED
REAR TRUCK ASSEMBLY 9642
"1" ENGRAVED
MOTOR BRACKET
FRONT TRUCK ASSEMBLY 9641
16 VOLT BULB
MOTOR CONDUCTOR PLATE
MOTOR WITH COUPLING TONGUE 9631
ARMATURE 9632
CONTACT OPENING
SLOTTED COUPLING
SHAFT & WORM GEAR 6934
SHAFT & WORM GEAR 6934
B
chassis

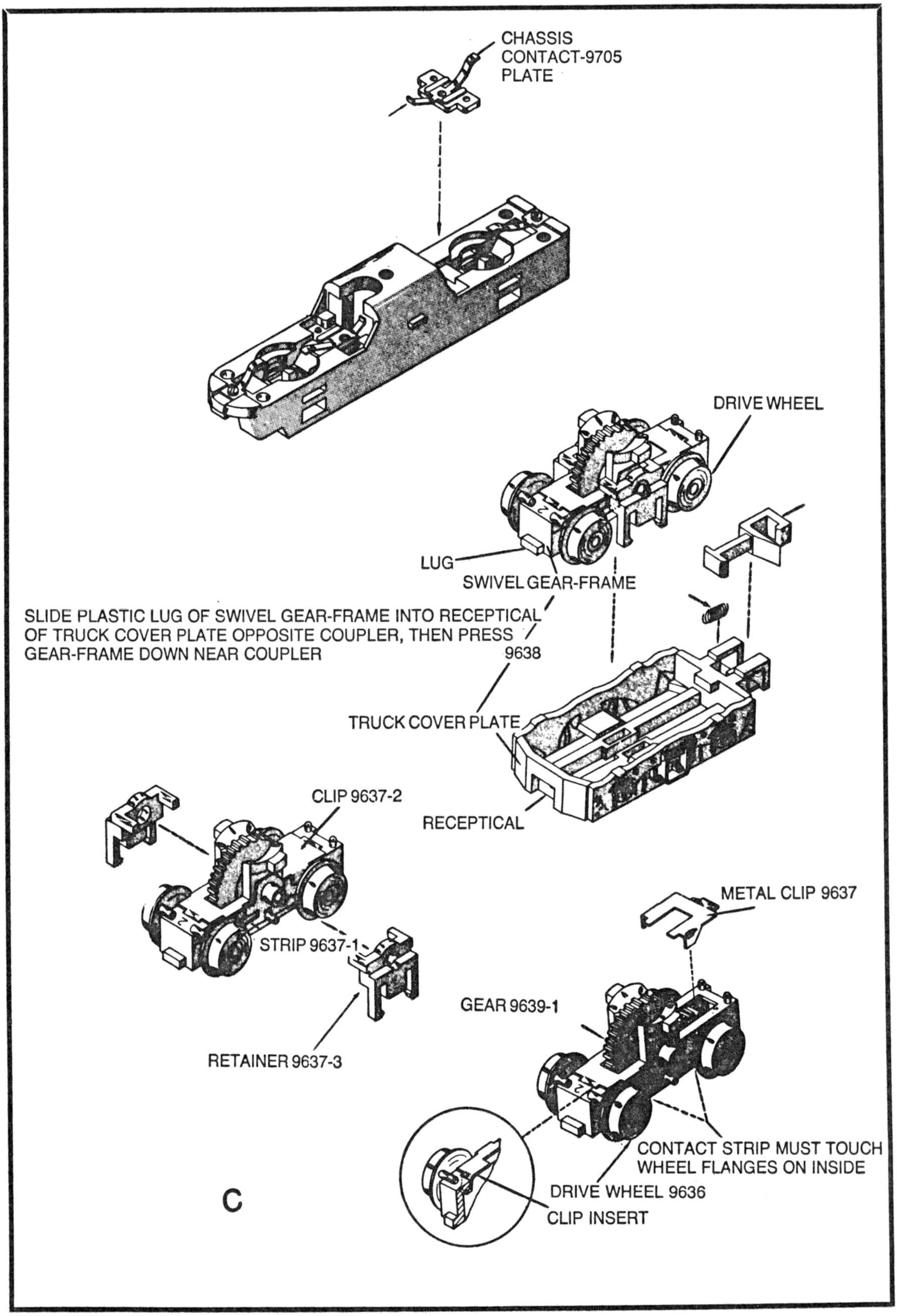
CHASSIS
CONTACT-9705
PLATE
DRIVE WHEEL
LUG
SWIVEL GEAR-FRAME
SLIDE PLASTIC LUG OF SWIVEL GEAR-FRAME INTO RECEPTICAL OF TRUCK COVER PLATE OPPOSITE COUPLER, THEN PRESS GEAR-FRAME DOWN NEAR COUPLER
9638
TRUCK COVER PLATE
RECEPTICAL
CLIP 9637-2
STRIP 9637-1
RETAINER 9637-3
METAL CLIP 9637
GEAR 9639-1
CONTACT STRIP MUST TOUCH WHEEL FLANGES ON INSIDE
DRIVE WHEEL 9636
CLIP INSERT
C

Index

Index

A

Accessible waterwings 109
Acorn 132
Alternate routes 56
Appearance, train 14
Around the wall plans 146
Arrangements, ladder 35

B

Big Z plan 179

C

Cars, open-top 60
Centennial peak branch 123
Center Layover Railroading 55
Centrifugal force 18
Changes, inappropriate 200
Changing
- curvature standards 201
- scale or gauge 189

Character profiles 80
Clearances and track centers 18
Clearances
- side 22
- vertical 22

Coffee Table
- railroads 108
- upper limit 122

Combination schematics 62
Configurations, layout 72
Constricted connecting railroad 91
Construction
- cookie cutter 70
- open grid 70
- track 68

Continuous track plan schematics 55
Convertible schematic plans 64
Cookie-cutter construction 70
Crossings 50
Curve turnouts 36
Curves 14
- vertical 28

D

Dieselizing or streammizing 210
Dogbones 60
Double track and single track 66

E

Easement 43
Easements and superelevation 14
Electrical controls & track plan 79
Elevations, track 76
Empty/Load Illusion 62
Equipment, narrow gauge 20
Essentials 172
Exhibitionist 147

F

Facilities, turning 90
Fiddle yards 91
Flat railroading 70
Freight car capacity 210
Freight railroad 178

G

Garage railroads 173
Geometry, turnout 30
Grand central junior 122
Grades
- and tonnage 22
- stiff 90

H

Hammerlock industrial district 96
Hand-laid, pre-fab or sectional track 46

I

Inappropriate changes 200
Iron Ranger 108

L

Ladder
- arrangements 35
- tracks 34

Layout
- configurations 72
- little big time 83
- oval 80
- prairie division point 83

Layouts, shelf-style switching 83
Limits
- lower 12
- sharp curve 132

Little big time layout 80
Log carrier 162

Long
  long train 138
  trains 122
Loop-to-loop 60
Lower limits 12
L-shaped pike 147

M

Main line, twice-around 96
Medium big time 129

N

N & Ho turnout recommendations 43
Narrow gauge equipment 20

O

Open grid construction 70
Open-top cars 60
Oval layout 80

P

Period railroad 52
Personal standards 11
Pike planning 64
Plan, Big Z 179
Planning, pike 64
Plans
  around-the-wall 146
  convertible schematic 64
Point-to-point 54
Prairie division point layout 83
Pretzel 129
Profiles, character 80

R

Radius & scale 14
Railroad
  freight 178
  period 52
Railroading
  center-layover 55
  flat 70
Railroads
  coffee table 108
  garage 173
  up-and-over 70
Ranger, iron 108
Reversing tracks 56
Rolling stock & track curvature 12
Routes, alternate 56
Run-around tracks 90

S

Savers, space 35
Scale & radius 14
Scale or gauge, changing 189
Schematic 52
Schematics
  continuous track 55
  combination 62
  semi-point-to-point 57
Semi-point-to-point schematics 57
Sharp curve limits 132
Shelf-style switching layouts 83
Short tail tracks 83
Side clearances 22
Size, standard 68
Space savers 35
Spaghetti on the rolling pin 147
Standard size 68
Standards
  changing curvature 201
  personal 11
  turnout 42
Stiff grades 90
Superelevation and easements 14
Super switching railroad 139
Switchbacks 83

T

Tilt 18
Tonnage and grades 22
Track
  centers and clearances 18
  construction 68
  curvature & rolling stock 12
  elevations 76
  hand-laid, pre-fab or sectional 46
  plan & electrical controls 79
Tracks
  ladder 34
  reversing 56
  run-around 90
  short tail 83
Trackwork 30
Traditional coffee table railroad 109
Train
  appearance 14
  long, long 138
Trains, long 122
Turning facilities 90
Turnout
  Geometry 30
  standards 42
Turnouts 30
  curve 36
  Wye & Equilateral 39
Twice-around main line 96

U

Underbed special 109
Up-and-over railroads 70

V

Vertical
  clearances 22
  curves 28

W

Wye & Equilateral Turnouts 39

Y

Yards, fiddle 91